WILL METZ

MUSIC THEORY for the SELF-TAUGHT MUSICIAN

HARMONY, COMPOSITION & IMPROVISATION

Or what to play, when, over what?

Backbeat Books

WILL METZ

Music Theory for the Self-Taught Musician

Level 2 — Harmony, Composition & Improvisation

A simple and logical way
to discover, understand, and master
the mysterious world of music theory,
without reading a single note!

Backbeat Books

Guilford, Connecticut

An imprint of Globe Pequot, the trade division of
The Rowman & Littlefield Publishing Group, Inc.
4501 Forbes Blvd., Ste. 200
Lanham, MD 20706
www.rowman.com

Distributed by NATIONAL BOOK NETWORK

Copyright © 2022 by Guillaume 'Will' Metz

All rights reserved. No part of this book may be reproduced in any form or by any electronic or mechanical means, including information storage and retrieval systems, without written permission from the publisher, except by a reviewer who may quote passages in a review.

British Library Cataloguing in Publication Information available

Library of Congress Cataloging-in-Publication Data available

ISBN 978-1-4930-6136-5 (paperback)
ISBN 978-1-4930-6137-2 (e-book)

∞™ The paper used in this publication meets the minimum requirements of American National Standard for Information Sciences—Permanence of Paper for Printed Library Materials, ANSI/NISO Z39.48-1992

CONTENT

Preface 4
Introduction 5

1 Chapter 1: Diatonic Harmonization of Scales or Modes
General points 13
Major scale and natural minor scale 21
Harmonic and melodic minor scales 33

2 Chapter 2: The Static Harmonic Context
About musical creation 39
Playing over a single bass note 53
Playing over a single interval or chord 67

3 Chapter 3: The Modal Context
Harmonic rhythm 87
Modal progressions 95

4 Chapter 4: The Tonal Context
The concept of key 107
Major diatonic tonal harmony 125
Minor diatonic tonal harmony 155
Creating melodies in a tonal context 179
Modal interchanges and modal sections 191
The Blues 239
Modal mixture and modulations 239

5 Chapter 5: Harmonic analysis and case studies
Standard major chord 277
Minor chord with modulation 297
Modal chart 307

Conclusion 315
Exercises 317

PREFACE

Knowing all the basic tools that allow one to play music—mastering scales, chords, and developing one's technical skills on the instrument—is usually not the hardest task. So many times aspiring musicians (and this includes me) reach that stage where they become quite comfortable with playing a lot of scales, modes, and chords, but struggle when it comes to improvising and composing. In other words, the bridge between knowing all the musical tools and using them appropriately to create music can be hard to cross. I cannot state how frustrating it can be for a musician to become aware of this vastly wide gap between their technical abilities on one side, and their inability to use this technique in musical contexts, such as improvising or composing. This type of situation often applies to "classically trained" (I try not to use that term) musicians or heavy metal enthusiasts who get to a point where their technique is flawless and their reading is as instinctive as talking or walking, yet when asked to improvise over the simplest chord progression, they become completely clueless.

Unfortunately, this frustration can lead to serious doubts about one's inherent capability to be creative. At that point, many musicians will simply assume that they are not meant to create or improvise and will settle for being interpreters who only play other people's music. What a pity! Because improvisation is a skill that *can* be developed just like everything else. Creative potential is not a "divine gift" that some have and others simply don't. Of course, natural and environmental predispositions exist, but the lack of those predispositions is not insurmountable.

This book is an attempt to deal with this uncomfortable situation and provide help to get out of it. Using the same logical, step-by-step approach as in my first book, I decided to break down the mechanics and rules of harmony, which is essential to fully understand the processes of improvising, composing, arranging, and many other aspects of musical creation. My goal is to unleash everyone's creative potential when it seems that it is nowhere to be found… And just like everything else, this starts with a phase of analyzing and understanding what's going on.

Please take some time to reflect on this: From the moment you start listening to music, you unconsciously build a reservoir of potential musical ideas. This little piece of melody, this lick or groovy rhythm will be stored in some part of your brain. When you learn how to tap into this reservoir of ideas, throw in some technique and musical knowledge and voilà! — the key to musical creativity. Now, that's easier said than done, obviously. The question is, how do you tap into this precious source of creativity? How can you draw inspiration from it, thereby allowing you to come up with interesting melodies or chord progressions, improvisations, and compositions?

Any guess? Oh, I hate to say this, lest I should sound like all the self-help gurus out there, but it's nonetheless true. It's practice! But guided, clever, practice! Creativity and what some may call "genius" is nothing like a divine epiphany and even the most respected composers relied and based their works on preexisting material.

INTRODUCTION

However, these so called "genii" knew how to draw from their "idea-wells," and worked very hard and systematically on their creations until they became masterpieces. The keyword here is work. Passion of course. But mostly work. Put enough work into anything, and people's minds will be so incapable of conceiving how much of it was necessary to accomplish the finished result that stands before their eyes (or ears), that they will attribute it to a stroke of genius, a miracle, or luck.

Could you be the next Mozart? Who knows… In any case, I truly hope that by reading this book and gaining a clear understanding of the material will allow you to meet and enjoy your creative self. It's time to leave the interpreter behind and become a creator.

Reminder about my method

So many books on music theory seem to be written for people who already have some knowledge of music. They use notes written on staffs (which assumes you should read notes already) or other notions that seem to exclude the possibility that there may be some people out there who want to learn more about music and yet know NOTHING about it. My challenge in this book and the previous one as well, was to write them as if my reader had never heard about music theory or even about music. This is admittedly unlikely if you are reading this book… but it's a matter of principle, teaching, and learning processes. I always hated it when my teachers assumed I should know more than I did. So I did my best to break down this fascinating yet intimidating science of music theory into several small logical steps and simple definitions that anyone, and I mean ANYONE, can understand. This includes you, my friend.

However, please don't start this book thinking that reading it will be enough to make you a brilliant musician. You will have to work and practice! As I've said before, music theory is like the operating manual of music. Reading it and knowing how to use it will be incredibly useful, accelerate your progress, and allow you to use all the cool "features" of music, but it's not enough. My uncle recently bought a drone, and I can assure you that reading the operating manual was necessary for him to know how to use it, but it definitely didn't prevent a couple of crashes or close calls. There is no miracle recipe or shortcut that can make you become a brilliant musician, while avoiding practice and hard work. And that's good! Because the key to happiness in life is to enjoy the process!

Finally, although I did my best to make things as understandable as possible, it doesn't mean you won't scratch your head at some points (most likely many of them). You still need to focus and make some effort to digest each point. Simple doesn't necessarily mean effortless.

INTRODUCTION

My method is based on:

- A well-defined goal, which is to understand the mechanics of harmony in order to know what notes to play in any harmonic context (think "a bunch of chords" for now, if the notion of harmonic context confuses you).
- Some notions and definitions that should be learned by heart without wasting too much time trying to understand them, as it would take us too far away from our initial subject.

Example: Understanding why a minor second interval is dissonant would require us to digress into advanced physics. It's very interesting, but it will not help you with your improvisation skills. Realizing that it is true as a matter of experience or just trusting me for now will avoid a waste of time and potential confusion.

Such notions will be presented in the following way:

 A minor second interval is dissonant.

Red line = Learn by heart

- Some notions and reasonings that should be understood so that you can easily find the result later, on your own. This pretty much applies to everything that is not next to a red line.
- A few well-chosen exercises to make sure you understand what's going on.

HARMONIZATION OF THE MAJOR SCALE IN TRIADS

Spell out the harmonization of the following scales:
A major, E major, Bb major, Eb major.

Everything in this book should obviously be applied directly to your instrument at some point, but when I feel that particular practice guides are needed, I will indicate it in the following way:

 Practice playing the harmonized scale...

INTRODUCTION

About learning processes

Lately in my teaching career, I've been spending a lot of time reflecting about thinking and learning processes. My main concerns have been to understand what REALLY understanding something means, as well as how to make sure that a student has attained that point of thorough understanding.

This question is important for several reasons:

1. It is a proven fact that most people lack the metacognitive skills allowing them to be aware of their own understanding of a subject. The simplified definition of metacognition is the ability to think about your own thinking. In other words, this means people will claim their understanding of something even though a simple inquiry would prove that they've got it all wrong! To put it even simpler, people don't know that they don't know. In an experiment, people of all ages and all professions and backgrounds were asked to draw a bicycle. Most people claimed with confidence that they knew how to REALLY draw a bicycle, which implies understanding how a bicycle works. The results were absolutely bemusing! Most people, regardless of their background and education level, failed miserably. Which brings us to the next point.

2. The way students are tested in the standard education system fails to expose major flaws in understanding. Why? Well, it's a combination of factors. First of all, most teachers are not at all aware of this phenomenon and most of them are probably victims of it themselves! Again, since the education system doesn't seem to care about this major cognitive issue, you can get a PhD while not really understanding what you are talking about (oh geez, I'm going to make enemies…). That's because school doesn't teach you how to think, but WHAT to think. The other problem about testing is that it only relies on grading. "You got more than 80%? Great! You pass and with a good grade to top it off." The thing is, it's not about the 80% you got right, it's about WHY you didn't get 100%. I guess my grandmother was right after all when the first thing she would ask me after I proudly presented my 99% to her was, "Where did you lose that one point?" Think about it this way: would you buy a calculator that gives you the right results 80% of the time? I mean, that's pretty good after all, right? Of course you wouldn't, and the first thing the programmers would do to this calculator is try to figure what is wrong with the process and at what point. Having 20% of your answers wrong can be the result of a deep misunderstanding, either of the subject itself OR of the previous knowledge required to understand the subject. It turns out that the only "acceptable" mistakes should be those caused by inattention. These are simply due to the fact we are only humans and that even though one's thinking process is solid, they can still make innocent mistakes here and there. But unless you are the most distracted person on the planet, with a good and solid understanding, your answers should be more than 90% correct.

INTRODUCTION

3. It seems to be very difficult (at least it is to me) to teach these metacognitive skills to people. Again, in virtue of the first point, people are very likely to say they understand when they in fact don't. Moreover, who is to say I MYSELF, as a teacher, am not still confused about some subjects? Many times I've been asked in class a question that pinpointed a flaw in my thought process which led me to rethink the way I think.

Studying learning processes led me to become interested in subjects I would have never suspected catching my attention, or at least not as an effect of teaching. It turns out that learning is to be analyzed mostly under the light of neurology and computer science.

There appears to be two main ways to acquire knowledge:

1. Experience
2. Expertise

Experience

Experience is acquired mostly by trial and error. You set a desired outcome to a situation (winning a chess match or making something sound good in music, for example), you try something out, and you compare the results of what you did to the outcome. If it worked, you conclude that whatever you did was the right thing to do. If it didn't, you try again until it does. Experience is precisely what self-taught musicians who know nothing about music theory tend to leverage. And you can become absolutely incredible at something using only experience! This has been proven countless times. From an outside perspective, it is very hard to tell if someone's mastery of a subject is only due to experience, and we naturally assume that experienced people really know and understand what they are doing. However, this is not true at all. Many very experienced people are absolutely incapable of knowing why or how what they are doing works. They only way you can learn from them is to put them in a particular situation, ask them how they would deal with it, observe, and then try to make sense of it. This is the reason why so many brilliant musicians are incapable of teaching their art. They literally have no clue why what they do works. What they do know is that it does work, because they have been in this situation a million times, and experience tells them it works.

Expertise

Expertise, on the other hand, comes from a complete rational understanding of the subject. It's what you gain when you ask yourself the question of why something works or doesn't work. It's precisely what you gain by trying to understand music theory, for example.

INTRODUCTION

What's very interesting is that you can have experience without having expertise OR expertise without experience. In the business world, for example, the role of a consultant is to provide expertise in fields where they probably have very little experience or none at all. Even more interesting is that in some cases, and particularly when a certain problem is to be solved, experience seems to be detrimental to problem solving, for it often harms objectivity and hinders one's ability to take a step back.

However, it is absolutely possible to have both experience and expertise in a particular subject, and this is what a well-rounded musician should aim for. Experience comes with practice and trial and error, and under the guidance and understanding of expertise, it usually leads to true mastery.

Prerequisite

In this book, I will assume that you are already comfortable with all the notions in my previous book. I will be using the same notations, the same vocabulary, as well as all the musical tools and concepts that I explained in the previous book, so I really encourage you to read it first if you haven't already. Not having a clear understanding of intervals, scales and modes, or not knowing how to spell or read a chord rather quickly will make it really hard, if not impossible, for you to understand this book.

Goals

Once again, to make progress in any field, it is essential to know what your goals are. Just a handful of clearly written-out goals is useful to avoid procrastination and to monitor one's progress. In this book, I would say that our two main goals are:

- To be able to understand and analyze all the main harmonic tonal and modal chord progressions.
- Knowing what scale or mode can be played in each musical context (single note, single chord, modal context, tonal context) to create melodies.

INTRODUCTION

About musical influences

As I pointed out earlier, the "idea-well" that each of us develops and uses to create, mostly comes from all the musical content that we play or listen to. In other words, it is absolutely essential to listen to A LOT of music in order to develop your creative potential. The more influences one has in terms of artists, genres, or instruments, the richer one's well of ideas will be.

Nowadays, thanks to the internet, most people are just a couple clicks away from accessing virtually ANY piece of music for free. Paradoxically, this leads to a quite recent problem: too many choices. Let's talk a little bit more about this.

When my grandparents or even my parents wanted to listen to music, their options were limited to the radio, CDs, vinyls, and cassette tapes. Moreover, there were fewer distractions, and I remember my mother saying that everyone back then would sometimes look forward to their favorite band's new album months before it was out! Once the new album was purchased (because you actually had to buy it), they would listen to it over and over again until the next one. My mother is not a musician, and yet she knows countless melodies and even instrumental solos by heart in so many different genres. What an incredible reservoir of ideas she could draw from had she decided to play music! I do believe that music lovers and musicians of the previous generations tend to have a much broader range of influences, and while I still wonder if this may just be a post-generational illusion, I also have another potential explanation. Despite that we can now listen to anything we want at any given time, we cannot actually listen to EVERYTHING, it would take more than a lifetime. We must choose what we listen to. Unfortunately, most of us don't spend our time exploring new bands and new original pieces of music. Instead, we naturally tend to listen to what we already know or to what is suggested to us. Have you ever noticed that if you try to walk randomly in a new place, you will most likely, unconsciously, land where you started? Human beings naturally tend to prefer what is known. Moreover, why would someone who wants to have a good time listening to music take the risk of listening to something they hate when they have a safe playlist of tunes they know they love? That and the fact we actually take more pleasure and secrete more endorphins by listening to tunes we've already listened to, and you have the prefect recipe for musical stagnation.

Oh boy... 27 years old and I already sound like a nostalgic old person, don't I? But this is not my intention. I certainly don't think that everything was better the way it was before and that we should destroy the internet and go back to vinyls. What I do believe is that we should always try to look at progress with a critical eye in order to make the most of it. In other words, try not to fall into the trap of listening to the same songs and same Spotify playlists over and over again. Be curious, try to look around creatively, and your resources for musical ideas will thank you for it.

INTRODUCTION

Tip

What I personally suggest in order to discover more artists and broaden your influences is to go "back in time" by looking at your favorite artist's influences and mentors. Again, ALL artists took their ideas from other existing artists. So go to Wikipedia, type in the name of an artist you like, find their influences and listen to their music. Then keep going back further and further. You might end up in very unexpected musical places.

Hang in there and don't give up!

After reading through this book from start to finish one last time, the main thought that went through my mind was, "Oh my God... That's a LOT of information." Well, first of all, you're welcome ;). This book, coupled with the first one, basically includes everything I know, give or take. But jokes aside, I want to warn you that it might take you a bit of time and focus to understand all the notions we will be exploring. But don't worry! You've got this. Take your time, be curious, and you will become a master of music theory in no time!

INTRODUCTION

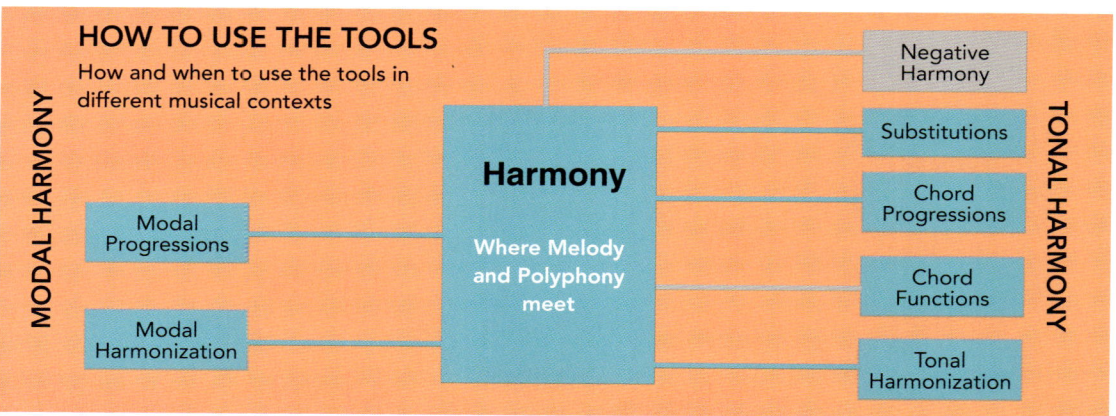

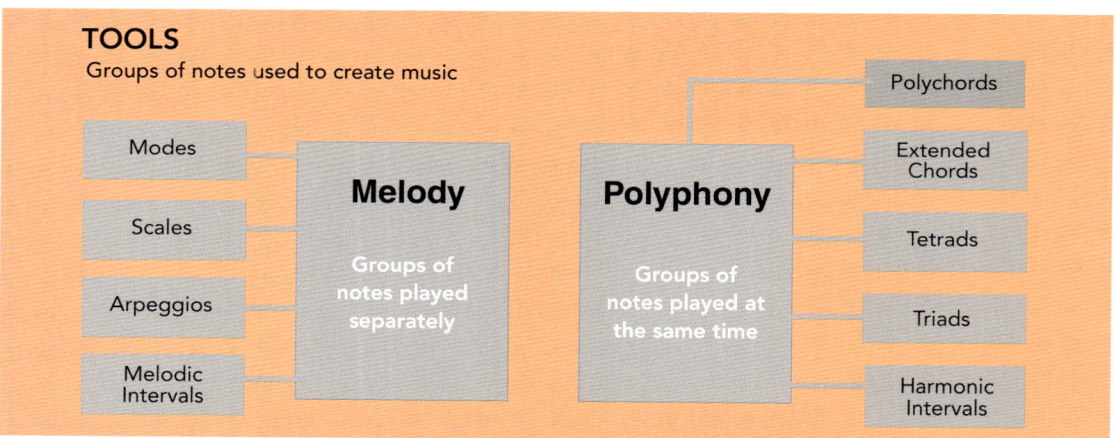

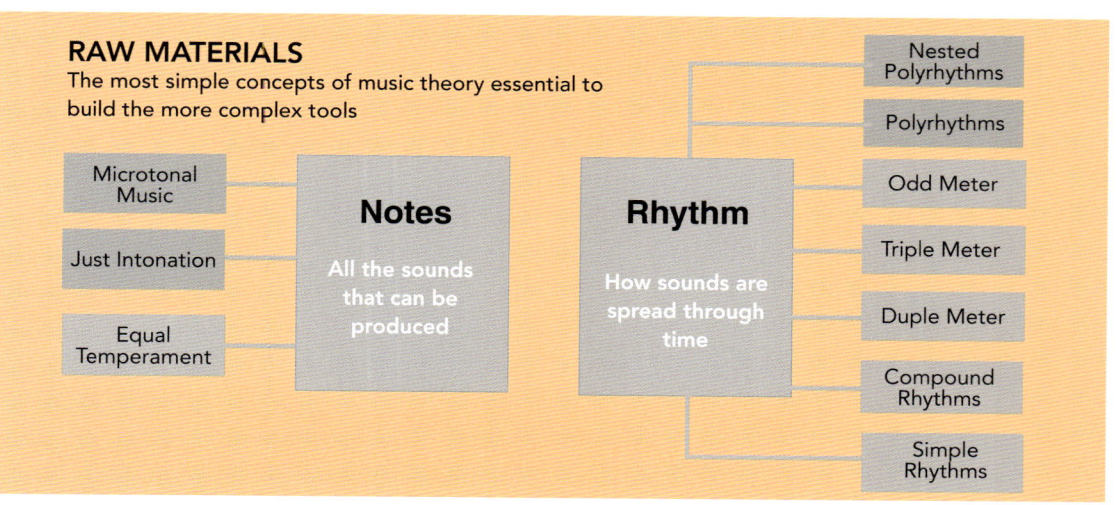

1

Diatonic Harmonization of scales or modes

GENERAL POINTS

GENERAL POINTS

Diatonic Harmonization

I like to see harmony as the **intersection between melody and polyphony**. It's the field of music that answers the question of which melodic tools one can play over different polyphonic tools and vice versa. In modern music, a piece of music is generally broken down into a main melody (or lead melody) played over a series of chords or a **chord progression**. The chords and their progression create a **harmonic context** which will give a particular "meaning" to the melody. A change in the melody or the harmonic context will necessarily change the sound and atmosphere of the musical piece.

The first link between melody and polyphony is made by what is called the harmonization of scales or modes, and more precisely, their **diatonic harmonization.**

Generally speaking, "harmonizing" means creating a collection of polyphonic units (harmonic intervals, or chords) using the bank of notes of a melodic tool (scale or mode).

> From now on, when I refer to scale, this will also include modes. Remember that technically modes are scales. So anytime you read the word "scale" you should think: "scale or mode".

The process of harmonizing a scale consists in generating a **collection of intervals or chords** of a **predefined type** (intervals of fifths, triads, tetrads, etc.) **and/or quality** (major, minor, perfect, etc.) **above each note of this scale**. This means each note of the scale will become the **root**, of an interval or chord. A harmonization is called **diatonic**, if all the notes of the intervals or chords generated, **belong to the scale being harmonized.**

In other words, the process of harmonizing is a bridge which allows to take melodic tools into the world of polyphony.

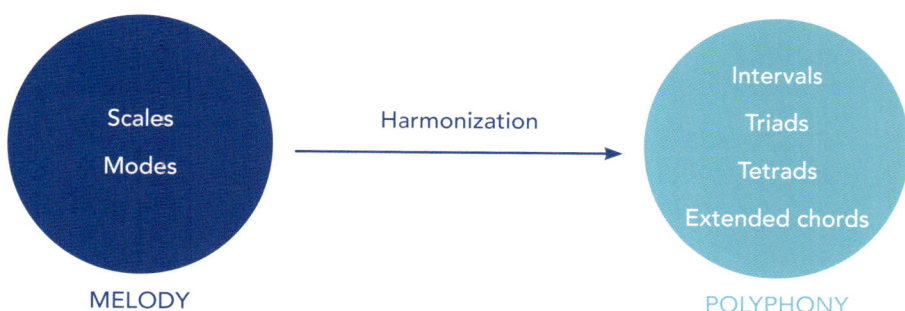

GENERAL POINTS

This definition of harmonization may sound like a mouthful, so let's clear it up with a few examples.

Example of a non-diatonic harmonization

Let's study the harmonization of the C major scale in major 3rds.

The process is simple:

1. Start with the notes of the C major scale

2. Above each note of the scale, add the note which is a major 3rd above:

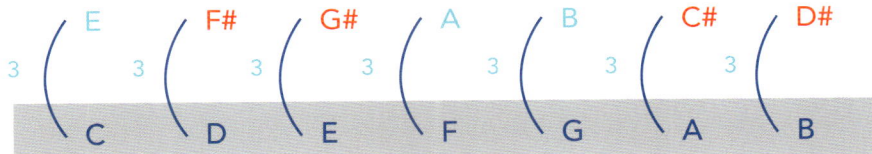

From a collection of single notes, we now have a collection of major 3rd intervals!

What can we notice here? Well, we clearly see that some of the notes (F#, G#, C#, and D#) generated in this harmonization do not belong in the notes of the harmonized scale (C major).

Conclusion: it is a non-diatonic harmonization.

GENERAL POINTS

Example of a diatonic harmonization

The harmonization of the C major scale in 5ths.

Step 1: Start with the notes of the **C major scale.**

Step 2: Define the type of intervals or chords that you want to generate when harmonizing the scale. We'll use intervals of 5ths in this example. You may notice that I specified the number but not the quality (perfect, augmented or diminished) of the interval—you'll understand why in just a moment.

Step 3: Above each note of the scale, add the note **of the C major scale** which is a 5th above.

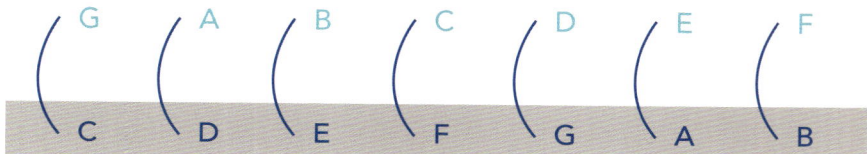

Step 4: Determine the quality of the 5th generated.

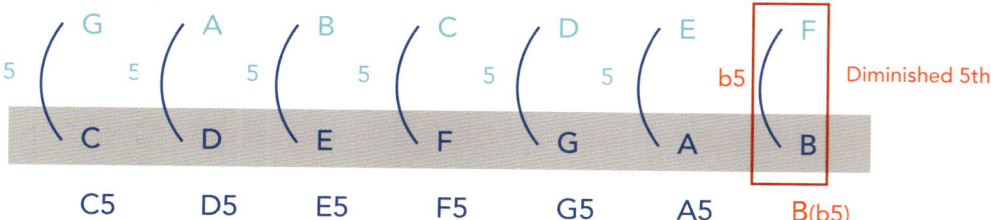

We can notice that the harmonization of the C major scale in 5ths generates **perfect 5ths** above each degree of the scale, except for the last one (above B). In this case, the **5th has to be diminished** in order for the harmonization to be diatonic.

■ Generalization

Let's see how we can generalize the concept of harmonization to any major scale. At this point, it will simply be a question of notation.

GENERAL POINTS

Harmonization of the major scale in 5ths

Scale notation	1	2	3	4	5	6	7
Harmonized scale notation	I5	II5	III5	IV5	V5	VI5	VII(b5)

In the harmonized scale, each note of the scale is written using a Roman numeral instead of an Arabic numeral. **This allows us to know that we are referring to an** interval or chord rooted on the note of a scale **rather than a single note.**

If the scale degree is not major or perfect, this also has to show in the harmonized scale notation:

Notice that next to each Roman numeral is another number. This is simply the standard notation of the interval or chord resulting from the harmonization. For example, the fifth interval rooted on the major 3rd of the major scale when harmonizing the major scale in 5ths is a **perfect 5th.**

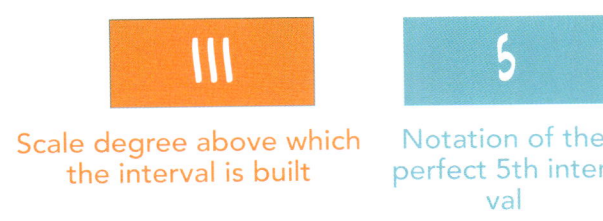

GENERAL POINTS

So, how should we name this III♭ interval? There are several options:

- Third degree of the harmonization of the major scale in 5ths
- Third degree interval of the major scale harmonized in 5ths

Now, let's use another example to make sure you understand the process. **We will harmonize the C natural minor scale diatonically, in 3rds.**

Step 1: Let's start with the notes of the C natural minor scale

Step 2: We are harmonizing this scale diatonically in 3rds so we will simply add above each note the note of the C natural minor scale found a third above.

Step 3: Determine the quality of each 3rd.

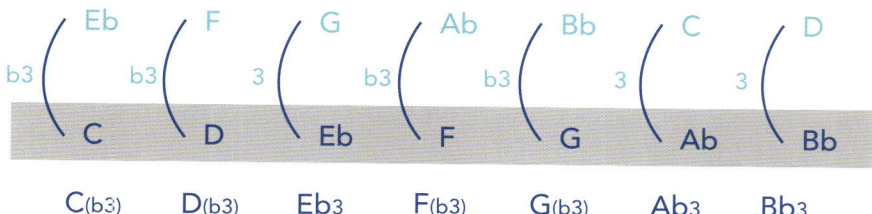

Again, you can notice that the 3rds generated can be either major or minor depending on the scale degree.

This information above could be generalized to the harmonization of any natural minor scale in 3rds:

GENERAL POINTS

Harmonization of the natural minor scale in 3rds

Scale notation	1	2	b3	4	5	b6	b7
Harmonized scale notation	I(b3)	II(b3)	bIII3	IV(b3)	V(b3)	bVI3	bVII3

Following the same principle, you can harmonize any scale or mode using any type of interval or chord.

The most common way to harmonize a scale is in **"stacks of 3rds,"** which will generate classic triads, tetrads, and extended chords. Remember that by "classic," I imply chords that are created by stacking different combinations of major and minor 3rd intervals on top of one another. Naturally, we will focus on the harmonization of the three most popular scales:

- **The major scale (and relative natural minor scale)**
- **The harmonic minor scale**
- **The melodic minor scale**

HARMONIZING SCALES IN DIFFERENT INTERVALS

I now invite you to complete **Exercise 1** in the Exercise section of the book. I will ask you to harmonize different scales and modes using different intervals.

1

Diatonic Harmonization of scales or modes

MAJOR AND NATURAL MINOR SCALE

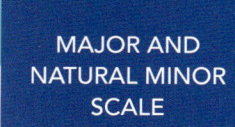

MAJOR AND NATURAL MINOR SCALE

Do you remember the classic triads, tetrads, and extended chords from the previous book? They are the ones created by piling up different combinations of major and minor 3rds. These chords are very important because they are used 99% of the time. This is why we will proceed to harmonize the most common scales, using these types of chords.

Diatonic harmonization of the major scale

Let's start by harmonizing the major scale by using classic triads, which are nothing more than a pile of two 3rds.

■ Harmonization of the major scale in classic triads

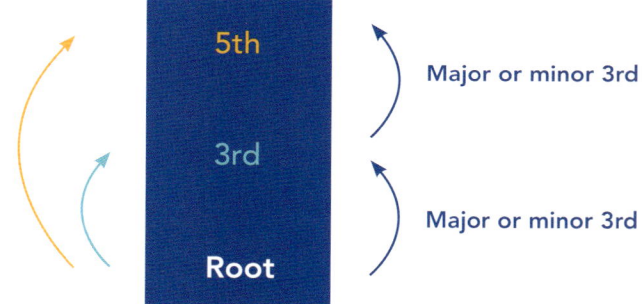

This means adding a 3rd and a 5th above each note of the C major scale and then analyzing which type of triad is generated from this process:

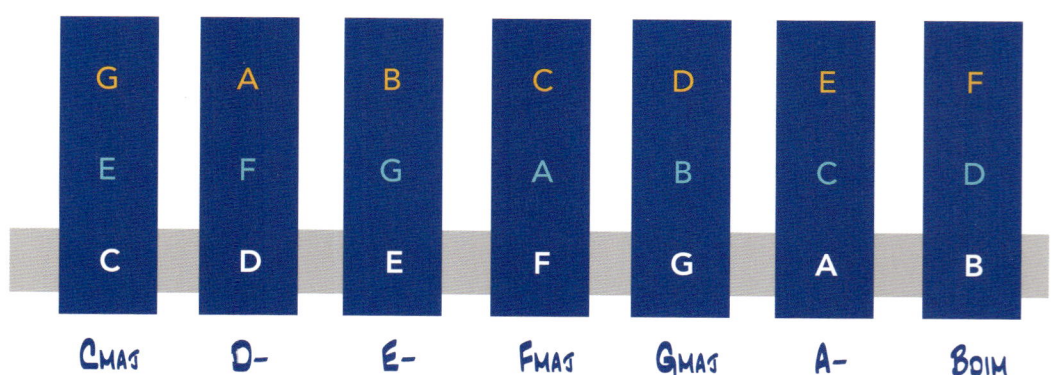

Very well! Now let's generalize what we just discovered above to any major scale. This constitutes a very important piece of information which must be remembered:

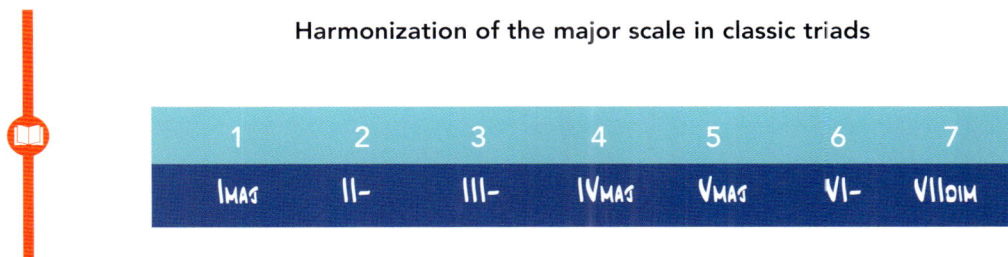

You may notice that this harmonization in triads also gives us the harmonization of the major scale in 3rds and 5ths! It makes perfect sense, since by definition, these triads are each made of a 3rd and a 5th. This can be very handy!

For example: since you know that the fourth degree triad of the harmonization of the major scale is a major triad, you know that the fourth degree interval of the harmonization of the major scale in 3rds will be a **major 3rd**. I know that this is an absolute mouthful and we will use shortcuts later on to refer to all this, but for now, try to read slowly and get used to those terms.

You should also notice that in the same way a scale has its own unique bank of notes (for a given tonic), the harmonized scale has its own **unique bank of chords or intervals**.

This is an interesting exercise which you would actually use quite a bit. Rather than harmonizing the major scale in classic triads, we will harmonize it in sus2 and sus4 triads.

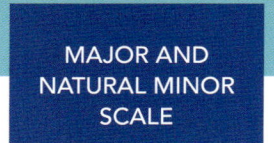

Harmonization of the major scale in classic tetrads

Let's now use the exact same logic while stacking another 3rd on top of each of the triads. This is equivalent to combining the information we found above with the harmonization of the major scale in 7ths. By doing this, we obtain the following series of tetrads:

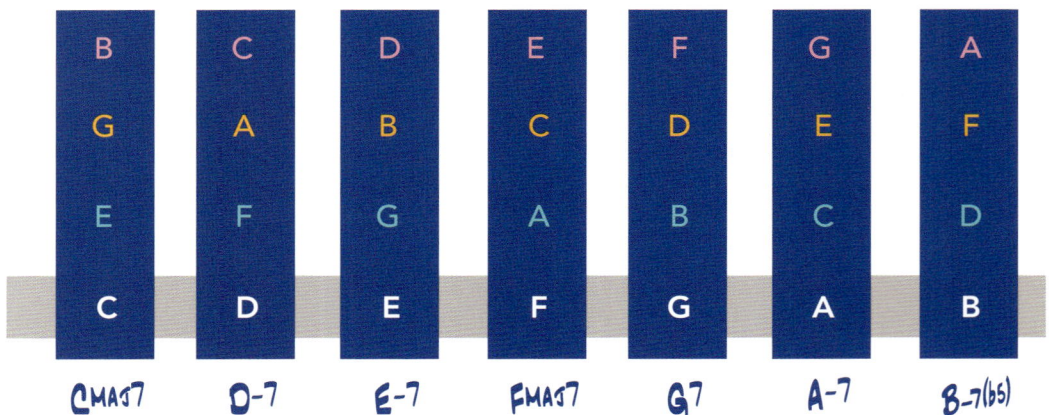

By generalizing this result we get:

Harmonization of the major scale in classic tetrads

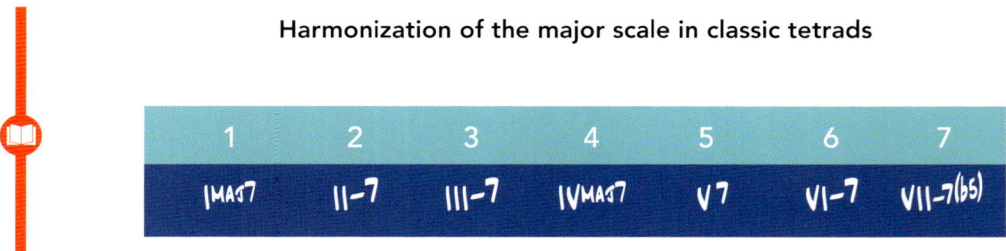

This result is also very important and **must be remembered by heart**. Generally speaking, you should always remember information relative to the major scale… It's the one you will (very likely) be using the most.

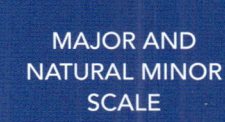

MAJOR AND NATURAL MINOR SCALE

■ Harmonization and extensions

Using the same logic while stacking up more 3rds, we can harmonize the major scale in extended chords of up to seven notes.

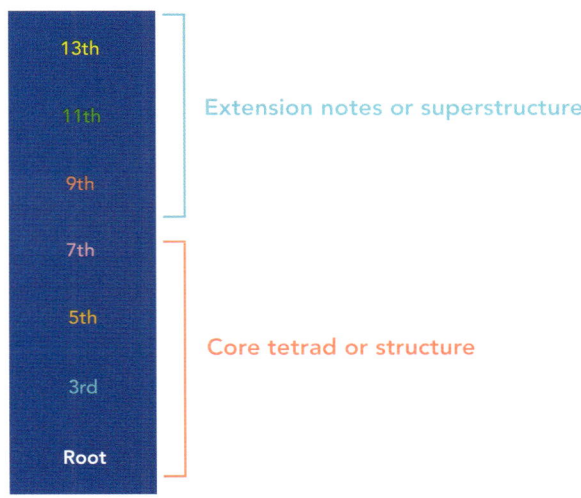

ABOUT EXTENSIONS (SUPERSTRUCTURE)

Why is it that we differentiate the four first notes of a chord (structure) from the 9ths, 11ths and 13ths (superstructure)?

A complete answer to this question would involve different fields and most likely take us too far away from the subject of this book. But one element of the answer (which to me is the most important from the musician's standpoint) is that the further "away" the notes of a chord are from the tonic, the more they seem to act as "color notes." Notions such as dissonance or consonance seem less important when notes are played at different octaves. The main sound quality of a chord is given by its **structure**, namely, the tetrad that forms the base of the chord. In classical music, the structure actually stops at the base triad and the 7th is already seen as an extension.

When you practice ear training (I really hope you do…) and try to recognize extended chords, this phenomenon becomes very clear. You will tend to recognize the structural tetrad first and then figure out what extensions are added to it.

MAJOR AND NATURAL MINOR SCALE

These chords are, as one could say, the "biggest" chords that can result from the diatonic harmonization of a scale, since they are made of all the possible notes of this scale. Adding another note to such a chord would mean one of two things:

1. That this note already belongs to the chord and would therefore not change the name of the chord.
2. That this note does not belong to the notes of the harmonized scale (or mode), which by definition would mean that the chord cannot come from the diatonic harmonization of this scale.

Let's see what we get for the C major scale:

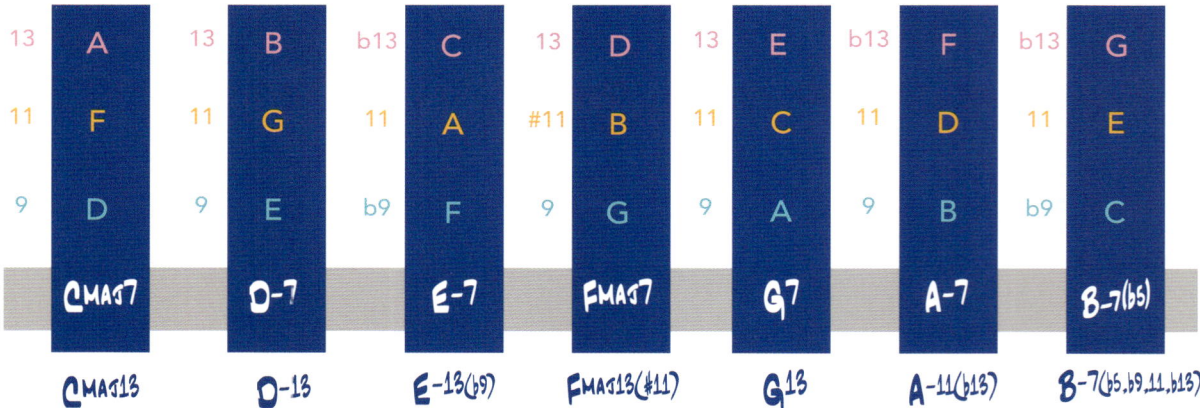

Ok, now I MUST stop here for a second considering how important the information above is. It's simply a goldmine of condensed information. Let's analyze this together:

1. **Each chord, depending on its root and degree in the diatonic scale, can be seen as the first degree of the harmonization** of a mode of the C major scale. Check it out:

The fourth mode of C major is? F Lydian, right?

F	G	A	B	C	D	E	F
1	2	3	#4	5	6	7	1

MAJOR AND NATURAL MINOR SCALE

If we take a look at the first degree of the harmonization of this mode we get:

Fmaj13(#11)

Lydian Mode

This chord is the same as the fourth chord of the harmonization of the C major scale. Moreover, this chord gives us ALL the information we need to know about the Lydian mode. From it, we can deduce that it is a *major mode* with a *perfect 5th* and a *major 7th*. Then, looking at the extensions of the chord, we can deduce the **2nd**, the **4th** and the **6th** of this mode.

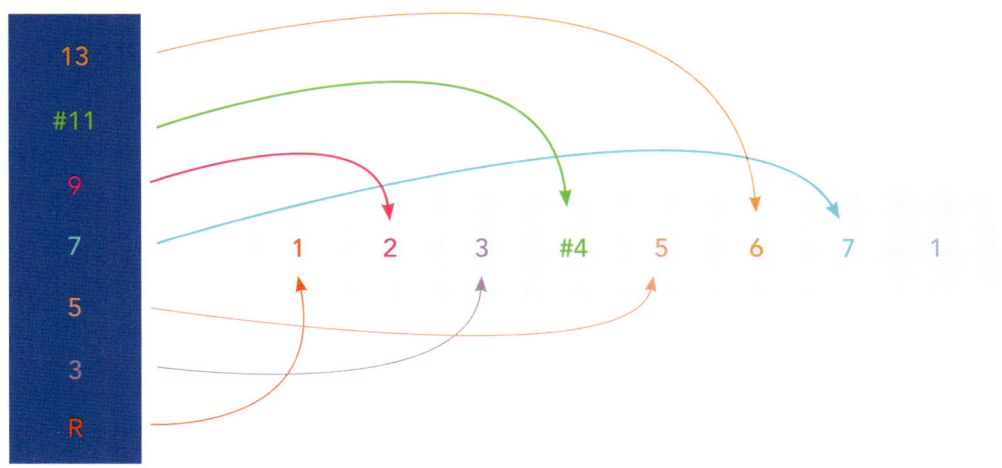

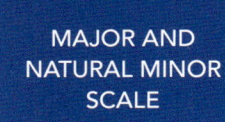
MAJOR AND NATURAL MINOR SCALE

2. **This harmonization gives us the diatonic harmonization of the scale in any other polyphonic unit (interval or chord) we wish to use:**

For example, say we wanted to know the diatonic harmonization of C major in 7ths. Well, I can refer to the nature of the 7th of each chord and BOOM. Want to harmonize in 2nds? Look at the 9th of each chord and voilà!

And now I bring you, the complete and generalized harmonization of a major scale :

Complete diatonic harmonization of the major scale

Degrees	1	2	3	4	5	6	7
Tetrads	IMAJ7	II-7	III-7	IVMAJ7	V7	VI-7	VII-7(b5)
Extensions	9 11 13	9 11 13	b9 11 b13	9 #11 13	9 11 13	9 11 b13	b9 11 b13
Mode	Ionian	Dorian	Phrygian	Lydian	Mixolydian	Aeolian	Locrian

How beautiful... Knowing this table itself condenses everything about the harmonization of the major scale, each of its modes, AND gives you a reminder about the constitutive and characteristic notes of all the modes of the major scale. If I was to forget everything I know about music theory and could keep ONE piece of information, I would remember this table. You can deduce everything from it! And as we will see later, it also gives you some good tips about how to improvise.

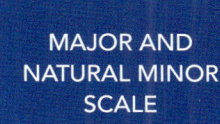

MAJOR AND NATURAL MINOR SCALE

Diatonic harmonization of modes

Technically, this part isn't really necessary since harmonizing a mode or a scale is exactly the same thing. This shouldn't surprise you since (again…) a mode IS a scale. However, you will find it relieving that since the major scale has already been harmonized, it is not necessary to do this work for every single other mode of the major scale. In a way, we have already harmonized all the modes.

But for the sake of practice and understanding, let's harmonize the F Lydian mode in order to obtain the same complete harmonization table we made above for the major scale.

F	G	A	B	C	D	E	F
1	2	3	#4	5	6	7	1

Let's start with the harmonization in tetrads:

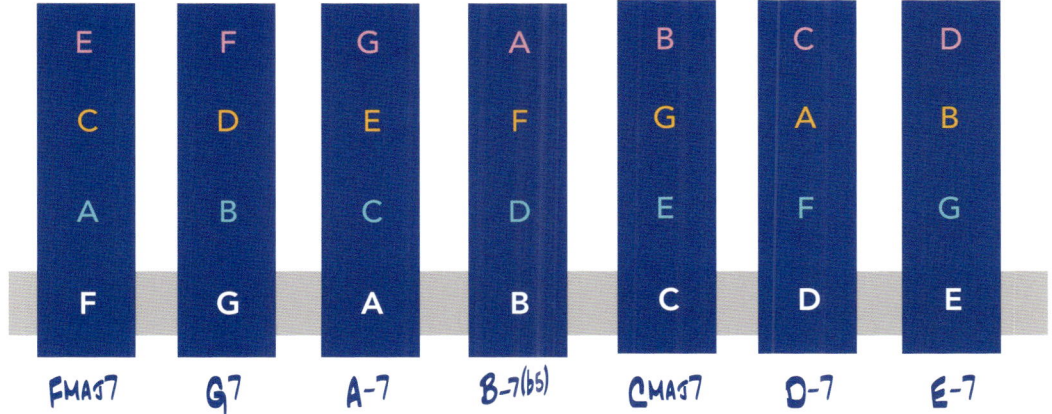

Now let's add the extensions:

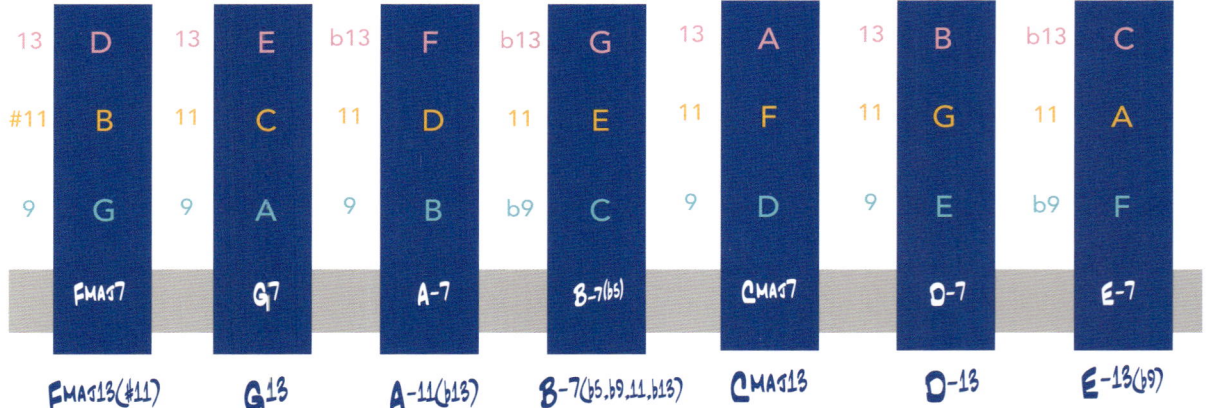

It's shouldn't be hard for you to notice that the harmonization of F Lydian is virtually the same as the harmonization of C major, except that the fourth degree of our C major harmonization becomes the first degree of the F Lydian harmonization. This will appear clearly in the following table.

Complete diatonic harmonization of the Lydian mode

Degrees	1	2	3	#4	5	6	7
Tetrads	IMAJ7	II7	III-7	#IV-7(b5)	VMAJ7	VI-7	VII-7
Extensions	9 #11 13	9 11 13	b9 11 13	b9 11 b13	9 11 13	9 11 13	b9 11 b13
Mode	Lydian	Mixolydian	Aeolian	Locrian	Ionian	Dorian	Phrygian
Relative Degrees in Major scale	4	5	6	7	1	2	3
Tetrads	IVMAJ7	V7	VI-7	VII-7(b5)	IMAJ7	II-7	III-7

MAJOR AND NATURAL MINOR SCALE

EXERCISE 3 — HARMONIZING ALL THE MODES OF THE MAJOR SCALE

> By using the harmonization of the major scale, your knowledge of modes and the F Lydian example given above, draw the table of the complete harmonization of the five remaining modes (mode 1 and 4 have already been studied).

Harmonization of the natural minor scale or Aeolian mode

If you have completed Exercise 3, you technically have already harmonized the natural minor scale since it corresponds to the sixth mode of the major scale—also called Aeolian mode.

This result is almost as important as the harmonization of the major scale (the natural minor scale is also very common), so I encourage you to remember it by heart. It's good to know how to deduce it, but you shouldn't have to do it each time.

Complete diatonic harmonization of the natural minor scale

Degrees	1	2	b3	4	5	b6	b7
Tetrads	I-7	II-7(b5)	bIIIMaj7	IV-7	V-7	bVI-7	bVII7
Extensions	9 11 b13	b9 11 b13	9 11 13	9 11 13	b9 11 b13	9 #11 13	9 11 13
Mode	Aeolian	Locrian	Ionian	Dorian	Phrygian	Lydian	Mixolydian

HARMONIC AND MELODIC MINOR SCALE

1

Diatonic Harmonization of scales or modes

HARMONIC AND MELODIC MINOR SCALES

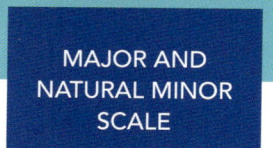

Harmonization of the harmonic minor scale

▪ Reminder

The harmonic minor scale is simply a natural minor scale with a major 7th instead of a minor 7th.

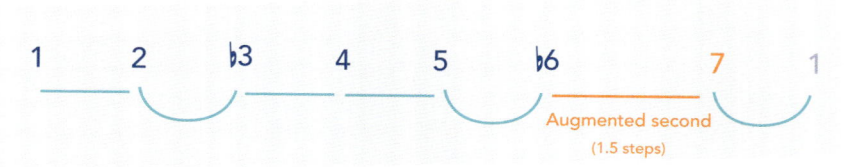

Harmonic minor scale

Again, let's start by studying the C harmonic minor scale and generalize the results:

C	D	Eb	F	G	Ab	B	C
1	2	b3	4	5	b6	7	1

Harmonization in triads:

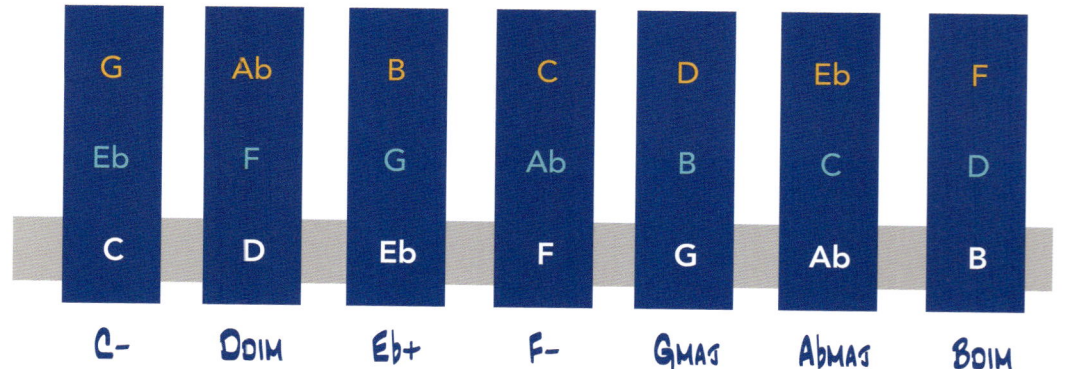

MAJOR AND NATURAL MINOR SCALE

Now let's pile up an extra third on top of these triads:

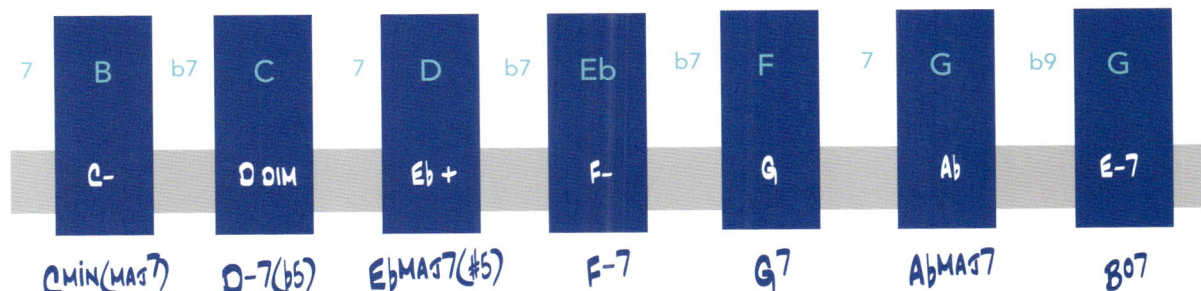

Playing each of these chords, you may notice that some of them have a very particular and unique sound. They are tinted with interesting dissonances which can sound a little weird at first, but often become very beautiful.

Now let's study the extensions of each of these chords.

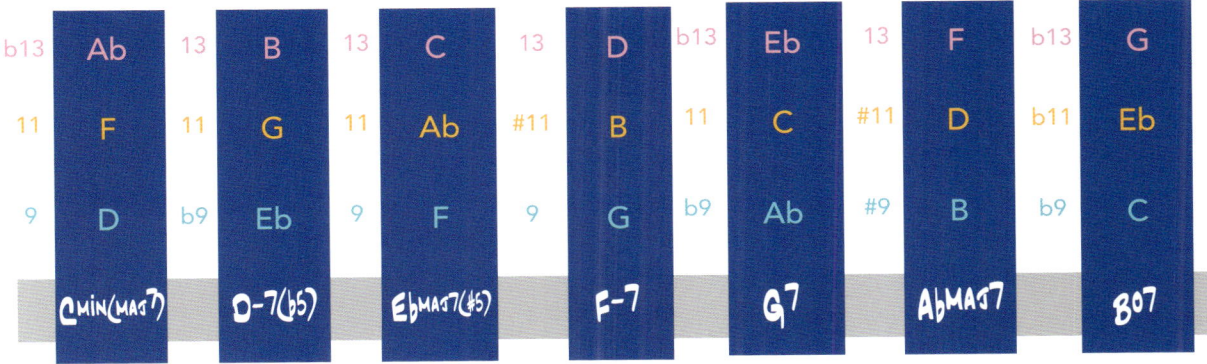

This allows us to draw the complete harmonization table of the harmonic minor scale.

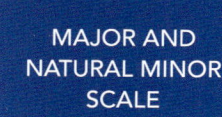
MAJOR AND NATURAL MINOR SCALE

Complete diatonic harmonization of the harmonic minor scale

Degrees	1	2	3	4	5	6	7
Tetrads	IMIN(MAJ7)	II-7(b5)	IIIMAJ7(#5)	IV-7	V7	bVIMAJ7	VII°7
Extensions	9 11 b13	b9 11 13	9 11 13	9 #11 13	b9 11 b13	9 11 b13	b9 11 b13
Mode	Harmonic Minor	Locrian Major 6	Ionian #5	Dorian #4	Phrygian Dominant	Lydian #2	Superlocrian bb7

By the way, if you haven't read my previous book or already have a solid understanding of chords and modes, it will probably be very difficult or even impossible to understand what's going on here. Don't try to force it... Read the previous book and come back to this one later.

Harmonization of the melodic minor scale
📖 Reminder

Again, let's start with a little reminder about the melodic minor scale: the melodic minor scale is simply a natural minor scale with a major 7th and a major 6th. It can also be seen as a Dorian mode with a major 7th or even a major scale with a minor 3rd.

The process of harmonization being identical to the one we've been using for all the previous scales, I will give you the result directly this time. Feel free to take a piece of paper and harmonize this scale yourself—I actually recommend it.

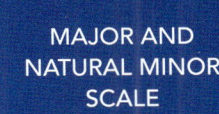
MAJOR AND NATURAL MINOR SCALE

Complete diatonic harmonization of the melodic minor scale

Degrees	1	2	3	4	5	6	7
Tetrads	IMIN(MAJ7)	II-7	IIIMAJ7(#5)	IV7	V7	bVI-7(b5)	VII-7(b5)
Extensions	9 11 b13	b9 11 13	9 #11 13	9 #11 13	9 11 b13	9 11 b13	b9 b11 b13
Mode	Melodic Minor	Phrygian Major 6th	Lydian #5	Lydian b7	Mixolydian b6	Locrian Major 2	Superlocrian

Conclusion

The concept of harmonization that we just discovered and elaborated upon in this part is extremely important because it is the foundation of musical analysis and composition. This is also why I decided to start this book with those key notions. We will be using all the above material countless times in the rest of the book, so it is very important that you eventually become familiar with it.

Now that we have all the tools we need, without further ado, we are going to dive into the mechanics of harmony, improvisation, and composition. Are you ready? Let's get started.

2

The Static Harmonic Context

ABOUT MUSICAL CREATION

ABOUT MUSICAL CREATION

The existential question of the improviser

Any musician who starts to dabble with improvising always has the same question in mind. Actually, I spend a lot of time asking myself the same question, and I think it never really ceases to occupy the mind of an improviser. This question is:

"What scale or mode can I play, right now, in this context, over this particular chord or chord progression?"

This question can also be formulated in the following way:

"What melodic tools can I use in this particular harmonic context?"

Asking yourself this question is perfectly natural… Even though some people still think that they just need their "ear" to improvise and to hell with rules, most people are hoping for a set of rational guidelines that can help them navigate with confidence the mysteries of improvisation and composition. Would *you* like such a set of rules?

Well, I have good and bad news for you. Let's start with the **bad news**:

> There is really only one rule in music: does it sound good or interesting to at lease ONE person (which can very well be just you)? Namely, is there one person at least that will be willing to give some of their attention to this music?

In a way, any sonic creation can be called "music." This judgment is so subjective and contextual that it is strictly impossible to have a universal rule or process that will guarantee the creation of an "absolutely beautiful" piece of music.

Now the **good news**:

> What we do have are countless musical analyses based on centuries of musical history and traditions, which allows us to see certain patterns, and thereby create a relatively complete inventory of "recipes" or guidelines that are known to work, in theory.

For example, we now know that a particular chord progression mixed with this particular melodic line will most likely sound "good" or "sad" or "Eastern" or "dissonant" to the ears of most people. We also know which scales, modes, and rhythms are mostly characteristic of traditional Indian, Arabian, or Japanese music, depending on the era and other factors.

But even those "recipes" have limits, since their reliability often depends on the musical preferences of the listener, the skills and sensitivity of the composer and also, frankly, on luck and apparent randomness, sometimes…

ABOUT MUSICAL CREATION

Yes, of course, there is a randomness in musical creation, and a large number of unconscious processes are always at work when someone is being creative! This is what gives some people the eerie impression of being "possessed" or "driven by other forces" while they are creating. It also does not help the false idea that you must be gifted to be a brilliant composer.

But just like in many other fields of human knowledge, musical "progress" (if there is such a thing) is often the result of involuntary actions. If you like cooking, you may know that MANY recipes were created by mistake or accident. If you were to ask the "genius" cooks responsible for those culinary breakthroughs, what would they tell you? "We didn't have anything to eat for the visit of the Tsar, so I took a bunch of snails in my garden and drenched them in butter, garlic, and parsley." (This is a true story.) And here you go: one of the most popular French dishes was born. Is this genius or random? You tell me.

So what should you do with all this information? Here is my answer:

Knowing the "recipes" that we know about harmony may not guarantee that you will revolutionize the world of music, but it WILL give you a **list of options**. Thanks to those options, with some practice, you will able to improvise very decently in many different situations. Moreover, the more you play and get familiar with those, the more your musical personality will take shape, along with the sharpness and sensitivity of your ear. Until one day, from your perseverance and practice, trials and errors, backed up with your knowledge and influences (and a bit of luck), you may create a world-renowned masterpiece. Or just a nice song or tune, which is fine. It usually takes many of the latter to get one of the former.

Again, allow me to draw an analogy with the art of cooking, which I also enjoy and is actually quite similar to music in my opinion. Knowing the rules and mechanisms of harmony is similar to having a good understanding of all the ingredients, as well as how they interact (this ingredient is bitter, but mixed with this other ingredient, it actually adds this type of flavor, and so on). It also means knowing a fair amount of standard, "classic" recipes that have stood the test of time. Any good cook knows their "classics" and can, from the top of their head, come up with at least a couple of recipes for each occasion and from different parts of the world and execute them perfectly. Most cooks will specialize in a particular type of cooking or favor certain techniques or cooking philosophies. This one may be a specialist of French cuisine and mostly uses the cooking style of Paul Bocuse, while this other one may be a genius in Italian cuisine. But regardless, most good cooks are well rounded enough that they know a little bit about all the most common styles of cooking. Little by little, a cook's palate will develop and get more precise, which will allow them to add some elements of "improvisation" in the recipes they follow. This is the phase where "making a recipe your own" or "adding your touch" becomes possible. At this phase, you start seeing imperfections in recipes or ways in which you would have done things differently. This phase is usually followed by the creation of a meal that does not follow any previous recipe—namely, a new, original recipe.

ABOUT MUSICAL CREATION

At first, in the early stages of "improvisation," a cook probably won't take the risk of creating a brand new recipe for this evening's service or big family dinner. They are more likely to serve her well-mastered recipes with perhaps a few, safe, personal modifications. Until one day, after much practice, her knowledge, palate, and know-how will communicate so efficiently that she will be able to improvise a recipe for the presidential dinner that same night, with a nearly unshakable confidence that it will be a success.

Well, that was quite the digression… Or it may appear to be. But I assume it is necessary, before learning about the mechanisms of composition and improvisation, to know a little about the psychology and philosophy of those two arts which are as sought-after as they are mysterious to most people. Let's start with a tough one: **what is the difference between composition and improvisation?**

Composition or improvisation

It is often difficult to clearly differentiate improvisation from composition and vice versa. Many compositions involve improvisation at least at some point in the process of their creation, and improvisation is undoubtedly a form of composition. I've looked around but failed to find a solid definition of what we refer to as "composing" and "improvising" especially in the field of music. The definitions I will give you here are clearly not the only possible ones. They are a combination of the various ones I have found, and of my personal interpretation of these words.

▪ Composition

The word "composition" comes from the Latin word componere which means "to put together." But it is important to notice that the word composition can refer to the process of composition (which is a dynamic meaning) as well as to the piece of music that results from this process (static meaning).

A composition is the final and—to some extent—permanent result of the process of musical creation. The process from which it originates is also referred to as composition. It often involves one or several phases of improvisation or exploration during which the author will find an idea (musical sentence, melody, or piece of melody, chord progression, etc…) that resonates with them in a way that seems pertinent. This idea is then refined and/or improved during a phase of arrangement (by adding more instruments, changing, or enriching the chord progressions, etc.) until reaching a point where the composer judges the piece of music to be at least temporarily finished and conclusive. It is not rare for a composer (or other arrangers) to rework the composition, which is thus always susceptible to changes and evolution.

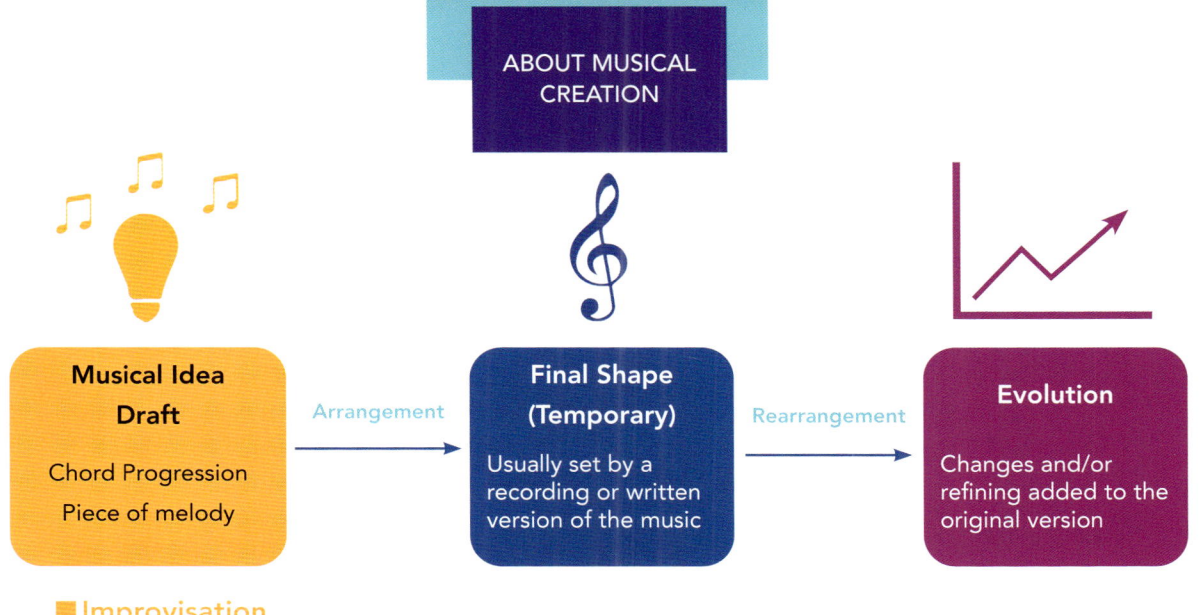

■ Improvisation

The word improvisation comes from French (yay homeland), and before this comes from the Latin word improviso which means "unforeseen; not studied or prepared beforehand." As the etymology clearly indicates, improvisation can be seen as an ephemeral and/or irreversible composition produced in the moment, without preparation. If it isn't written, memorized, or recorded while it is being executed, an improvisation most likely only has one life and will never be played exactly the same again. Another element of improvisation, at least in the way musicians or public speakers see it, is that it is immediately put to the test. A musician is often said to be "improvising" when they are doing so in front of an audience that can immediately witness the result of this process.

Finally, improvisation can be done "ex nihilo" (out of nothing), which means the improviser has virtually NO musical constraints while improvising. Often however, improvising is done in a certain predefined musical context which to some extent frames and constrains the improviser. In jazz and rock for example, musicians are often asked to improvise during "solos." Those solos are often melodies improvised over a predefined harmonic context (or chord progression) played by other instruments, thereby narrowing down the possibilities of the improviser, who is no longer responsible for the whole composition. This being said, it is not uncommon to see some musicians improvise an ENTIRE piece of music in front of an audience, so brilliantly that it is almost impossible to tell whether or not the work was previously composed or not. Needless to say, this implies a considerable level of mastery.

■ What we will be focusing on

In the end, it is relatively pointless to spend too much time arguing about the subtle differences between composition and improvisation. To summarize it, if you are working on a tune in your room, alone, or in a studio with your band, with no time constraints, you are composing.

ABOUT MUSICAL CREATION

If you are playing something on the spot that hasn't been previously prepared (or at least not entirely), whether it's a solo or an entire tune, you are improvising. Again, both are often essential to creating a complete piece of music.

The main difficulty with improvising, especially in a live situation, is that you clearly don't have a lot of time to THINK about what you play. On the other hand, you can spend a week choosing the perfect note or chord when you are composing. This means that improvising requires an instinctive understanding and reactivity beyond the rational understanding. However, I am by no means implying that composing is "easier" than improvising.

To eliminate any ambivalence, from now on I will use the word "creating" to refer to both composing and improvising.

Creating in music usually implies one of the following processes:

- Creating a melody over a preexisting harmonic context. This is what you would do if asked to compose or improvise a melody, line, or solo over a certain chord progression.

- Creating a chord progression or harmonic context around a preexsiting melody. This process is also called harmonizing or reharmonizing. It's what you would do if a singer came up with a melody and asked you to come up with a chord progression for this melody. When done in a context of improvisation, this process is also called "comping." In this case, you would be harmonizing on the spot.

- Creating both of the above simultaneously. This requires a great degree of mastery and an instrument that allows you to play melodies and chords at the same time (the piano is the best example).

These processes can also be combined! For example, it's not rare for someone to start writing a tune by coming up with a melody. Then they have to figure out what chords would work best for this melody. The chord progression can then lead to modifying the original melody or creating a new part based on the harmonic context.

> **So, which of these processes will we be exploring?**
>
> **I believe that the best way to start is to understand the first process: how to create a melody (improvised or composed) in a certain harmonic context.**
>
> Once you become conformable with this first process of creation, it will be much easier to reverse engineer it and come up with chords for a melody. Starting the other way around would be nonsense in my opinion.

ABOUT MUSICAL CREATION

In this book, we will mostly be focusing on what to play melodically in a certain harmonic context. We will explore some elements of harmonizing or reharmonizing, but going too deep into these notions would require another book on the subject.

> To make it simple, I will be putting myself in the shoes of someone who is given a particular harmonic context and is asked to improvise or create a melody in it.

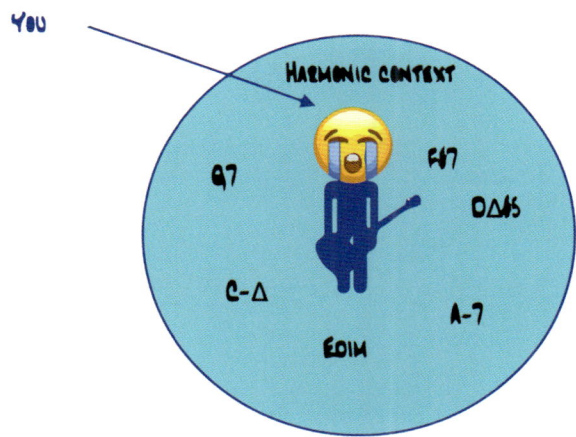

Different contexts of improvisation

What are the situations in which you are likely to be asked to improvise as a musician? There are four main scenarios :

■ 1 - The "lead sheet"

A lead sheet will give you the chord progression of the tune (only the name of the chords, the way you play them is subject to interpretation) as well as the main melody written bellow on a staff. One thing is sure, you will run into many lead sheets as a musician for it is the most common way of writing music nowadays, especially modern music

ABOUT MUSICAL CREATION

ABOUT MUSICAL CREATION

■ 2 - The chord chart

    A chord chart is like a lead sheet that doesn't include the melody. Sometimes it will include some rhythmic indications about how or when to play the chords. It may also include some pieces of melody when it is relevant (for example, if it's a line that must be played by all instruments in unison). Part of my promise here in this book is to not use notes written on a staff, so we will mostly be using chord charts. But remember that if you are given a lead sheet and don't know how to read music, you can still read the chord part! Unless you are asked to play the melody… Then, well, you either fake it (which I don't recommend), confidently admit that you don't know the song and cannot sight read, or last but not least, pretend that you don't know the song while you actually know it and pretend like you're reading it (which I may or may not have done in the past).

    The chord chart of the example above would be:

All Of Me

(Medium Swing)   Gerald Marks

[A]
| $\frac{4}{4}$ $C_{\Delta 7}$ | ✗ | E_7 | ✗ |
| A_7 | ✗ | D_{-7} | ✗ ‖
[B]
‖ E_7 | ✗ | A_{-7} | ✗ |
| D_7 | ✗ | D_{-7} | G_7 ‖
[A]
‖ $C_{\Delta 7}$ | ✗ | E_7 | ✗ |
| A_7 | ✗ | D_{-7} | ✗ ‖
[C]
              $F^{\#}_{o7}$ $C_{\Delta 7}/G$
‖ $F_{\Delta 7}$ | F_{-6} | E_{-7} | A_7 |
| D_{-7} | G_7 | C_6 $E^{\flat}_{o7}$ | D_{-7} G_7 ‖

■ 3 - The chord chart given orally, on the spot

This is a much-dreaded situation, especially when you don't have a lot of experience with it. You finally decide to play and hop on stage at the jam session as you hear some of the hosts talk about a tune that you love and know perfectly. But suddenly, the tide seems to turn radically, and one of the musicians suggests a tune that you don't know AT ALL… of course. For a moment, you look around and hope that you won't be the only one preferring the original tune, the one you took all your courage to go up there and play. You hope that someone will help you, save you. But little by little, you are left with the eerie realization that all the other musicians know this newly suggested tune. Worse than that! They prefer it much more and all agree that it will be the one that will be played. All eyes are now on you, and you are still wondering if nobody can spot the obvious fear on your face. Then, the person guilty of this ugly change of events, driven by a profound sense of empathy, tells you: "It's super easy! Check it out, it starts in 7/8 with Gb-∆, and then it only modulates about six times…" followed by the utterly dreaded, "You'll hear it!"

At this moment, you understand that it's over. You'll have to sit back and hope they don't give you a solo that you know will be a disaster. The audience is waiting. You desperately ask the musician closest to you to give you the chord progression one more time. But it's too late. Mercilessly, the drummer starts:

"Three, four…"

Normally, if you are not used to this type of situation, you will fail, like everyone else. Try to laugh about it.

However, with a bit of practice, you'll get used to it and know how to seemingly fake your way through. After you've encountered enough chord progressions, you start seeing patterns and similarities which allow you to understand what's going on quite quickly.

■ 4 - The "all-by-ear" situation

This is by far the hardest scenario. You are basically asked to figure out the tune on the spot by ear, without any information. This obviously takes some skills.

The importance of ear training and the limits of "playing from the mind"

Let's come back to the parallel with cooking: In order to create or improvise a recipe, it is very important to know your ingredients more than on a theoretical level. You must know how they taste and smell on their own AND when combined! If your palate is bad, you won't really know what you're doing.

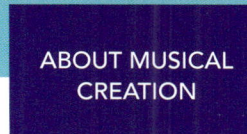

ABOUT MUSICAL CREATION

It's virtually the same thing in music! You can know all the theory in the world and understand perfectly what's going on on paper, but if you don't know what a major scale, the lydian mode, the major chord, and all the other musical "ingredients" that exist actually SOUND like, you will never be able to improvise efficiently.

■ The limits of logical playing or "playing from the mind"

You simply cannot use logic only when it comes to music and even more so when it comes to improvising! Thinking takes TIME. You may be the fastest thinker in the world, but by the time your brain figures out what scale would be the most appropriate to play on a particular chord, the chord will be long gone and you'll have to think about the next chord. Nevertheless, if you spend enough time training your ear in order to quickly and efficiently recognize all the different musical tools (intervals, scales, modes, chords, rhythms), you will be able to use much faster neural circuits that allow you to react promptly and improvise coherently. On an experimental level, it feels like you are hearing what you want to play in advance while your body immediately and intuitively follows (whether it's your finger, feet, or vocal chords). It feels like you are playing exactly what you want without having to think about it, which creates a very satisfying sense of flow, which I hope you will get to experience.

For this reason, I really encourage you to train your ear and to start NOW as you go through this book. Eventually, you should be able to recognize and SING (for the voice is the best way to internalize the sounds) ALL the concepts we will be discovering in this book AND the tools explored in the previous book.

Building these skills will take time, a lot of practice, and trial and error. But don't despair, you will get there!

Understanding is necessary but not sufficient. In you music you music be able to HEAR.

Balance between melodic, polyphonic, and rhythmic complexity

In order for music to be pleasing, it is often better to avoid "overloads of musical information." Granted, some styles of music seem to purposely ignore this piece of advice (think about some bebop jazz, fusion jazz, "free" jazz, or some metal or classical music). But when you add too much complexity to the melodic, polyphonic, and even rhythmic dimension of a tune, you may chase away many listeners and be left with a restrained niche of nerdy musicians. And if this is your goal, then who am I to judge? Just be aware of this fact.

Now, what exactly do I mean by "richness or complexity"? This might need some clarifying. Complexity to me can be added with:

ABOUT MUSICAL CREATION

- **Density**. For example, a lot of notes in a chord, or a lot of chords in a tune, many different notes in a melody, etc.

- **Debit.** Debit refers to how much musical information is being played in a certain amount of time. How fast the notes are being played or how fast the chords change or even how many notes the drummer is playing per bar, etc.

- **Dissonance or tension.** We'll talk more about tension later, but dissonance—which refers to chords or notes which create a feeling of tension or instability—can also add complexity to a tune.

- **Unpredictability.** Again, humans take pleasure in the repetition of predictable patterns. Moreover, when we listen to a tune, we all have a subconscious idea of how it's going to evolve by comparing it to similar tunes we know. When this pattern of predictability is broken, it adds a felling of complexity to the tune.

It's always important to find a balance between the amount of melodic, polyphonic, and rhythmic information. Imagine that you are in a room that has three different heaters and that you are trying to maintain a comfortable temperature in this room. If you turn one of the heaters up, you will inevitably have to lower either or both of the other heaters to maintain the temperature.

In this book, **we will not be focusing on the rhythmic aspect of improvisation, so we'll just go ahead and take this out of the equation. But please be aware that it also plays a major part.**

In many cases, you will find this rule to be respected because if you overload all these parameters, it may just sound like nonsense, chaos or simply like "too much is going on." Again, you may find some connoisseurs or musicians that will get it and admire the technical skills involved, but you WILL limit your audience.

I consider myself a music nerd and open-minded listener and yet have once been tempted to ask for my money back at a free-jazz concert. It was technically very impressing but it sounded, well… VERY BAD.

Each genre of music tends to favor different aspects when it comes to complexity. Traditional African music, for example, emphasizes rhythm much more than anything else. There is also often singing involved (which corresponds to melody) but very little harmonic context.

On the other hand, classical western music tends to favor the polyphonic aspect over rhythms and melody.

ABOUT MUSICAL CREATION

High Melodic Complexity ⟷ **High Polyphonic Complexity**

- Modal music
- Asian and Indian traditional musics
- Some African music
- Certain types of jazz

- Tonal music
- Classical music
- Swing

Again, there are styles of music which are complex in all aspects. Bebop jazz and some heavy metal are two examples of such genres. Well... ask a random person in the street who is not a music fanatic if they like either of these styles. I guarantee that most of the time the answer will be negative. Hell... I'm not the biggest fan of bebop or heavy metal! I respect the technique involved, but I hardly ever listen to theses types of music.

Without further ado, let's dive into it! We will start with the left hand of the spectrum—a simple harmonic context—and work our way towards the right by adding polyphonic complexity little by little and studying how this changes our melodic options.

2

The Static Harmonic Context

PLAYING OVER A SINGLE BASS NOTE

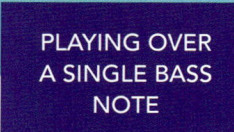

So, before exploring our melodic options over a rich chord progression that changes every bar at 240bpm, we are going to start with the simplest harmonic context that you will find:

The context of a single note played in the background

In this situation, the polyphonic information is basically none. Polyphony will only be limited to the **intervals formed with the note and each note the melodist will be adding to it.**

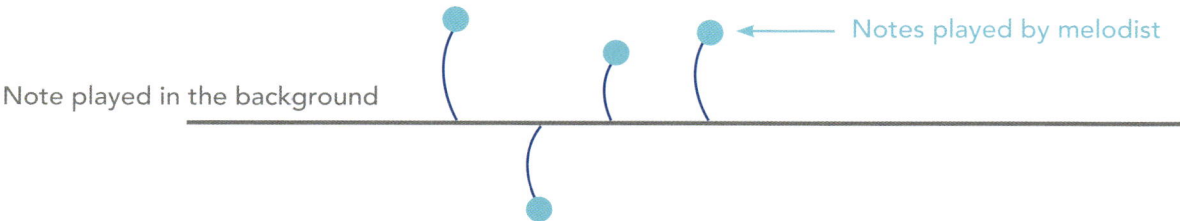

Now, even though any note at any pitch could technically work to create a harmonic context, it's always best to use a low-pitched or bass note to really "ground" the context. Remember that the harmonic context is always carried by the bass since the ear naturally uses the lowest pitched note as a reference. This is also why melodies tend to be played at higher pitches! To put it differently, the note played in the background has to be lower than any (or at least most) of the notes you will be playing as a melody. **Such a note is sometimes called a pedal or drone note.**

So basically this context is you playing over **one note that never changes**. In this context, the only musical information you have is a **tonic**. As I said in the previous book, our ear naturally uses the lowest note in a musical piece as reference note or **tonic**.

For example, let's study the case of a static **C note**, played by the bass.

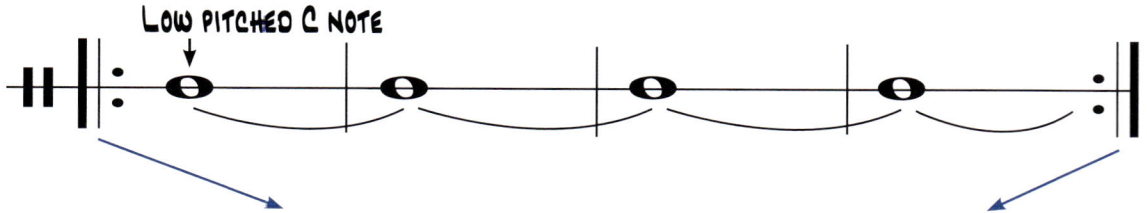

These symbols indicate that the measures between them are repeated once. However, in this case, let's just assume that the measures are repeated indefinitely, or as long as the melodist keeps on going.

PLAYING OVER A SINGLE BASS NOTE

 This symbol is called the neutral clef, which basically means the notes written here only give us rhythmic information. You can somewhat read rhythms by now, right? You should be able to if you had read the previous book...

Let's also not worry about any notion of time signature or rhythm for now, since we want to focus on our options in terms of pitches. These will apply to any rhythm or time signature.

The first thing to point out is that regardless of the note palette or collection of notes played by the melodist, it will be perceived as being played **OVER the note C**. In other words, the only element "imposed" by the harmonic context is the note C.

Question: What does it mean for C to be "imposed" in this case?

It means that whether you like it or not, **from the point of view of the listener**, C IS part of the scale or mode that you are playing over. Even if you decided to improvise over this C without actually playing the note C, it is still heard when the music is considered in its entirety. Not only that, but being the lowest note, **C will naturally be the tonic of whatever scale or mode you play**. The musical context you have will always look like this:

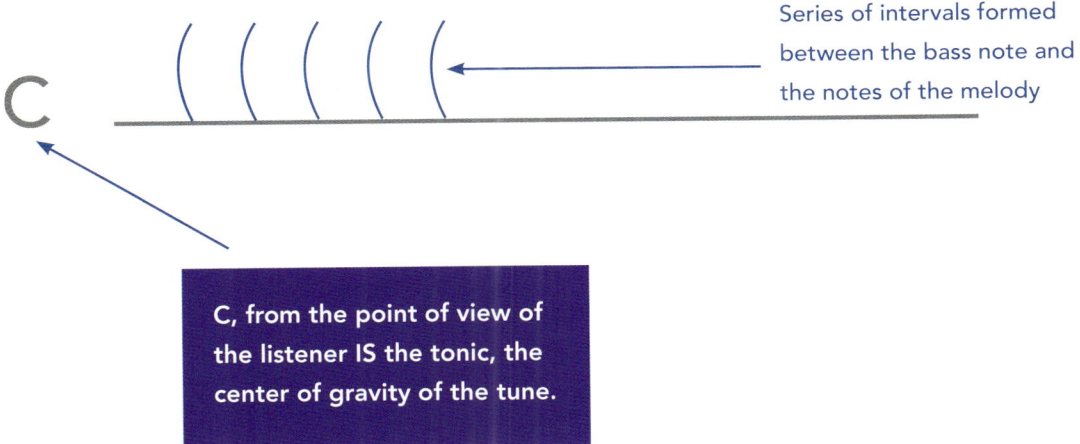

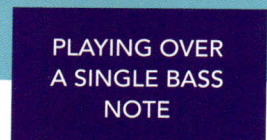

PLAYING OVER A SINGLE BASS NOTE

Okay, so what notes can we choose in this context? What will sound good or bad? What scales or modes can we play? Well, sadly, I still need to introduce a few other notions before we answer these questions.

What is thought versus what is heard - the point of view of the listener

I must introduce you to the difference between **what you think when you play and what is heard.** I believe keeping this in mind will help you considerably, especially when it comes to improvising and composing. If you study the whole system of a piece of music in its entirety, whether it is live or not, it always involves many processes and points of views:

- What each musician is thinking when they are playing (the mix of thought process and intuition that leads them to play what they play).

- What each musician hears from the other musicians.

- What the listeners hear and receive which is the result of the two previous points.

You may have heard before that when playing, you should always devote a major part of your attention to listening. But listening to what, exactly? I've asked myself this question for a long time. You shouldn't just listen to what you play, nor should you only listen to what your fellow musicians are playing. Instead, you should put yourself in the shoes of a third person listener who has NO CLUE whatsoever of what each musician is thinking and is just receiving the final result of what is happening on stage or in the studio.

This subtlety in mindset and perspective will soon become very handy for what we will be studying here. For example, I can think very hard, "I'm going to play the C major scale now" and start playing what is obviously C major in my mind. But if the bass player decides to play a D in the background, my thought process doesn't matter. The listener will be receiving or hearing the **D Dorian mode**! Remember? The D Dorian mode corresponds to the notes of the C major scale played over the second note of this scale, which is D. If this doesn't make sense, back to the first book ;).

Being aware of this will make your life MUCH easier, especially when things get a little tricky and complex. We will see that you can often "think" in terms of very simple scales and tools and yet, by leveraging the fact that listeners hear the band as a whole, give the impression of playing in a complex and sophisticated way.

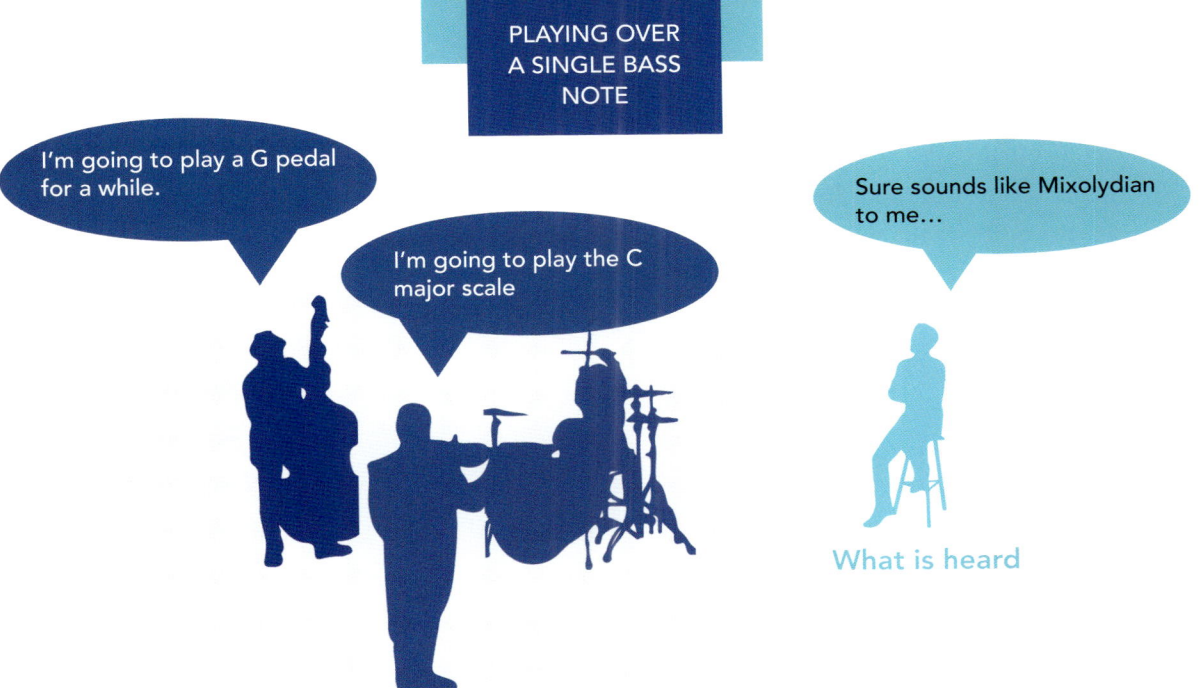

What is thought by each musician

About consonance and dissonance

As I explained in the first book, the particular sound of a scale or a mode is given by the group of intervals formed between the notes of the scale and its tonic. Each interval has a characteristic "color" or sound which can be more or less consonant or dissonant.

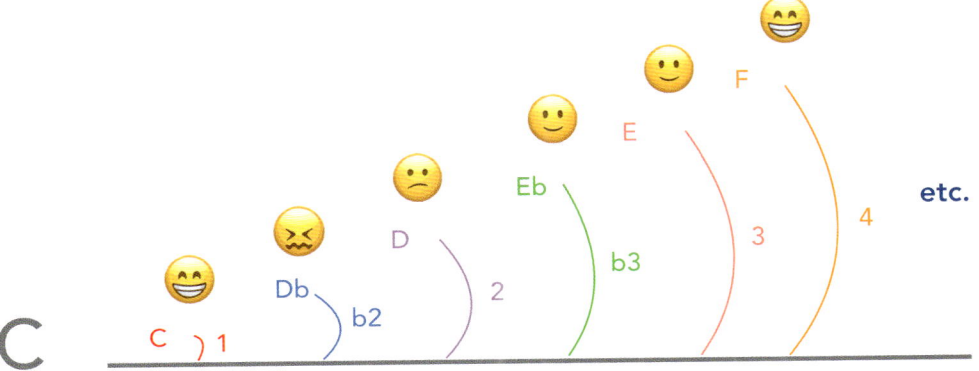

PLAYING OVER A SINGLE BASS NOTE

Consonance and dissonance involve a big part of subjectivity and it is very important not to give those two notions a positive or negative connotation. A dissonance can sound awful to you and beautiful to someone else. It can also sound good in a particular context and not so much in other situations.

You will come to notice what really matters is how consonances and dissonances are distributed, how they alternate, and in which context they are used.

Despite being subjective notions, there are physical and rather objective characteristics to intervals that allow us to attribute to each interval a certain level of consonance or lack there of.

PLAYING OVER A SINGLE BASS NOTE

Name	Example	Notation	Consonant or Dissonant	Level of consonance or dissonance
Perfect Unison	C - C	1	Consonant	Perfect consonance
Augmented Unison	C - C#	#1	Dissonant	Strong dissonance
Minor 2nd	C - Db	b2		
Major 2nd	C - D	2	Dissonant	Moderate dissonance
Augmented 2nd	C - D#	#2	Consonant	Moderate consonance
Minor 3rd	C - Eb	b3		
Major 3rd	C - E	3	Consonant	Moderate consonance
Perfect 4th	C - F	4	Consonant	Perfect consonance
Augmented 4th	C - F#	#4	Dissonant	Strong dissonance
Diminished 5th	C - Gb	b5		
Perfect 5th	C - G	5	Consonant	Perfect consonance
Augmented 5th	C - G#	#5	Consonant	Moderate consonance
Minor 6th	C - Ab	b6		
Major 6th	C - A	6	Consonant	Moderate consonance
Augmented 6th	C - A#	#6	Dissonant	Moderate Dissonance
Minor 7th	C - Bb	b7		
Major 7th	C - B	7	Dissonant	Strong dissonance
Perfect Octave	C - C + 1 octave	8 (or 1)	Consonant	Perfect consonance

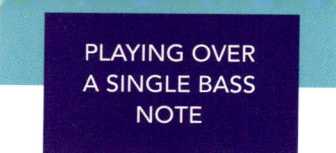

PLAYING OVER A SINGLE BASS NOTE

This means that when you play a melody over a single bass note, depending on the scales or modes that you decide to play, you will create a series of more or less dissonant/consonant intervals.

■ Specific cases of compound intervals (bigger than one octave)

You will notice as a matter of experience that the more a note is distant from a root (in terms of pitch), the less clearly "consonant" or "dissonant" the resulting intervals will become. For example, a minor 9th—which is the compound version of a minor 2nd—will be less dissonant than a minor 2nd. This explains why most of the time, dissonant notes (or dissonant extensions) in a chord tend to be played at a reasonable distance from the root.

Again, make sure you play all the intervals, listen to them, and learn to recognize them.

Tension and resolution mechanisms

A **dissonant** interval usually generates a feeling of tension. Physically speaking, the two sound waves tend to clash, thereby inducing a relatively displeasing or unstable sensation. Naturally, the person listening to such a sound will want it to end, on some level, to resolve to a more stable or pleasing sensation.

Unconsciously, your brain will start imagining which notes could and/or should change in order to put an end to the displeasing interval. It's like it was unconsciously thinking:

"If only one of those two notes could go up or down a half step, it would sound SO MUCH better."

When the musician(s) decide(s) to satisfy this urge, by changing one of the notes in order to create a more consonant interval, it will create a great sense of relief in the listener's mind. The tension is then said to be resolved. It's a similar feeling to the one you would feel after wearing shoes that are too small for an entire day and finally taking them off.

Most of western music is based on this principal of tension followed by a resolution, as we will see in the chapter dedicated to the tonal context.

This phenomenon leads us to define the notion of **stable notes** (as well as stable intervals and chords). A stable note (or interval or chord) is the closest note that can be played, in order to resolve a dissonant interval. A note (or interval or chord) creating a dissonance is also called an **active note.**

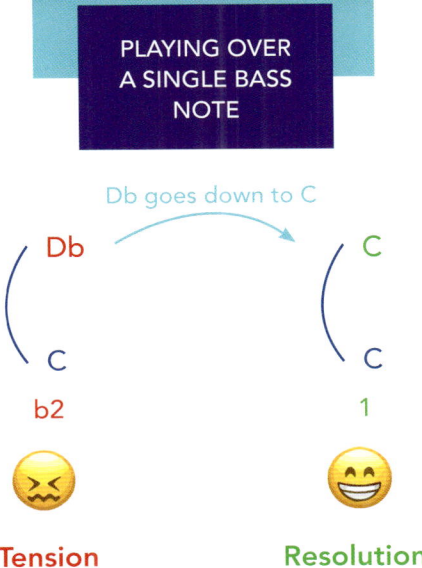

■ Always a half step from the "right" note

You may have heard some people say that *"you are always only a half step away from the right note."* This statement actually has some truth to it. Indeed, if you look at the table of the intervals above, you'll notice that any dissonant interval is always either immediately followed or preceded by a consonant interval.

So if you're soloing and you land on a note that makes you want to shed a tear, don't worry, you can save the day by sliding up or down one half step. If you're playing jazz, you might actually make people believe that the bad note was played on purpose.

■ Reciprocal resolution and double resolution

A dissonant interval can be resolved by changing the higher OR the lower note of this interval to a more stable note. You can also change BOTH notes to create a more consonant interval.

 Given one possibility of resolution, its reciprocal resolution consists in creating the same consonant interval but by changing the other note.

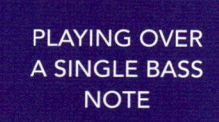

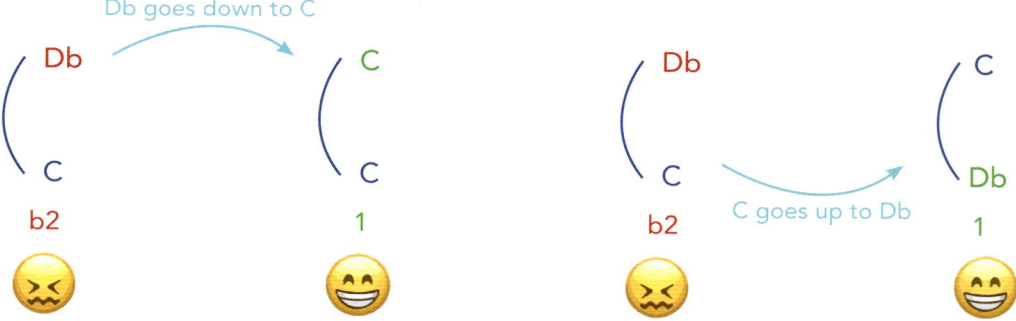

 A **double resolution** consists of changing both the notes of an interval in order to create a more consonant interval

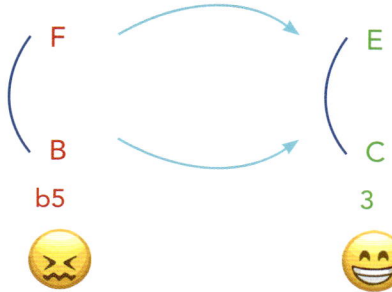

Okay, let's get back to our melodic creation studies! We are (still) in the case of a single note played at a low pitch (bass note) over which we are trying to create a melody. If the bass player shows good behavior and actually stays on that given note, I, the improviser or composer, am entirely responsible for creating either consonant or dissonant intervals and for choosing to resolve the dissonant intervals or not.

Remember that the tonic will always be the most stable note. If you play the tonic (that means the same note as the bass player at any octave you want), tensions will be resolved and EVERYONE will agree that this note is consonant.

Now, can you potentially decide NOT to ever play the tonic? Of course! You can do whatever you want. But playing the tonic is always a grounding feeling and most improvisers and composers rely on it for this precise reason.

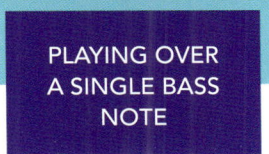

PLAYING OVER A SINGLE BASS NOTE

Context of a static bass note: summary

Creating a melody over a static bass note is the simplest polyphonic context one can encounter, which gives the melodist almost total melodic freedom. There are many cultures that use this type of musical context, and it can be interesting to listen to some Indian, African, or Asian traditional music (even though some don't use our equally tempered system).

Whether or not it is played by the melodist, the note played by the bass **belongs to the scale or mode played** and IS the **tonic** of this scale or mode. **It is also the most stable note that can be played.**

Note: When talking about notions which apply to any note, I will simply use a generic note X in honor of the math nerd I used to be (and still very much am...)

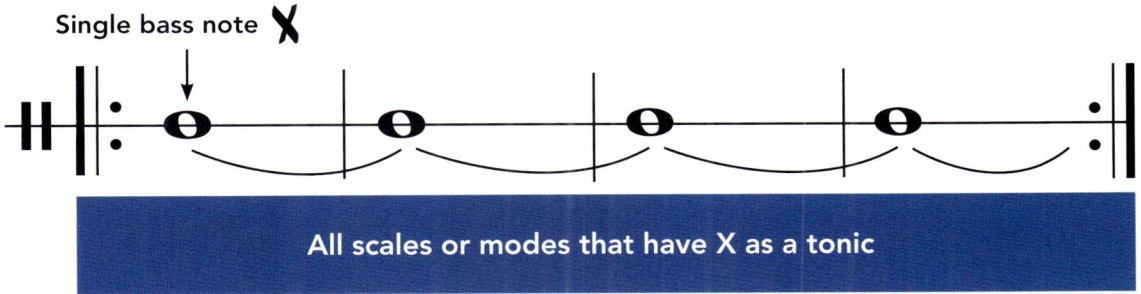

Melodic Options

Now, you may be tempted to say that this does not give you much of a guideline. What we discovered above is that in the context of a static note, you can play ANY mode or scale that has this note as its tonic. Well, that's a lot of options. So this leads to the following question:

Are there modes or scales among all the possible ones that are preferable or "sound better" than others?

Again, this is a tricky question, but the short answer is: Of course! But sound better or preferable TO WHOM? To you? To your listeners? Sometimes you can't be in alignment with the tastes and preferences of everyone. What is certain however, is that the more you practice and explore all the options with the guide of theory and logic, the more you will know which notes are appropriate and the more control and freedom you will have over what you create. You'll even sometimes be able to ignore all rules about scales and modes and just let your fingers go where your ears guide them, since you will know exactly how they sound in advance.

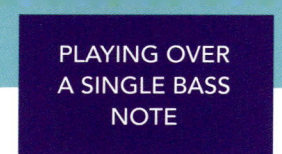

PLAYING OVER A SINGLE BASS NOTE

This, by the way, is what "playing by ear" REALLY means. Not to be confused with the notion of just trying out a bunch of notes with no sense of control due to a lack of knowledge. Playing by ear takes an incredible degree of mastery, so it always surprises me to hear some unexperienced musicians us this term.

It also very much depends on the context and the style of music you are playing. If you are partaking in a religious ceremony somewhere in the Middle East (they use a lot of single-note harmonic contexts) and start ripping a blues scales, you'll probably politely be asked to stop.

The five commandments of the melodist

This book wouldn't be very useful if the conclusion was only "just play anything you want and figure it out." My goal is to give you some guidelines and the rules used by most experienced improvisers and composers, so we need to somehow limit our options. I am guessing that when improvising, you want to create melodies that are somewhat pleasing, and this can be done by following this advice:

1. **Try to limit dissonant notes (or intervals) by including stable notes**

    If the note palette you chose is made exclusively of dissonant notes, and does not contain enough stable notes, people will just think you don't know how to play. It's just a fact.

2. **Don't play too many notes! Show your audience that you know what you're doing and are actively and carefully choosing the notes you play.**

    If you just play all the notes (a.k.a. the chromatic scale) all the time without making clear choices of notes, it will sound like nonsense! There is always a happy medium to find between naive, conservative, consonant playing, and complete cacophony.

3. **Use the appropriate scales and modes as your guideline but not absolute truth.**

    When it comes to creating melodies, figuring out what main scales or modes you can use as a guide should always be your fist concern. But once you have an idea of what to play, feel free to explore other options which do not necessarily make theoretical sense!

PLAYING OVER A SINGLE BASS NOTE

4. **Adapt to the musical genre or style**

   You have to know what scales or modes to favor depending on what genre or music you are playing! Of course, some scales, such as the major scale or the pentatonic scales, are used in almost every genre. But there are genres in which some scales or modes can be inappropriate. Try playing a Superlocrian lick in bluegrass jazz and look at the faces of the other musicians.

   How do you know what's appropriate? That's what **musical culture** is for! You need to listen to music and play a variety of different genres to build a sense of what each style is supposed to sound like.

5. **Favor melodies that can be sung.**

   People relate to music with the one instrument almost everyone has: their voice. If what you are playing is so complicated and chaotic that it would take a scat expert to sing it, you are probably not playing the best melody. You can sometimes ignore this rule for solos if you want to add a technical element just to show off how badass you are, but still... the most legendary solos of all time are usually solos you can sing.

PLAYING OVER A SINGLE INTERVAL OR CHORD

2

The Static Harmonic Context

PLAYING OVER A SINGLE INTERVAL OR CHORD

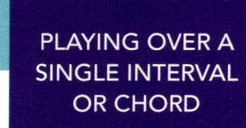

It's now time to add more notes to our harmonic context. This time, rather than just one bass note, we will be looking at the case of a **single interval or chord played in the background** over which we have to create a melody.

We'll consider that the lowest note of this interval or chord is the lowest note played, and therefore the tonic of whichever melodic tool we use to create our melody over it.

You'll see that the principles for creating melodies over an interval or a chord are very similar. Let's start with intervals and work our way up from there.

Context of a single interval

Let's start by studying the case of a 5th interval with a root of C.

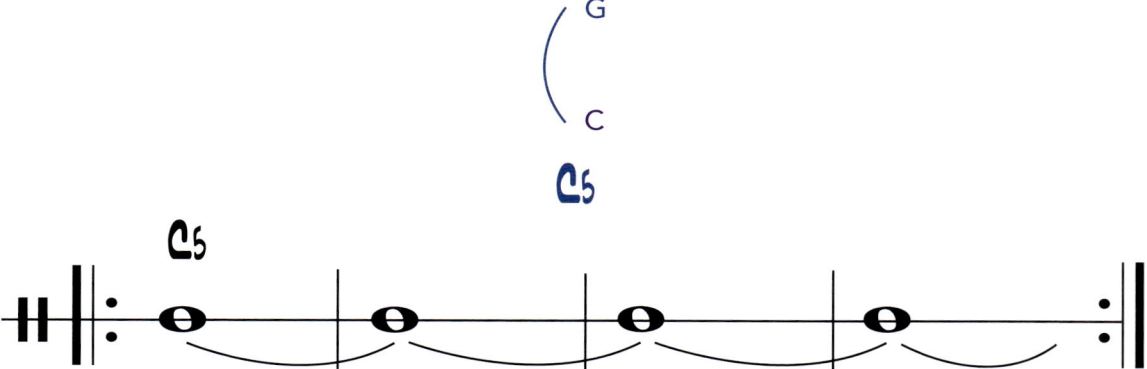

What does this imply?

1. Our collection of notes now contains **two imposed notes** (i.e., notes that are part of it whether we want it or not). C, which will be the tonic, and G, the perfect 5th above C. These two notes are stable notes of the harmonic context and can therefore be played at will to create relief.

2. Each time we play a note, this note will interact with the two notes of the interval, giving us a total of three intervals. Put differently, each note played will create a TRIAD (group of three notes).

PLAYING OVER A SINGLE INTERVAL OR CHORD

Example:

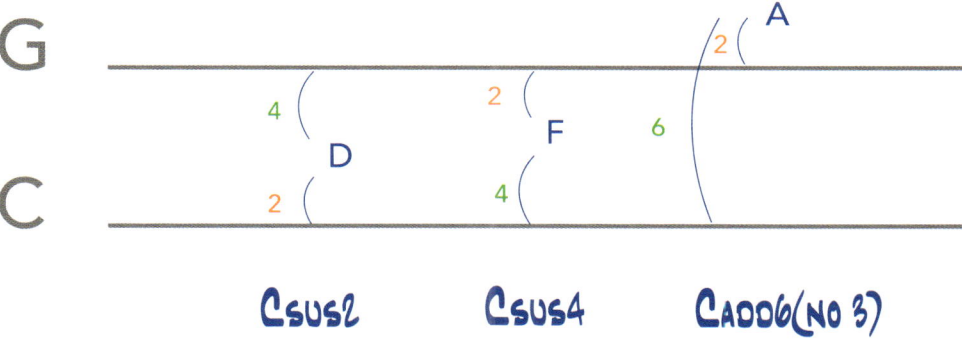

Csus2   Csus4   Cadd6(no 3)

You can notice that adding information in the harmonic context limits my freedom when creating a melody for two reasons:

1. Each note I play is at risk of creating a dissonance with two notes. So if I want to play consonant intervals or chords, options can quickly become limited.

2. I can no longer play a scale that does NOT include the perfect 5th. I can THINK in terms of a scale without a perfect fifth, but to the listener, listening to the music as a whole, the 5th is there, it's being played whether I like it or not.

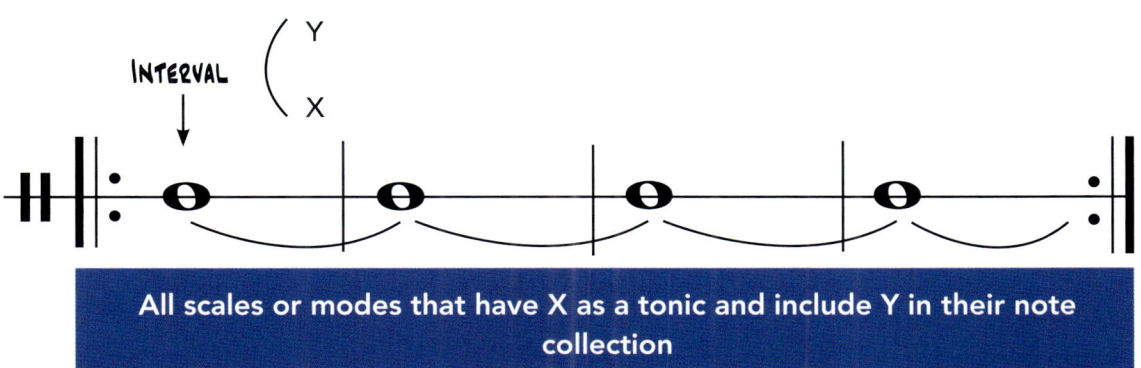

All scales or modes that have X as a tonic and include Y in their note collection

Melodic Options

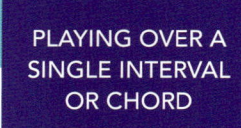

Again, at this point, knowing that X and Y are part of our note palette for whichever melodic option we decide to use over the context of a single interval, does not help us much. It still leaves us with way too many options! Yet, knowing what to choose in a predetermined context is the whole purpose of this book. So we need to add some principles in order to limit our options.

■ Relevance of melodic tools used to create melodies

As I stated previously, knowing what you can theoretically use to improvise is one thing, but knowing the most relevant options is really what this is all about. And relevance comes from finding a balance.

A good improvisation must be coherent and almost sound like a composed melody. The notes should be carefully chosen with the right dose of "prettiness" and tension. And this often requires using other scales than the chromatic scale.

Sure, the chromatic scale technically is compatible to all contexts, since it includes ALL the intervals. But I promise you that it would only take a minute of constant chromatic playing for you to realize that it quickly becomes indigestible. We need to focus on the scales that you will ACTUALLY USE.

And this is why, from now on, we will be only studying the compatibly of all the "common scales/modes" (defined in the previous book) with given harmonic contexts. You will see this already gives us a LOT of options to pick from. We will exclude the chromatic scale from our list of options since it's technically compatible with any context, but often includes too many dissonances to be considered a relevant option.

PLAYING OVER A SINGLE INTERVAL OR CHORD

Major scale	7 notes	Diatonic
Natural minor scale	7 notes	Diatonic
Harmonic minor scale	7 notes	Non-diatonic
Melodic minor scale	7 notes	Non-diatonic
Major pentatonic scale	5 notes	Non-diatonic
Minor pentatonic scale	5 notes	Non-diatonic
Whole-tone scale	6 notes	Non-diatonic
Minor blues scale	6 notes	Non-diatonic
Major blues scale	6 notes	Non-diatonic
Half-whole diminished scale	8 notes	Non-diatonic
Whole-half diminished scale	8 notes	Non-diatonic

In this book, I will be giving you the most "common" (which may already not seem so common to you) melodic options. Feel free to go beyond these possibilities.

Let's go back to our context of a static interval and see which of the above scales and modes can efficiently be played over it.

$$\begin{pmatrix} G \\ C \end{pmatrix}$$

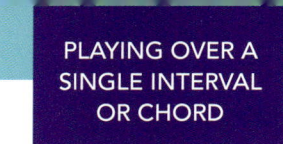

PLAYING OVER A SINGLE INTERVAL OR CHORD

 It's as "simple" as answering the following question: What are the scales and modes that have C as a tonic and a perfect 5th as part of their note palette?

Tonic = C							
Imposed notes = Perfect 5th (G)							
Major scale modes	Harmonic minor scale modes	Melodic minor scale modes	Pentatonic scales	Blues scales	Whole-tone	Diminished
Ionian	Harmonic minor	Melodic minor	Major	Major	Whole-tone	Half-whole
Dorian	Locrian maj 6	Phrygian maj 6	Minor	Minor		Whole-half
Phrygian	Ionian #5	Lydian #5				
Lydian	Dorian #4	Lydian b7				
Mixolydian	Phrygian dom.	Mixolydian b6				
Aeolian	Lydian #2	Locrian maj 2				
Locrian	Superlocrian bb7	Superlocrian				

 The modes in green cells are the ones compatible in the given harmonic context.

Now I am sure you still can't help yourself from wondering… well, WHY???? Why for example would the C Locrian mode "not work" in the contact of a static perfect 5th interval based on C?

Well, my friend, go ahead and try it! The fact is that the Locrian mode has a diminished 5th, which will not only clash with the tonic (the diminished fifth is a pretty dissonant interval), but with the perfect 5th played in the background.

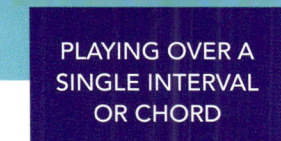

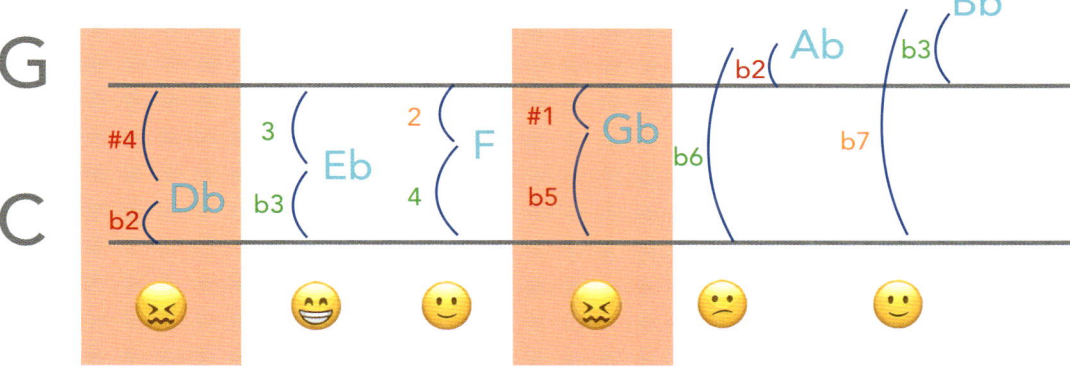

Interaction of the notes of the Locrian mode with the notes the interval

Okay… But then if we look at the C Phrygian mode (which is basically a C Locrian mode with a perfect 5th), it still has a minor 2nd (Db)!! Which will create the exact same dissonance! So why would this one work better than the other?

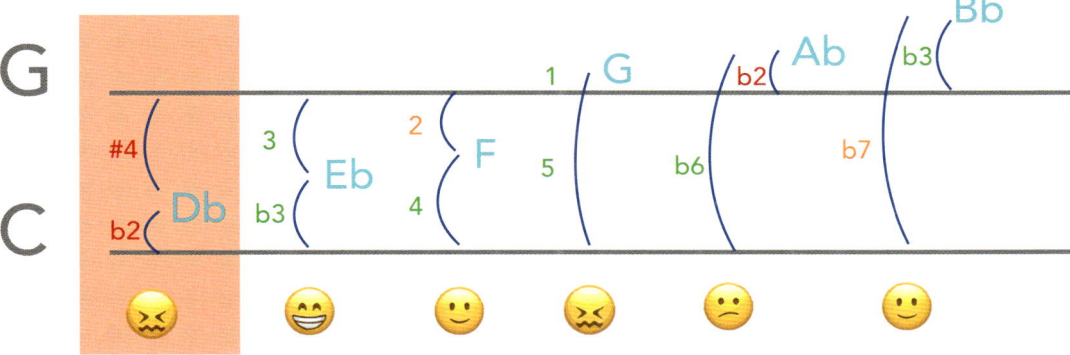

Interaction of the notes of the Phrygian mode with the notes the interval

The answer is that the Phrygian mode works BETTER than the Locrian mode because it will include fewer dissonant intervals. It's true that the Phrygian mode is relatively dissonant with its minor 2nd, but the Locrian mode is even more dissonant. Therefore, the Phrygian mode is a **more balanced option** and will be much more appropriate. **This is why we will assume that the Phrygian mode "works," while the Locrian mode doesn't offer a perfect 5th interva**l. Could you still play the Locrian mode or at least "think Locrian" over this interval? Yes, you could! But try it out and you will realize that it may be a little too tensed.

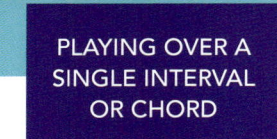

PLAYING OVER A SINGLE INTERVAL OR CHORD

I really want to insist on and work with the options that work BEST. So we will be applying this logic from now on. If I didn't decide to focus on the options that are most appropriate, I would have to fall back to the "whatever works and anything can work" option, which is not at all a decent guide to improvisation.

Moreover, you'll notice that this gives you A LOT of options already, and we will see later that it is possible to use any of the compatible scales or modes above as a main guideline, while adding passing tones, modulations and chromatic notes if you think it's useful.

EXERCISE 4 — DETERMINING THE MELODIC POSSIBILITIES OVER DIFFERENT INTERVALS

Given different intervals, highlight the different relevant melodic options that can be used when these intervals are used as a harmonic context.

Context of a single chord

■ Adjusting our thermostats

At this point, I hope you can understand that the phenomenon we just noticed can be extrapolated into this general fact:

> **Anytime you add a note to the harmonic context, you add polyphonic information, thereby reducing your melodic possibilities.**
>
> **Of course, you can always theoretically play everything (chromatic scale), but we are trying to figure out the most efficient possibilities, which means limiting ourselves to the most common scales and modes.**

-1 degree of melodic freedom — Melodic Complexity

+ 1 note (or degree of complexity) — Polyphonic Complexity

PLAYING OVER A SINGLE INTERVAL OR CHORD

To make sure you understand the process, let's study the case of a static triad.

■ Context of a single triad

Again, in order to study the general case of any triad, I will be using the generic notes X, Y, and Z, which means that they can in theory be any note you want as long as they form a triad.

Let's study the case of a C major triad.

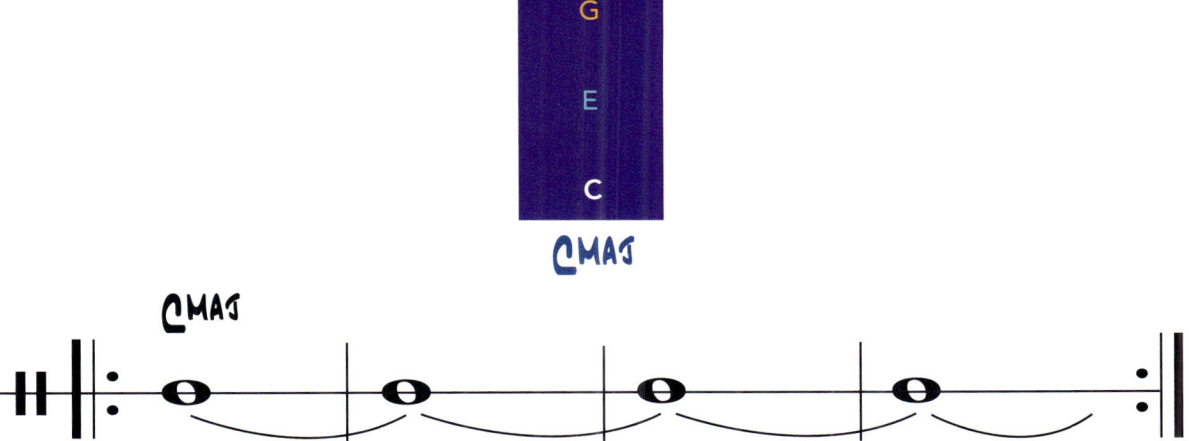

1. Our bank of notes now contains three imposed notes. Assuming the chord played is consonant, each of its notes will be stable. The root of the chord C will take the role of tonic of any scale or mode we chose to play.

2. Each note played will interact with three other notes. This generates six intervals for each note played. You can see that the number of intervals generated grows very rapidly as notes are added to the context.

PLAYING OVER A SINGLE INTERVAL OR CHORD

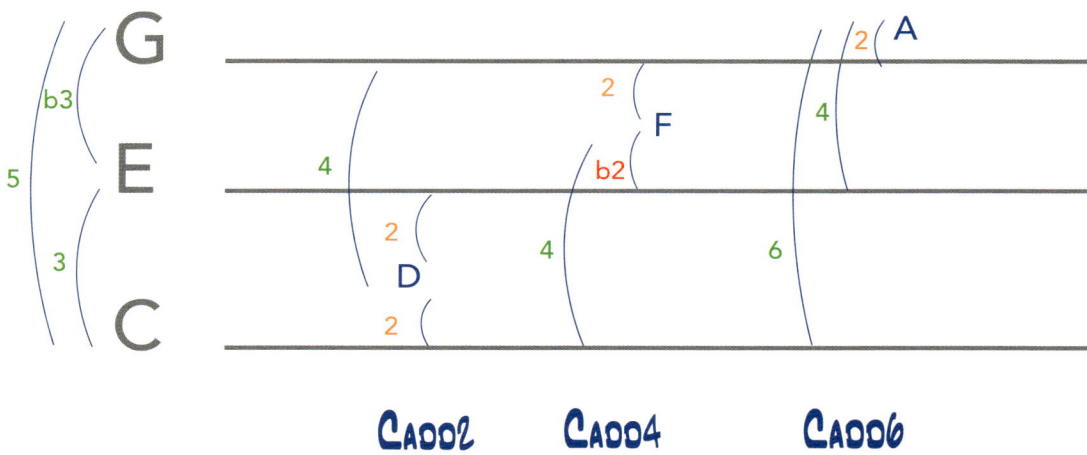

Notice that the more you add notes to the harmonic context, the harder it becomes to play notes that ONLY create consonant intervals with all the notes of the context. At one point, your ear simply cannot process all the intervals and perceives everything in terms of chords, which become new sonic units, heard as a whole.

You can't go wrong with arpeggios

Remember this:

In the context of a triad or any other chords containing at least three notes, the only notes that can potentially generate only constant intervals are simply the notes of the chord.

Therefore, the safest options to create a melody over a chord is to play the arpeggios of this chord.

In our example, C, E, and G are the only notes that will only generate consonant intervals.

Composers and improvisers actually happily take advantage of this rule, and you will notice that many melodies are based partly and sometimes entirely on arpeggios. Do you know what this means?

Work on your arpeggios! They can (and they will) save you!

PLAYING OVER A SINGLE INTERVAL OR CHORD

But remember that dissonant does not mean ugly or bad. Many beautiful chords include dissonant intervals, which gives them just enough tension to make them more beautiful and interesting than chords that are 100% consonant. Moreover, playing only arpeggios over a chord will admittedly sound consonant and coherent, but it can become boring.

What is important is to resolve tensions using the stable notes that are available in the given context.

So in the case of our C major triad, what are the modes that have C as a tonic, a major 3rd and a perfect 5th as part of their bank of notes?

Tonic = C						
Imposed notes = Major 3rd (E) + Perfect 5th (G)						
Major scale modes	Harmonic minor scale modes	Melodic minor scale modes	Pentatonic scales	Blues scales	Whole-tone	Diminished
Ionian	Harmonic minor	Melodic minor	Major	Major	Whole-tone	Half-whole
Dorian	Locrian maj 6	Phrygian maj 6	Minor	Minor		Whole-half
Phrygian	Ionian #5	Lydian #5				
Lydian	Dorian #4	Lydian b7				
Mixolydian	Phrygian dom.	Mixolydian b6				
Aeolian	Lydian #2	Locrian maj 2				
Locrian	Superlocrian bb7	Superlocrian				

Towards the static modal context

The more notes you add to a chord creating a static harmonic context, the more you narrow down your melodic options. Now you may ask yourself, what happens if we just keep adding notes to the chord played as a harmonic context?

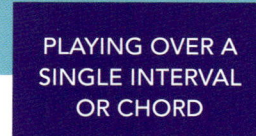

PLAYING OVER A SINGLE INTERVAL OR CHORD

Indeed, each note added to the context becomes "imposed" which means, as we've already seen, that it automatically belongs to the collection of notes of the scale or mode chosen to improvise. If you keep adding notes, you will eventually end up with a chord that **includes ALL the notes of a particular mode or scale**. In this case, the only compatible melodic options (or most compatible) will be reduced to this **ONE scale or mode**, which is made of the exact same notes as the chord.

If we focus on classic chords (the ones made of stacked-up thirds), we notice that these can contain up to seven different notes at most. And just so you know, the biggest chords you will encounter will likely have seven different notes at most. If you lay these seven notes horizontally (in a melodic way), seeing them as the collection of notes of a scale of which the tonic is the root of the chord, you will find that **each seven-note chord contains the exact same notes as one of the three most famous heptatonic scales, or one of their modes**. These scales are:

- The major scale
- The harmonic minor scale
- The melodic minor scale

Let's take an example:

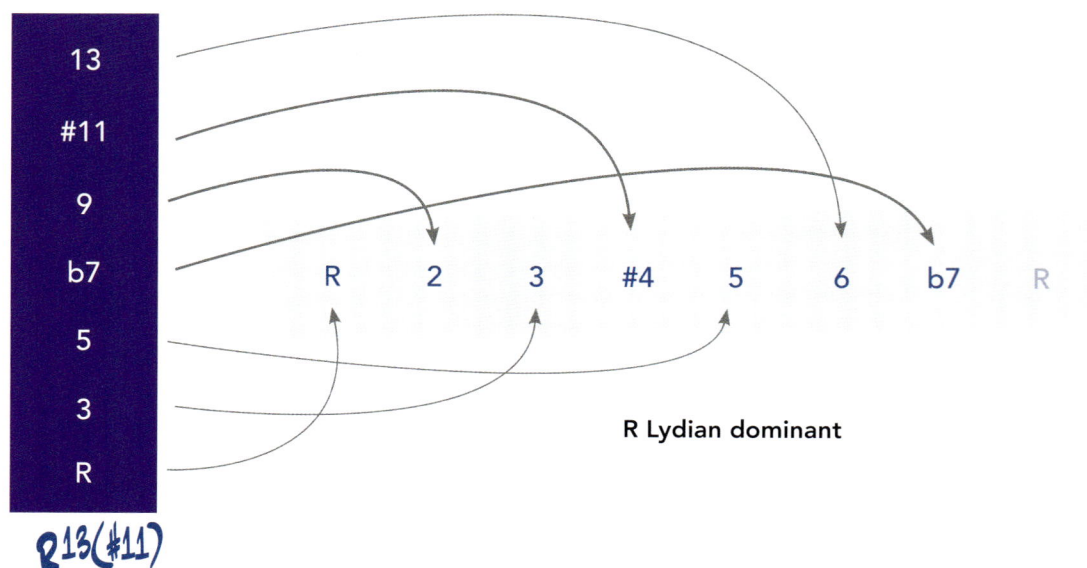

PLAYING OVER A SINGLE INTERVAL OR CHORD

You can see that the chord shares the exact same notes as the Lydian dominant mode. This means that if you limit yourself to the melodic options we have been choosing from, the most coherent option to improvise over this chord is inevitably **the Lydian dominant mode**.

Conversely, you can also start from the Lydian dominant mode and notice that the chord R9 (#11, 13) simply corresponds to the first degree of the harmonization of the R Lydian dominant mode. This means that if you harmonize this mode in stacks of 3rds, the chord built upon the tonic of the mode will be this exact chord.

At this point, playing the mode is almost equivalent to playing the arpeggio of this "big" chord. Although remember that even if a scale and a chord share the same notes, they are built for different purposes and you will most likely play a mode differently than you would an arpeggio.

This is our first encounter with what is commonly called a **modal context**.

A modal context is a harmonic context of which the polyphonic complexity (notes of the chord played) limits the relevant melodic possibilities of improvisation to ONE mode and ONE ONLY. In other words, the notes of the chord that constitutes the harmonic context are exactly the notes of a particular mode and the root of the chord is the tonic of this particular mode.

Now, I am aware that this may sound like a lot to digest. So let's use another example. It's much simpler than it seems.

Let's say we are asked to improvise or create a melody in the following context:

PLAYING OVER A SINGLE INTERVAL OR CHORD

CMAJ13(#11) =

| 13 |
| #11 |
| 9 |
| 7 |
| 5 |
| 3 |
| C |

=

| A |
| F# |
| D |
| B |
| G |
| E |
| C |

As you know, the most relevant options to improvise in this context are the scales or modes that have C as a tonic AND contain all the notes of this chord. By using our table of options we would get:

Tonic = C						
Imposed notes = 3,5,7,9,#11,13						
Major scale modes	Harmonic minor scale modes	Melodic Minor scale modes	Pentatonic scales	Blues scales	Whole-tone	Diminished
Ionian	Harmonic minor	Melodic Minor	Major	Major	Whole-tone	Half-whole
Dorian	Locrian maj 6	Phrygian maj 6	Minor	Minor		Whole-half
Phrygian	Ionian #5	Lydian #5				
Lydian	Dorian #4	Lydian b7				
Mixolydian	Phrygian Dom.	Mixolydian b6				
Aeolian	Lydian #2	Locrian maj 2				
Locrian	Superlocrian bb7	Superlocrian				

PLAYING OVER A SINGLE INTERVAL OR CHORD

Note: The major pentatonic scale and major blues scale only work because they contain FEWER notes than the ones present in the harmonic context. Essentially, when playing these scales you are playing the Lydian mode, minus a certain number of its notes.

You also could have found this result differently! Check it out:

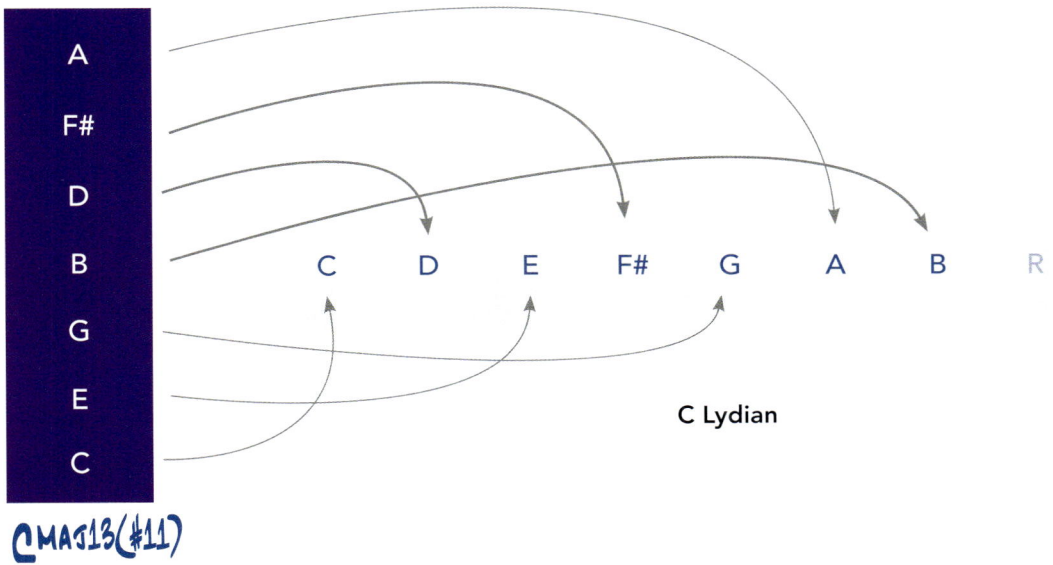

CMAJ13(#11)

This chord is the first degree of the diatonic harmonization of the C Lydian mode. And very logically, the best mode to improvise with in this context will be: the C Lydian mode! (It's always so satisfying when things just make sense, isn't it?)

This forms a first useful connection between the harmonization of scales and modes AND improvisational tools:

 The chord corresponding to first degree of the complete harmonization of a scale or mode (i.e., the chord that contains all the notes of this scale or mode) taken as a single static chord harmonic context, limits the coherent melodic choices to this mode or scale ONLY.

PLAYING OVER A SINGLE INTERVAL OR CHORD

Examples:

Chord	First degree of the harmonization of	Context	Best choice for melodies
IMIN(MAJ13)	Melodic minor scale	Melodic minor	Melodic minor
I13	Mixolydian mode	Mixolydian	Mixolydian
I7(#11)	Lydian dom. mode	Lydian dom.	Lydian dom.

Caution: You may (but this is very unlikely) encounter chords that don't seem to be compatible with any of the scales or modes that we are currently working with when studying melodic options. This is very possible since there are many more scales and modes in addition to the ones I introduced. I purposely excluded some of the more bizarre or obsolete ones (harmonic major scale, double harmonic major, etc.) to avoid any counterproductive overload of information. If you ever find yourself in this situation, first of all, congratulations! You are definitely part of a minority if you have to look into the harmonic major scale to answer your creative ambitions. But in any case, you can find those resources online very easily. It would make no sense for me to list a bunch of other scales and modes at this point.

When pentatonic scales come in handy

In the middle of all these modes and confusing rules, we will see that pentatonic scales can save the day and become a delightful breath of fresh air.

If you remember correctly, pentatonic scales are simply scales of five notes, and the most common ones are the major and minor pentatonic scales. These scales respectively derive from the major scale and natural minor scale in the following way.

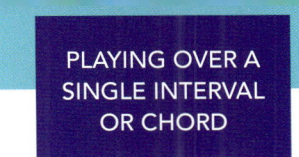

PLAYING OVER A SINGLE INTERVAL OR CHORD

Major Pentatonic Scale

Minor Pentatonic Scale

Now here is where things get interesting. Let's start by comparing all the main **major modes**.

 A major mode is a mode of which the first degree harmonization in triads is a major triad.

The main major modes are:

- Ionian
- Lydian
- Mixolydian
- Lydian dominant

Ionian	1	2	3	4	5	6	7	1
Lydian	1	2	3	#4	5	6	7	1

PLAYING OVER A SINGLE INTERVAL OR CHORD

Mixolydian	1	2	3	4	5	6	b7	1
Lydian Dominant	1	2	3	#4	5	6	b7	1

The only notes that make these modes different are their **4th or their 7th**. This is why they are the characteristic notes of all major modes.

This means that if you take these notes out of the original mode, you create some kind of "master key scale" that can be played in place of all major modes. And this is precisely what the major pentatonic scale is. This is incredibly useful because it means that essentially you can play the major pentatonic scale in place of any major mode.

This little trick is especially useful when you are struggling to figure out what precise mode you should be using. When in doubt, just default to the appropriate pentatonic.

Now let's look at what happens with minor modes.

 A minor mode is a mode of which the first degree harmonization in triads is a minor triad.

The main minor modes are:

- Aeolian
- Dorian
- Phrygian
- Phrygian maj 6

Aeolian	1	2	b3	4	5	b6	b7	1
Dorian	1	2	b3	4	5	6	b7	1
Phrygian	1	b2	b3	4	5	b6	b7	1
Phrygian maj 6	1	b2	b3	#4	5	6	b7	1

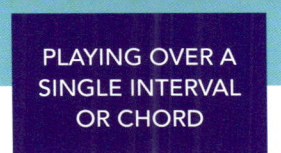

PLAYING OVER A SINGLE INTERVAL OR CHORD

The only notes that make these modes different are their 2nd or their 6th. This is why they are the characteristic notes of all minor modes.

The minor pentatonic scale, which is built by ridding itself of these two notes, is a master key to all the main minor modes. This means that it can be played in place of any of those modes.

As you can see, pentatonic scales offer the advantage of being much more versatile than scales of seven notes or more. This is entirely due to the fact that they have fewer notes and therefore, fewer chances of clashing with the harmonic context.

You can see them as an intermediate option between playing arpeggios or playing the scales of seven notes or more.

Indeed, while playing the arpeggio of a chord is taking no risks at all, playing a compatible pentatonic scale allows you to add a few notes without taking much more risk of playing clashing notes.

Let's summarize this with a cute little illustration representing the level of "risk" involved when playing different melodic tools in a harmonic context. Of course the word "risk" is to be taken lightly. Nobody will die if you play something that sounds bad.

Risk simply refers to the likeliness of one or several notes of this tool clashing with the context.

To sum it up

- The melodic possibilities of a composer or improviser depend on the harmonic context which can be more or less polyphonically complex (from one single note on the bass to seven-note chords or sometimes more).

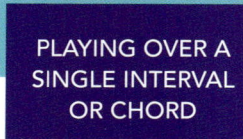

PLAYING OVER A SINGLE INTERVAL OR CHORD

- You can theoretically always play ANYTHING you want, meaning you could always use the chromatic scale in every context. But unless your ear is absolutely perfect, by doing this, you will take the risk of playing too many dissonant and not-willingly chosen notes. The listeners will perceive it as a lack of control and as "wrong notes." Therefore, the best option is to limit yourself to the more standard melodic tools that are summed up in the tables used above.

- The more notes you have in the harmonic context, the more you will be limited in your melodic choices.

- An efficient default solution is to limit your melodic choices to the notes of context only. If your context is a static chord, this basically means playing arpeggios of this chord.

- A chord that contains all the notes of a scale or mode will limit the improviser to ONE most coherent option. If the chord comes from the first degree of harmonization of a certain scale, the most coherent choice will be to play this scale.

- Finally, you can also use pentatonic scales, which can be seen as "master key scales," since they are compatible over a variety of harmonic contexts. The major pentatonic scale works in place of any major mode, and the minor pentatonic scale in place of any minor mode.

EXERCISE 5: DETERMINING THE MELODIC POSSIBILITIES OVER DIFFERENT CHORDS

Given different chords, highlight the different relevant melodic options that can be used when these intervals are used as a harmonic context.

3

The Modal Context

HARMONIC RHYTHM

Harmonic rhythm

For now, we have limited ourselves to a **static** harmonic rhythm, which means that we were only considering a single note, interval, or chord. But although there are some styles of music that actually use these contexts and stay on the same note or chord forever, others improvise over it. These situations are relatively rare. It is indeed rare for an entire piece of music to be based on one single chord for the whole duration of the music. In most cases, chords will change over time, following a certain progression and logic. The fact that chords change over time at a certain speed creates the notion of **harmonic rhythm**.

 The harmonic rhythm of a piece of music corresponds to how often chords change over time, relative to the general tempo of the tune.

It is extremely difficult to talk about harmonic rhythm in writing only, without referring to actual musical examples. There are some elements that you will have to hear. The rules of harmonic rhythm are mostly based on the way rhythm is experienced, and up to this day, I believe it still hasn't been entirely explained in a truly intellectually satisfying way. Getting deep into this would be enough to write another book on the topic.

So why is harmonic rhythm **relative to the tempo of the tune**? Because if the tempo of your tune is 240 bpm and the chords change once every two bars, it will feel like the chords change often. But this feeling only comes from the fact that the tempo is VERY fast! The harmonic rhythm, however, would be considered slow. A piece of music with a tempo of 60 bpm, where chords change twice per bar, would have its chords change at the same rate as the previous tune, but this time the harmonic rhythm would be considered fast.

 **The harmonic rhythm is based on a number of chords per bar and not on the perceived speed at which chords change.**

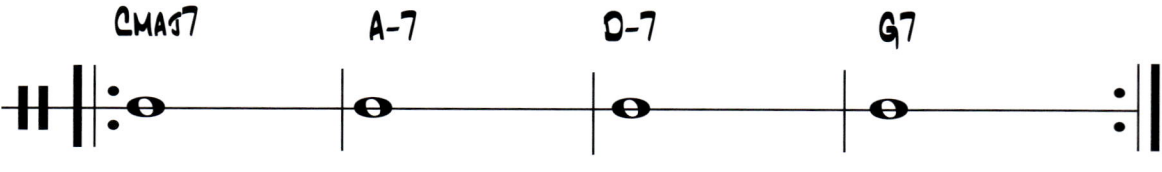

Slow Harmonic Rhythm

HARMONIC RHYTHM

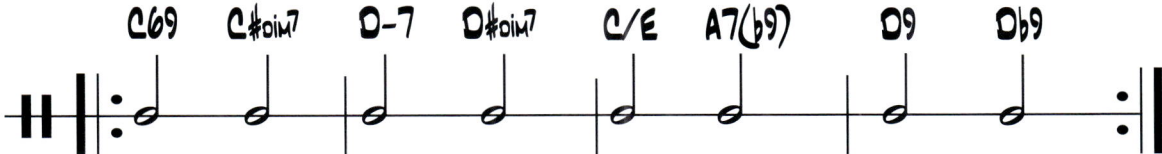

Moderate Harmonic Rhythm

Fast Harmonic Rhythm

There are many more elements that normally have to be taken into consideration when analyzing harmonic rhythms (structure and form of the tune, time signature, meter, etc.), but this would take us on too big of a detour and is not necessary when it comes to melodic options for improvisation. **Everything we will be exploring here in terms of melodic options applies to any tempo, meter, or time signature.**

All the elements of musical analysis that I will be giving here are the ones that are indispensable to introduce. But the complete analysis of a musical piece can go MUCH further.

■ Regularity of the harmonic rhythm

The harmonic rhythm is said to be "regular" when all the chords are of equal length. Any change in regularity, whether punctual or prolonged, creates an irregularity. **However, punctual changes in the harmonic rhythm are often not interpreted as a change in the general harmonic rhythm per se.**

Most pieces of music have a relatively regular harmonic rhythm:

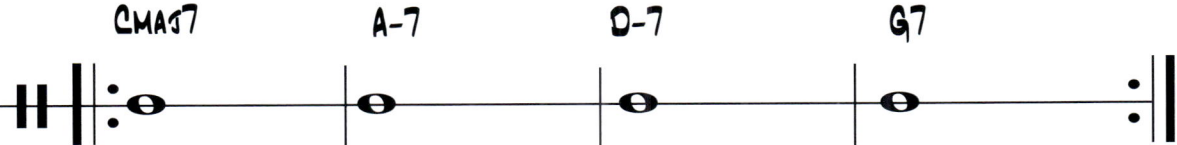

Regular harmonic rhythm

HARMONIC RHYTHM

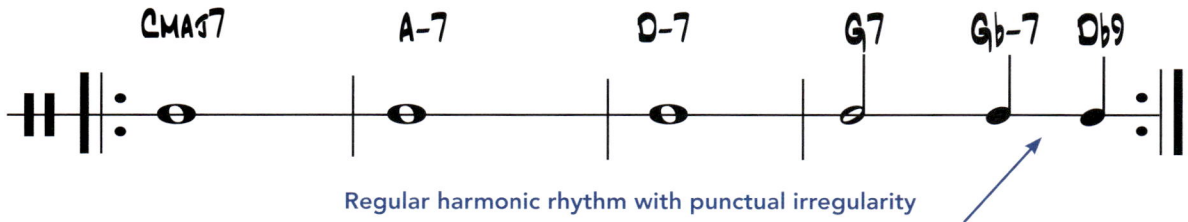

Regular harmonic rhythm with punctual irregularity

This punctual irregularity does not impact the general harmonic rhythm of the tune, which will still be one chord per bar.

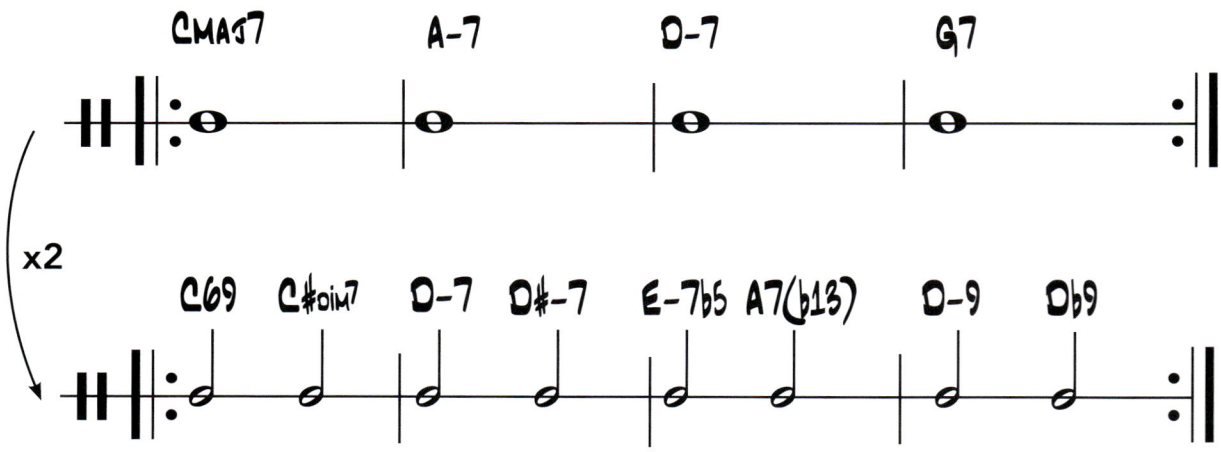

Regular harmonic rhythm but doubled after bar 4

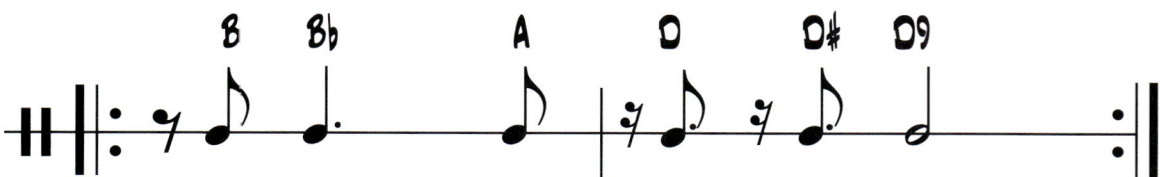

Irregular or syncopated harmonic rhythm

HARMONIC RHYTHM

■ Strong and weak beats of the harmonic rhythm

Any rhythm is made of an alternation of "strong" beats and "weak" beats. It is quite complicated to explain this phenomenon on paper, so you will have to believe me here. I do encourage you to verify this by listening to several pieces of music. You will most likely feel that some beats seem more "important" or impactful than others. Strong beats, for some reason, seem to have more impact than weak ones.

Most of the time, the first beat is a strong beat. Then strong and weak beats alternate throughout the tune.

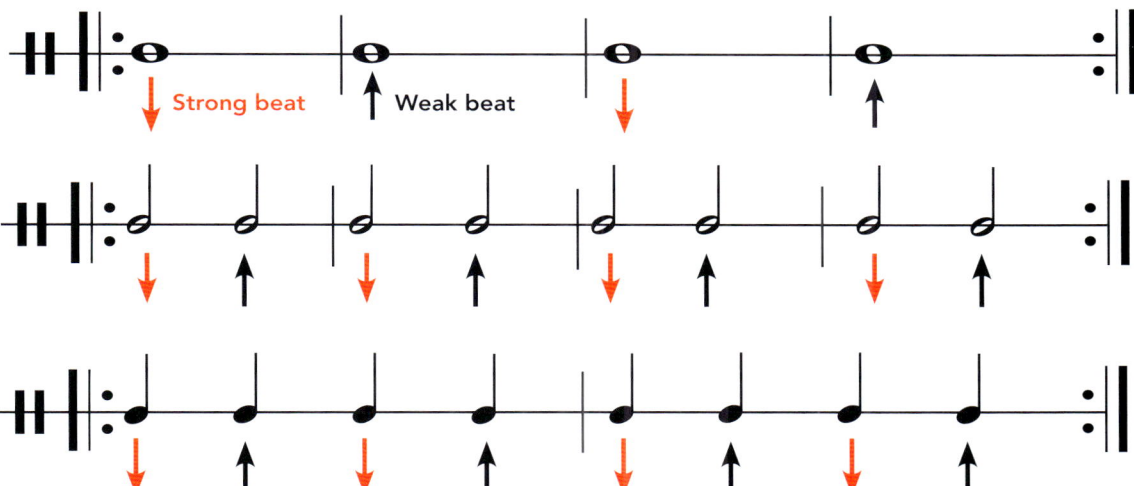

This phenomenon also applies to the harmonic rhythm of a musical piece, which means the "effect" or impact of chords will change whether they are played on strong or weak beats of the harmonic rhythm.

Now, remember the two following points:

- Punctual irregularities do not change the harmonic rhythm.
- A prolonged change in harmonic rhythm (doubling the rhythm or dividing it by two) changes the strong and weak beats of the harmonic rhythm.

HARMONIC RHYTHM

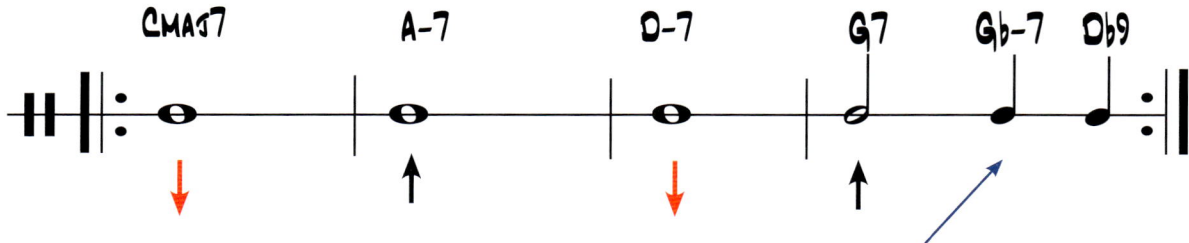

This punctual irregularity does not impact alternation of strong and weak beats. Therefore, the Gb-7 and Db9 are still part of the weak beat in this bar.

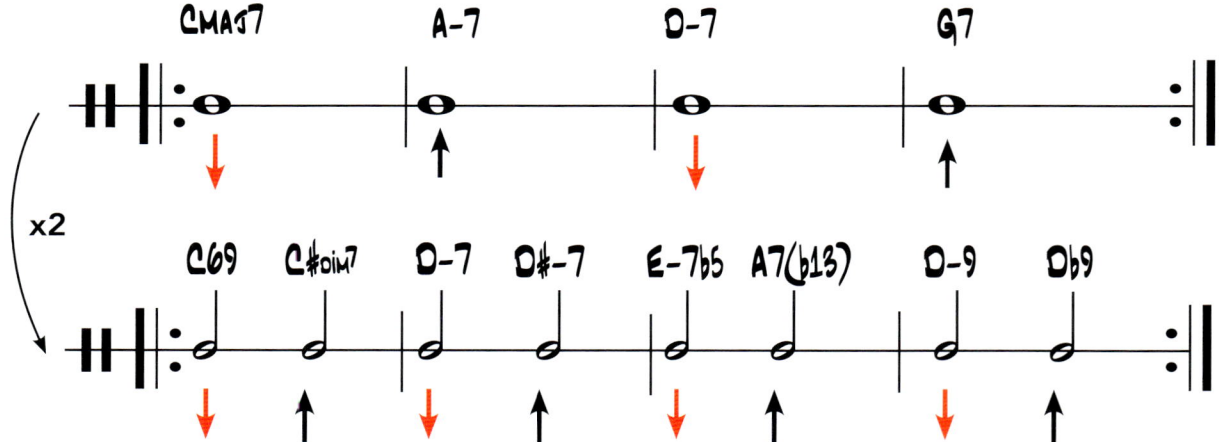

Notion of chord progression

As soon as there is a chord change in a tune, some thinking needs to be done, and you can't simply think in terms of static context. The chord change should be analyzed to determine the relationship between the two chords (if there is one). There are usually three options:

- **There is no categorized relationship between the chords, and they can simply be seen as two isolated static contexts.**

    In this case you can improvise on each chord using the techniques and rules we covered in the previous chapters.

- **The two chords form a modal progression (which is the subject of this chapter).**
- **The 2 chords are part of a tonal progression (subject of the following chapter).**

HARMONIC RHYTHM

To know what situation you are dealing with, you must:

1. **Study the possible relationship between the chords depending on the context.**

2. **Take the harmonic rhythm into account.**

First, we will be studying modal progressions.

HARMONIC RHYTHM

3

The Modal Context

MODAL PROGRESSIONS

MODAL PROGRESSIONS

Modal chord progressions

A modal context, as we've seen in the previous chapter, can be created by playing the first chord of the complete harmonization of a mode.

For example, to create a C Lydian context, I could simply play:

CMAJ13(#11)

The problem of this chord is that it is much too "dense"—meaning it contains way too many different notes.

One can easily notice that a chord that contains too many different notes can be slightly overwhelming to listen to. In general, any overload of information in music is risky. It's the same thing in cooking where putting in too many ingredients at once can overcharge the palate and make the meal "too rich." A few fresh, properly chosen ingredients are what you need! So what do you do if you REALLY want to serve all those ingredients within the same meal? Well, you could serve it in several courses!

And this is where modal progressions come in handy. Rather than playing this massive seven-note chord, we are going to divide it into two or three chords of a more reasonable size, which will allow us to play all those notes we want but at different points in time (in several courses ;)).

To do this, we are going to carefully choose other chords from the harmonization of the mode. And in order to avoid chords that are "too big," we will limit the size of the chords to three or four notes (sometimes five).

MODAL PROGRESSIONS

■ What chords to choose?

For obvious reasons, all modal progressions contain the first degree of the harmonized mode. This chord is usually emphasized, for it is rooted upon the tonic of this mode, which allows the listener's ear to use this note as a harmonic reference.

The goal of the other chords is to **bring out the other extensions of the mode** that were taken out of the original chord in order to break it down into more "digestible" chords.

 This is why when it comes to modal progressions, we ought to compare the notes of each chord to the tonic of the mode and not the root of each of the chords.

Let me explain. Let's take the example of the Lydian mode. Again, the full seven-note Lydian chord being too big, we are going to reduce it to a tetrad.

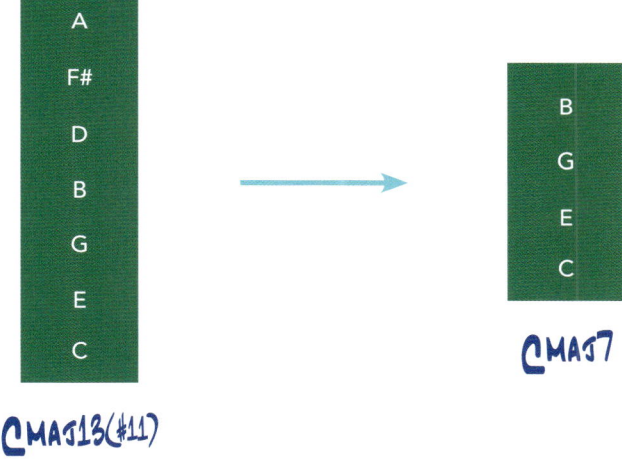

Yes, but… doing this also deprives the chord of the characteristic notes of the Lydian mode (9th, 13th and more particularly, augmented 11th). Our goal is to find the other chords in the harmonized scale that contain those extensions:

MODAL PROGRESSIONS

Degrees	1	2	3	#4	5	6	7
Tetrads	IMAJ7	II7	III-7	IV-7(b5)	VMAJ7	VI-7	VI-7
Interval between each note of the chord and the tonic of the mode	7 5 3 1	1 13 #11 9	9 7 5 3	3 1 13 #11	#11 9 7 5	5 3 1 13	13 #11 9 7

Again I want to emphasize the fact that in this table, we are studying **what interval each note of each chord forms with the tonic of the mode, not the root of each chord**. We are looking for which chord contains the extensions characteristic of the Lydian mode.

By looking at this table, we notice that in the case of the Lydian mode, the chords that contain all the extensions that are lacking in the first degree chord are:

II7   VII-7

Since the most characteristic note of the Lydian mode is the #11, we could also use the chords that contain this extension, even if they don't contain ALL the other extensions.

~~IV-7(b5)~~   VMAJ7

So why did I cross out the #IV-7b5 from our list of options? Well, it turns out that for some reason (which I don't really know, honestly), chords based on a diminished triad are not the best to create a modal context. Unless of course you are trying to create the modal context of a mode which is based on a diminished triad (the Locrian mode for example). I guess a better way to put it is that if you can go without using a diminished based chord, you probably should.

MODAL PROGRESSIONS

This allows us to divide our big seven-note chord the following way:

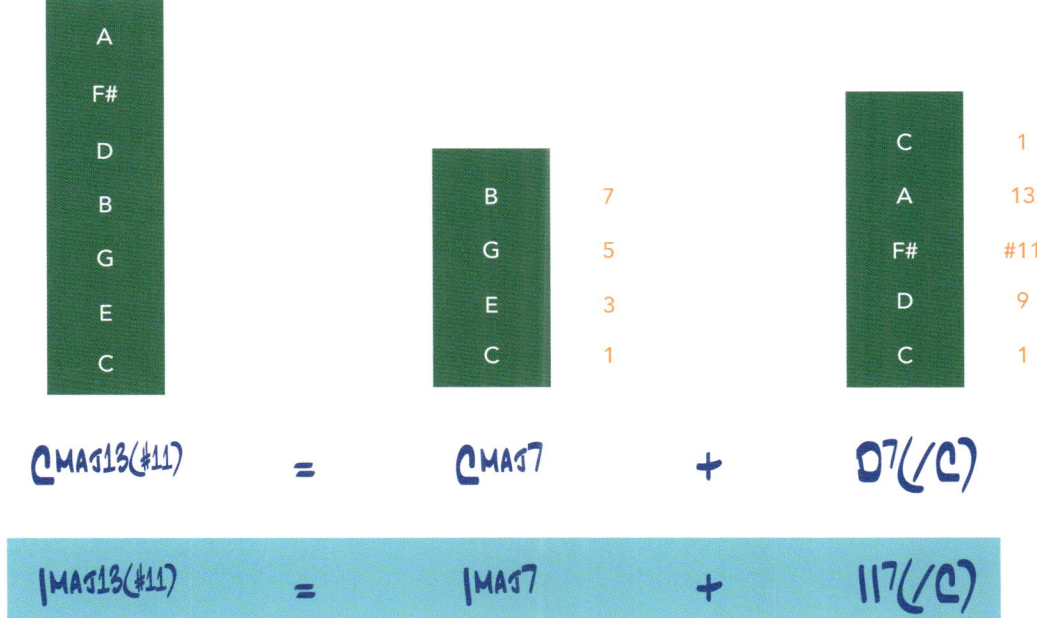

The second chord is labeled D7/C, since technically the notes of the chord are still considered in relation to the tonic of the mode. However, this doesn't mean you HAVE to play C on the bass constantly. The fact that the bass note temporarily goes from C to D is not a big deal as long as C is more emphasized by it being played more often or via the harmonic rhythm.

So instead of playing:

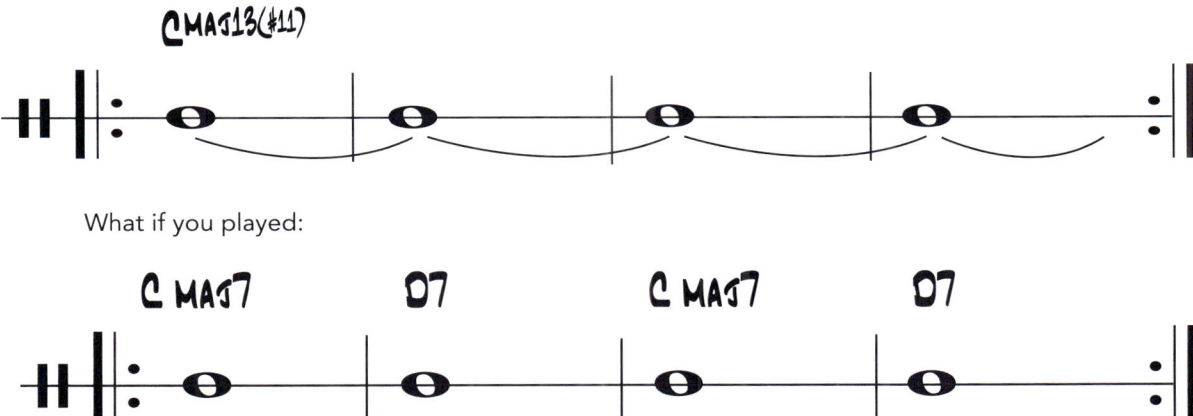

MODAL PROGRESSIONS

Some could say that when the chord switches to a D7, since the root changes, the context should technically change as well. And if C is no longer the tonic, how can we still be in C Lydian? This objection makes sense. You very well could see the above progression as two different static contexts, alternating.

But if you pay attention to the harmonic rhythm, you will notice the following fact:

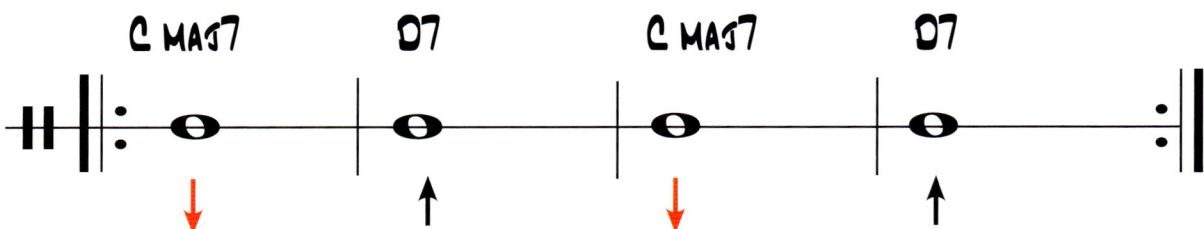

The C chords are played on strong beats of the harmonic rhythm, which will therefore give them more harmonic impact. Your ear will technically hear a different mode when the bass switches to D (which would be a Mixolydian mode), but the emphasis on C will still give an all-over impression of C Lydian.

In the end, the way the melody is built over these chords will give you the final clues about how you should interpret the context. But without any melodic indications, this context WILL be considered Lydian.

The notes of the D7 are seen (or heard) as extensions of the C△7 chord.

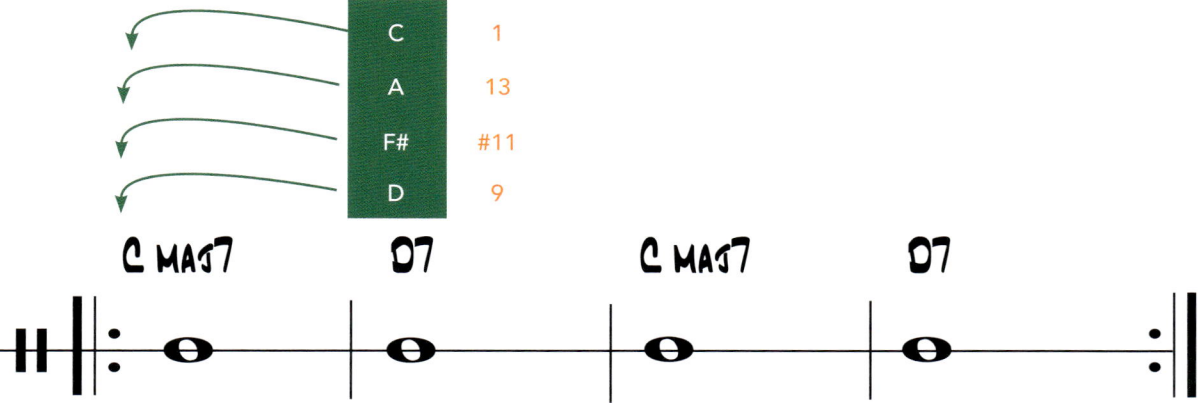

MODAL PROGRESSIONS

 Generally speaking, in order to create a modal harmonic progression, you can use an alternation of several chords (usually two or three) that come from the harmonization of that mode. The progression is often based on the first degree chord and the goal of the other chords is to bring out the remaining extensions of the mode. This alternation is often called a modal progression or modal cadence.

From a improvisational perspective, it will actually make your life much easier.

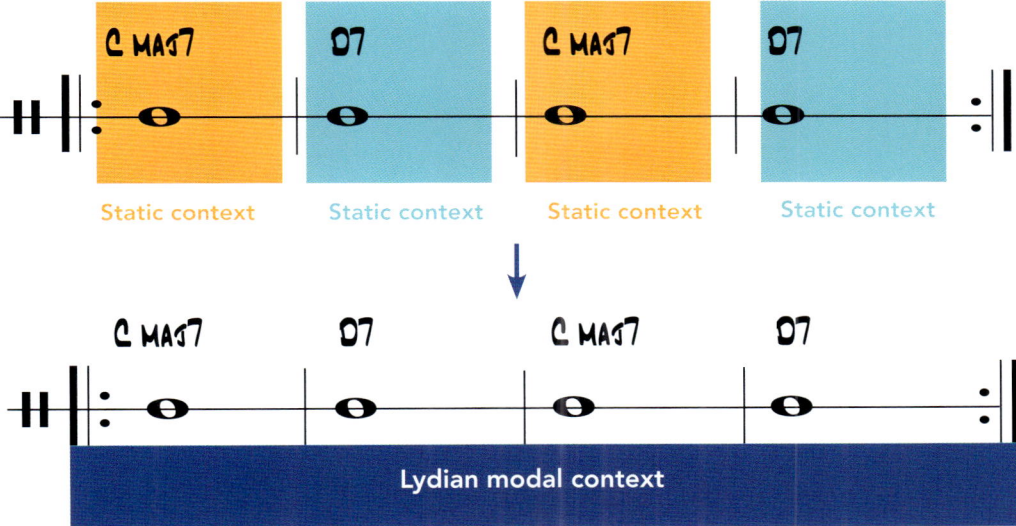

■ Use of a pedal note or pedal point

Above I told you that it was not necessary for the bass to stay on the tonic of the mode during a modal progression. It is, however, quite common to see bassists (or other instruments playing the role of the bass) stay on that note which is then called a pedal point or pedal note. This comes from the fact that on an organ, bass notes can be played and sustained indefinitely using the pedal keyboard.

■ A good tip for modal progressions

 To create a modal progression for a particular mode, you can alternate between the first degree of the harmonized scale and the two nearest degrees, namely, the second and seventh degree of the harmonized scale. This rule is always true unless one of the degrees is based on a diminished triad. It is always preferable not to use these chords in modal progressions.

MODAL PROGRESSIONS

This trick can be easily demonstrated. Indeed, any of the tetrads used as the first degree of the harmonized scale or mode will be a combination of the following notes :

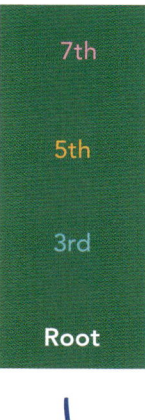

And therefore, the two surrounding chords will look like this:

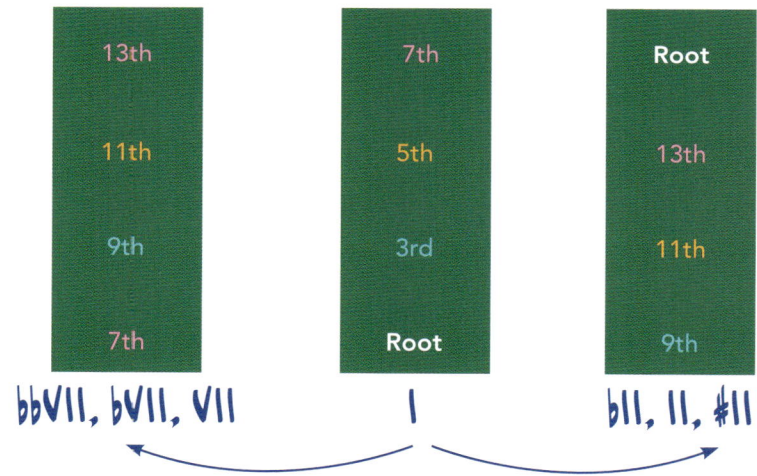

A short inventory of modal cadences

All modal progressions are created using the process we just discovered, so feel free to explore and come up with your own progressions. There are, however, some important and common modal progressions that you should know in order to use them and recognize them easily when composing or improvising.

MODAL PROGRESSIONS

Here is an inventory (rather complete yet not exhaustive) of the most common modal progressions. You will also notice that it is necessary to understand and master the harmonization of all the different modes and scales in order to be comfortable with modal contexts and progressions.

Ionian mode

Progression over four bars	IMAJ7	IVMAJ7	IMAJ7	IVMAJ7
Extensions in each chord	1, 3, 5, 7	11, 13, 1, 3	/	/
Example in C	CMAJ7	FMAJ7	CMAJ7	FMAJ7

Dorian mode

I-7	II-7	I-7	II-7
1, b3, 5, b7	9, 11, 13, 1	/	/
C-7	D-7	C-7	D-7

I-7	IV7	I-7	IV7
1, 3, 5, 7	11, 13, 1, b3	/	/
C-7	F7	C-7	F7

IMAJ7	II-7	bIIIMAJ7	II-7
1, b3, 5, b7	11, 13, 1, 3	b3, 5, b7, 9	9, 11, 13, 1
C-7	D-7	EbMAJ7	D-7

MODAL PROGRESSIONS

Phrygian mode

I-7	bIIMAJ7	I-7	bIIMAJ7
1, b3, 5, b7	b9, 11, b13, 1	/	/
C-7	DbMAJ7	C-7	DbMAJ7

Phrygian dominant mode

I7	bIIMAJ7	I7	bIIMAJ7
1, 3, 5, b7	b9, 11, b13, 1	/	/
C7	DbMAJ7	CMAJ7	DbMAJ7

Lydian mode

IMAJ7	II7	IMAJ7	II7
1, 3, 5, 7	9, #11, 13, 1	/	/
CMAJ7	D7	CMAJ7	D7

IMAJ7	VII-7	IMAJ7	VII-7
1, 3, 5, 7	7, 9, #11, 13	/	/
CMAJ7	B-7	CMAJ7	B-7

MODAL PROGRESSIONS

Lydian dominant mode

I7	II7	I7	II7
1, 3, 5, b7	9, #11, 13, 1	/	/
C7	D7	C7	D7

Mixolydian mode

I7	V-7	I7	V-7
1, 3, 5, b7	9, #11, 13, 1	/	/
C7	G-7	C7	G-7

I7	bVIIMAJ7	I7	bVIIMAJ7
1, 3, 5, b7	11, 13, 1, 3	/	/
C7	BbMAJ7	C7	BbMAJ7

Aeolian mode

I-7	bVII7	I-7	bVII7
1, b3, 5, b7	b7, 9, 11, b13	/	/
C-7	Bb7	C-7	Bb7

EXERCISE 6 — IDENTIFYING MODAL CONTEXTS BASED ON CHORD PROGRESSIONS

Deduce the modal context from the given chord progressions.

THE CONCEPT OF KEY

4

The Tonal Context

THE CONCEPT OF KEY

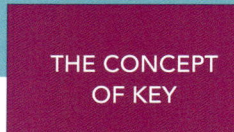

THE CONCEPT OF KEY

Introduction

Even though we did introduce the concept of chord progressions in the previous chapter, we never truly left the field of static harmonic contexts! Here you must be thinking: "so what about modal progressions?" Well, you must know by now that modal progressions actually only exist to emphasize and bring out the notes of one chord while spreading those notes over two chords in order to use smaller chords (with fewer notes). Therefore, these contexts are still of a very limited harmonic complexity.

The tonal context, on the other hand, is extremely rich harmonically and based on a beautiful theoretical coherence—and it sounds amazing. This system was mostly developed in the "classical" era of music where it was actually formalized and where its rules were settled and theorized. The tonal context always gravitates around a particular major or minor SCALE. And I insist on the word SCALE here! Why not a mode? Because the harmonic mechanisms that allow for the creation of a tonal context (perfect cadence, resolution of the tonal tritone) are exclusively found within the harmonization of the major scale and the natural minor scale (with borrowings from the harmonic and/or melodic minor scales). Another characteristic of the tonal system is its reliance on tension/release mechanisms between chords which allow for emphasis of the tonal center of the piece, namely, the "key" of the tune. In a tonal context, the harmonic progression follows a particular logic that goes way beyond splitting a chord in half. For this reason, harmony, in the tonal context, is named **functional harmony**. The melody in this case is just part of a greater system of harmonic mobility.

Indeed, in a modal context, the only role of the harmonic context is to emphasize the melody which usually has a lot of freedom. In a tonal situation, the chords also tell a story in which the melody is no longer necessarily the protagonist. If you look into the history of the tonal context, you will notice that it originally comes from several melodies being played or sung at the same. The way these melodies move was dictated by different harmonic rules such as counterpoint. It is only long after this art of "poly-melodic" music that the notions of chords and other vertical harmonic analysis tools were born. But originally, tonal music comes from different stories told at the same time which all together formed a coherent piece of music in which the higher voice (generally thought of as melody) was only one voice among the others (listen to fugues from Bach to get a good idea of what this all means).

The reappearance of melody as being a "more important" voice in a piece of music reappeared when lyrics started to be added to orchestral music with the emergence of opera. Now, most of modern music puts the emphasis on the sung melody and the lyrics, while at the same time being mostly tonal!

THE CONCEPT OF KEY

Singing melodies as a way to tell a story is not new at all. Most cultures have always had some popular singing (the Troubadours in France in the Middle Ages, Aoidoi and Rhapsodists in ancient Greece, etc…). But the main difference is that most of these types of singing were done in a modal context more than a tonal context!

Chords, in tonal music, typically follow a relatively fast harmonic rhythm (one chord per bar or more). In such a context, it becomes complicated to see each chord as a separate modal context or static context, since the chords change very often. The only way to coherently and properly improvise or compose a melody in the situation is to **stick to the notes of the scale which those progressions are based** on, thereby defining what we call the **KEY** of the tune!In such a context, most of the richness is carried by the polyphonic part. The chords and the way they charge and alternate create tension and then resolve it. Sometimes the key can change, temporarily or permanently. **But generally, in a tonal context, there will always be a big emphasis on the "key" scale, its bank of notes on a melodic level, and the chords generated by its harmonization, on a polyphonic level.**

This part of the book is dedicated to the study of the tonal context, which is by far the most used context in western modern music (pop, rock, jazz, classical, metal…)

Make sure you read "Appendix A: More about tonality" on page 328 before continuing.

Tonality and the concept of "key"

The key of a musical piece is the major or minor scale that forms the basis of this musical piece. This means:

- That the melody mostly uses the collection of notes of this scale.
- That the great majority of the chords used come from the harmonization of this scale.
- That the tonic of the scale is emphasized in the melody.
- That the first degree chord of the harmonized scale is emphasized by the harmonic progression.

Example: Being in the key of C major implies:

- That the melody will be mostly made of the following notes:

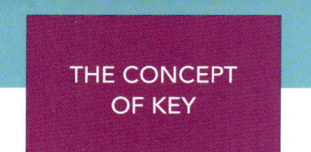

THE CONCEPT OF KEY

- **That the chords in the tune will belong to the harmonization of C major**

Note: Just like for the modal context, the chords used usually don't have more than four or five notes in order not to be too "indigestible."

Tetrads	CMAJ7	D-7	E-7	FMAJ7	G7	A-7	B-7(b5)
Extensions	9 11 13	9 11 13	b9 11 b13	9 #11 13	9 11 13	9 11 b13	b9 11 b13
Mode	Ionian	Dorian	Phrygian	Lydian	Mixolydian	Aeolian	Locrian

- The tonic C is emphasized in the melody. We will soon discover what this means exactly, but for now, just admit that this is mostly done by starting or especially finishing with this note by repeating it often within the tune or by playing it in "strong" moments or the harmonic rhythm.

- The C chord, with or without extensions, is emphasized by what we call **cadences**, which we will study in great detail. These cadences create a tension/release mechanism which by "releasing" on the C chord on key moments of the piece and its harmonic rhythm, will settle this feeling of C as being the **"center of gravity" of the tune**.

■ Characteristics of the key of a tune: the key signature

When improvising or composing in a certain key, it becomes essential to be able to quickly figure out which scale the key is based upon. This information can be accessed very simply thanks to a particular characteristic of major and minor scales.

THE CONCEPT OF KEY

We saw in the previous book that each major scale—and therefore its relative minor scale—generated a unique bank of notes for a specific tonic. **This bank of notes is characterized by a certain number of sharpened OR flattened notes which constitute a unique signature for each tonic.**

I insist on the "OR" in the previous sentence because you will notice that major scales CANNOT have sharps and flats simultaneously for a given tonic.

Here is a table of all major scales, organized by the number of sharps or flats they contain.

Number of #'s or b's	1	2	3	4	5	6	7	1
7	C#	D#	E#	F#	G#	A#	B#	C#
6	F#	G#	A#	B	C#	D#	E#	F#
5	B	C#	D#	E	F#	G#	A#	B
4	E	F#	G#	A	B	C#	D#	E
3	A	B	C#	D	E	F#	G#	A
2	D	E	F#	G	A	B	C#	D
1	G	A	B	C	D	E	F#	G
0	C	D	E	F	G	A	B	C
1	F	G	A	Bb	C	D	E	F
2	Bb	C	D	Eb	F	G	A	Bb
3	Eb	F	G	Ab	Bb	C	D	Eb
4	Ab	Bb	C	Db	Eb	F	G	Ab
5	Db	Eb	F	Gb	Ab	Bb	C	Db
6	Gb	Ab	Bb	Cb	Db	Eb	F	Gb
7	Cb	Db	Eb	Fb	Gb	Ab	Bb	Cb

THE CONCEPT OF KEY

You may not yet realize it, but this table gives a lot of information, if you look closely. Let's dive into it.

- **Number of accidentals for each key**

By just simplifying the table above, you will notice that the number of sharps or flats for each tonic follows a particular logic:

Number of #'s	0	1	2	3	4	5	6	7
Major Key	C	G	D	A	E	B	F#	C#
Minor Relative	A	E	B	F#	C#	G#	D#	A#

Perfect 5th — 5 — 5 — 5 — 5 — 5 — 5

Number of b's	0	1	2	3	4	5	6	7
Major Key	C	F	Bb	Eb	Ab	Db	Gb	Cb
Minor Relative	A	D	G	C	F	Bb	Eb	Ab

Perfect 4th — 4 — 4 — 4 — 4 — 4 — 4

Those two tables should be known BY HEART. Why? Because the number of sharps and flats in a key already tell you a lot about what scale you will be using. However, those tables do not tell you what notes carry these accidentals (sharps and flats). So we still need to figure that out.

- **What notes carry the accidentals**

Let's start with the scales that contain sharps.

THE CONCEPT OF KEY

Tonic of the scale	Accidentals						
C							
G	F#						
D	F#	C#					
A	F#	C#	G#				
E	F#	C#	G#	D#			
B	F#	C#	G#	D#	A#		
F#	F#	C#	G#	D#	A#	E#	
C#	F#	C#	G#	D#	A#	E#	B#

THE CONCEPT OF KEY

Now let's look at the keys that contain flats.

Tonic of the scale	Accidentals						
C							
F	Bb						
Bb	Bb	Eb					
Eb	Bb	Eb	Ab				
Ab	Bb	Eb	Ab	Db			
Db	Bb	Eb	Ab	Db	Gb		
Gb	Bb	Eb	Ab	Db	Gb	Cb	
Cb	Bb	Eb	Ab	Db	Gb	Cb	Fb

Interestingly enough, intervals of 4ths and 5ths are complementary intervals, which means that they are inversions of one another.

- If I go up (or down) a 5th, then I need to go up (or down) an extra 4th to complete an octave. Naturally, this means if I go up (or down) a 4th, I need to go up (or down) an extra 5th to complete an octave. It will all make more sense with the following illustration.

THE CONCEPT OF KEY

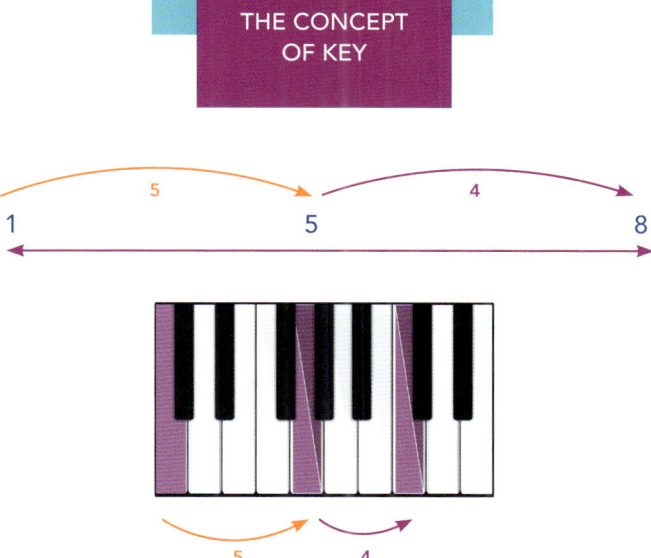

- Starting from any note, going up any interval or down its inversion, will lead to the same note (an octave below or above). And the reverse is also true, obviously. This is a direct consequence of what is above.

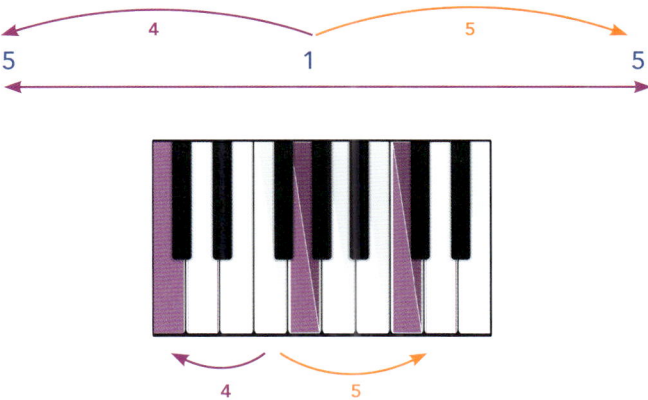

■ Circle of 5ths and circle of 4ths

As you may have noticed, the number of sharps and flats in a key, as well as which notes carry those accidentals, are based on **cycles of 5ths and 4ths**. This is why what we call the **circle of 5ths** is SO important in music theory. You MUST know it perfectly, in all directions starting from any note. And since going up a 5th is equivalent to going down a 4th and vice versa, you only need to know ONE circle to know both the circle of 5ths and the circle of 4ths! You just have to learn it clockwise and counterclockwise.

THE CONCEPT OF KEY

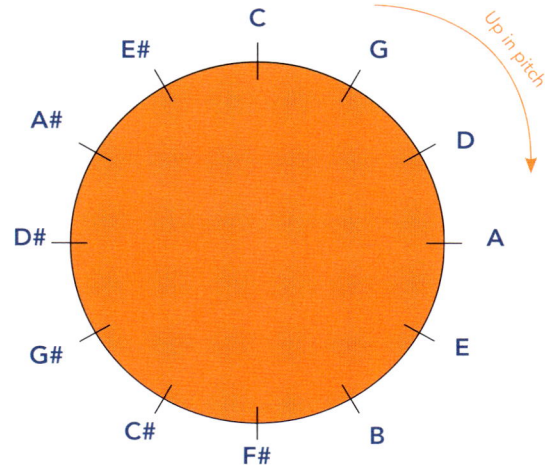

Circle of 5ths

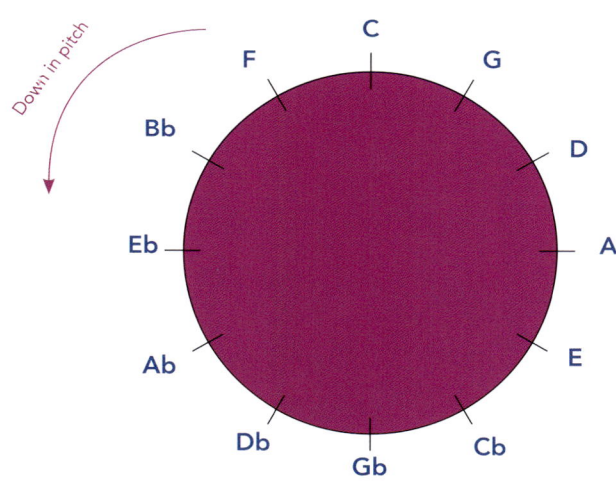

Circle of 4ths

You might realize by looking closely at the two circles above, that the use of enharmony is necessary to preserve coherence and make the circles more convenient to use. For example, in the circle of 5th, the jump from E# to C is actually a diminished 6th since a perfect fifth above E# would actually be a B#. Without this approximation and use of enharmony, each turn around the circle would make more and more accidentals appear, which would make it confusing an impossible to use (after B# we would have F## and C## etc.). It would end up looking more like a spiral than a circle. So just keep this in mind! The goal of the circles of 4ths and 5ths is mostly to help you navigate keys and chord changes, not to be exact in describing intervals.

THE CONCEPT OF KEY

Notice how the circle of 5ths and circle of 4ths are actually the same circle! Both can be condensed in the following way:

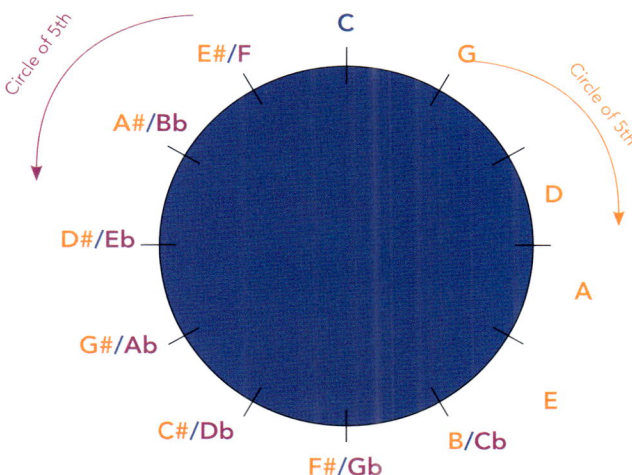

Going clockwise around the circle means going up the circle of 5ths while going counter clockwise means going up the circle of 4ths.

The circle of 5ths alone allows us to find:

- The number of accidentals (# or b) for each key (and conversely, the key, depending on the number of accidentals).
- What exact notes carry those accidentals in each key.

In the tables above, we notice the fact that the number of sharps increases as you go UP the circle of 5ths and the number of flats increases as you go up the circle of 4ths, which is the same as going DOWN the circle of 5ths:

THE CONCEPT OF KEY

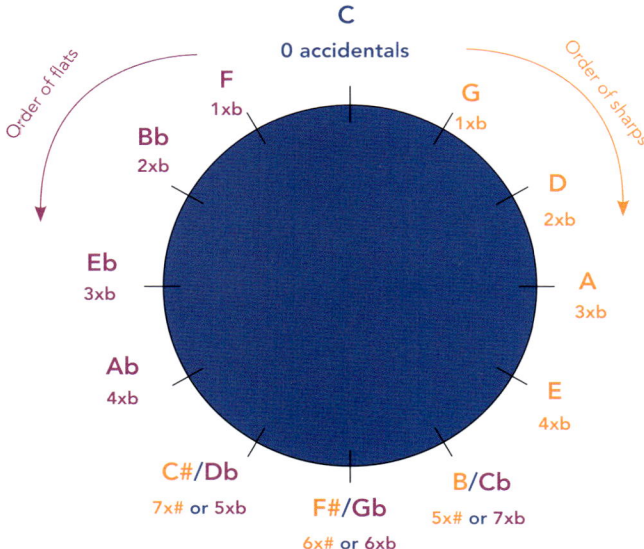

Since going up the circle of 5ths makes sharps appear, it is also referred to as the **order of sharps**. The other way, the circle of 4ths is called **order of flats**.

The trick to finding which notes are sharpened or flattened is the following:

- **For the keys with sharps, the first accidental is always F#. Then, simply go up the circle of 5ths until you reach the right number of accidentals. You can also check your result by making sure that the last sharpened note of your key is the major 7th of the scale.**

Example: Let's say that we are trying to figure out the number of sharps and what notes are sharp in the key of A major.

Simply start by going up the circle of 5ths starting from C to determine the number of sharps: C (0) -> G (#) -> D (##) -> A (###). So in A major, there will be three sharp notes in the note palette.

Now, to determine what notes are sharp, you start from F# and go up the circle of 5ths until you reach three accidentals. F# (1)-> C# (2)-> G# (3). And just to double check, we can verify that G# (our last sharp note) is indeed the major 7th of A major. If this is true, you are good.

- **For the keys with flats now, the first accidental will always be Bb. Then, simply go down the circle of 5ths—which AGAIN is the same as going up the circle of 4ths—until you reach the right number of accidentals. You can always double check by making sure that the second-to-last flat note is the tonic of the scale.**

Example: Say we are trying to determine the number of flats and what notes are flat in Db major.

Start by going down the circle of 5ths starting from C to find out how many flats I have in this key: C(0)-> F (b)-> Bb (bb)-> Eb(bbb)-> Ab(bbbb)-> Db(bbbbb). So there are five flats in this key.

Now to figure out what notes are flat, I simply start from Bb and go down the circle of 5ths until I reach five accidentals: Bb-> Eb -> Ab -> **Db** -> Gb. And we can double check our result by making sure that Db (the tonic) is the second-to-last flat note. Which it is indeed!

■ Key signature

I know that this book is supposed to not include any staff, but regardless, you have to be able to decode a key signature. Have you ever seen something like this:

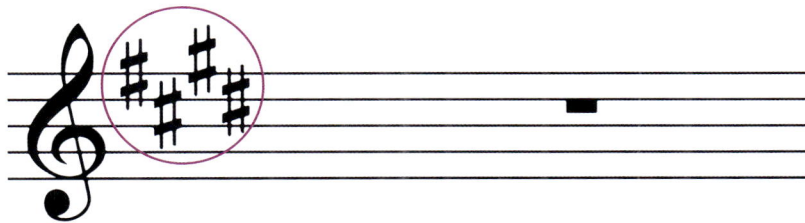

Even if you don't know how to read (yet), I am pretty sure you have already seen a key signature somewhere. The key signature indicates which notes will be sharp or flat throughout a piece of music. Therefore, the key signature also clearly indicates how many sharps or flats are in the key of any particular tune.

For those of you who can read music, this is probably already a well known fact! For the other ones, you don't even need to read to use this tool, so dry up those tears. **Just look at whether you are dealing with sharps or flats, count them, and you have your key!**

THE CONCEPT OF KEY

 EXERCISE 7 FIND THE MAJOR AND RELATIVE MINOR KEY ASSOCIATED WITH KEY SIGNATURES

Remember, the number of accidentals is enough to find the key, but you should also know what notes carry these accidentals.

■ Constitutive and non-constitutive accidentals

I think it is important to distinguish the accidentals that are present in the key signature—which technically apply throughout the entire tune unless they are changed or canceled by other accidentals—from the accidentals that occur during the tune for a limited amount of time. In order to make this distinction, I usually refer to the accidentals in the key signature as constitutive accidentals. By default, all other accidentals can be simply called accidentals or non-constitutive accidentals. This is where the word comes from originally: accidentals temporarily or "accidentally" change the pitch of a note for a limited amount of time. The effect of such an accident typically ceases at the end of the measure in which it occurs.

 **A non constitutive accidental is an accidental that generates a note that does not belong to the original key scale. Reasons for such accidentals are diverse (modulation, passing note, chromaticism, etc…) and we will study some of them later.**

Relative key

Everything we have seen so far only concerns major keys. But as you know, each major scale has a relative (natural) minor scale, and thus each major key has a relative minor key and vice versa.

Relative keys, just like relative scales, are made of the same bank of notes, and therefore have the same constitutive accidentals or key signatures, but their tonic and tonal center are different.

A minor key will always, by default, be based on the natural minor scale. However, we will soon see that the two other minor scales (harmonic and melodic) are often used to complete some necessary harmonic mechanism within the minor key. Remember: a scale is not the same thing as a key, because a key is more based on the harmonic progression than on the notes of the scales. But for now, when you think minor key, just think natural minor scale. In the rare cases where a tune was to be based entirely on the harmonic or melodic minor scales, the key signature will still, most likely, be that of the natural minor scale. The accidentals necessary to obtain the harmonic or melodic minor scale from the natural minor scale will simply be written throughout the tune as non-constitutive accidentals.

THE CONCEPT OF KEY

"Neighbor" keys

The neighbor keys of any key are simply the closest keys (in terms of shared notes) to this original key. The minor (or major) relative key seems to be an obvious neighbor key since relative scales share all their notes. The other closest keys are the ones that surround the key of origin in the circle of 5ths and their relative keys. To sum it up, the neighbor keys of any major key are:

- **The relative minor scale.**
- **The keys that are directly before and after in the circle of 5ths, and their relative minor scales.**

    Which gives us a total of five neighbor keys.

Examples: What are the neighbor scales of C major?

The keys found directly before and after in the circle of 5ths are:

- **F major** and **G major**
- The relative minor scale of C major is **A minor**.
- The relative minor of **F major** is **D minor.**
- The relative minor of **G major** is **E minor.**

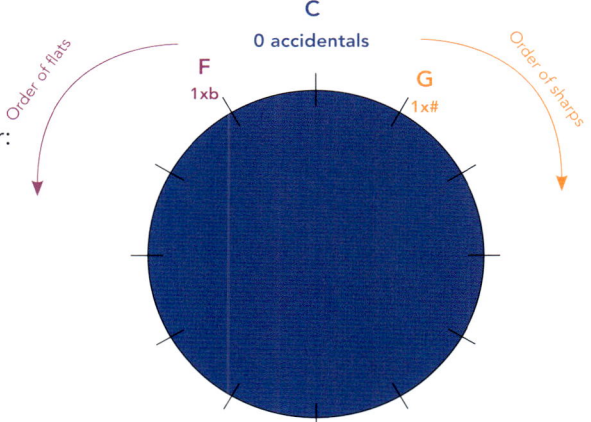

Which gives us the five neighbor tones of C major:

- F major
- D minor
- G major
- E minor
- A minor

THE CONCEPT OF KEY

It's important to talk about neighbor keys since modulations and key changes are often done towards those keys. For now the important part is that you understand what neighbor keys are. Their use will be studied later.

The degrees of the diatonic scale

In the tonal system, each note or **degree** of a diatonic scale plays a certain harmonic and melodic role and is therefore given a particular name.

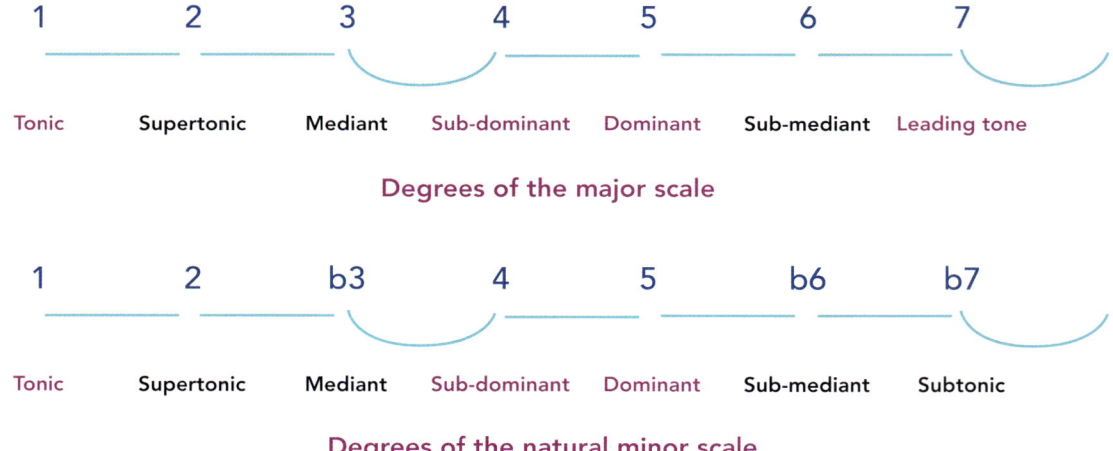

Knowing all these names is a plus but you must be familiar we the following degrees:

°1 - **Tonic**: The tonic, as always, is the center of gravity of the key, both melodically and harmonically. If there was one note to remember, it would be this one since everything else is articulated around it.

°5 - **Dominant**: This degree, as we will see, mostly has a harmonic importance. The chord built on this degree of the harmonized scale creates a tension that releases perfectly on the first degree chord. However, it also plays a melodic role, since the melodic movement from the 5th to the 1st degree is particulary efficient to emphasize the key.

°7 - **Leading tone**: The leading tone has both a harmonic and melodic importance. Melodically, being only a half-step away from the tonic creates a strong sense of "pull" or "melodic tension"(*) towards the tonic. Harmonically, this tone is also present in the dominant chord.

THE CONCEPT OF KEY

(*): Even though tension can be brought by the melody, the tension can only really exist if more than one note is being played! Polyphony and harmony—because they can generate dissonances—are necessary to create any sort of tension. A note on its own has no tension at all. And some may say that just a melody alone can create this sense of "pull" from the leading tone to the tonic, but this is ONLY because of memory retention. If the melody is well crafted, your brain will unconsciously remember the lowest note played (the tonic) and cognitively generate polyphony by comparing the notes played to this memory of a tonic.

Those three notes are important as they are involved in the most important mechanisms of tensions/release that the tonal system is based on.

Okay! We now have exposed the main characteristics of the tonal system and studied some vocabulary which will be very useful in the next part. We've discoved that a key can be major when based on the major scale or minor when based on the minor scale, and can be recognized by the number of accidentals in its bank of notes.

But we still have a long way to go! For example, you may have been asking yourself the following question:

"The key signature does not tell us if the key of the tune is the major key or its relative minor key! Since they both have the same notes, their key signatures are identical, so how do we know which one we are dealing with? This is a great question that will be answered soon. The answer is to be found not in the collection of notes but in the harmonic progression, which again is the main mechanism at work in the tonal system.

MAJOR DIATONIC TONAL HARMONY

4

The Tonal Context

MAJOR DIATONIC TONAL HARMONY

MAJOR DIATONIC TONAL HARMONY

Introduction

As I said above, tonal harmony mostly relies on harmonic tension/release mechanisms. These mechanisms are created within the chord progression (harmonically) but also by the melody and the way each note interacts with the polyphonic context—the chords played "underneath" the melody.

In a way, you can compare tonal or functional harmony to a piston motor which generates movement through a succession of compressions and reliefs.

Historically, tonal harmony was simply seen as several melodies played at the same time and was very much analyzed "horizontally." The vertical analysis of harmony using the notion of chords is more recent, and makes a lot of sense in modern music, where most pieces can be broken down to a melody played over a chord progression.

This means that harmonic analysis in the tonal system is actually neither purely horizontal nor vertical. Indeed, there is more than the simple vertical analysis of each chord! We also need to study what happens from one chord to the other. In this way, we can call this a "diagonal" vision of music. Chords change and alternate in time according to the harmonic rhythm. Some chords will create a sense of tension, while others will create a sense of stability which will generate a feeling of release in contrast with the tensions. Those tension/release alternations will guide the listener throughout the tune and will often—at key moments— release on the tonal chord of the tune which will give the impression of "being back home." The melody will always be intertwined with the harmonic progression, since from the point of view of the listener, each melodic note will be part of the chords underneath it! The choice of notes will be mostly limited to the notes of the key scale, BUT this still gives the melodist some freedom in terms of what note to choose. They will be able to choose more or less dissonant notes, as we will see, to participate in the whole harmonic mechanism.

I'm sure by now you are more than fed up with all my talking here and simply can't wait to learn how to create a melody over a tonal chord progression, whether through the form of improvising or composing. But first we MUST study this "motor" of tonal harmony and its mechanisms.

For coherence and simplicity reasons, we will start with the major tonal context. You will then find it easier from there to understand the minor context since it is quite similar to the major one, even though it does present some interesting and noticeable differences.

MAJOR DIATONIC TONAL HARMONY

Degrees and harmonic functions

Major diatonic total harmony, as the name indicates, is based on the diatonic harmonization of the major scale. Each degree of the harmonized scale has a certain function depending its degree of stability or tension.

The three harmonic functions a chord can have in diatonic tonal harmony are:

- The function of tonic
- The function of dominant
- The function of sub-dominant

The Tonic

The chord that creates the most stability in a tonal context is always going to be the **first degree triad of the harmonization of the major scale** which the tune is based upon. The root of the chord is the tonic of the key scale which gives an impression of "being back home." Your "ear" (or really, your brain and memory retention) will naturally want to hear this root. Moreover, the major 3rd interval between the tonic and the median (third of the scale) brings out the major aspect of the key. The 5th, which is the most constant interval that can be formed with the tonic, other than the octave, simply amplifies the importance of the tonic. But in a way, if you HAD to take a note out of this triad, the 5th would be the first one to leave out because it is not as important as the tonic and the major third.

MAJOR DIATONIC TONAL HARMONY

Example in C:

Since this chord is built upon the tonic of the scale, it is called the **tonic chord** (no surprises here).

Even though the chord built on the first degree of the harmonized scale is, by far, the most powerful tonic chord, it is not the only one that can be found in the harmonized scale. Indeed, there are two other chords that create a good impression of stability. These two chords share two out of three notes with the main tonic chord and are the chords built on the third and sixth degree of the harmonized scale:

You will find that these chords are often played in strong moments of the harmonic rhythm in order to bring out the tonal center of the tune. Many tunes will start with the tonic chord and **most tunes will especially end with it**, to create a sense of conclusion on the tonal center. At this moment, the listener thinks, "The tune is obviously over, and it brought us back home, safe, on our beloved and stable tonal chord."

- The tonic chords in a major scale are the chords that bring out the key center.
- The main tonic chord is the triad built on the first degree (tonic) of the scale
- There are two other tonic chords in a major scale: the one built on the third degree and the sixth degree.

MAJOR DIATONIC TONAL HARMONY

A question of genre

In all the styles and genres that are influenced by jazz, some dissonances will be "allowed" even in the tonic chord. In this case, we can extend what we just leaned to the first tetrad of the harmonized scale.

The tonic chords will thus be:

IMaj7
MAIN TONIC CHORD

III-7
MEDIANT

VI-7
SUB-MEDIANT

In all the other genres (classical, rock, pop, etc.), tonic chords tend to be played as triads for extra consonance and stability.

■ The Dominant

Now the question is: what chord will be most appropriate to create the tension that will then resolve on the main tonic chord (Imaj)?

In tonal harmony, the main chord used to create this tension is the chord built on the **fifth degree of the harmonized scale**. Since this chord is built on the dominant scale degree, it is called the **dominant chord** (how original).

MAJOR DIATONIC TONAL HARMONY

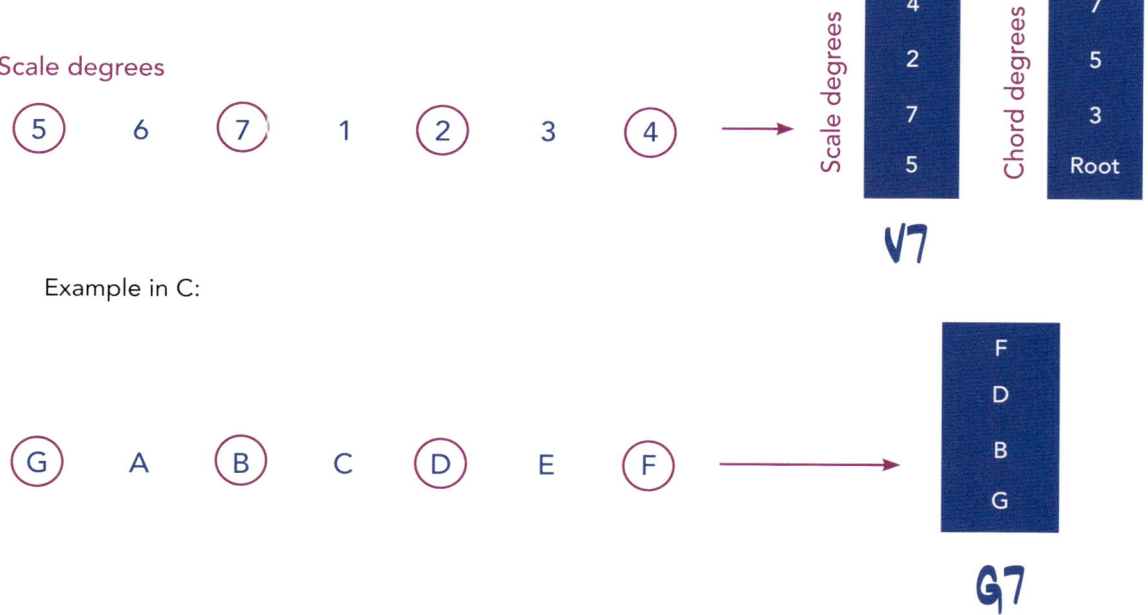

This chord works perfectly as a tension chord leading to the tonic for several reasons:

1. It allows a root movement by 5th (a descending 5th from the fifth degree towards the first), which for reasons that are honestly quite mysterious to me (probably a mix of cultural and physical reasons), are particularly strong for resolution purposes.

2. The 3rd of this chord is the leading-tone of the scale which naturally wants to resolve to the tonic, a half-step above.

3. When the dominant is played as a tetrad (dominant 7th), it contains a tritone, which is a particularly dissonant interval. This tritone reinforces the feeling of tension, which thereby creates an even more intense feeling of release when resolved on the tonic chord Imaj.

MAJOR DIATONIC TONAL HARMONY

Double resolution of the tonal tritone

The interval formed between the 3rd and the 7th of the dominant chord (which respectively corresponds to the 7th and the 4th of the scale), is a very unstable interval: the diminished 5th, also called the tritone. When the dominant chord is followed by the tonic chord, this interval resolves on the major 3rd interval formed between the tonic and the mediant of the scale. This major 3rd is not only much more consonant and stable, it also reinforces the feeling of being in a major key and brings out the tonal center.

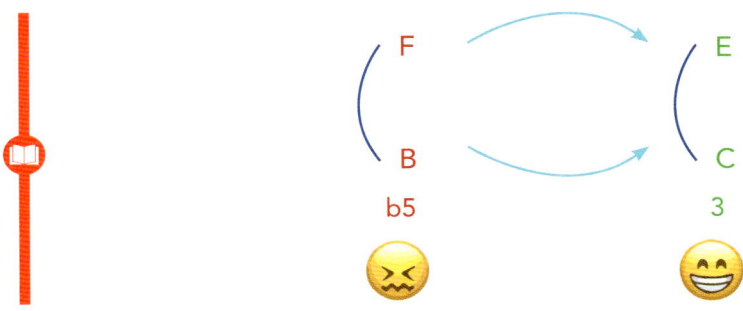

The resolution of the tonal tritone is probably the most important and powerful tonal mechanism.

In a major scale, there is only one tonal tritone. The natural minor scale, on the other hand, does NOT have a tonal tritone, and we will see that this is somewhat "problematic."

By extension, any other chord that contains this tonal tritone is also called a dominant chord. In the diatonic harmonization of the major scale, there is one other chord that contains the tonal tritone.

By the way, this is why chords of the type X7 are always referred to as "dominant chords." But this is a language misuse. We will see that an X7 type chord does NOT necessarily have the role of the dominant, per se, AND we just saw that there are dominant chords that are not of the type X7. For this reason, I encourage you to call these chords **dominant 7th chords** or simply 7th chords.

MAJOR DIATONIC TONAL HARMONY

■ The Sub-Dominant

Sub-dominant chords, like dominant chords, create a sensation of "instability" that is, however, not as strong as that created by dominant chords. These chords generate more of a "suspension" than a real tension. In case you are wondering, the word sub-dominant comes from the fact that the main sub-dominant chord is built upon the fourth degree of the scale. Yet, the fourth degree of the scale is equally distant from the tonic going down, than the dominant degree is, going up. Thus the word "sub" dominant.

This is not necessarily that important in practice, but it's good to know where names come from.

Even though sub-dominant chords can be directly resolved to the tonic chord, their main role is to prepare the dominant chord with a milder instability, which is why they are also called predominant chords. Sometimes you don't want tension to escalate too quickly, right? You can think of the sub-dominant chord as a warm-up that prepares your ears for more tension, before finally being resolved.

This suspension is mostly due to the fact that sub-dominant chords contain the tonic (1) and the fourth (4) of the scale. These two notes form a perfect 4th interval (or perfect 5th if you invert it). The fourth—being a half-step away from the major 3rd of the key—naturally wants to resolve on the 3rd, which creates tension. The main sub-dominant chord is naturally the one built on the sub-dominant degree (fourth degree), but the second degree chord works as well, since it includes the notes responsible for the sub-dominant quality:

- Sub-dominant chords create some degree of instability, but not as much as dominant chords. They are mostly used to prepare for the dominant chord.

- The main sub-dominant chord is the major chord built upon the fourth degree (sub-dominant) of the major scale.

MAJOR DIATONIC TONAL HARMONY

Example in C:

If we briefly go beyond the harmonization of the major scale in classic triads, we can also find two other very popular sub-dominant chords: **the suspended chords.**

Because they also contain the characteristic fourth interval of sub-dominant chords, the following chords are also sub-dominant:

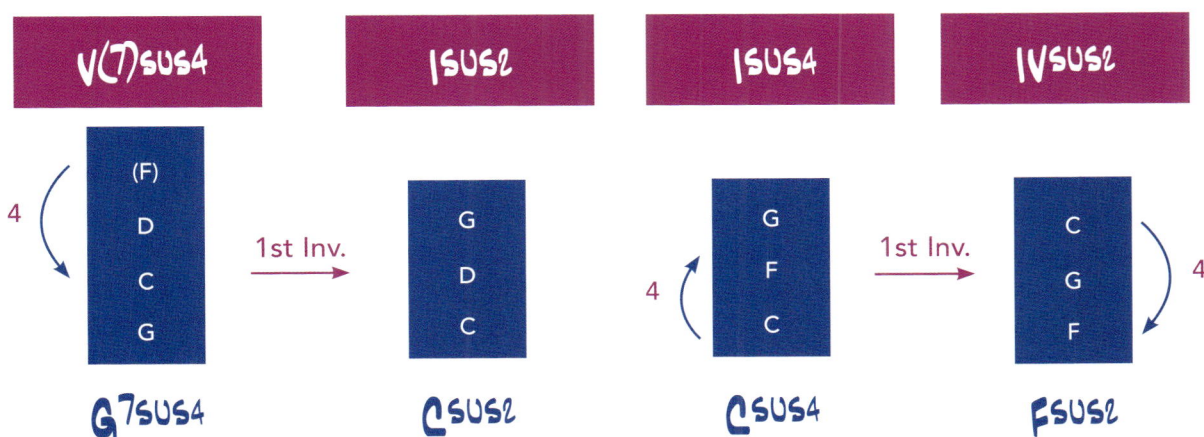

Technically, Gsus4 needs to include F, the minor 7th, to qualify as a subdominant chord, but in practice, the triad is enough to create the desired effect of suspension. The Csus2 and Fsus2 work because they are inversions of Gsus4 and Csus4.

MAJOR DIATONIC TONAL HARMONY

> **ATTENTION**
>
> You can notice that Vsus4 is built on the dominant degree (fifth degree), BUT has the function of a SUB-DOMINANT chord, when suspended. Why? Because it no longer contains the tonal tritone or the leading tone that makes this chord dominant.

Now let's sum up all the chords and their harmonic function:

Degrees	1	2	3	4	5	6	7
Tetrads	IMAJ7	II-7	III-7	IVMAJ7	V7	VI-7	VII-7(b5)
Function	T	S-D	T	S-D	D	T	D

"Authorized" extensions

Everything we have studied so far only applies to chords with a maximum of four notes (tetrads). The root and the two or three notes that are closest to it form the main structure of the chord and are always the ones that matter most when studying harmony. **It is, however, time to look into extensions in the tonal context.**

Even though all the extensions we are going to study directly come from the diatonic harmonization of the major scale, we will see this doesn't mean they should all be used.

■ On the first degree chord

In tonal harmony, the first degree always takes the role of the most stable chord. This means it should only contain extensions with no or very mild tension. The most stable solution will always be the classic major triad without any extensions.

MAJOR DIATONIC TONAL HARMONY

However, as I said before, in some particular styles, especially jazz, you can add the major 7th which, although dissonant, is considered appropriate even on stable chords. But be careful with this major 7th! Even in jazz it is sometimes avoided, especially when the first degree chord is used as a conclusive chord—the last chord of the tune—and replaced by less dissonant extensions. The question is: what extensions CAN I use without adding too much tension? The best extensions to serve this purpose are mainly the 6th (or 13th) and the 2nd (or 9th). The 9th is surprisingly a very mildly dissonant interval and the 6th quite consonant. Still, these extensions will most likely be added in jazz or more modern styles. Very rarely—if not ever—will you see any of the following chords as a conclusive chord in classical music.

Make sure to avoid using the 4th or 11th! For several reasons:

1. If the chord has a major 7th, the 4th and the major 7th will form the tonal tritone, which is very unstable, and has quite the opposite purpose of stability.

2. Even without a 7th, the 4th is only a minor 2nd above the 3rd of the chord, and minor 2nds are always VERY dissonant, which defeats the purpose of a stable chord.

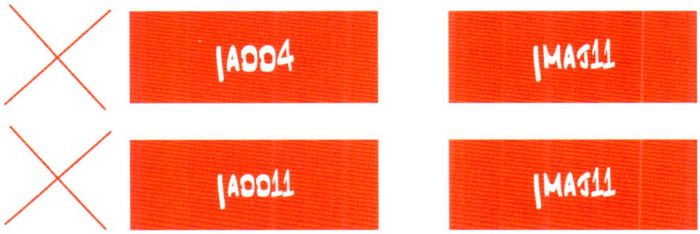

MAJOR DIATONIC TONAL HARMONY

■ On the second degree chord

The second degree is used in a tonal context as a sub-dominant chord. You can therefore add the extensions that will create a moderate dissonance. The one note to avoid here is the 6th or 13th, which would form the tonal tritone with the 3rd of the chord.

The 9th, 11th (and minor 7th, of course) are very acceptable in most cases.

Note: Here we can notice an important difference between modal and tonal situations. The second degree chord corresponds to the first degree of the Dorian mode. In a Dorian situation, it would not only be accepted but advised to play the major 6th, which is the most characteristic note of this mode. But this only works in a modal situation! In a tonal context, this chord is part of a bigger system of which the aim is not at all to bring out the colors of each mode!

If you do happen to see a minor chord with a major 6th, this probably indicates a Dorian modal context.

■ On the third degree chord

The third degree is also a tonic chord and must therefore only contain stable extensions. This means you should avoid the minor 9th and minor 13th.

The 9th, 11th (and minor 7th, of course) are very acceptable in most cases.

MAJOR DIATONIC TONAL HARMONY

■ On the fourth degree chord

The fourth degree chord is sub-dominant. This means the tonal tritone should be avoided, which implies avoiding the augmented 4th or 11th.

Attention! In some tunes (especially in jazz), you might see this extension, which usually has two explanations:

1. To emphasize the fact that it is indeed the fourth degree chord and not the first degree chord of a modulation—of which there are plenty in jazz.

2. To show that it is a Lydian modal context. Again, as I just explained in the case of the second degree chord and the Dorian mode, the #11 is actually a note you want to insist on in a Lydian context and avoid in a tonal context.

■ On the fifth degree chord

The fifth degree chord is dominant and is pretty much meant to be as tensed as possible. So you can go all in in terms of extensions! In fact, we will see later on that it is quite common to borrow extensions from the harmonization of other scales to make this chord even more dissonant. The only extension that tends to be avoided is the 4th (or 11th), which actually tends to give this chord more of a sub-dominant quality. It is not completely forbidden, however.

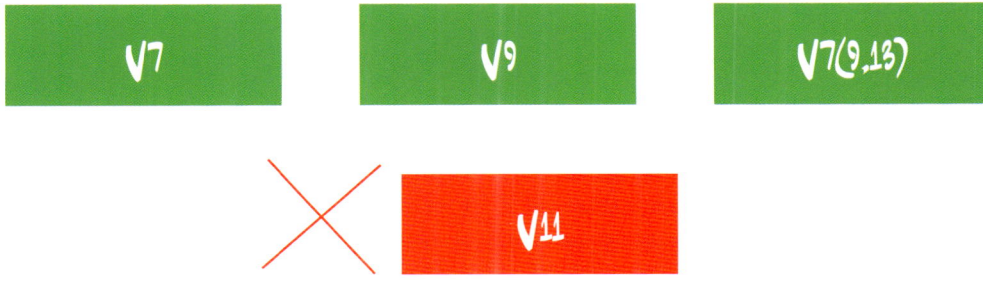

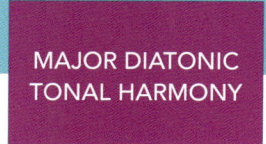

MAJOR DIATONIC TONAL HARMONY

■ On the sixth degree chord

This chord is a tonic chord which means the minor 13th should be avoided since it clashes with the 5th of the chord (creating a minor 2nd interval). Other extensions are welcome.

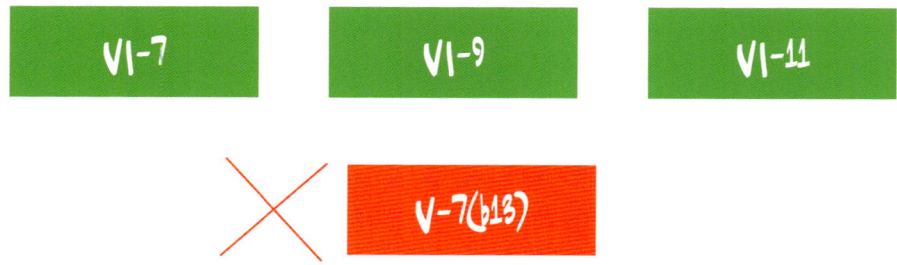

■ On the 7th degree chord

This chord is a tonic chord which means the minor 13th should be avoided since it clashes with the 5th of the chord (creating a minor second interval). Other extensions are welcome.

Degrees	1	2	3	4	5	6	7
Tetrads	IMAJ7	II-7	III-7	IVMAJ7	V7	VI-7	VII-7(b5)
Extensions	9 11 13	9 11 13	b9 11 b13	9 #11 13	9 11 13	9 11 b13	b9 11 b13
Function	T	S-D	T	S-D	D	T	D

MAJOR DIATONIC TONAL HARMONY

Perfect major authentic cadences

Cadences (from Latin cadere which means "to fall") are the most common system of chord progressions in the tonal system. The word "fall"—used to refer to those progressions—obviously does not come out of nowhere. Cadences bring out the "gravitational" characteristic of tonal music of which the center is, as we said earlier, the first degree tonic chord.

> The strongest cadence is the perfect authentic cadence which links the **fifth degree dominant chord in root position** to the **first degree tonic chord in root position**. The word "perfect" is most likely used in its original meaning which is "completed." The perfect authentic cadences is the progression that will give the strongest sense of resolution in a given key. Here is the notation we will be using:

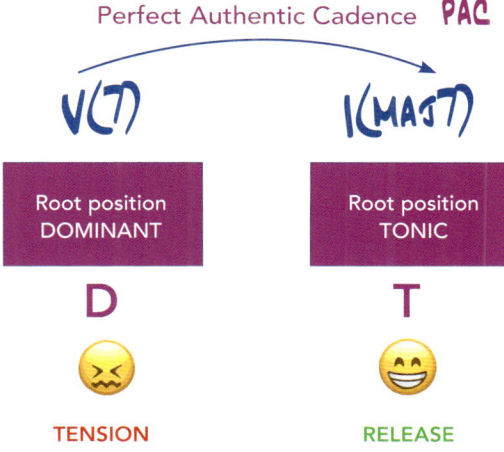

Examples:

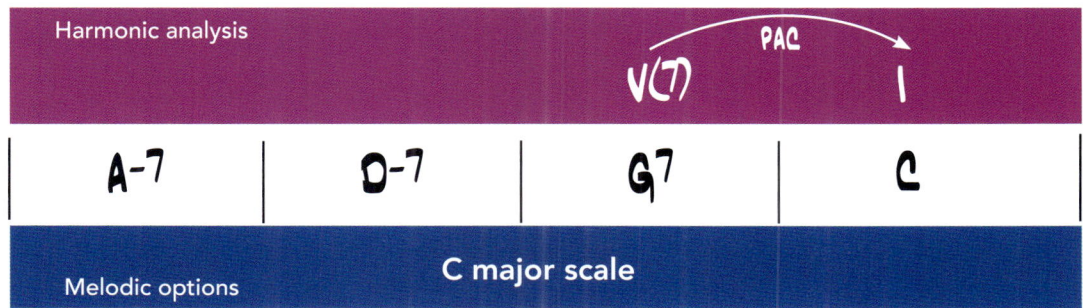

MAJOR DIATONIC TONAL HARMONY

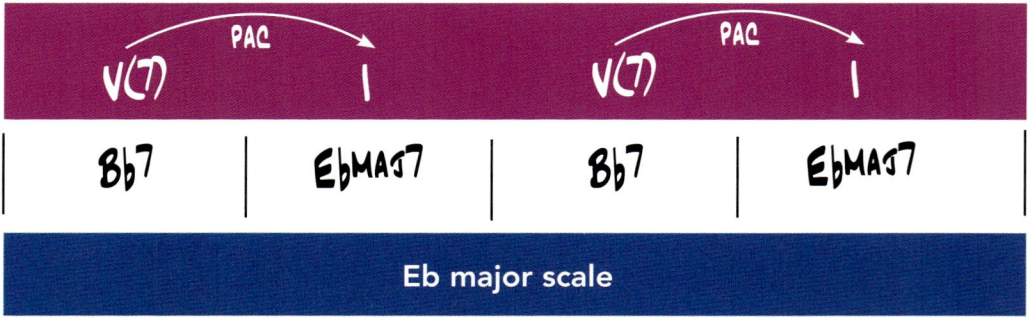

By default, you don't need to systematically indicate that the cadence is perfect and authentic (PAC) which will be implied in the absence of an indication that the cadence is NOT perfect. So in the second example above, the cadences are perfect even without the "PAC" being specified.

Moreover, you don't have to necessarily specify all the extensions of each chord (7, 9, 11, 13…). What matters is the degree! You can also indicate the quality of the main triad or tetrad that the chord is based on. But this too isn't necessary since you're supposed to know the quality of each chord for each degree.

Perfect authentic cadences are the most important harmonic movements of tonal music. This means you MUST know how to:

1. **Recognize such a progression immediately.**
2. **For a given first degree tonic chord, find the dominant chord that precedes it.**
3. **For a given fifth degree dominant chord, find the first degree tonic chord it resolves onto.**

And this is the purpose of the following exercise. One piece of advice: use the circle of 5ths.

Recognize the perfect authentic cadences in the given chord progressions.

MAJOR DIATONIC TONAL HARMONY

Imperfect authentic cadence

An imperfect authentic cadence is also a cadence of the following type:

Imperfect Authentic Cadence **IAC**

D → T

However, it includes all the possibilities excluded in a PAC, meaning:

1. When one of the chords (or both) is NOT in root position.
2. When another tonic chord other than the first degree is used.
3. When another dominant chord other than the fifth degree is used.

Examples in C major :

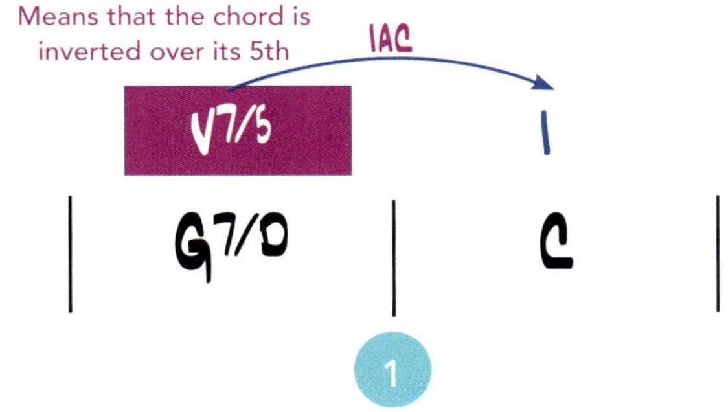

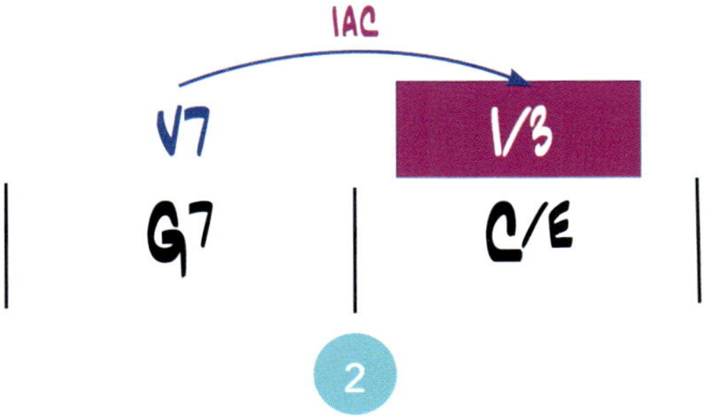

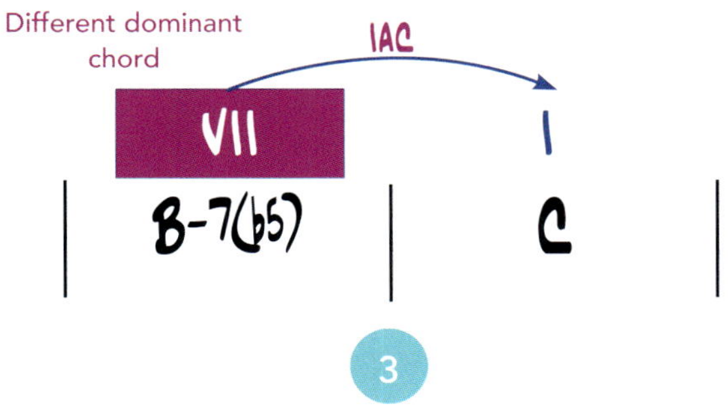

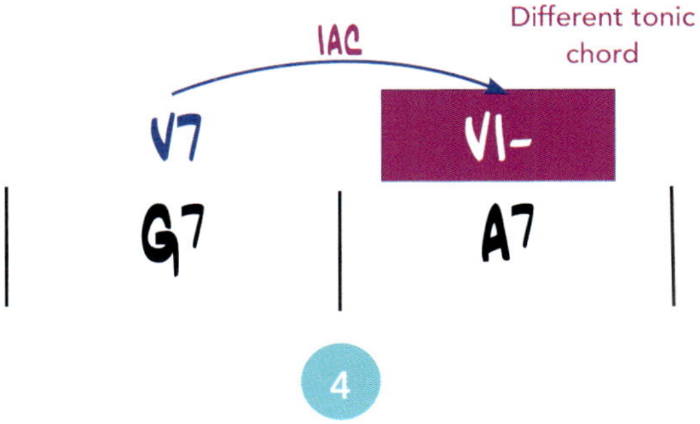

1. Means that the chord is inverted over its 5th — V7/5 → I — G7/D | C

2. V7 → I/3 — G7 | C/E

3. Different dominant chord — VII → I — B-7(b5) | C

4. Different tonic chord — V7 → VI- — G7 | A7

MAJOR DIATONIC TONAL HARMONY

Now at this point you might already be telling yourself, "Why the hell should I be learning all this stuff? This does not seem to have anything to do with improvising at all!"

Normally I would just answer, "Chill out, focus and be patient, it will make sense soon," but just to give you an extra boost in motivation, let me clarify why all of this is important. Finding these tonal progressions within a tune allows you to know exactly whether or not you are dealing with a tonal piece of music AND what key the tune is in. Knowing that allows you to deduce what scale the piece is built upon and this scale is precisely the one you will use to create or improvise. Now do you get it? Are you reassured? Great! Let's keep on going.

Plagal cadence

The plagal cadence is more of a "suspension"/resolution than a tension/resolution mechanism. The effect is not as strong as in an authentic cadence but is still very common and characteristic of tonal harmony. In this progression, the sub-dominant chord resolves directly to the tonic chord.

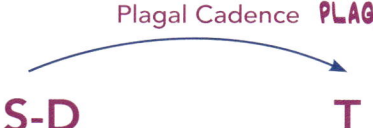

Therefore, there are many possible plagal cadences within a key, but the most common is the one that involves the fourth degree sub-dominant chord resolving to the first degree tonic chord.

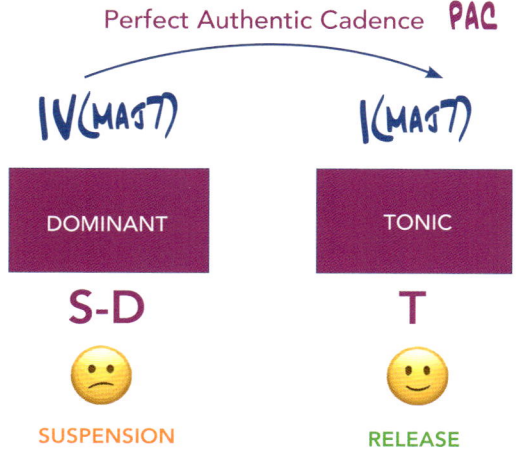

Example:

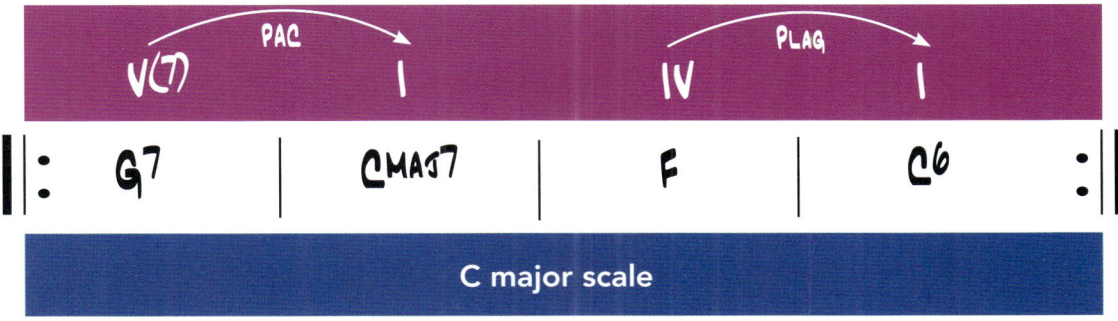

Complete cadence

A complete cadence is a series of three harmonic functions and is defined as follows:

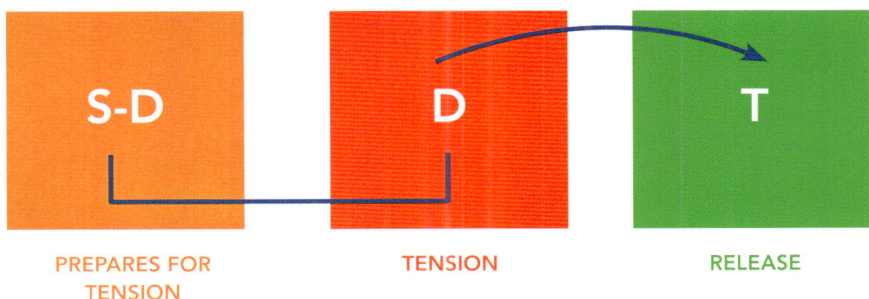

    This is probably the strongest tonal progression. You know how every good joke is based on three parts? The first two build a pattern, and the third part surprises us by braking the pattern. This is exactly what happens here! The sub-dominant starts a feeling of suspension and instability. It is then followed by the dominant chord, even more tensed and unstable than the previous. But the third chord interrupts the pattern by creating a comforting sense of tonal stability. This mechanism amplifies the conclusive aspect of the tonal chord.

    The most common complete cadences are the famous "II V I" and "IV V I."

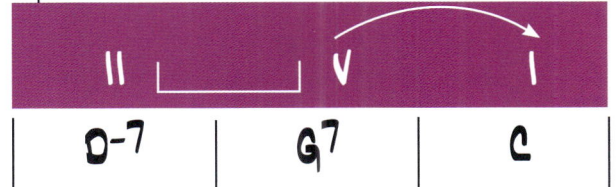

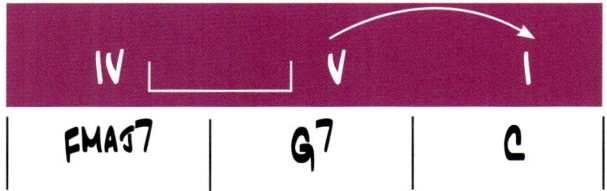

The II V I progressions are the most common progressions in jazz. It is absolutely indispensable to be able to recognize them, especially if you want to study jazz at any point. Just like for cadences, you should spot them automatically without thinking.

And again, you can use our beloved circle of 5ths!

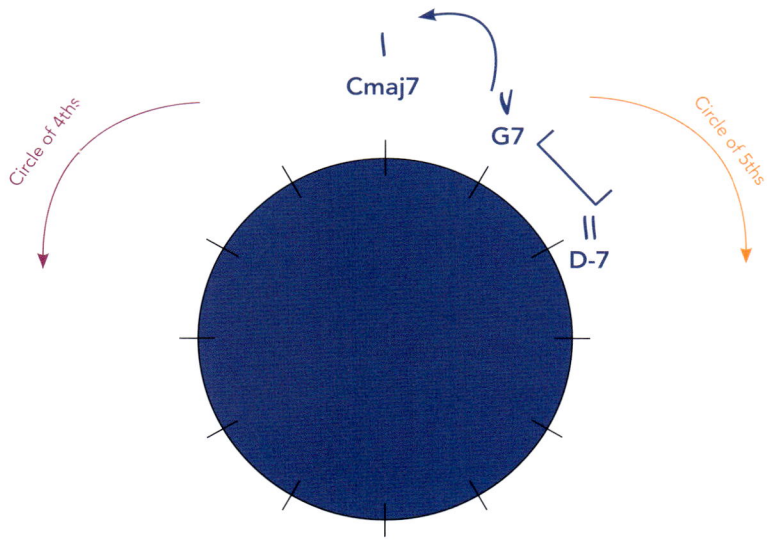

EXERCISE 9 — RECOGNIZING COMPLETE CADENCES

Find the complete cadences in the given chord progressions.

MAJOR DIATONIC TONAL HARMONY

There are plenty of variations of the complete cadences that can be used. Let's look into them.

■ Complete cadence with delayed resolution

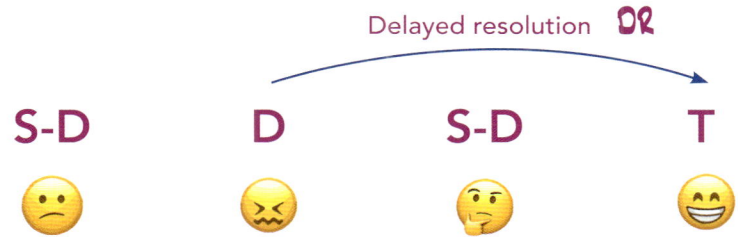

This variation of the "basic" complete cadence is even more powerful and is often found at the very end of a piece or at the end of a part.

The sub-dominant is played again, between the dominant and the tonic, which prolongs the sense of instability and creates a feeling of "double-resolution." This cadence involves:

1. **A plagal cadence.**

2. **A delayed resolution of the dominant chord.**

> **A delayed resolution (DR) applies when one or several chords are played between the dominant chord and the tonic chord on which it resolves.**
>
> **However, the dominant and tonic still have to be relatively close together. Close enough to remember that a dominant chord has not yet been resolved. If the tonic chord is too far apart from the dominant, it will be called an interrupted cadence, as we will see.**

Even though the final cadence (S-D to T) in this progression is plagal, it is not as strong as the resolution of the dominant to the tonic. Remember, the S-D chord played after the dominant is just there to amplify the authentic cadence by delaying the resolution. This is why the plagal cadence will not be indicated in the analysis.

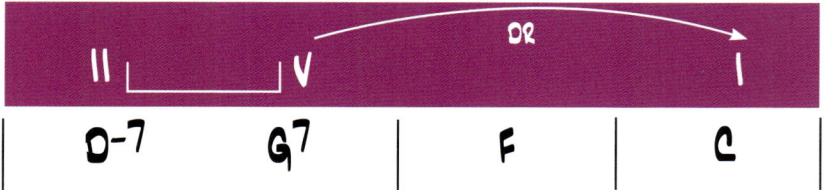

■ **Complete cadence with double-preparation**

This type of cadence also allows an amplified sense of release by prolonging the moment of tension that precedes it. What should be a "preparation of tension, tension and resolution" becomes "preparation of tension, tension, wait what? Where is my resolution?" The listener simply cannot wait to hear the tonic chord! So when it is finally played, the satisfaction is even greater!

Incomplete cadences

Incomplete cadences are the ones that only involve two of the three harmonic functions that must be present in a complete cadence. This means imperfect cadences always take one of the following forms:

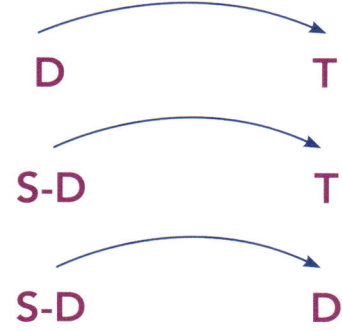

MAJOR DIATONIC TONAL HARMONY

Don't let words induce any negative feelings towards cadences that are "imperfect" or "incomplete." It doesn't mean they are bad and should be played less than the "perfect" and "complete" ones.

The attributes of "completion" and "perfection" can be combined which gives us four possible combinations:

- **Perfect Complete Cadence**

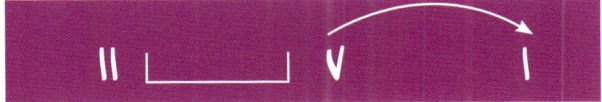

- **Perfect Incomplete Cadence**

- **Imperfect Complete Cadence**

- **Imperfect Incomplete Cadence (Poor cadence...)**

Interrupted or evaded cadence

An interrupted or evaded cadence is a cadence where the expected resolution of the dominant chord simply doesn't happen. The tension is left unsatisfied, with no resolving tonic chord. These cadences are most likely to be found in the middle of a tune because of their utterly inconclusive characteristic. But again, rules are meant to be broken and you will always find some little smarty pants, especially in jazz, ending a piece with an interrupted cadence, which will most likely leave the listener with a sense of frustration.

When analyzing a tune, make sure the resolution isn't simply delayed before calling it an interrupted cadence

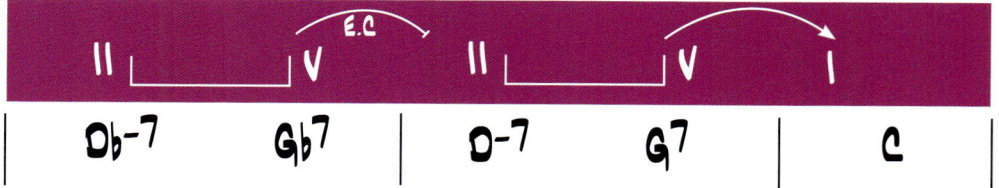

In the example above, you can clearly see what seems to be II V I in Cb major. Except that the I (Cb), never comes! Instead, the cadence is interrupted and the context modulates to another key. Interrupted cadences are very often used for the purpose of modulation, which we will explore very soon.

Question: Is the following cadence an imperfect cadence or an evaded cadence?

Technically, this is an imperfect cadence that concludes on the VI degree chord which plays the role of tonic chord. But some will argue that it could also be an indication of the tune modulating to the key of A minor —in this case A- would be the first degree chord of the A minor key. This would make this the cadence an evaded cadence. To avoid confusion, I think it's better to reserve the name "evaded" to progressions that land on a chord that cannot be seen as a tonic chord. If by analyzing the piece in its entirety you did find out the piece was modulating in A minor at this moment, I would simply interpret the progression as follows:

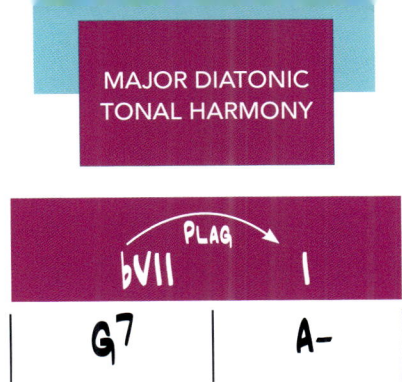

The reason for that is that in minor tonal harmony, the bVII degree is considered sub-dominant. If this doesn't make sense right now, it's normal: we have not studied minor tonal harmony yet. So you'll have to take this as a given for now.

As we will see, it is important to know whether or not you are modulating to the minor relative key, or simply playing the VI chord while staying in the major key since it will influence the way you improvise. On the VI chord of a major key, you should still be focusing on playing in the major key, whereas on the I chord of the minor relative key, you will want to bring out the minor characteristics of the key and should no longer be "thinking major."

Note: Ambiguities and disagreements in naming cadences

I can already hear the complaints and arguments of many, outraged about the above definitions, especially for people having studied classical music. There are more subtleties—which come from counterpoint and other older forms of composing—that can come into play when naming a cadence. For example, for a cadence to be perfect, not only do the chords of the cadence have to be in root position, but the highest note of the tonic chord HAS to be the tonic. Okay… But the problem is that these definitions exclude a lot of more modern types of music. The reality is that, in jazz for example, a perfect cadence does not have to respect the rule I just exposed. In general, the rules have become more lenient and it is better to have a more flexible vocabulary, easily defined, that can accurately describe ALL types of music, than a load of overly complicated definitions that ignore the way music evolves.

If we start naming each cadence differently for each particular type of voicing, it would take years of studying and a book as big as the dictionary to learn all of them. What we want are catalogs and categories.

Our goal here is to analyze just enough to be able to create melodies (either composing or improvising) in a particular musical context. The way you would improvise over a perfect cadence, whether the tonic is or isn't the highest note of the tonic chord, would be exactly the same.

MAJOR DIATONIC TONAL HARMONY

Some will say, "Oh, we could talk about this for hours." Well, guess what? If you can talk for hours about how to name a cadence, that means there is something fundamentally wrong with the nomenclature you are using. Names are meant to be easily given and should make communication simpler, without much room for interpretation. So I am not saying I am right in the way I name cadences. But I do know that using those definitions is sufficient to avoid confusion and improvise or compose confidently. "So how do I name a prefect cadence with the tonic as the high note of the tonic chord?" Well, you just did, and I perfectly understood you. There doesn't have to be a name for everything, especially if it generates confusion.

Cadences and harmonic rhythm

The impact of cadences is largely influenced by the harmonic rhythm and particularly dependent on where in the harmonic rhythm they are prepared or resolved.

As seen in the previous chapter, weak and strong beats alternate throughout any piece of music. Whether the beats are weak or strong largely depends on how many chords are found in each bar.

- **A strong cadence is a cadence that resolves on a strong beat of the harmonic rhythm.**

- **The cadence found at the end of a piece or part is called conclusive cadence. If it is also a strong cadence, it is called a strong conclusive cadence.**

- **A weak cadence is a cadence that resolves on a weak beat of the harmonic rhythm. If such a cadence is also conclusive, it will be called weak conclusive cadence.**

- **A half-cadence is a cadence in which the dominant chord is played on a strong beat of the harmonic rhythm.**

Now at this point you may ask yourself again, "Why in the world are we studying those things and are they really useful for someone that just wants to improvise some shredding solos?" Let me tell you why! You won't improvise or compose a melody the same way on a cadence that concludes a part or a piece of music, or on a cadence that doesn't resolve or sits on the dominant on a strong beat. In each of those situations, the melody should amplify and serve the harmonic progression.

MAJOR DIATONIC TONAL HARMONY

Diatonic substitution

A diatonic substitution consists of replacing a chord by another chord of the harmonized scale that serves the same harmonic function. For example:

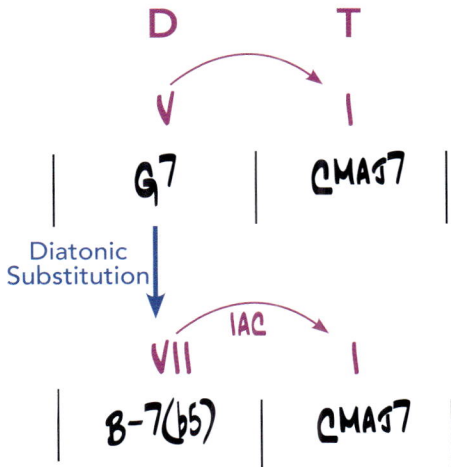

A substitution is usually used in three different cases:

1. Remember the difference between what is heard versus what is thought? Well, in the case of substitutions, the improviser could be "thinking" a substitution instead of the actual chord which will influence what they play. For example, in the chord progression above, when the improviser reads the first line (actually written), he or she could imagine that the G7 is actually a B-7b5 and play a B-7b5 arpeggio. Nothing really changes in that case, apart from the way the tune is perceived and interpreted. The B-7b5 arpeggio will sound less obvious than a G7 arpeggio. In other words, quick mental diatonic substitutions, when improvising, can expand your panel of melodic options.

2. In the case of the rearrangement of a tune—which basically means re-writing a preexisting tune in a different way—you can rearrange all aspects of a tune (the rhythm, the melody, the tempo, etc.), and changing the harmony is one of the options commonly used. A diatonic substation in that case is a great way of changing the harmony not too drastically.

MAJOR DIATONIC TONAL HARMONY

3. In the case of a person accompanying and playing the chord progression, that person could decide to include a substitution in order to slightly change the preexisting tune. This works like an "improvised rearrangement" in some way.

Improvisation and melody creation

"Okay, so this is great and all but for now, apart from studying loads of musical analysis, we have not seen ANYTHING on improvisation or creating melodies." Well, allow me to disagree. Actually, everything we have been talking about so far is nothing BUT the art of improvising. To improvise or compose correctly, you NEED to understand the harmonic context you are in. Understanding and knowing all the mechanisms we have been studying allows you to do precisely this: know what key you are in in order to confidently choose the scale (or mode or arpeggio) you can play in. Recognizing harmonic mechanisms and being able to fully analyze music is the only way to rationally approach improvisation. If this sounds like too much, well I recommend going back to the old fashion "playing it by ear" and using your "feelings" or "intuition." Which is another way of saying that you simply don't know what you are doing.

Let's take an example:

Here is what you need to improvise over. Oh, and sorry, you don't get to listen to it before. So go ahead! Come on! Improvise! One, two, three… Does that sound impossible to you? Not if you've been paying attention. Let's take a closer look:

```
||: FMAJ7  | D-7  | G-7  | C7  |
   FMAJ7   | D7   | G-7  | C7  :||
```

Notice once again, that I did not include a time signature in the example above. Simply because all the rules that we are discovering here apply to any time signature!

If you know your cadences, you should immediately see this very obvious one:

MAJOR DIATONIC TONAL HARMONY

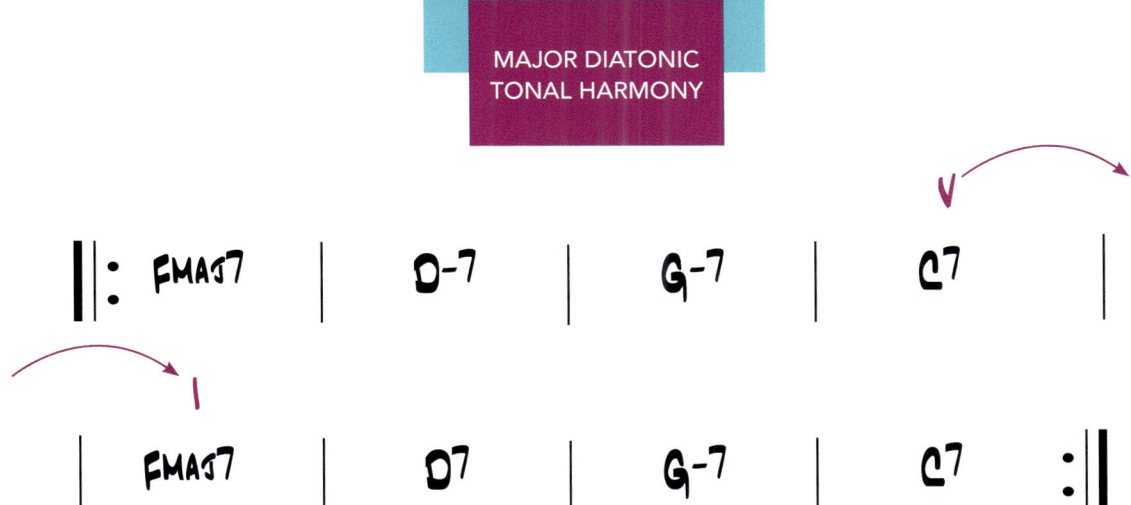

C7 is the fifth degree dominant chord in the key of F major. At this point, you are allowed to suspect that the key might be F major. So let's analyze the other chords and see if they belong to that key.

Let's look at the chord right before the C7. You can see it corresponds to the second degree chord II-7 in F major.

If you keep going, it won't take long for you to see that ALL the chords of this progression belong to the harmonization of F major.

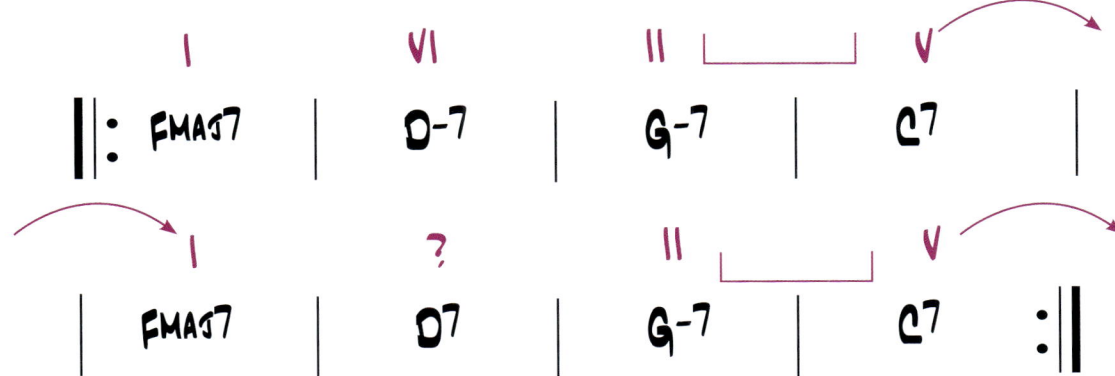

Conclusion: Except for this "stranger" chord on bar 6 (the D7), all the other chords indicate the key of F major, so to improvise you can use the F major scale (which again also includes the pentatonic and obviously the arpeggios of each chord). You can even survive the D7 chord by simply playing a D7 arpeggio, even if you don't understand the context yet.

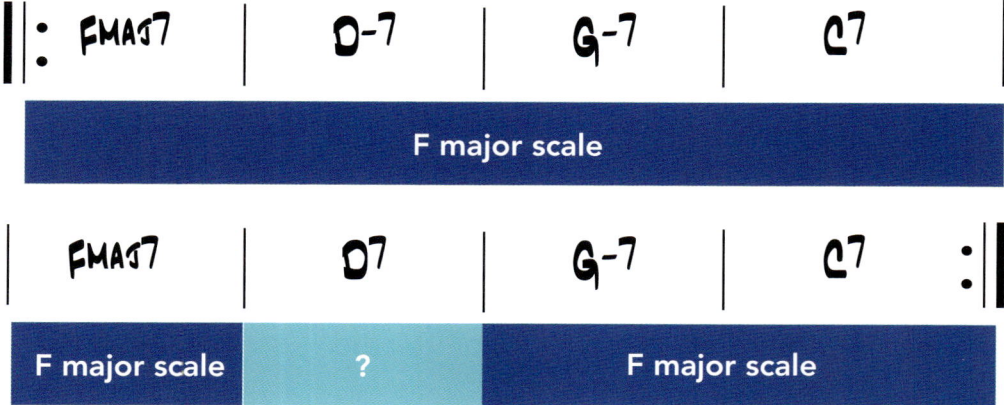

    This is precisely why music analysis is so powerful and useful. Someone who can quickly analyze a piece of music could play or improvise over the above chord progression without having played over it EVER before. They might not play the best solo. But at least it will work!

    Now back to this weird D7 chord that seems to come out of nowhere and that does not belong to the harmonization of F major. How do we explain this chord? We will see this in just a little bit. We will also dive deeper into the possibilities of melodic creation. I simply wanted to dissipate any confusion or thoughts that could be distracting. So I hope this was enough to make you realize that with what we have seen, you already know a lot more than most people about improvising.

4

The Tonal Context

MINOR DIATONIC TONAL HARMONY

MINOR DIATONIC TONAL HARMONY

It's now time to dive into the particularities of the minor tonal context. You will find that there are a lot of similarities with the major context. However, there are some notable differences. For example, we will see that the natural minor scale does not, in itself, contain the chords that allow building proper cadences. This is what made it necessary to borrow some chords from the harmonization of the harmonic and melodic minor scales.

Degrees and functions

Let's look at the harmonization of the natural minor scale:

Degrees	1	2	b3	4	5	b6	b7
Tetrads	I-7	II-7(b5)	bIIIMAJ7	IV-7	V-7	bVI-7	bVII7

■ Tonic Chords

The most important and stable tonic chord of the natural minor scale is the chord built on the first degree of the scale. The root of this chord is the tonic of the scale, and the minor 3rd interval between the root and the 3rd of the chord reflects the minor character of the key.

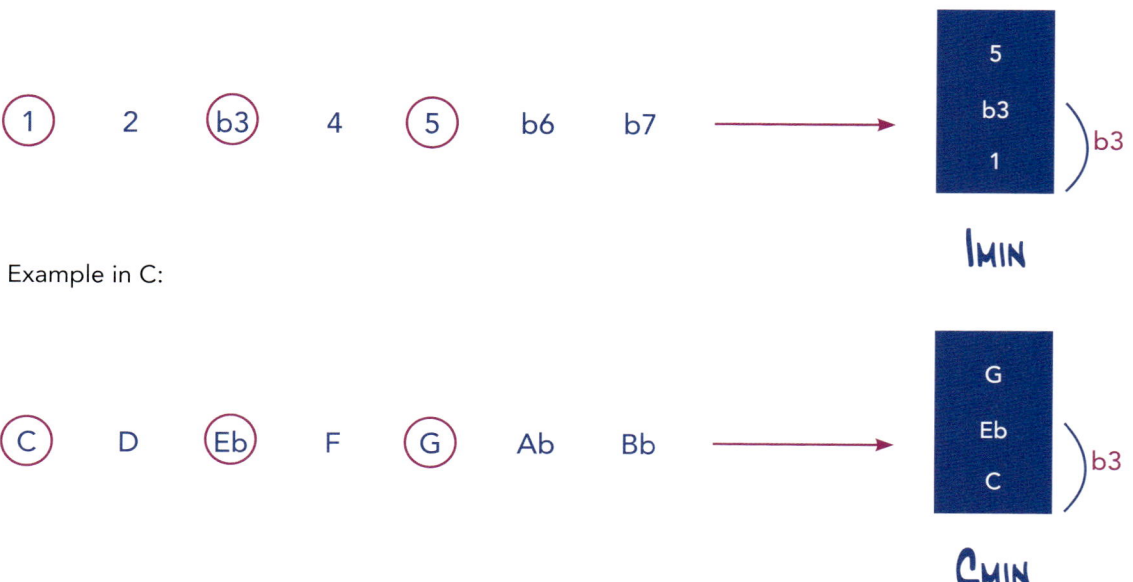

Example in C:

MINOR DIATONIC TONAL HARMONY

Just like for the major context, the chord is more stable as a triad, but the minor 7th can be added in genres that allow fore dissonance (namely: "jazz").

Another stable tonic chord is the chord based on the minor 3rd of the scale:

■ Dominant chords

Well, here we have a problem... We know that a dominant chord needs to contain some degree of tension. But most importantly, it must include the tonal tritone. The resolution of the tonal tritone to the first degree chord is really what anchors the sense of tonality. Remember: it's the mechanism that makes our "tonal motor" work. So what options do we have in the natural minor scale?

Let's put ourselves in the key of C natural minor. The first degree tonic chord will be:

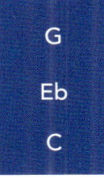

The tonal tritone in this key is:

MINOR DIATONIC TONAL HARMONY

So we want a chord that contains those two notes in order to allow the following resolution:

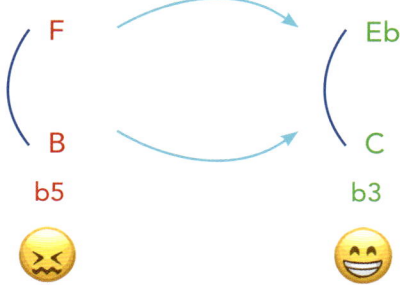

Resolution of the tonal tritone in C minor

Let's see if we find any candidates!

- ### The II-7b5 chord

This chord has a tritone indeed, but not the tritone we want!

Tonal Tritone

Moreover, the interval of 4th between C and F, just like in a major context, gives an impression of tonal "suspension" which makes this chord sub-dominant.

Popup quiz: This chord is not dominant in the key of C minor, but it IS dominant in a specific major key. Can you tell which one?

It's the VII-7b5 degree of Eb major. Which happens to be the relative major scale of C minor. It all makes sense!

MINOR DIATONIC TONAL HARMONY

Let's see if we find any candidates!

- ## The bVII7 chord

This chord also has a tritone, but again, not the right one.

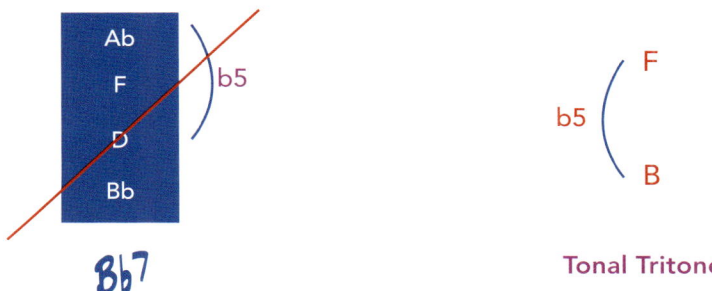

Tonal Tritone

In a minor context, this chord is (because it includes the fourth degree) is also sub-dominant.

 So **even though we seem to be running into a little bit of an issue here and still haven't found the right chord, we nevertheless discovered something useful: The dominant chords of a major key are sub-dominant in its relative minor key!**

This is very useful to create some effective "surprises" amid the chord progression. For example, in C major, a G7 could resolve two ways:

- On the first degree of the major key with an authentic cadence.

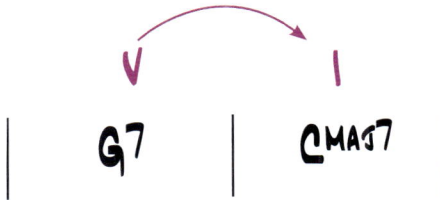

- Or towards the FIRST degree of the relative minor key which a plagal cadence which implies a modulation (change of key):

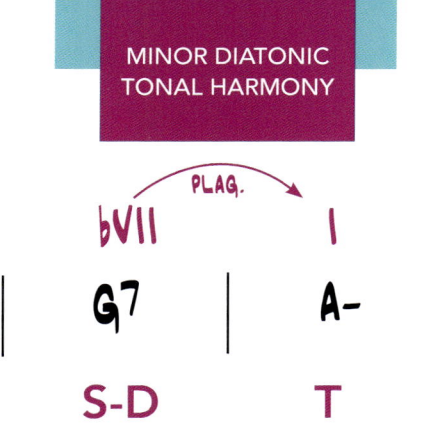

Does this ring a bell? We studied this exact chord progression in the section on evaded cadences.

- ## What about the V chord?

We could also look at the fifth degree of the natural minor scale remembering that the most effective resolution of a dominant chord requires a bass movement from the fifth degree to the first degree (V to I).

Unfortunately, the fifth degree chord in the harmonization of the natural minor scale is NOT a dominant seventh chord and does not include a tritone.

The following progression would therefore give some sense of resolution, but clearly not enough, since the V-7 chord is simply not "tensed" enough.

Actually, the V-7 degree chord in a minor key doesn't really have any specific function. It doesn't give the sense of stability of a tonic chord and is not tensed enough to feel dominant or sub-dominant. It's actually kind of useless from a tonal standpoint. But luckily there is a solution!

If the chord is not dominant, why not just make it dominant?

Let's see what happens if we pop the minor third of this chord up a half-step:

MINOR DIATONIC TONAL HARMONY

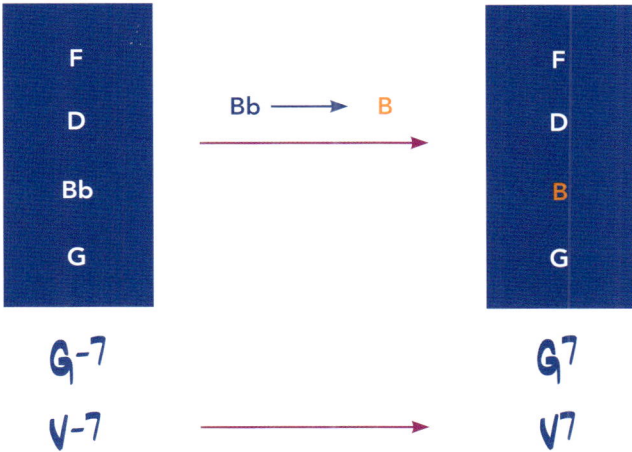

So by changing this fifth degree chord and simply increasing the pitch of its third by a little half-step, this chord becomes the perfect candidate as it has the tonal tritone we were looking for!

Okay, but here you might say that if we start allowing ourselves to tweak around the notes of the chords the way we want to, we can make anything appear. In the meantime, when I change this note, I am no longer in C minor! C minor does not have a natural B but a Bb in its note palette.

Well, that's true. But! Let's look at what scale we create by applying this little change:

Oh lord... This can't be!... It's... It's the harmonic minor scale!!

It's okay! Take a few deep breaths. You must be quite overwhelmed by the beauty of this discovery right now. What did we discover?

1. **We have just discovered the origin of the "harmonic" minor scale. It's a minor scale that has, above all, a harmonic advantage that allows to palliate the absence of a dominant chord in the natural minor scale.**

MINOR DIATONIC TONAL HARMONY

2. We have also just discovered the notion of modal borrowing or modal interchange. A borrowing or interchange is a temporary, short-lived change in key, either towards another key or towards a modal section. Modulating towards a modal section is called a modal borrowing or modal interchange (or sometimes modal mixture). For the length of this section, we would temporarily be in a static modal context, which we studied a while ago.

Indeed, even if during this one chord, we find ourselves having to use the notes of the C harmonic minor scale, it's actually the fifth mode of this scale that we would be playing: the phrygian dominant mode or Mixolydian (b2, b6), since our bass will be the fifth degree of the scale. Again, you might "think" in terms of harmonic minor, but the mode heard will inevitably be the Phrygian dominant mode.

Degrees	1	2	3	4	5	6	7
Tetrads	IMIN(MAJ7)	II-7(b5)	IIIMAJ7(#5)	IV-7	V7	bVIMAJ7	VII°7
Mode	Harmonic minor	Locrian major 6	Ionian #5	Dorian #4	Phrygian dominant	Lydian #2	Superlocrian bb7

From a melodic standpoint, the harmonic minor scale is simply a natural minor scale with a leading tone. This allows to create the tensions and the harmonic and melodic "pull" that are required in the tonal system.

So here is what our harmonic context will look like in the case of a minor V to I cadence.

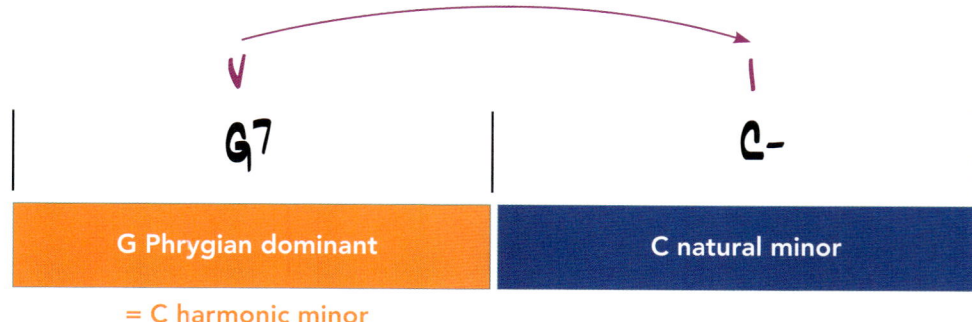

MINOR DIATONIC TONAL HARMONY

- ## The VIIdim7 chord

Harmonizing the harmonic minor scale gives us another dominant chord that includes the tonal tritone and resolves beautifully on the first degree tonic chord. Let's look into it:

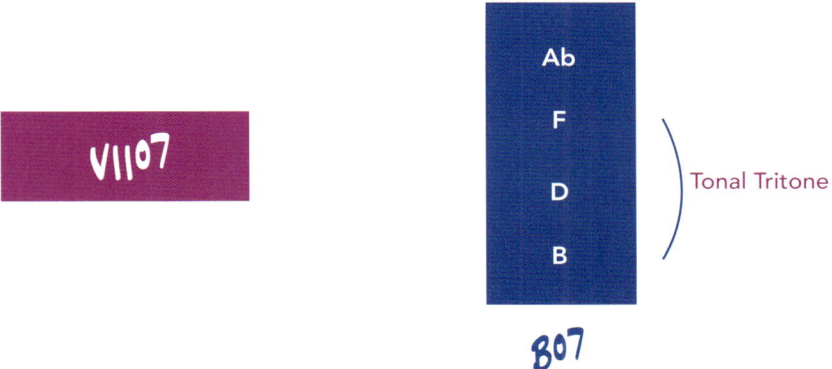

Now, the cool thing with fully diminished chords is that they are symmetrical by inversions. This makes sense when you remember that they are made of three stacked-up minor 3rds. This means that all the inversions of a diminished chord are also root position diminished chords.

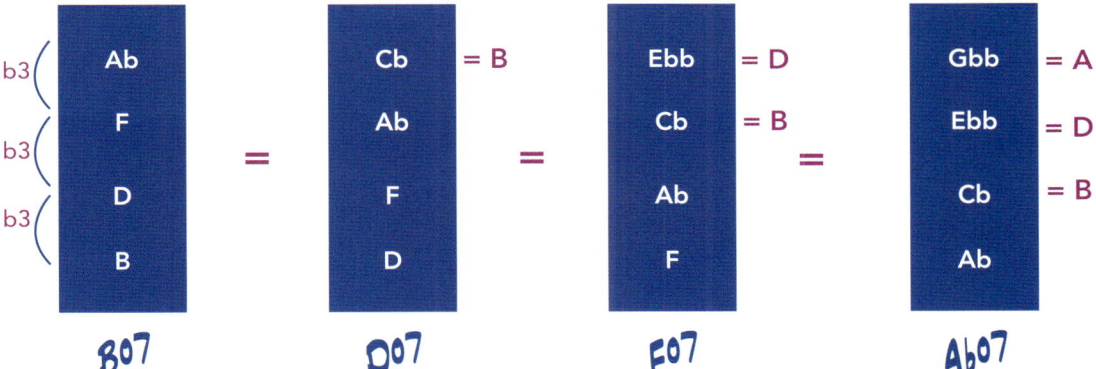

So borrowing from the harmonization of the harmonic minor scale didn't only allow us to have one dominant, but two and even five dominant chords if you include the inversions of the dominant diminished chord!

Question: Why don't we simply base the minor key off of the harmonic minor scale?

If you were asking yourself this question, then congratulations! Indeed, why not? Why bother with the natural minor scale at all if it lacks dominant chords? Well, first, there are pieces of music that ARE based exclusively on the harmonic minor scale. But it's a bit rare for several reasons:

MINOR DIATONIC TONAL HARMONY

1. The harmonic minor scale is extremely colorful (sometimes too much), and it actually has more of a modal quality. If this is your intension, then so be it! But sometimes you also might want to be able to play in a minor key without having to sound like you're playing Middle Eastern music or Flamenco. So the natural minor scale will be predominant and you just have to borrow the dominant chord from the harmonic minor to create proper cadences.

2. There are simply NO tonic stable chords in the harmonic minor scale. In the harmonic minor scale, degrees I and bIII become:

Those chords are very unstable, and this is not at all what we want for tonic chords.

■ Sub-dominant chords

The sub-dominant chords in the natural minor scale are also the ones that create an impression of suspensions. They have to include the fourth degree of the scale:

MINOR DIATONIC TONAL HARMONY

To sum it up

Let's gather all the information we've seen so far about chord functions in the minor key.

Degrees	1	2	b3	4	5	b6	b7
Tetrads	I-7	II-7(b5)	bIIIMAJ7	IV-7	V-7	bVI-7	bVII7
Function	T	S-D	T	S-D	/	S-D	S-D

Natural minor scale

Degrees	1	2	b3	4	5	b6	7
Tetrads	IMIN(MAJ7)	II-7(b5)	IIIMAJ7(#5)	IV-7	V7	bVIMAJ7	VII°7
Function	T	S-D	T	S-D	D	S-D	D

Harmonic minor scale

Degrees	1	2	b3	4	5	b6	7
Tetrads	IMIN(MAJ7)	II-7(b5) II°7	III MAJ7(#5)	IV-7 IV°7	V7	bVIMAJ7 bVI°7	VII°7
Function	T	S-D D	T	S-D D	D	S-D D	D

Harmonic minor scale Including the inversion of the diminished chord

MINOR DIATONIC TONAL HARMONY

Role of the melodic minor scale

We know that the harmonic minor scale is mostly used for "harmonic purposes." So what do you think the melodic minor scale is going to be used for?

The melodic minor scale plays a melodic role since it is not nearly as "colorful" as the harmonic minor scale but yet still has a dominant fifth degree, the tonal tritone, a leading tone, and all that good stuff. Even on the dominant chord itself, playing the Phrygian dominant mode can sound a little too "Middle Eastern," which is not always appropriate. This characteristic color of the harmonic minor scale comes from the augmented 2nd interval between the minor 6th and the major 7th:

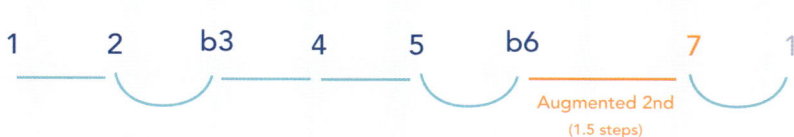

So how is the melodic minor scale different? It simply has a major 6th, which eliminates the one-and-a-half-step interval:

Now what about the fifth degree chord? Will it still be the right type of chord? Yes, it will!

Degrees	1	2	b3	4	5	6	7
Tetrads	IMIN(MAJ7)	II-7	IIIMAJ7(#5)	IV7	V7	VI-7(b5)	VII-7(b5)
Mode	Melodic minor	Phrygian major 6th	Lydian #5	Lydian b7	Mixolydian b6	Locrian major 2	Superlocrian

MINOR DIATONIC TONAL HARMONY

The new borrowed mode, the Mixolydian b6, is the perfect compromise in a minor cadence when you don't want the melody on that part to sound too sonically colored.

Looking at the different harmonic functions of the chords of melodic minor, we get:

Degrees	1	2	b3	4	5	6	7
Tetrads	IMIN(MAJ7)	II-7	IIIMAJ7(#5)	IV7	V7	VI-7(b5)	VII-7(b5)
Function	T	S-D	T	S-D	D	/	D

For the same reason as the harmonic minor scale, you will very rarely see tunes that use exclusively the melodic minor scale. It is, however, a very good scale to borrow a couple of colors from in natural minor contexts.

"Authorized" extensions

Just like in a major key, some extensions are more "authorized" than others, depending on the chord and its function. However, things are going to get a little more complicated than in the major key since we are now taking into account the extensions of three minor scales, and each one brings different extensions to the table.

■ On the first degree chord

The most stable chord is the minor triad. This triad will most often be seen as the first degree of the natural minor scale, but the first degrees of the two other minor scales are also based on this triad. Technically, as a composer or improviser, you can choose to interpret this triad as you wish. But remember, the harmonic minor scale and melodic minor scale have a particular sound. Use them wisely and willingly.

I-   Natural minor scale (NM)
     Harmonic minor scale (HM)
     Melodic minor scale (MM)

MINOR DIATONIC TONAL HARMONY

13	MM	
b13	NM HM	
11	All	Scale each extension comes from
9	All	
7	HM MM	
b7	NM	

I−

■ **On the second degree**

This degree is sub-dominant and is most often found in the following form:

II−7(b5)

Remember that a sub-dominant chord should prepare for the tension of the dominant and therefore have some degree of dissonance, without including the tonal tritone. For this reason, the b9 and 13 extensions will not work.

13	MM HM
b13	NM
11	All
b9	All
b7	All

II−7(b5)

MINOR DIATONIC TONAL HARMONY

However, it is quite common to see a natural 9th played as an extension of this chord. This natural 9th can be obtained by borrowing from the sixth degree of another melodic minor scale. The exact name of this context is Locrian major 2. There is no particular logic behind this modal interchange other than the fact that it seems to "work well."

So the complete table of authorized extensions is actually:

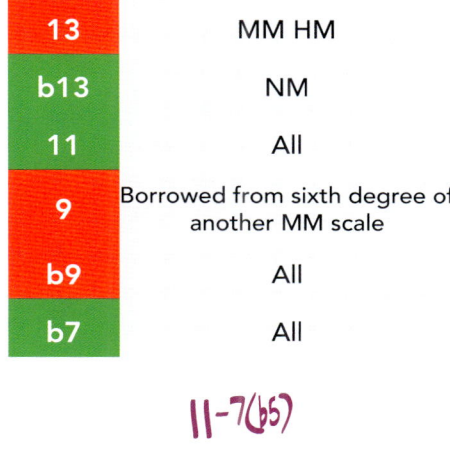

Example:

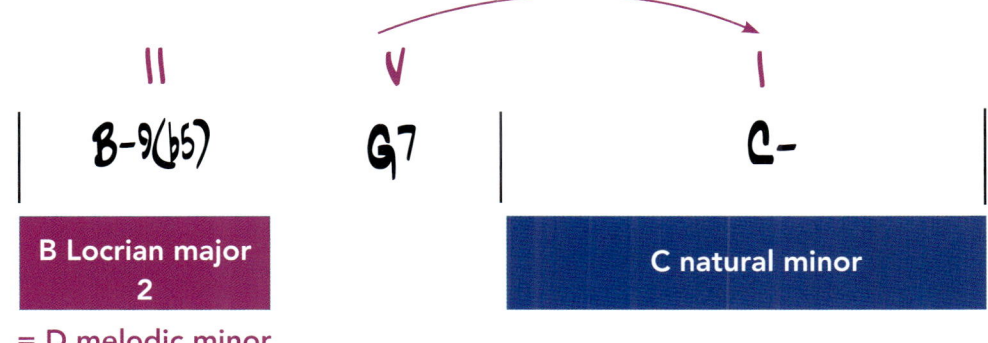

The last case scenario is the case where the second degree is borrowed from the melodic minor scale. In this case, the chord is not based on a diminished triad, and the authorized extensions are:

On the third degree

This chord allows the same extensions as the first degree tonic chord in a major context (see above). It is a tonic chord, so it should be relatively stable. The augmented 5th borrowed from the harmonic and melodic minor scales can be added in styles that allow some extra tension. The 11th is too unstable as it is only a half step away from the 3rd. The augmented 4th borrowed from the melodic minor scale is possible but again very tensed. It should be used with great care. The 9th and 13th are perfectly acceptable and color the chord without adding too much tension.

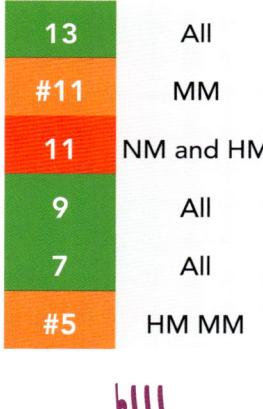

On the fourth degree

This degree is sub-dominant and will therefore allow some moderate tension, but not the tonal tritone. The #11 brought by the harmonic minor scale is not used because it creates excessive dissonance. Finally, the IV7 chord borrowed from the melodic minor scale can be used. Even though this chord is of a X7 form, it is STILL sub-dominant.

MINOR DIATONIC TONAL HARMONY

■ On the fifth degree dominant

The fifth degree dominant chord is a chord that can (and sometimes ought to) be tensed and unstable. So, theoretically, you can add any accidental you wish, even though some extensions will be more preferable than others depending on the context, as we will discover shortly.

However, you should always be aware of the accidentals you use and familiar with the particular sound they create. Each accidental has a particular color and should be used with total control. Again, this is why ear training is so important.

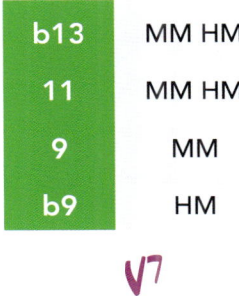

■ On the sixth degree

Because it is barely ever used and doesn't really have any role, we will put aside the VI-7b5 of the melodic minor scale. If you do encounter it, it will be seen as a passing chord. The characteristic of this mode is Locrian major 2, and as we saw, it is more often borrowed as the II-7b5 to add a major or natural 9th.

For the other cases, this degree is sub-dominant which allows the following extensions:

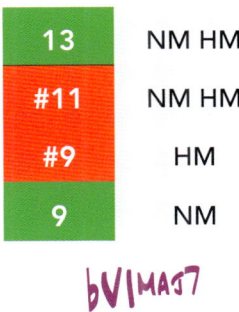

MINOR DIATONIC TONAL HARMONY

■ On the sub-dominant seventh degree

As a sub-dominant chord, this degree will allow the following extensions.

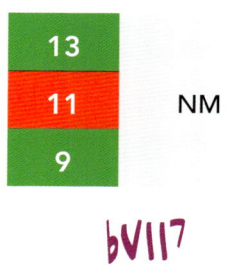

■ On the dominant seventh degree

The seventh degree of the melodic minor scale (VII-7b5) is rarely used in this classic tetrad form. We will see that it is, however, used in another configuration.

The fully diminished form from the harmonic minor scale is used quite often and all the extensions are technically allowed .

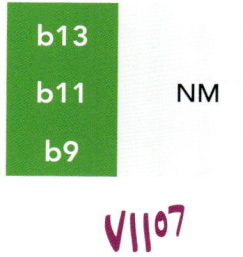

Passing chords

The question is, is the non-dominant form of the fifth degree chord (the one coming from the natural minor scale) used at all? It actually is! And this allows us introduce a concept we have not yet seen so far. The V-7 chord is used as a passing chord.

 **A passing chord, in general, is a chord without any particular harmonic function that is played to link two chords that do have a harmonic function. The main types of passing chords are:**

MINOR DIATONIC TONAL HARMONY

- **Chromatic passing chords**

| Key: C Major | III
E-7 | bIII(CHROM)
Eb-7 | II
D-7 | |

Chromatic passing chords are a great alternative to dominant chords when it comes to creating a "tension-resolve" mechanism.

- **Non-dominant diminished passing chords**

We will study these shortly

Even though the fifth degree of the natural minor scale does not belong to the main categories described above, it is still used as passing chord.

To conclude

As you noticed, the minor key is a bit more complex than the major key. In most minor tunes, the harmonic progression is based on not one but three different minor scales that all have a different harmonization and different corresponding modes and extensions. This means you should be comfortable with the three main minor scales. On the positive side, this gives a lot of options for creating interesting chord progressions and melodies. It's one of the reasons I always prefer minor keys: you can go much deeper and bring out such a variety of sounds and feeling which are simply unavailable in major harmony. Luckily, even in a major tune, you can borrow from minor modes, as we will see, to bring some of this minor richness and delicate complexity to balance out the simplicity of a major key.

It's also not uncommon, in a minor context, to borrow from other minor modes such as Dorian and Phrygian. Don't panic! It takes time to carefully study the three minor scales and get used to switching from one to the other. But as long as you understand the principle, you will make progress.

MINOR DIATONIC TONAL HARMONY

Degrees	1	2	b3	4	5	b6	b7
Triads	I–	IIdim	bIII	IV–	V–	bVI	bVII
Extensions	b7 9 11 b13	b7 b9 11 b13	7 9 11 13	b7 9 11 13	b7 b9 11 b13	7 9 #11 13	b7 9 11 13
Function	T	S-D	T	S-D	Passing	S-D	S-D

Natural minor scale

Degrees	1	2	b3	4	5	b6	7
Triads	I–	IIdim	bIII#5	IV–	V	bVI	VIIdim
Extensions	7 9 11 b13	b7 b9 11 13	7 b9 11 13	b7 9 #11 13	b7 b9 11 b13	7 #9 #11 13	bb7 b9 b11 b13
Function	T	S-D	T	S-D	D	S-D	D

Harmonic minor scale

MINOR DIATONIC TONAL HARMONY

Degrees	1	2	b3	4	5	6	7
Triads	I-	IIoIM	bIII#5	IV-	V	VIoIM	VIIoIM
Extensions	7	b7	7	b7	b7	b7	b7
	9	b9	9	9	9	9	b9
	11	11	#11	#11	11	11	b11
	13	13	13	13	b13	b13	b13
Function	T	S-D	T	S-D	D	Passing	D

Melodic minor scale

Minor cadences

Now it gets simpler, I promise, since the minor cadences are based on the same chord functions as major cadences.

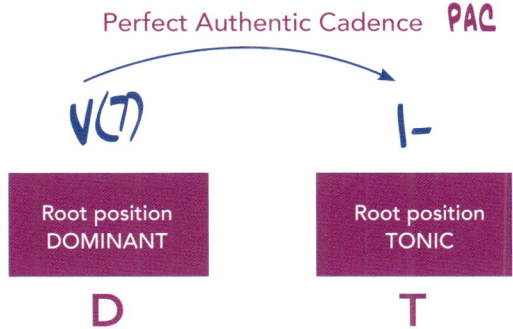

Perfect Authentic Cadence **PAC**

V(7) → I-

Root position DOMINANT — D

Root position TONIC — T

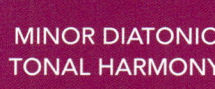

MINOR DIATONIC TONAL HARMONY

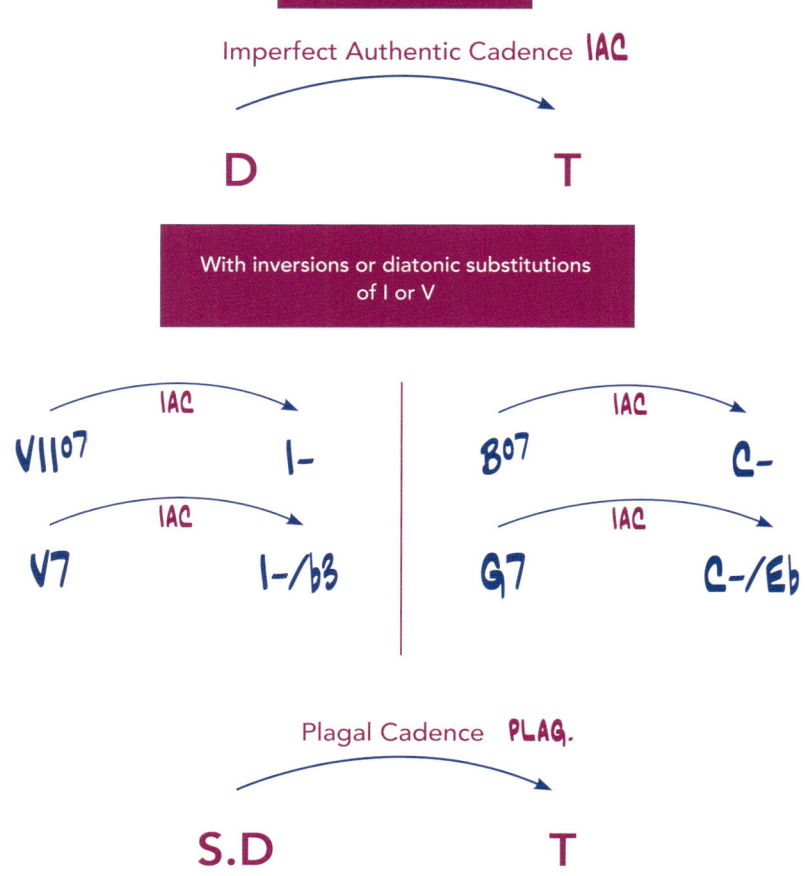

MINOR DIATONIC TONAL HARMONY

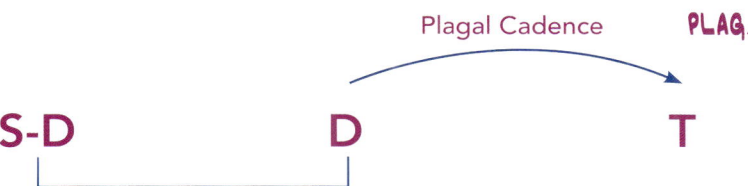

Just like for the major context, the goal is to know and be able to recognize the minor cadences in order to know when you are indeed in a minor context. This information will tell you what you can use to create melodies. You also need to know which of the three minor scales the context implies! It takes a bit of practice, but you'll get used to it.

MINOR DIATONIC TONAL HARMONY

4

The Tonal Context

CREATING MELODIES IN A TONAL CONTEXT

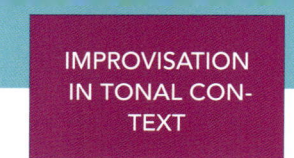

IMPROVISATION IN TONAL CONTEXT

Rhythm changes and the I-VI-II-V

Before moving forward, I would like to introduce you to one of the mot common chord progressions, especially in jazz: the I-VI-II-V. This chord progression is sometimes referred to as rhythm changes. This is due to the fact that the famous tune "I Got Rhythm" by George Gershwin is based entirely on this chord progression. But history aside, recognizing this progression in a tune allows you to determine easily the key in which you are in and therefore, makes improvisation much easier.

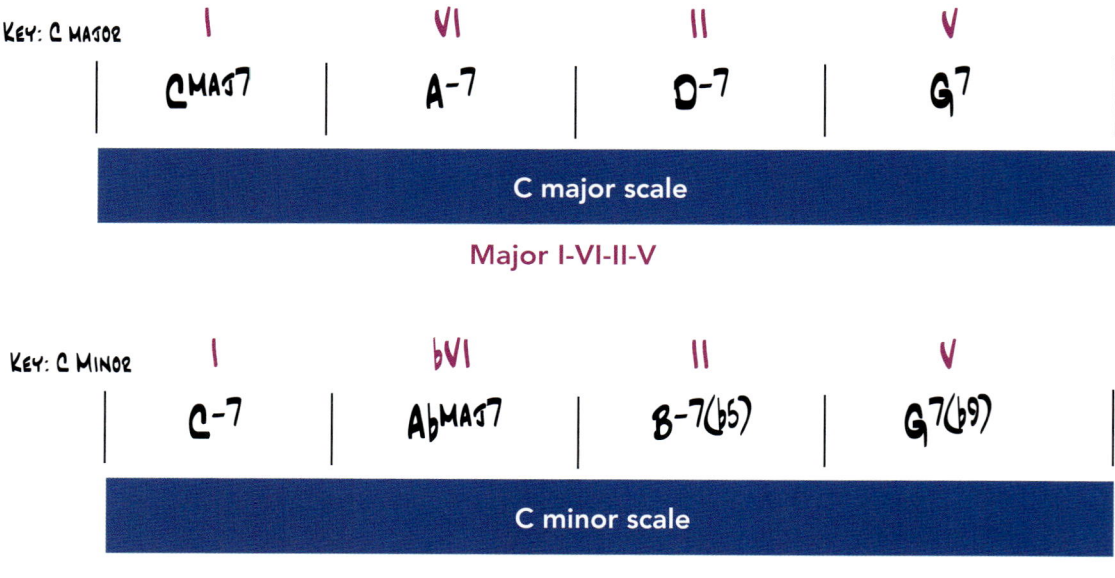

Now that we have studied the rules and mechanisms of major and minor contexts, and thereby learned how to recognize these contexts, the question is: what can you play in those contexts?

But first, let me remind you the rules of the game: There are no rules. What I will be telling you here is advice and tips that will guide you through what has been proven to work and is commonly used in certain musical contexts. But this being said, the only rule is always: "how does it sound?" What I will be teaching you HAS to be practiced since it will give you a variety of tools and options to create and improvise in common musical situations. Once you master this, feel free to explore and to break the rules.

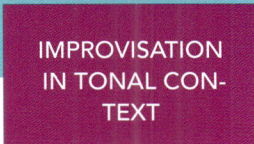

IMPROVISATION IN TONAL CONTEXT

Knowing is good, recognizing is essential

My friends, without waiting any longer, I give you: the key of improvisation. The goal is to recognize, using the analysis of chord progressions, what context you are in (major, minor, or modal, and what key). This is really 80% of the work. Once you know you are in a C minor key for example, you know what to play: the C minor scale. You must accept your duty of becoming a master at chord progression recognizing.

Let's take a concrete example and assume that you need to improvise over the following chord progression:

- The least dangerous way of improvising over this chord progression would be to play arpeggios over each chord. You simply can't go wrong with limiting yourself to the notes of the harmonic context.

- Another way we could be looking at this chord progression is by thinking of each bar as a static modal context. Because why not? For each bar you could apply the rules of improvising in a modal context. For example:

KEY: C MAJOR

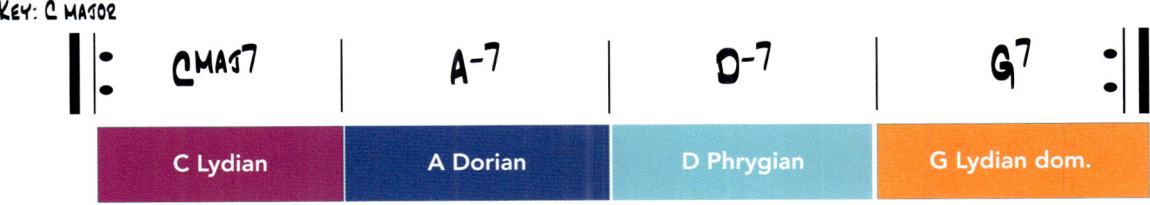

On each chord considered independently, each of the modes suggested above technically "works" if you follow the modal improv guideline we saw in the first part of this book. And you know what? If you did experiment with that, you might think it sounds good! If the tempo is slow enough for example, and there is enough time to establish a modal context on each chord, it may be very interesting (I'm actually going to go try this out right now).

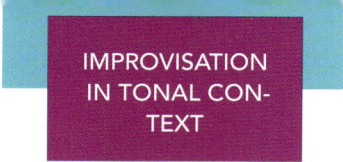

However, if you improvise like this all the time, meaning, if you see everything as a modal context, you will quickly realize that:

1. **It may sound messy, incoherent, or straight up bad.**

2. **If the tempo is too quick, it will become intellectually impossible.**

So how can we make it easier? We can simply change the way we look at the chord progression and analyze it under the light of tonal harmony. Remember that at least 90% of the music you know is mainly tonal, so it makes more sense to actually start analyzing a piece by assuming it will be tonal.

Remember that unlike modal music, tonal music tends to simplify melodic options by favoring one main scale and therefore, one main collection of notes. Variation will be added through interchanges, modulations or chromaticism, which we will study shortly.

After little practice, you will quickly be able to see that the chord progression is actually a I-VI-II-V in C major.

And if you can recognize this chord progression quickly, you're done! The key is C major during this chord progression, and the C major scale can be your main tool for creating melodies.

Now let's say you are not familiar with rhythm changes. You could still figure out what key you are in:

1. **All the chords belong to the harmonization of the same scale (C major).**

2. **This chord progression includes a perfect authentic cadence (which happens to resolves on a strong beat).**

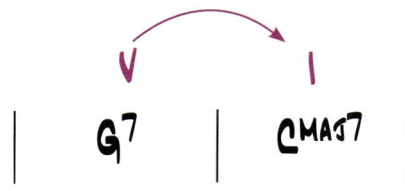

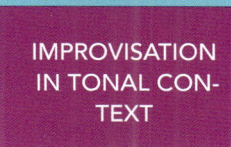

So if you analyze the chord progression you will obtain:

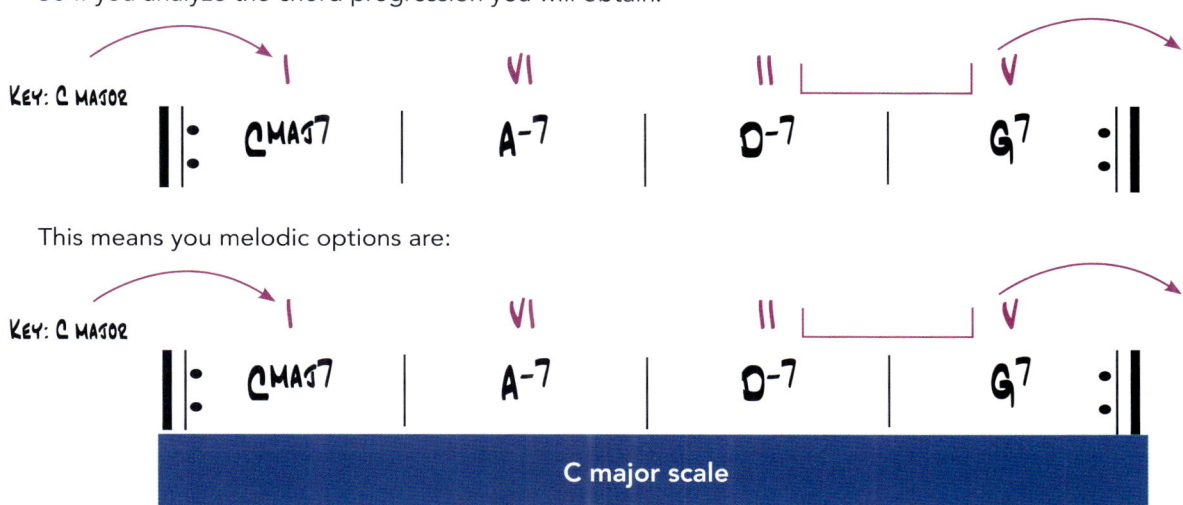

This means you melodic options are:

You just have to play the C major scale during this whole chord progression. Isn't it amazing? Four chords! One scale! This is just too easy...

Wait is that really all there is? Well... Nope. Of course not. Because even if you can technically play C major the whole time, the choice of notes, the way you play them, when, and in what order—all these parameters and many others are REALLY what are going to make the melody you create sound good. This comes from practice, ear training, and trial and error. BUT at least your options in terms of improvisation are now narrowed down, and you have a guide to follow. And this is what this book is all about: teaching you options.

■ Notes to "avoid"

Each note of the melody you play over a certain chord progression will necessarily become, in the general perspective, a note of the chord you are playing over. Depending on what note you play, it can be a structural note (chord tone) or an extension (non-chord tone). And as we just saw, certain extensions in the tonal context should be avoided, or at least, used with caution. The same caution should be applied with these notes when used to create melodies.

Therefore, let's add these notes to our improvisation guide:

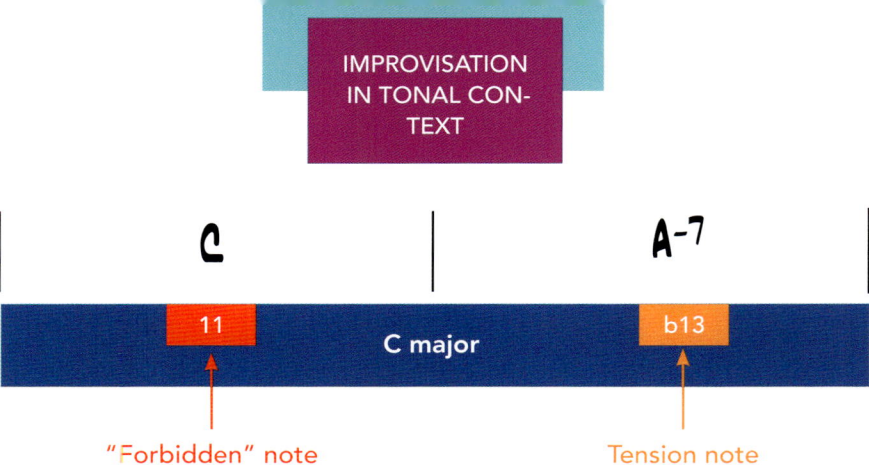

■ Scale thought versus mode heard

If you have a good understanding and knowledge of modes (which were described in the previous book), you should remember that when I play the collection of notes of a particular scale, **if the bass plays a note different from the tonic of the scale, I will not "technically" be playing this scale anymore. Instead, I will really be playing a particular mode of this scale (or a totally different scale).**

Wait whut?! This simply means that even though you are thinking in terms of key and using one simple scale, each time the bass changes away from the tonic, you will hear a different mode. To put it differently, if I was to isolate a bar in which the bass does not play the tonic, you will hear a mode rather than the scale of origin. Now you may think we are going a little bit too far here. Indeed, we just said that the tonal system emphasized the KEY, without any modal thinking or interpreting. And even though this is true, we will see that making this difference can be very useful. What difference? Well… the difference between scale PLAYED (the way you think) and the mode HEARD (what is actually heard by the listener).

For the rest of this book, I will indicate:

The scale or mode that should be thought when improvising, on the bottom of the chords.

The scale or mode that will be technically "heard," regardless of what thought process is going on in your brain while you are creating a melody.

Now, please understand that the mode or scale thought is not a rule or an absolute. Every improviser has a different thinking process! So I will give you what is to me the easiest or most efficient way of "thinking" while improvising.

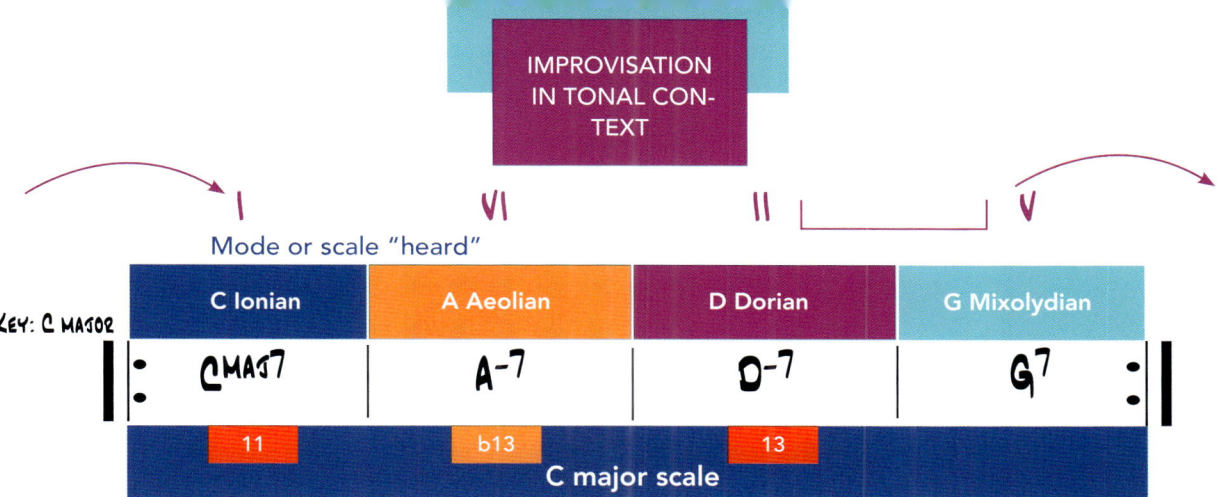

About arpeggios

We already talked about this, but allow me to insist on the fact that the most obvious and consonant notes that you can play over a chord progression will always be the arpeggios of these chords. They are incredibly efficient and can be used:

- **By playing them in a very obvious, straight forward way.**

- **By using the scale but emphasizing the notes of each chord and thereby articulating the melody around them.**

Arpeggios ALWAYS work. If you are lost, you can't go wrong with them, whether it's a modal or a tonal context. Don't hesitate to use them or fall back to them. But this doesn't mean you shouldn't know how to NOT use them.

Ornaments and melodic approaches

Once the harmonic context has been defined, it is quite common to punctually break the "rules" of melodic creation. When done in the right way, it can actually make your melodies much more interesting. There is a handful of those accepted "exceptions" that are very often used:

■ Anticipation

An anticipation corresponds to the fact of playing a tensed or "forbidden" note on a chord, knowing that this note will be consonant or accepted on the following chord.

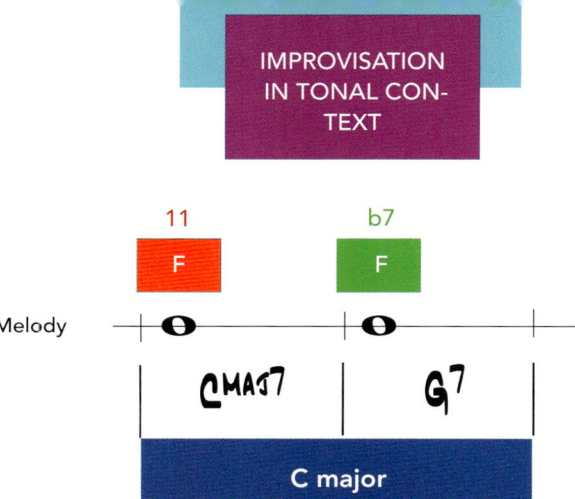

Appoggiatura

An Appoggiatura is a tensed or "forbidden" note played on the first part of a chord but resolved before the chord changes.

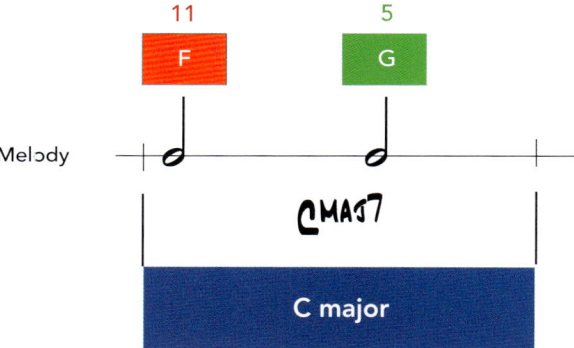

Cambiata

There are several meanings and interpretations of what a Cambiata is. In French, it translates to embroidery or "embellishment," which I think makes more sense. A Cambiata is a series of non chord tones (more dissonant) surrounding an actual chord tone. The tension in those more dissonant notes amplifies the sense or consonance of the structural note, which emphasizes it.

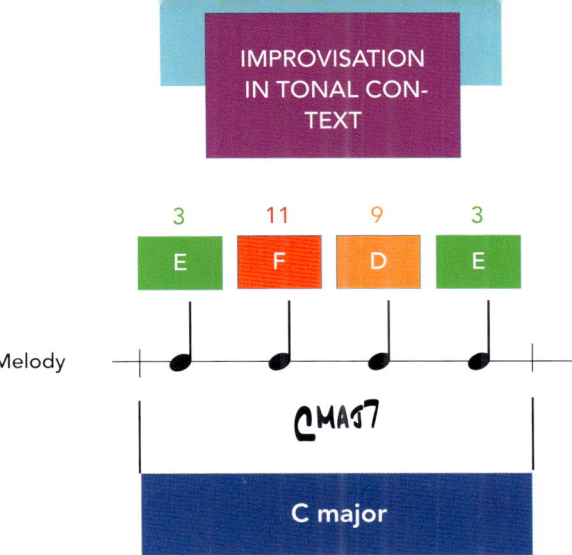

Passing note

A passing note is a dissonant note played between two consonant notes of a diatonically ascending or descending melody.

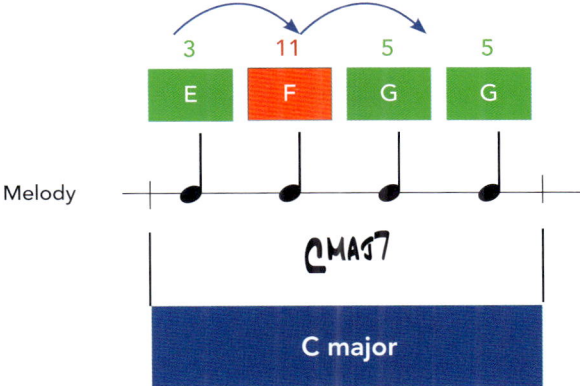

Retardation

This is the "opposite" of an anticipation in a way. A retardation is a consonant chord tone that prolongs onto the following chord as a tension (non-chord tone) of this new chord. It then resolves to a consonant chord tone of the new chord.

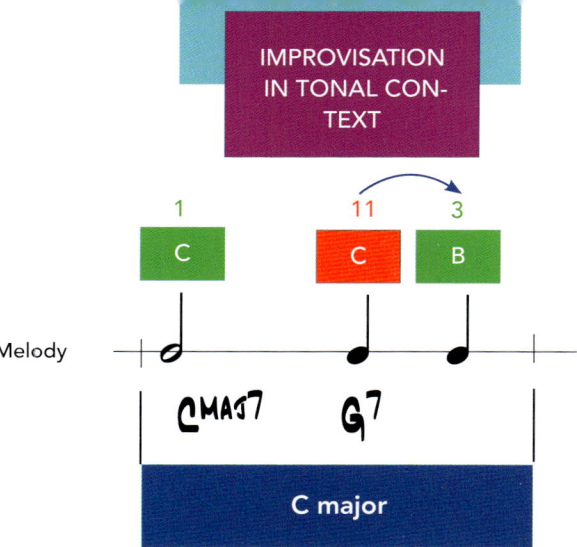

Playing "out"

Playing out refers to voluntarily playing away from what theory and analysis would recommend in order to purposely create tension and dissonance. You may think:

"Oh that I can do for sure! All this time I was just playing 'out,' cool…"

Sorry but this doesn't work! Playing out is more of an effect than it is a guide to improvising… Moreover, playing out can only be efficient when it is nicely balanced with some good old "in" playing. Too bad…

Trust me, anyone can easily tell the difference between an experienced player playing out and some simple nonsense.

> **And this is pretty much how creating melodies works in tonal situations. The most important step is to be able to recognize the context you are in by using all the tools we just discovered. This will give you a list of options that you can use. Most of the time, in a tonal context, the options will be limited to one scale with some borrowings (in the case of a minor context). You can then also use arpeggios, some melodic ornaments, and your melodies should sound decent. But remember! Understanding is actually the easy step. The quality of your compositions and improvisations will only grow with practice and trial and error. And this simply takes time.**

Now it is time to focus on all the different ways in which chord progressions can take us AWAY from the original key. We have actually already seen such a mechanism in the case of minor tonal harmony! Remember that on the fifth degree dominant, the scale temporarily changes.

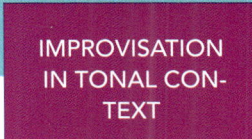

IMPROVISATION IN TONAL CONTEXT

This is often referred to as a modal borrowing, since you will temporarily "borrow" a chord from the harmonization of another scale, to create to desired sound. Modal borrowings are also often referred to as modal interchanges or modal mixture. I am sure you can understand the reasoning behind these names.

This is one of many ways that exist to wander away from the center key. Let's explore them!

MINOR DIATONIC TONAL HARMONY

4

The Tonal Context

MODAL INTERCHANGES AND MODAL SECTIONS

MODAL INTERCHANGES AND MODAL SECTIONS

Modal interchange vs modulation

In a given key, a modal borrowing means that one or several of the chords in this progression don't belong to the harmonization of the main key scale (major or natural minor). Instead, these chords belong to the harmonization of a para lel mode. The borrowing results in a temporary change of the harmonic context. It must be short enough not to be considered a modulation. Modal borrowings are also referred to as modal interchanges.

A modulation corresponds to a lasting change of the original key towards another key.

A modal section is in some ways, a "modulation" towards a modal context. If the modal section is too short, it will simply be considered a modal borrowing, so the change has to last for a consequent amount of time. Most of the time, modal sections can be recognized with a particular modal cadence, or a static chord with some characteristic extensions.

Although there are differences in the ways you can go away from a key, they can be all referred to as "modulations," in a broader meaning. There are several ways in which you can modulate, and I will give you the main categories.

Tritone substitutions

The tritone substitution, even though it may sound difficult, is actually a very simple mechanism. Remember the tonal tritone between the 3rd and the minor 7th of a dominant chord? Let's use an example:

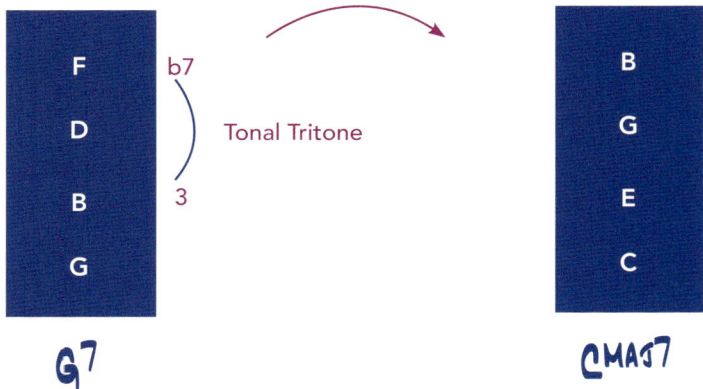

MODAL INTER-CHANGES AND MODAL SECTIONS

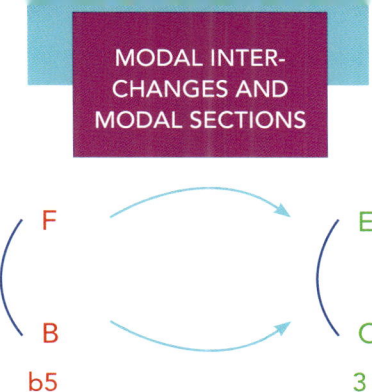

One of the particularities of a tritone is that it is exactly half of an octave. Indeed, a tritone (whether it is seen as an augmented 4th or a diminished 5th) is made of three steps, and an octave is made of 6 steps.

This means that the inversion of a tritone is also a tritone. This means that for each dominant chord, there MUST be another dominant chord that shares the SAME tritone, but inverted! Let's try to find it!

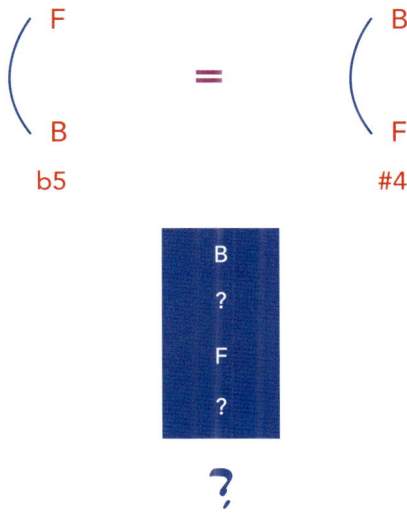

The mystery chord

So we need a dominant chord (meaning an X7 type chord). It should have a major 3rd and a perfect 5th, so we should have something like:

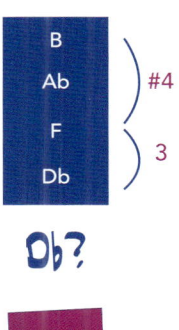

Db?

MODAL INTERCHANGES AND MODAL SECTIONS

Unfortunately, this chord does not have a minor 7th. Oh well. Nice try, I guess. Let's move on. Wait! Actually, we may still have a chance. Let's look at the notes of a Db7.

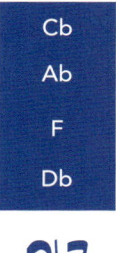

Boom!!! That's easy, B = Cb. Again, an enharmonic comes to save us. This means we found a chord that has the same tonal tritone and will therefore give some of the same sense of tension and resolution BUT that doesn't belong to the key of origin.

The question is, what scale DOES it belong to?

Technically, this chord can belong to several scales. But traditionally, when you look for the scale or mode a borrowing is from, you should always use the CLOSEST POSSIBLE SCALE in terms of common notes.

Instinctively, you could say this Db7 is the fifth degree dominant chord in Gb major.

But there is actually a scale that offers fewer differences while still having a Db7. This scale is the Ab melodic minor scale. The fourth degree of this scale is indeed a Db7 and the corresponding more is Db Lydian dominant.

Db	Eb	F	G	Ab	Bb	Cb	Db
1	2	3	#4	5	6	7	1

Now if you look at the interval between the root of the original dominant chord (G7) and the tritone substitution, you will find that it is... a tritone! In other words, the tritone substitution chord is found a tritone above the root of the 5th degree dominant chord:

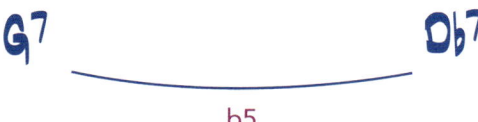

MODAL INTERCHANGES AND MODAL SECTIONS

Since this interval is symmetrical, the tritone substitution of Db7 would be:

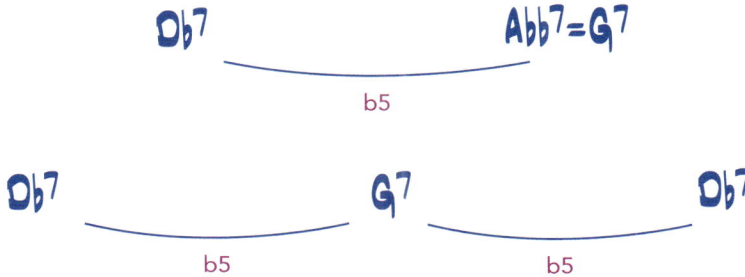

"Chromatic" resolution

If you look at the way the bass moves from a dominant chord to the tonic chord (in the case of a perfect cadence), it either goes up a 4th or down a 5th. When the dominant chord is substituted however, the bass moves down a minor 2nd and is therefore said to resolve chromatically. The sense of tension and release is thereby even stronger since it adds another melodic tension! The Db can be seen as another leading tone that is a half step above the tonic rather than below.

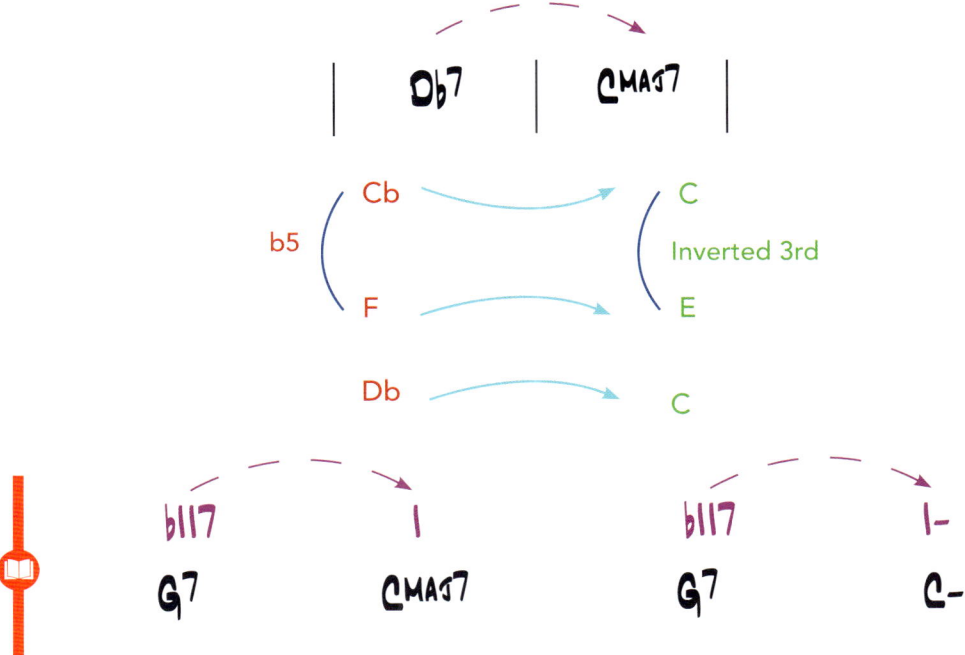

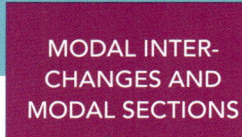

MODAL INTERCHANGES AND MODAL SECTIONS

Every dominant 7th chord has a tritone substitution. The substitute is also a dominant 7th chord of which the root is found a tritone above (diminished 5th) or below (augmented 4th) the root of the original dominant 7th chord. The tritone substitution of a tritone substitution is simply the original dominant 7th chord.

The root of the substitute can also be found a minor 2nd above the root of the first degree tonal chord the original dominant chord resolves onto.

The tritone substitution chord is interpreted as first degree of the Lydian dominant mode (which is the 4th degree of the melodic minor scale). Therefore, it can carry the following extensions:

$$Db7(9, \sharp11, 13)$$

This means that the tritone substitution implies a borrowing from the Lydian dominant mode.

KEY: C MAJOR

| D-7 | Db7 | CMAJ7 | CMAJ7 |

| 13 C major scale | Db Lydian dom. | 11 C major scale |

This symbol, which represents the movement of a sub-dominant chord towards a dominant chord, is in a dotted line because of the chromatic movement of the base.

Secondary dominant chords

Secondary dominant chords are used to add some tension/release mechanisms to preexisting chord progressions. Again, it sounds more complicated than it is, so let's dive into it.

The principle is based on the fact that all the chords that are based on a major or minor triad can be seen as first degree tonic chords in at least ONE key. This means that for any chord based on a major or minor triad, there is a fifth degree dominant chord that resolves onto it in a certain key. For example:

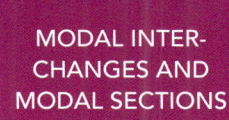

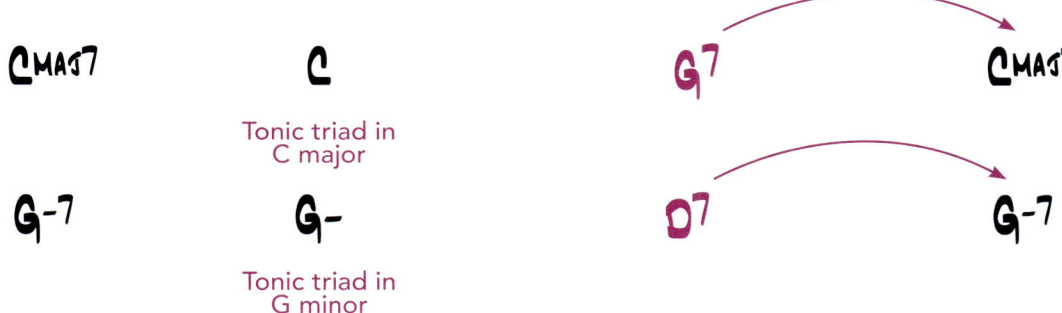

Moreover, dominant 7th chords (of the X7 type) themselves are based on major triads and can therefore be seen as tonic chords. Again, in a tonal resolution, what's most important is the resolution of the tonal tritone on either a major or minor 3rd interval. The other extensions of the chord are not that important. We will see that in blues for example, dominant 7th tetrads are used as tonic chords!

However, resolving a dominant 7th type chord on another dominant 7th chord will always leave the listener with a feeling of incompletion and unresolved suspension. Naturally, because of our natural inclination for tonal resolution, hearing a C7 chord will have us expect the following resolution:

Replacing this major triad or major 7th chord with a dominant chord will just create a new instability which will now be expected to resolve as follows:

MODAL INTERCHANGES AND MODAL SECTIONS

When such a sequence of dominant chords is resolved, the sense of relief is even greater.

 **So, in a given key (major or minor), a secondary dominant chord is a dominant 7th chord which does not belong to the harmonization of the original key and which is added to the chord progression in order to resolve on a scale degree chord other than the tonic chord (I).**

■ Harmonic sequences (inception of dominant chords)

A harmonic sequence, generally speaking, is a succession of chords of the same type whose root notes moves up (ascending) or down (descending) a consistent interval, from one chord to the other.

The descending 5th (or ascending 4th) harmonic sequences of dominant chords are extremely popular because they create a constant feeling of "false resolution." It's simply the extrapolation of what we saw above, taken to the extreme. Each dominant wants to resolve on a stable chord which is replaced by its dominant form, and on and on.

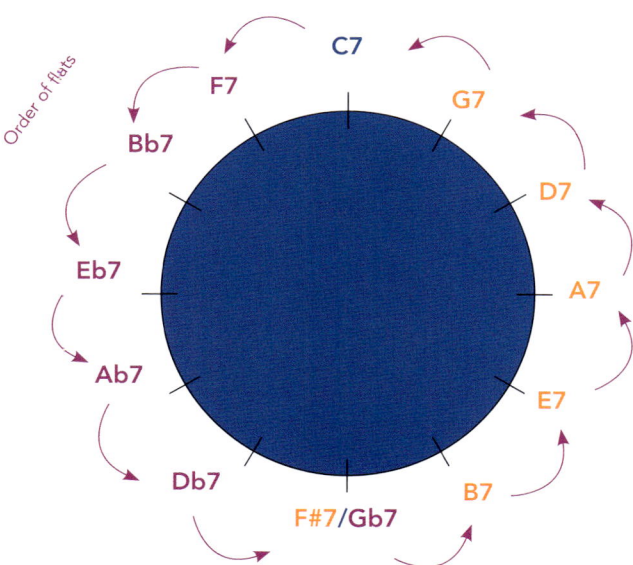

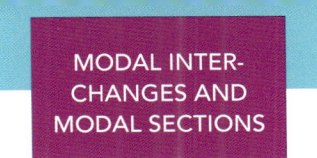

MODAL INTER-CHANGES AND MODAL SECTIONS

Again, in order for a chord to have a secondary dominant, there has to be at least one key in which this chord can be seen as the first degree tonic chord (and therefore, in this key, it will necessarily have a fifth degree dominant chord). This means that some chords do not have any secondary dominant chords:

VII-7b5   II-7b5   VIIo7

Why? Because there is simply no key in which these scales can be seen as stable, first degree, tonic chords.

Q: What about chords based on augmented triads?

Well, even though they feel "unstable," remember that they are considered to be tonic chords in the harmonic and melodic minor scales. So yes, they do have a secondary dominant, it works.

G7 → CMAJ7(#5)

> Just remember: any dominant 7th chord which is added to resolve on a chord that is NOT the I(maj) or I(min) of a tune is a secondary dominant chord. Moreover, secondary dominant chords can themselves resolve on other secondary dominant chords.

Now it's time to find out how secondary dominants are notated in music analysis. Let's start as an example to make sense of the general notation.

Let's say that I am in the key of C major and that I am dealing with the following chord progression:

KEY: C MAJOR | CMAJ7 | A7 | D-7 | G7 |

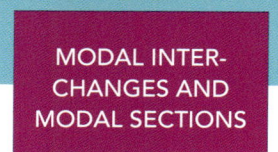

As a good little new analyst, you should recognize that all these chords belong to the harmonization of C major except for one.

A7 does not belong to the harmonization of C major (A-7 does, however). So how can we make sense of this chord? Well, it turns out that A7 is the fifth degree dominant chord in the key of D minor, where it resolves on a D-7. Conclusion: A7 is a secondary dominant of our second degree chord and it will be written:

You would say that A7 is the "five of the two chord."

In general, if X is the degree of a chord in a given key, then the secondary dominant of this chord will be written:

"Five of the X chord"

Now what about the secondary dominant chords of secondary dominants? Which remember are called harmonic sequences. How will we notate this?

Let's use our previous example and imagine, while still being in C major, that we found the following chord progression:

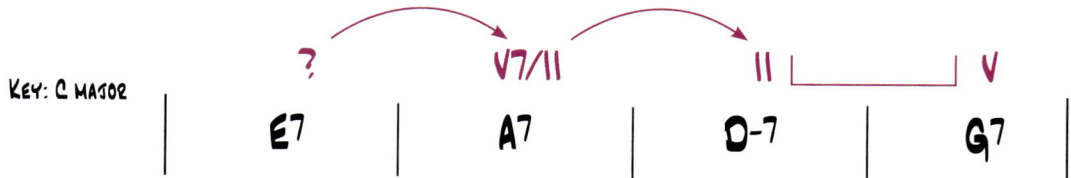

MODAL INTERCHANGES AND MODAL SECTIONS

Here, E7 is a secondary dominant of A7. So what should we write?

V7/V7/II ?

Well, you can see how this notation would easily become quite confusing, especially if we have a long harmonic sequence. V7/V7/V7/V7/… is not a very efficient notation. So instead we will ignore the fact that A7 does not belong to the scale and still consider the E7 resolves on the sixth degree (VI) of C major. Now I get it, this is quite confusing since the sixth degree should be a VI-7 chord! But harmonically, it makes more sense this way, since E7 is technically "supposed" to lead to the VI degree. Now the fact that "surprise!" it turns out to be a dominant chord, is not as important. So you will write:

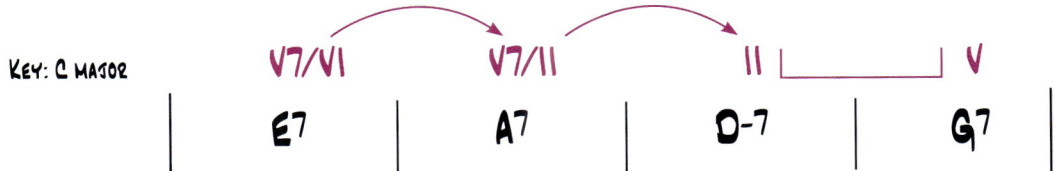

So when naming secondary dominants, you need to work your way backwards, from right to left, starting from a chord that actually belongs to the harmonization of the original key. Remember that any sequence of secondary dominant chords will eventually (most of the time) resolve onto a "normal" chord. As you work your way backwards, you will eventually find a chord that belongs to the harmonization of the original scale, the chord that precedes the harmonic sequence, and then you are out of trouble.

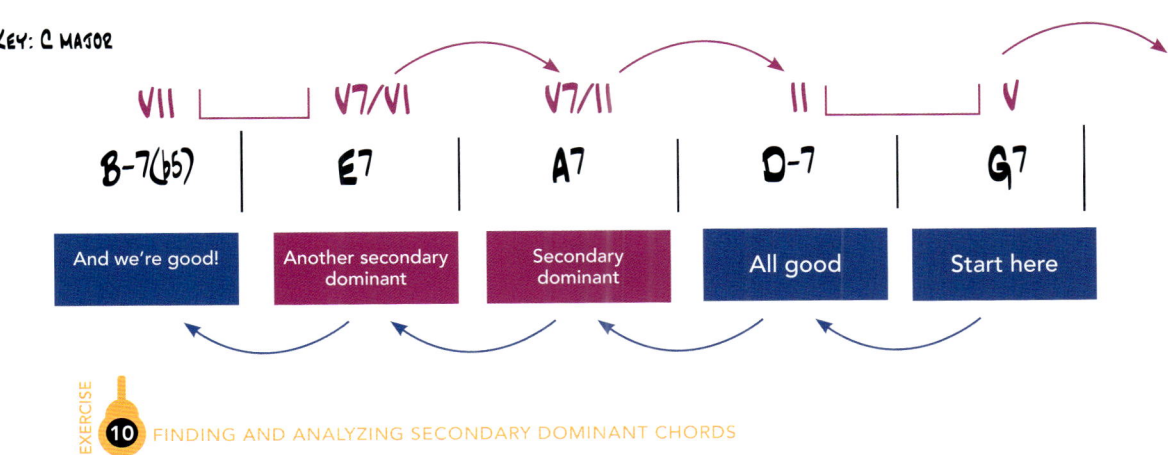

EXERCISE 10 FINDING AND ANALYZING SECONDARY DOMINANT CHORDS

Analyze the given chord progressions and find the secondary dominant chords.

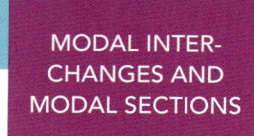

MODAL INTER-CHANGES AND MODAL SECTIONS

■ Borrowing from neighbor keys

In any given key, the use of a secondary dominant induces a modal borrowing from one of the neighbor keys. Let's explain this:

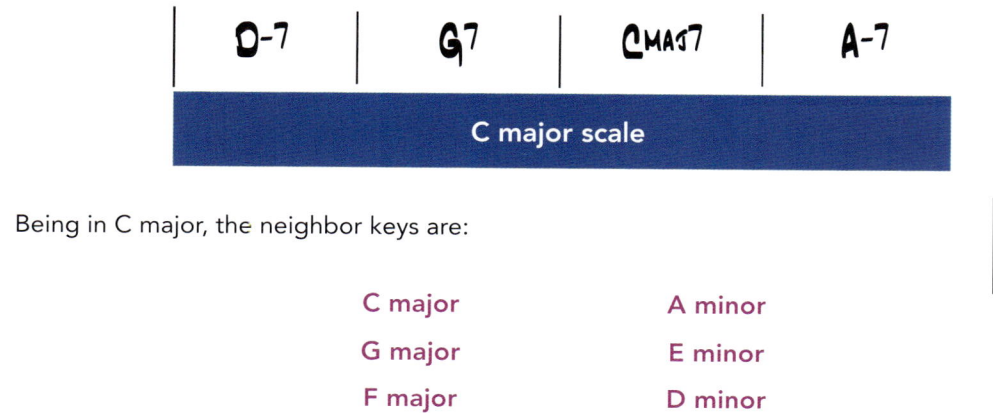

Being in C major, the neighbor keys are:

              C major   A minor
              G major   E minor
              F major   D minor

Imagine that we wanted to approach the first chord, D-7, with a secondary dominant chord. Again, this chord is a first degree tonic chord in the key of D minor and therefore can be preceded by the fifth degree dominant chord of this key:

This is a V to I cadence in the key of D minor. As seen in the chapter on the minor tonal context, this implies a modal borrowing from the D harmonic minor scale (or A Phrygian dominant mode to be exact), or potentially the D melodic minor scale.

This is why some people prefer to consider the minor neighbor scales in their non-natural minor form (harmonic or melodic). I see no problem with that, and to some extent it actually makes more sense.

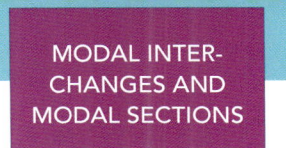

MODAL INTERCHANGES AND MODAL SECTIONS

So our improvisation guide would be:

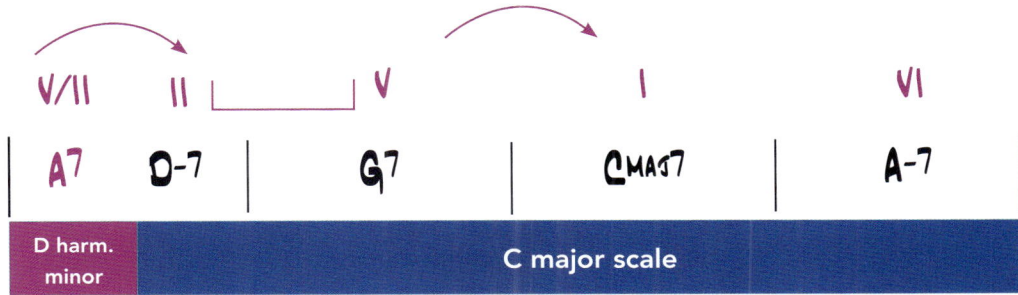

Now let's assume that we want to use a secondary dominant on the G7:

Even if the cadence does not resolve completely on G7, for the duration of the D7 chord, the progression should be interpreted as follows:

This is a V to I cadence in the key of G major, which is, of course, a neighbor key of C major. On the D7, this will imply a modal borrowing from D mixolydian.

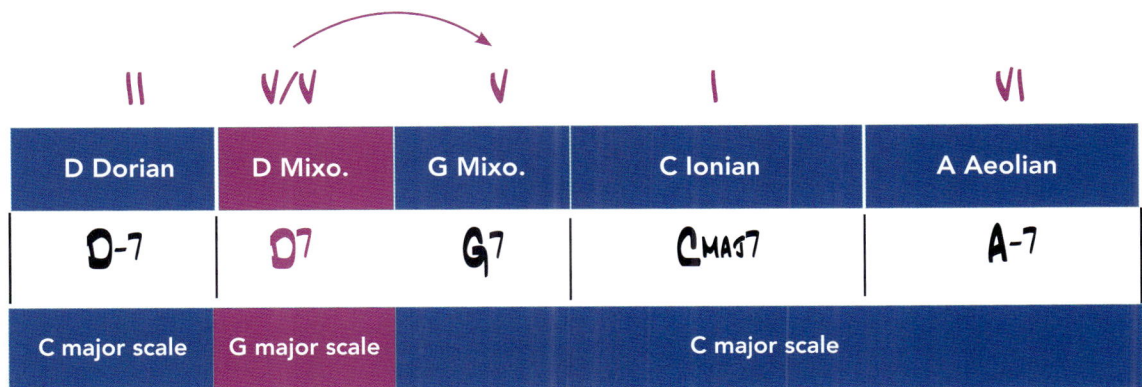

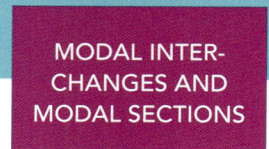

MODAL INTER-CHANGES AND MODAL SECTIONS

Now let's approach the A-7 with a secondary dominant chord:

This cadence takes us to the key of A minor (harmonic minor and melodic minor over the E7 and natural minor over the A-7). And again, A minor is a neighbor key of C major.

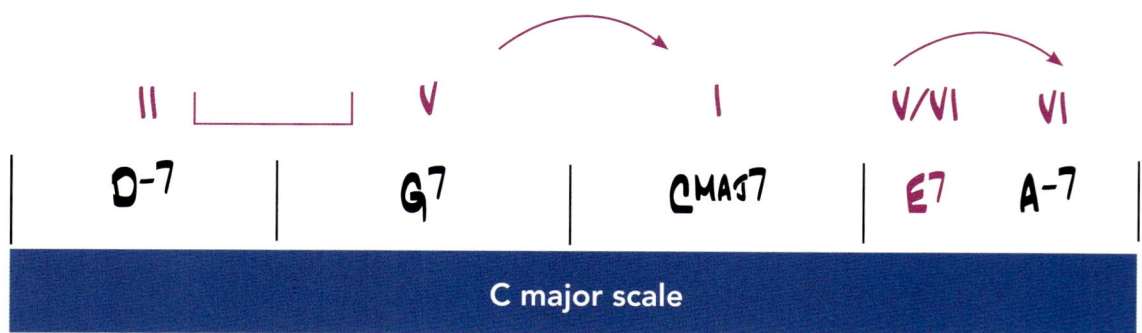

By now you may have realized that in any given key, a secondary dominant applied to any chord that belongs to the harmonization of this key will induce a modal borrowing from one of the five neighbor keys. Obviously, this does not apply to the VIIb5 degree, which does not have a secondary dominant. This phenomenon translates to the relative minor scale.

Degrees	1	2	3	4	5	6	7
In C major	C	D-	E-	F	G	A-	Bø
Secondary dominant	V7/I = V7	V7/II	V7/III	V7/IV	V7/V	V7/VI	
In C major	G7	A7	B7	C7	D7	E7	
Modal borrowing from		D harmonic minor	E harmonic minor	F major	G major	A harmonic minor	

204

MODAL INTERCHANGES AND MODAL SECTIONS

Degrees	1	2	b3	4	5	b6	b7
In A minor	A-	Bdim	C	D-	E-	F	G
Secondary dominant	V7/I = V7		V7/bIII	V7/IV	V7/V	V7/bVI	V7/bVII
In C major	E7		G7	A7	B7	C7	D7
Modal borrowing from	A harmonic minor		C major	D harmonic minor	E harmonic minor	F major	G major

EXERCISE 11 — DETERMINE THE IMPROVISATION GUIDE OF PROGRESSIONS INCLUDING SECONDARY DOMINANTS

Write the improvisation options underneath the given chord progressions.

Substitution of secondary dominant chords

Now this is when things can get a little messy. Each of the secondary dominant chords can also be substituted, either diatonically or using tritone substitutions.

Remember that tritone substitutions replace an ascending 4th or descending 5th movement of the roots of each chord with a descending chromatic movement.

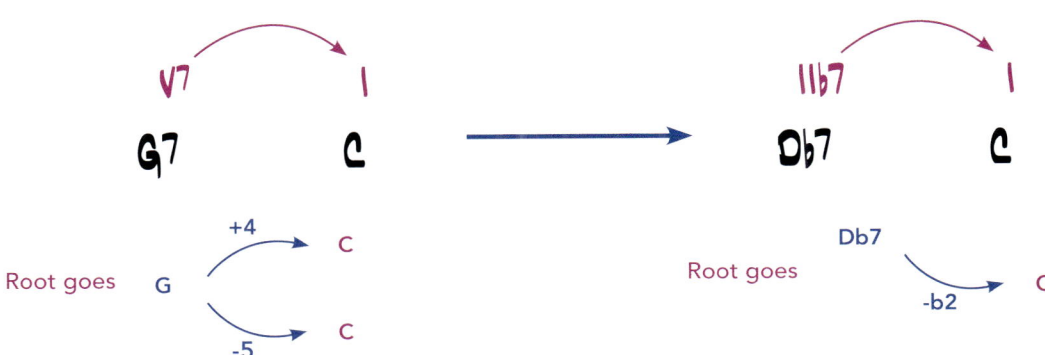

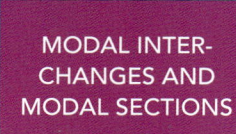

MODAL INTER-CHANGES AND MODAL SECTIONS

Applying these substitutions to a harmonic sequence of dominant chords will therefore transform a progression in 5ths (or 4ths) into a chromatic sequence of dominant chords.

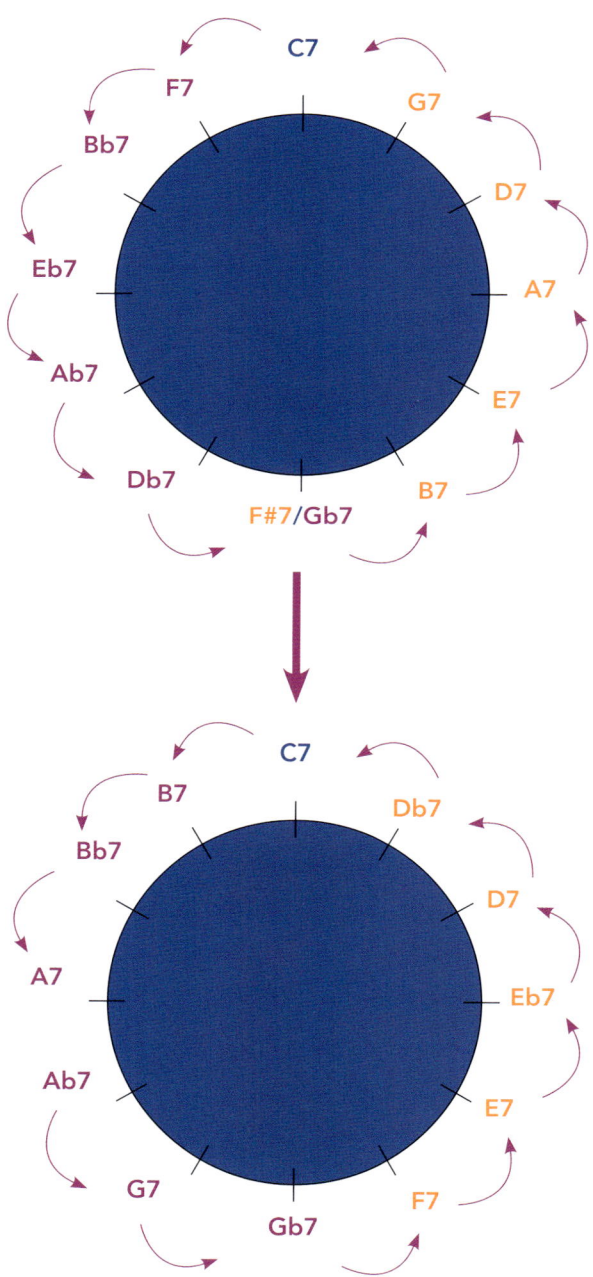

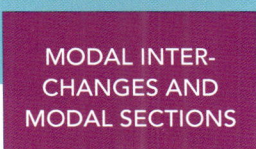
MODAL INTER-CHANGES AND MODAL SECTIONS

The substitution of a secondary dominant chord will be notated the following way:

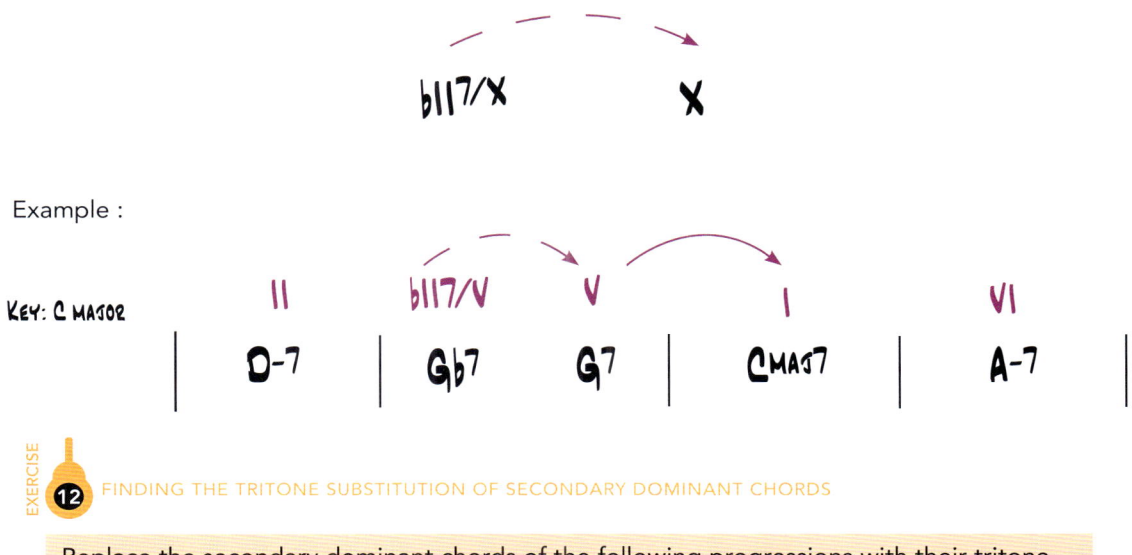

Example :

EXERCISE 12 — FINDING THE TRITONE SUBSTITUTION OF SECONDARY DOMINANT CHORDS

Replace the secondary dominant chords of the following progressions with their tritone substitution.

Secondary Cadences

Any dominant chord (participating in a V to I type progression), whether it is a secondary dominant or not, can be preceded by a sub-dominant chord, thereby creating the following type of progression:

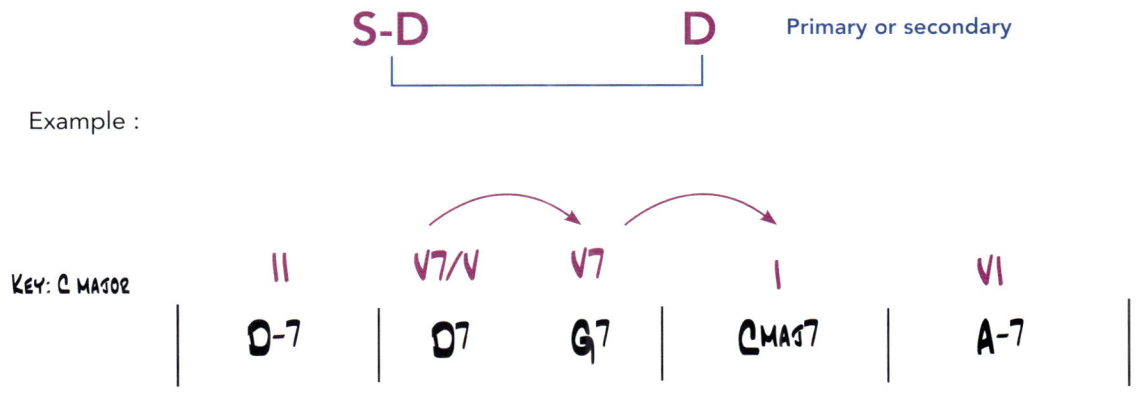

Example :

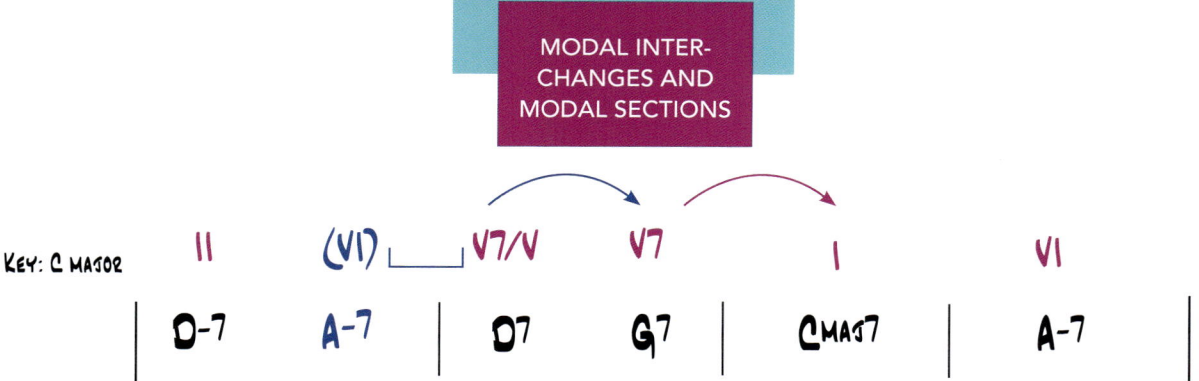

In this example, the secondary dominant turns out to belong to the harmonization of the key of origin. Therefore you can indicate the degree of this chord in relation to the key of origin as a reminder, in parenthesis, if you wish. BUT it is not at all necessary, because you need to understand that in this case, A-7 plays the role of a "II chord" in the key of G major, in order to create a complete cadence resolving on G. That this chord happens to be in the original key is really irrelevant. There are many cases in which the secondary sub-dominant chord will not belong to the key of origin, an in this case, you do not have to make sense of it.

Example:

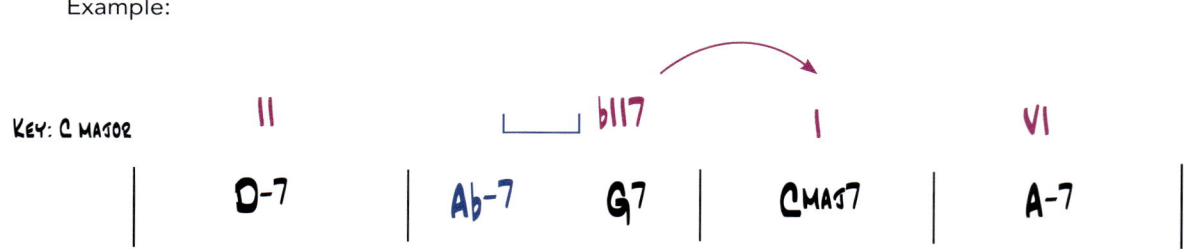

In this case, G7 is substituted with its tritone substitution Db7, which is then proceeded by Ab-7, the II-7 secondary dominant in the key of Gb major. However, Ab-7 does not belong to C major in any way, so it is customary to indicate the bracket but leave the function of the chord blank.

 **When a chord is proceeded by a secondary dominant, which in turn is proceeded by a secondary sub-dominant chord, the resulting cadence is called a secondary complete cadence. And any chord that can be seen as a tonic key can take part in a secondary complete cadence.**

MODAL INTERCHANGES AND MODAL SECTIONS

Secondary Cadences

Now when you combine all those possibilities with all the possible substitutions, you realize that it gives you a LOT of options to expand a very simple chord progression. Those tricks can be used to analyze music, but also, conversely, to enrich preexisting chord progressions. And this is used all the time in composition and especially arranging and rearranging. Remember that rearranging implies taking a preexisting composition and modifying it, either rhythmically, melodically, or harmonically (or all of the above). Well, when it comes to harmonic rearranging, secondary progressions and substitutions offer a lot of options.

Let's take an example. I am writing a tune and come up with the following chord progression.

But I just feel like the harmonic progression is too slow and too simple, namely: I want to add more chords while keeping the essence of the progression intact.

It's a very simple progression in C major. Let's say I want to make this more jazzy by spicing up the chord. I could start by simply adding some jazzy extensions to those chords:

Okay, that's a little bit better. But the IV (Fmaj7) as a sub-dominant is not very jazzy. Let's use a diatonic substitution and replace it with another sub-dominant chord: the II-7.

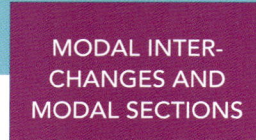

Now that's jazzy! But not quite enough. I want more chords per bar to have a faster harmonic rhythm!

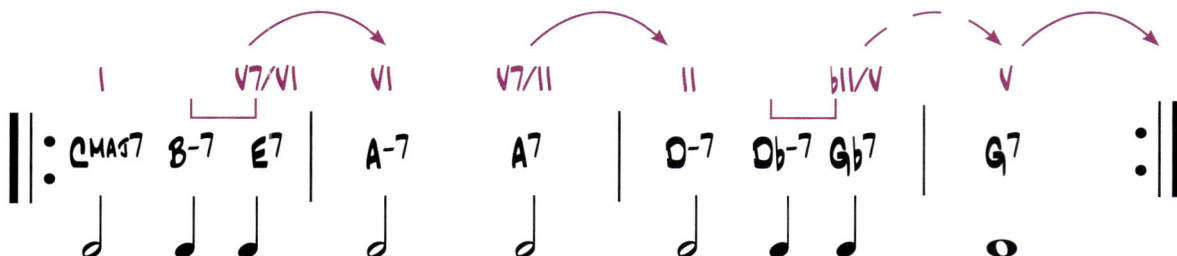

Now we're talking! From four chords to nine, this is pretty good. And you could keep going… But again, more chords is not necessarily better. It depends on the result you are looking for. The good news is, you can also go the other way around. That means that if I had been given this complicated jazzy nine-chord progression, by analyzing it properly, I can eliminate all the secondary progressions to strip it down to its simplest form. This is quite amazing. I sometimes call it "dearranging."

Substitutions and diminished chords

Sorry, but we are not quite done with substitutions. Remember that in minor tonal harmony, the VII-dim7 chord is a dominant chord that can be used to resolve on the first degree tonic chord.

Therefore, in a minor context, you can always use a diatonic substitution and replace the fifth degree dominant chord with the seventh degree diminished chord.

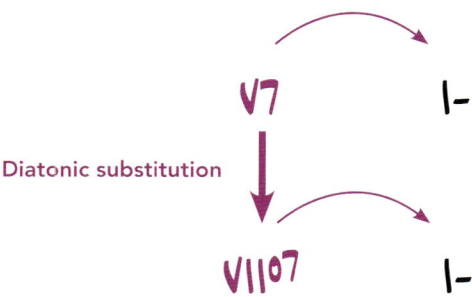

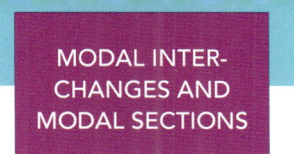

This, hopefully, doesn't come as much of a surprise. But it doesn't stop there:

You can also, in a major context, borrow this chord from the minor context to resolve on the first degree major chord! This type of cadence will be called a "minor/major" cadence, and we will see there are other cadences of this type.

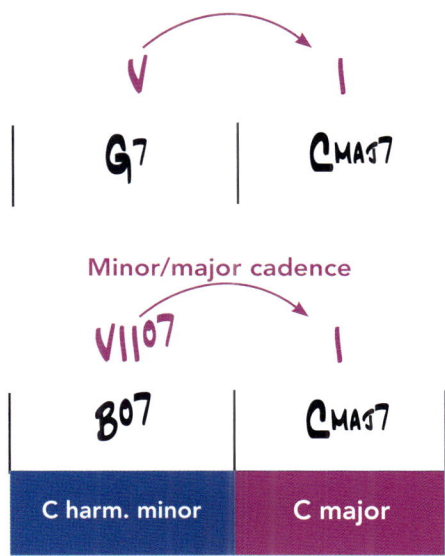

And this type of substitution can also apply to secondary dominant chords.

Extensions on dominant chords

As I already pointed out, the role of dominant chords is to build tension which is then released on the tonic chord. The more tension is created, the greater the satisfaction when it resolves. This means that you can pretty much add any extension you want to a dominant chord, even the most dissonant ones, since the point of the dominant chord is to create tonal tension. And even though some extensions are mostly used in jazz, the use of particularly tensed extensions can be traced back to classical music. For example, the Neapolitan chord, analyzed with the tools of modern music, is equivalent to a V7(b9,b5). My point is: any extension or combination of extensions on a dominant chord is technically acceptable as long as it creates the desired sound and tension.

MODAL INTERCHANGES AND MODAL SECTIONS

The main questions are:

- What are the extensions that work best depending on the context?

- Depending on the extensions I chose (or the ones indicated in the music) what scales/modes can I use over the resulting chord?

$$X7 \begin{pmatrix} \flat 9 \\ 9 \\ \sharp 9 \\ 11 \\ \sharp 11 \\ \flat 13 \\ 13 \end{pmatrix}$$

Well, it turns out that anytime a dominant chord is played, and especially when it is extended, you should analyze it as a temporary static modal context. Why? Simply because adding extensions that don't belong to the original key scales implies a temporary modal interchange. And this takes us back to the beginning of this book.

You simply have to look at what notes are given by the harmonic context and deduce what scales and modes are most compatible accordingly. This means that the more extensions are given by the harmonic context, the more your melodic possibilities will be reduced, and conversely, if no extensions are imposed, you will have many available options.

Let's look at all those possibilities. We will see that some modes are quite obvious while others, not so much.

Technically, since a dominant 7th chord is made of a root, a major 3rd, a perfect 5th, and a minor 7th, the modes used over such a chord should include these intervals in their definition. This is equivalent to saying that the first degree tetrad that comes from the harmonization of these modes should be a dominant 7th chord. And although most of the modes used to improvise over extended dominant 7th chords will indeed follow this principle, we will see that some modes don't. This means they are not technically compatible, but become compatible with a little tweaking and some enharmonic tricks. So let's start with the modes that naturally generate a dominant 7th chord when looking at their first degree harmonization. Then, we will look into some less obvious possibilities.

MODAL INTERCHANGES AND MODAL SECTIONS

■ Modes naturally including a dominant 7th

The Mixolydian Mode

The Mixolydian mode, fifth mode of the major scale, is the most obvious solution when in comes to improvising over a X7 type chord, especially in a major context. In a given major key, this mode will be naturally heard. Even if you stick to the major scale (scale thought), each time the dominant chord is played, the heard mode will be Mixolydian.

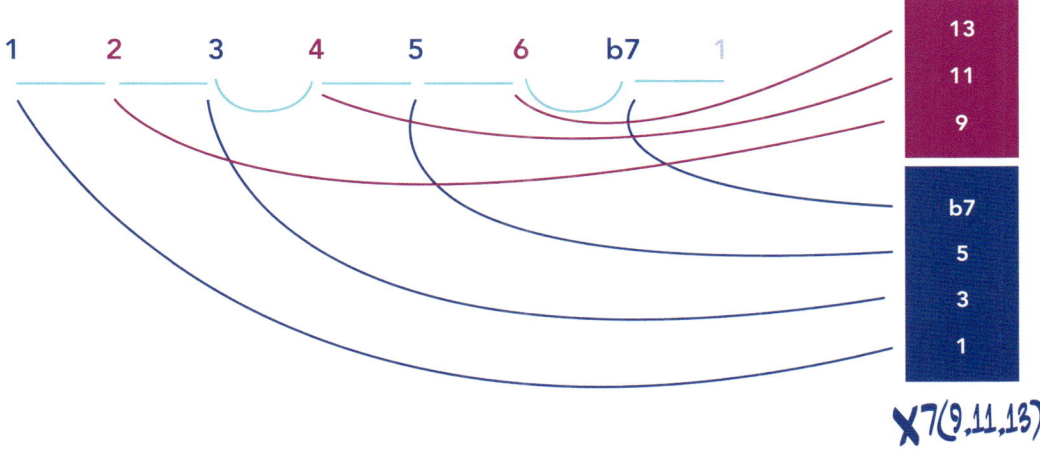

Please understand that what this means is that the Mixolydian mode can be played on any dominant 7th chord that includes any number and combination of the extensions above. So technically, all the following chords:

X7   X9   X11   X13   X7add11   X7add13   X9add13

And we could technically add all the suspended chords to this list. So for obvious reasons, I am not going to write all these chords every time. You should know how to name chords appropriately by now, just understand that all the chords above come from different combinations of extensions.

Now, as I said, the Mixolydian mode has a context in which it excels, which is on the V chord of a major authentic cadence:

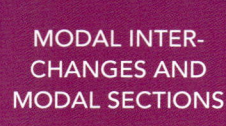

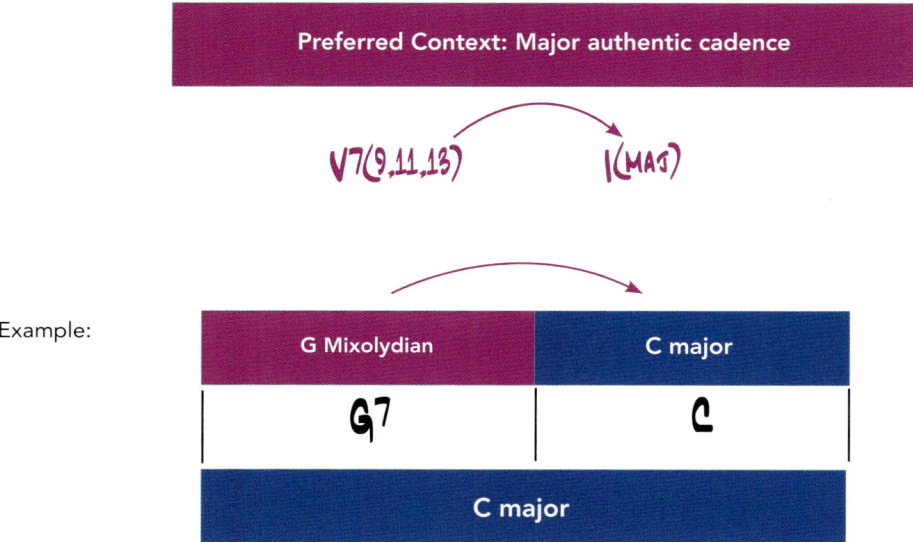

Example:

The Phrygian Dominant mode

The Phrygian dominant mode is the fifth mode of the harmonic minor scale. As we saw above, this mode naturally occurs when playing the fifth degree dominant in a minor context. It will therefore be the most coherent choice when the dominant chord is part of a minor cadence. The most common extension(s) that imply this mode are the b9 and/or b13.

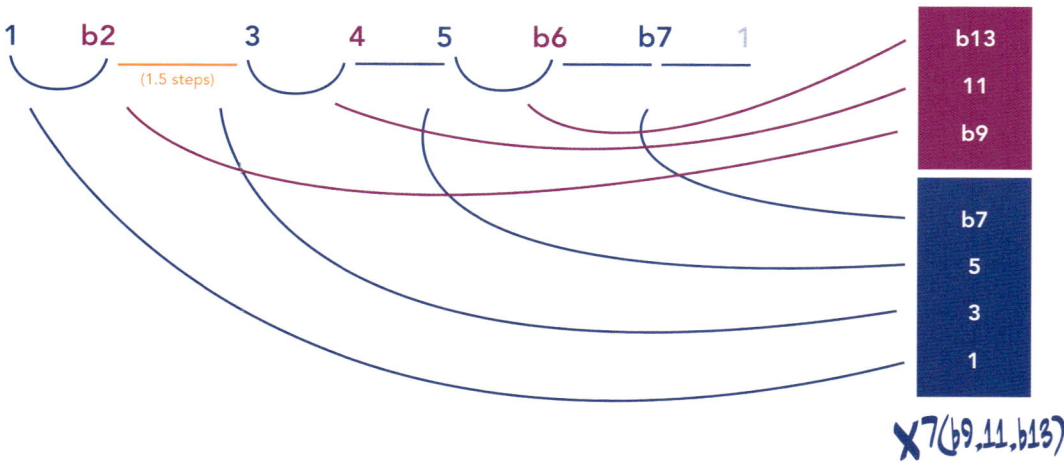

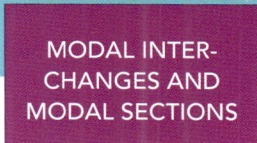

MODAL INTER-CHANGES AND MODAL SECTIONS

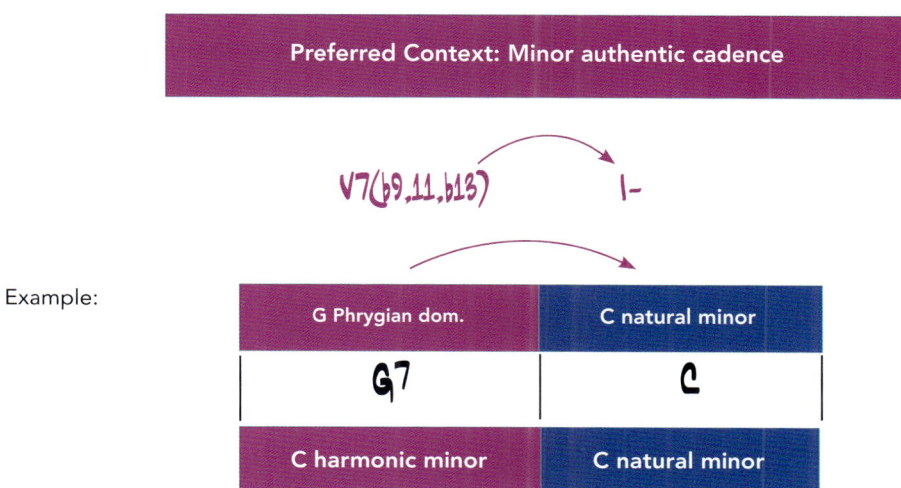

The Mixolydian b6 Mode

This mode is an alternative to the Phrygian dominant mode in a minor cadence. It can be used when there is no indication about the nature of the 9th during a minor cadence. To me, the chord that most obviously implies this mode is X7(b13). This chord gives you freedom when it comes to the nature of the 9th while indicating the presence of a b13.

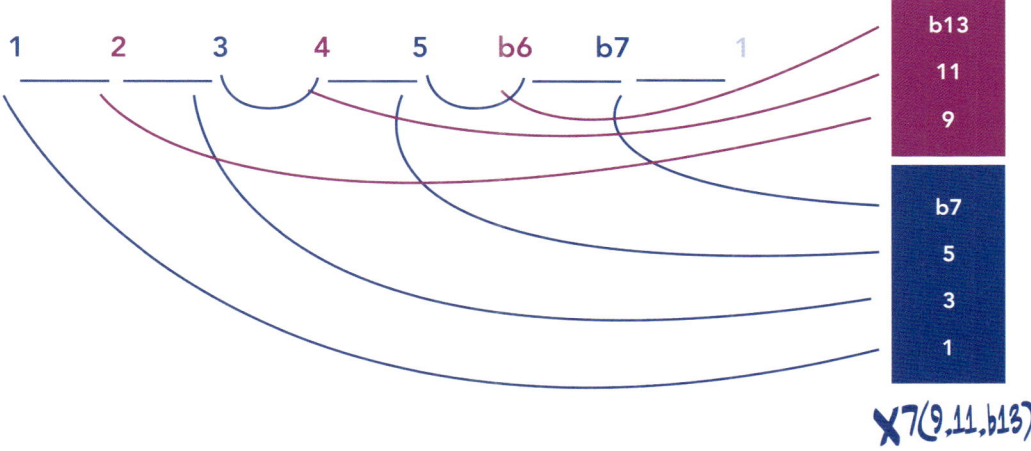

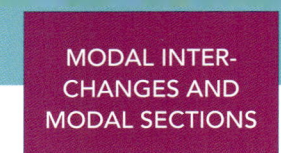

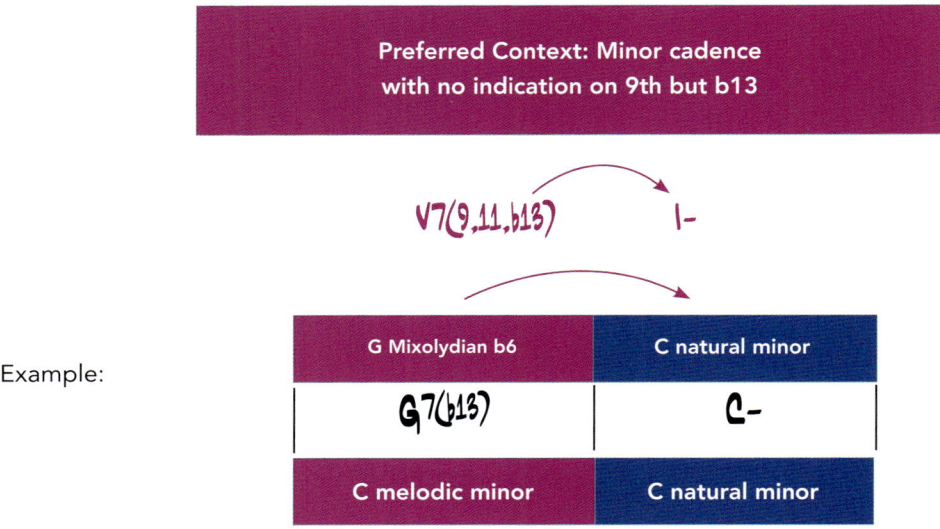

Example:

The Lydian Dominant mode

The Lydian dominant mode is mostly useful on tritone substitution dominant chords. It can also be used on sub-dominant, dominant 7th chords. The clearest indication in terms of extensions that this mode is implied is the presence of a #11.

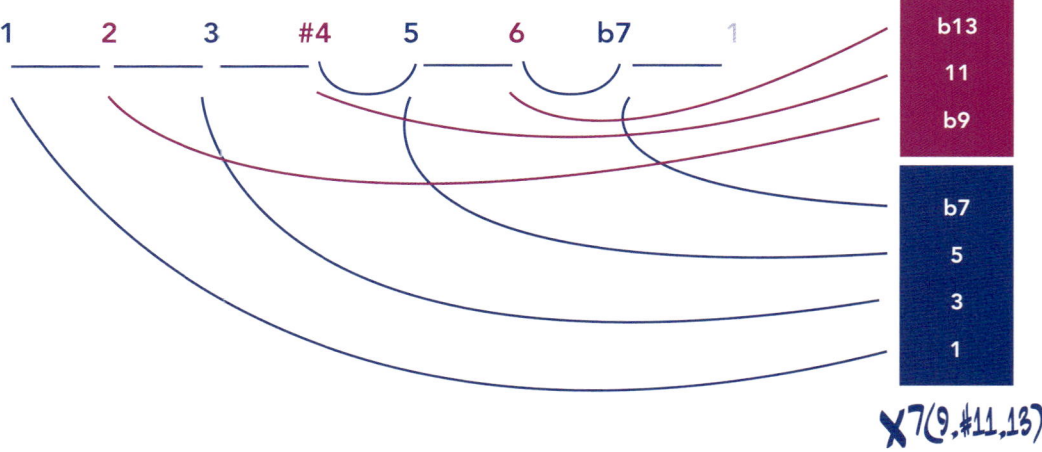

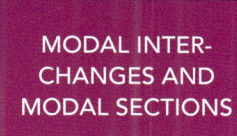

MODAL INTER-CHANGES AND MODAL SECTIONS

- Tritone substitution chord
- IV7 sub-dominant chord
- X7#11 chords

Example:

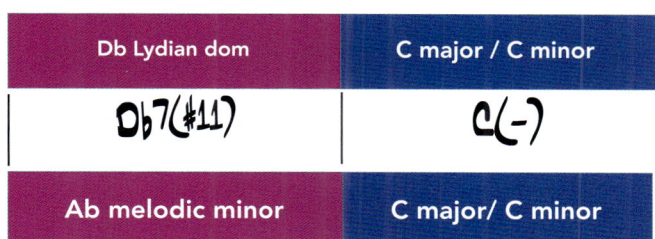

Db Lydian dom	C major / C minor
Db7(#11)	C(-)
Ab melodic minor	C major/ C minor

■ Modes that work without normally including a Dom 7th

The Superlocrian mode

As I said in the first book, the Superlocrian presents some ambiguities.

Technically, this mode is the seventh mode of the melodic minor scale and is associated with a half-diminished chord. Now, a half-diminished chord has a MINOR 3rd and a DIMINISHED 5th, which is not what we are normally looking for. Again, we are looking for scales or modes that are compatible with a dominant 7th chord, which has a major 3rd and a perfect 5th.

Degrees	1	2	3	4	5	6	7
Tetrads	I min(maj7)	II-7	III maj7(#5)	IV 7	V 7	VI-7(b5)	VII-7(b5)
Extensions	9 11 b13	b9 11 13	9 #11 13	9 #11 13	9 11 b13	9 11 b13	b9 b11 b13
Mode	Melodic Minor	Phrygian Major 6th	Lydian #5	Lydian b7	Mixolydian b6	Locrian Major 2	Superlocrian

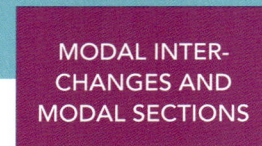

However, this mode is practically never used over seven degree half-diminished chords. Remember that the Superlocrian mode can be rewritten in a non-diatonic way with the following intervals:

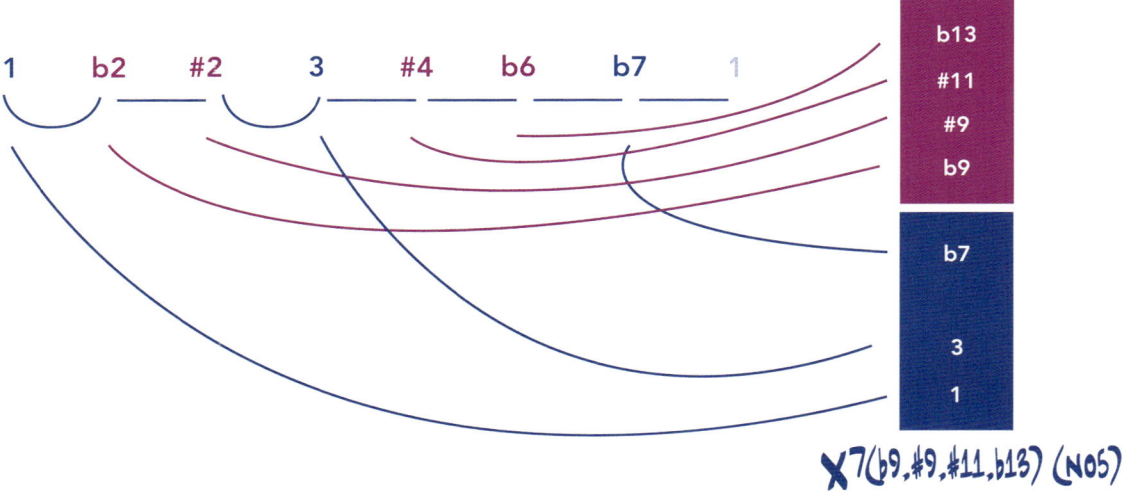

The absence of the 5th doesn't really matter since, again, the perfect 5th in dominant chords does not really contribute to the color of the chord. In reality, it amplifies the importance of the root and can be counterproductive in some case. It is common to not play the 5th in chords that include a perfect 5th, since it is not as characteristic as the 3rd, the 7th and other extensions. If you had to get rid of one note in a chord, choose the 5th.

Note: This is only true if the 5th is perfect. The 5th is obviously important and colorful when it's augmented or diminished.

This chord is often named "altered" and is written:

And this explains why the Superlocrian mode is also sometimes referred to as the altered mode.

The Superlocrian mode can also be written in the following ways:

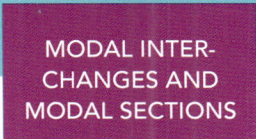

In this case, the main structural tetrad would be an X7b5, and with the extensions, we would have:

Or even:

I, however, find these interpretations to be more confusing since they imply a lot of chromaticisms in the way the mode is written. But in the end, you must realize that we are just talking about the same thing, written in different ways.

Superlocrian is perfect anytime you want to encounter an altered chord OR want to add a lot of tension to a dominant 7th chord, within a cadence.

Example:

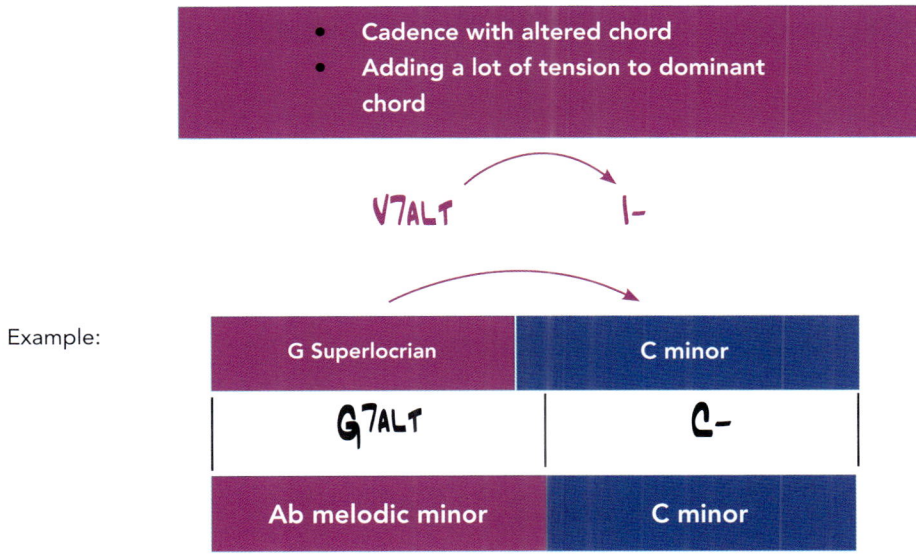

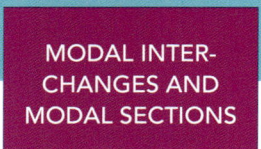

MODAL INTER-CHANGES AND MODAL SECTIONS

The half-whole diminished scale

Just like for the Superlocrian mode, it is not immediately obvious why this scale works on a dominant 7th chord. This comes from the fact that if you harmonize this scale in triads, it does not generate a dominant chord. However, by using some enharmonic tricks and harmonizing this scale differently, we will see that it actually works beautifully.

This diminished scale has eight notes, which means that it MUST present at least one chromaticism at one point. However, depending on the context, this chromaticism can appear in different ways. Let's look at several ways the diminished scales can be written.

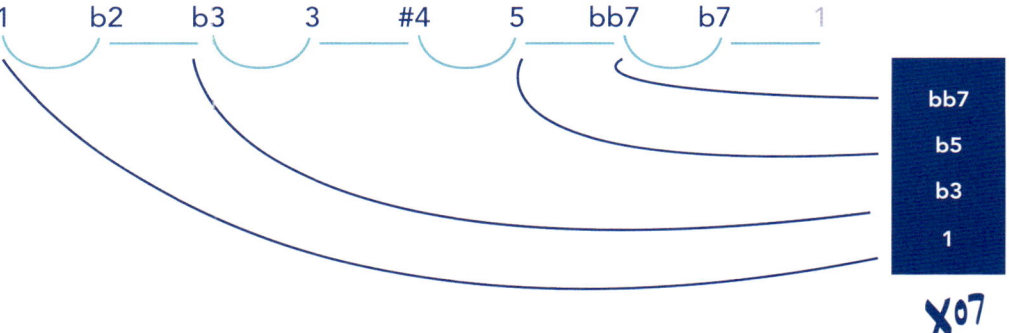

According to this interpretation, the diminished scale is compatible with a fully diminished chord. This is true, but it's not what we are looking for. Let's rewrite our scale:

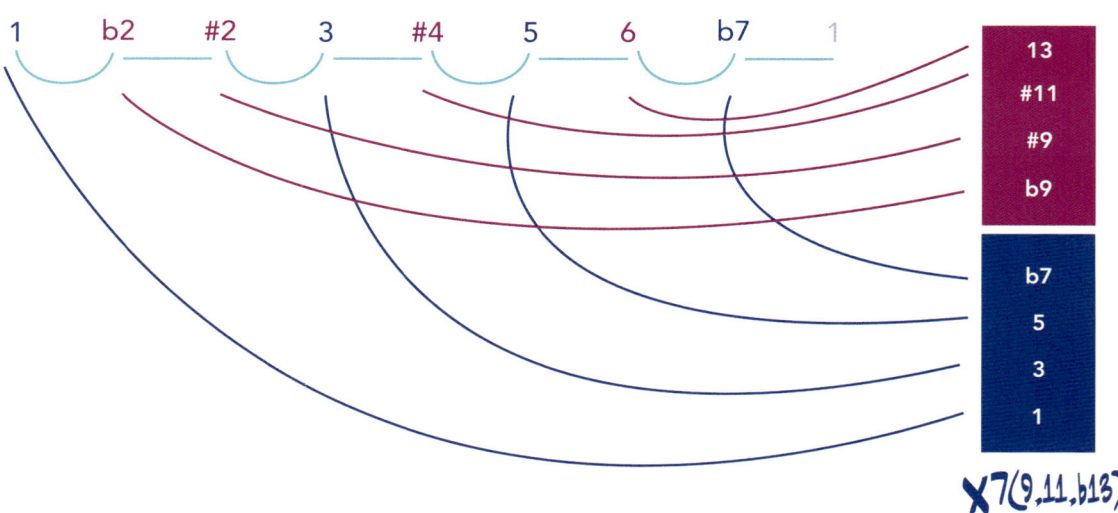

MODAL INTERCHANGES AND MODAL SECTIONS

Now, that's much better! Written this way, the diminished scale can clearly generate a dominant 7th chord with some very interesting and colorful extensions! This scale can be used in a lot of contexts but mostly works on a V7 resolving on a I major or I7 in my experience. This scale provides a lot of dissonances but is not AS dissonant as the Superlocrian mode since it has an extra note in common with the major scale.

The whole-tone scale

The whole-tone scale only has six notes and therefore can be written in different ways thanks to enharmonics.

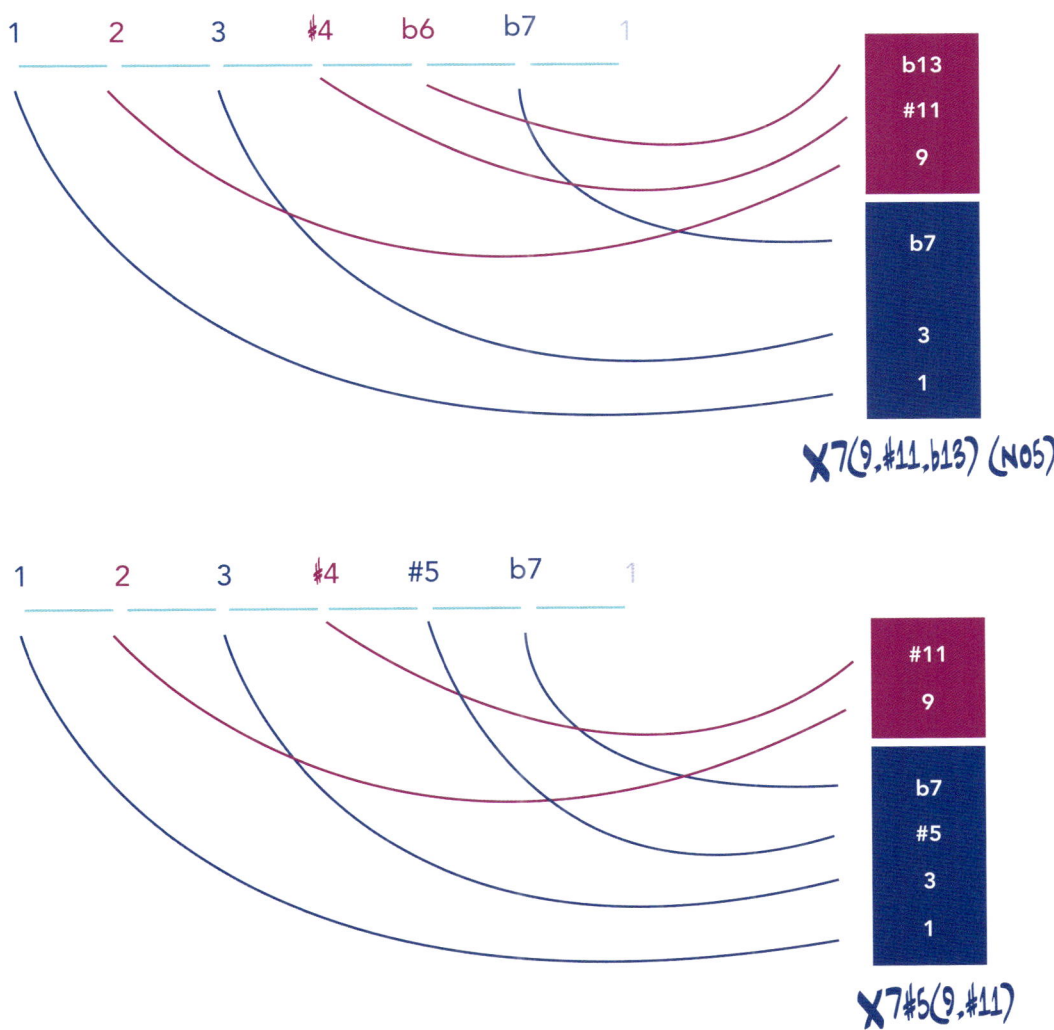

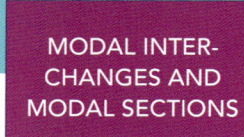
MODAL INTERCHANGES AND MODAL SECTIONS

There is no particular context in which this mode works. As long as the extensions are possible or clearly indicated by the harmonic context, it is always an option. Just try playing it and getting familiar with the way this scale sounds, and try playing it in your cadences over the dominant chord. It sounds very interesting, but it can be hard to use this scale tastefully sometimes.

The Phrygian major 6th

This mode is the second mode of the melodic minor scale. Just like the last three modes we've studied, it's not obvious why this mode should work on a dominant 7th chord, so let's study it a little.

This mode generates a minor 7th tetrad, so again, it technically shouldn't work. But it does if we use the magic of enharmonics:

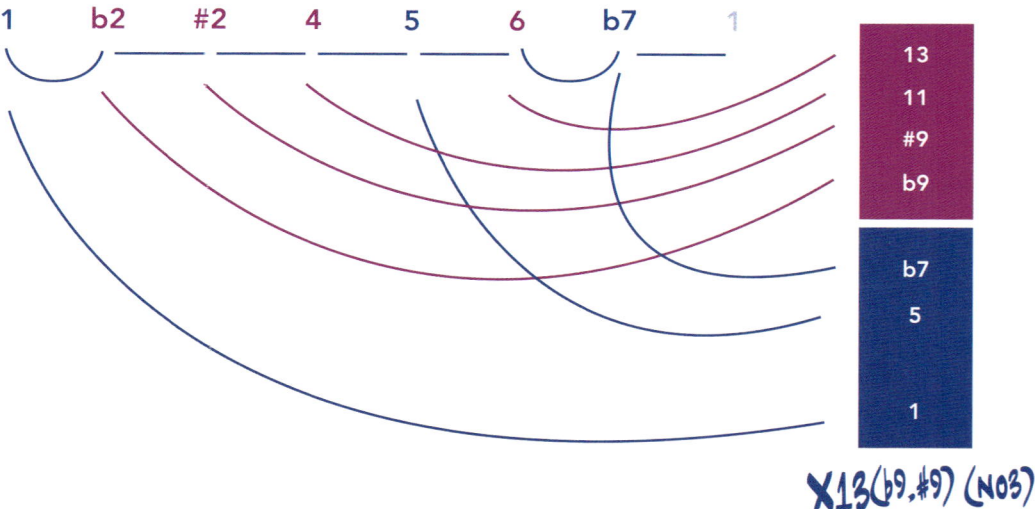

The great thing about this mode is that it really only adds the b9 and #9 extensions, while the other notes are identical to the Mixolydian mode. Sure, it doesn't have a major 3rd, but you don't necessarily have to emphasize this note all the time, or you could just add it to the scale as a passing note.

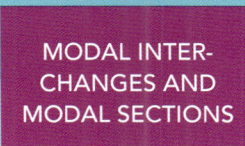

MODAL INTER-CHANGES AND MODAL SECTIONS

The major pentatonic scale

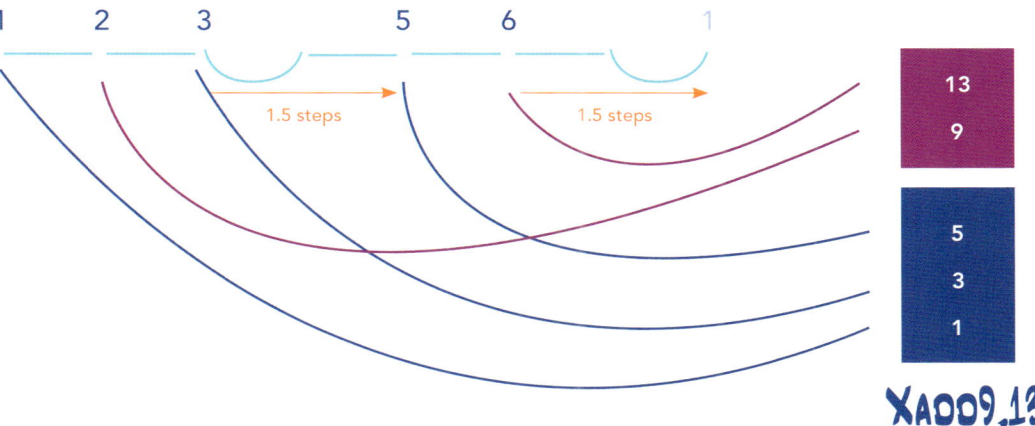

The major pentatonic scale, even though it doesn't have a mind 7th, works on all dominant 7th chords with a major 9th and a major 13th. This scale is usually used in place of the Mixolydian mode, but it would also work as a replacement for the Lydian dominant mode, since the nature of the 11th doesn't matter when playing the pentatonic scale.

The minor pentatonic scale

The minor pentatonic scale, as its name implies, is technically more appropriate in a minor context. But mostly because of blue,s which we will study very soon, it is accepted on dominant 7th chords with the following interpretation:

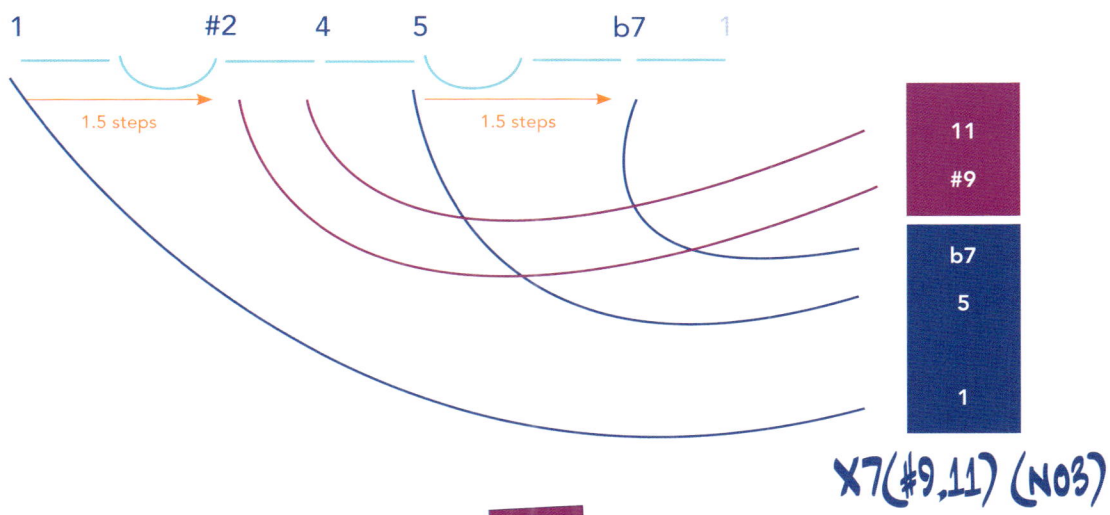

MODAL INTERCHANGES AND MODAL SECTIONS

Before we move forward, I want to make it clear that all the extended dominant chords that we've studied above are meant to be used in tonal situations. Extensions are added to create tension which results in a modal interchange, but the purpose of the extensions is to reinforce tonality. In this case, some elements of modal music are used to enrich and strengthen tonal music. Now that we know all the different scales and modes that can potentially work on a dominant 7th chord and their compatible extensions, it's time to take a little break and think about it for a bit.

There are several things that should be taken into account when you are deciding what mode or scale to play on a dominant chord:

- **What CAN you play:** What is the broadest spectrum of options that are compatible with the dominant chord you are dealing with, when taking the extensions into account? When you simply think about what you CAN play, not having any extensions leaves you with a TON of options, so you need to use another guide.

- **What SHOULD you play:** Given the style of music and/or other indications, such as what scene you are writing for in a movie, what mode or modes are going to be the most appropriate within this context? For example, if you are gigging in a country band and you see a dominant 7th chord in the chart, I would strongly recommend using Mixolydian or a major pentatonic. I can guarantee you that people will look at you funny if you pull out a Superlocrian lick. Too jazzy, bro!

MODAL INTERCHANGES AND MODAL SECTIONS

- **What does the harmonic context tell you:** If you look at the chord progression in a broader way, what is the dominant chord really used for? Is it a blues? (We will study this shortly.) Is it a major or minor context? Again, if you are in a minor context and you see a dominant chord, part of a V I cadence, you can absolutely play and should play the Phrygian dominant or Mixolydian b6 mode and "assume" that since it's a minor context, those are the modes that are implied.

- **What sounds are you looking for:** This is kind of similar to rule number two, but at the end of the day, regardless of the rules, what do you want to hear? What do you think will sound good or appropriate? And this is where, again, ear training and experimenting and listening to a lot of music will refine the way you navigate through those situations.

So now that we've established the inventory of the scales that can potentially be used on dominant chords, I would like to give you a summary of all the different dominant chords you might encounter, with different extensions. For each case, I will give you what modes are most appropriate.

In a style that accepts all types of dissonances (again, jazz typically), over a dominant 7th chord, without any given extensions, you can play any of these modes:

Mixolydian	9,11,13
Phrygian dominant or Mixolydian b2 b6	b9,11,b13
Mixolydian b6	9,11,b13
Lydian dominant or Mixolydian #4	9,#11,13
Superlocrian	b9,#9,#11,b13
Half-whole diminished scale	b9,#9,#11,13
Whole-tone scale	9,#11,b13
Phrygian major 6th	b9,#9,11,13
Major pentatonic	9,13
Minor pentatonic	#9,11

MODAL INTERCHANGES AND MODAL SECTIONS

■ What mode for what extensions

Again, allowed doesn't mean preferable. There are modes that are technically allowed but won't sound as good or coherent as others. So I decided to make this distinction:

In yellow, I will give you the compatible modes. This means they technically can be played but won't necessarily sound good. In green you will find the modes that are preferred or implied. In red you will find modes to avoid.

X7

Without any given extensions, a dominant 7th chord leaves a lot of possibilities. So this will depend on the context. The safest, most consonant choices, however, will always be the Mixolydian scale in a major context and a Phrygian dominant or Mixolydian b6 scale in a minor context.

Mode	Extensions
Mixolydian	9,11,13
Phrygian dominant or Mixolydian b2 b6	b9,11,b13
Mixolydian b6	9,11,b13
Lydian dominant or Mixolydian #4	9,#11,13
Superlocrian	b9,#9,#11,b13
Half-whole diminished scale	b9,#9,#11,13
Whole-tone scale	9,#11,b13
Phrygian major 6th	b9,#9,11,13
Major pentatonic	9,13
Minor pentatonic	#9,11

A dominant 7th chord with a natural 9th is quite common and is compatible with all the following modes. The most consonant and compatible mode is the Mixolydian mode.

Mode	Extensions
Mixolydian	9,11,13
Phrygian dominant or Mixolydian b2 b6	b9,11,b13
Mixolydian b6	9,11,b13
Lydian dominant or Mixolydian #4	9,#11,13
Superlocrian	b9,#9,#11,b13
Half-whole diminished scale	b9,#9,#11,13
Whole-tone scale	9,#11,b13
Phrygian major 6th	b9,#9,11,13
Major pentatonic	9,13
Minor pentatonic	#9,11

MODAL INTERCHANGES AND MODAL SECTIONS

X13

This chord necessarily implies Mixolydian. .

Scale	Extensions
Mixolydian	9,11,13
Phrygian dominant or Mixolydian b2 b6	b9,11,b13
Mixolydian b6	9,11,b13
Lydian dominant or Mixolydian #4	9,#11,13
Superlocrian	b9,#9,#11,b13
Half-whole diminished scale	b9,#9,#11,13
Whole-tone scale	9,#11,b13
Phrygian major 6th	b9,#9,11,13
Major pentatonic	9,13
Minor pentatonic	#9,11

X9sus4

This rather common chord usually implies a Mixolydian mode, but technically, there's another possibility: the Lydian b6 scale in a minor context.

Scale	Extensions
Mixolydian	9,11,13
Phrygian dominant or Mixolydian b2 b6	b9,11,b13
Mixolydian b6	9,11,b13
Lydian dominant or Mixolydian #4	9,#11,13
Superlocrian	b9,#9,#11,b13
Half-whole diminished scale	b9,#9,#11,13
Whole-tone scale	9,#11,b13
Phrygian major 6th	b9,#9,11,13
Major pentatonic	9,13
Minor pentatonic	#9,11

MODAL INTERCHANGES AND MODAL SECTIONS

X7(9,13) — Without any indications on the nature of the 11th, by default, the most compatible mode will be Mixolydian, but technically, Lydian dominant also works.

Mode	Tensions
Mixolydian	9,11,13
Phrygian dominant or Mixolydian b2 b6	b9,11,b13
Mixolydian b6	9,11,b13
Lydian dominant or Mixolydian #4	9,#11,13
Superlocrian	b9,#9,#11,b13
Half-whole diminished scale	b9,#9,#11,13
Whole-tone scale	9,#11,b13
Phrygian major 6th	b9,#9,11,13
Major pentatonic	9,13
Minor pentatonic	#9,11

X7(#11) — This notation often implies the Lydian dominant mode, but it is compatible with three others.

Mode	Tensions
Mixolydian	9,11,13
Phrygian dominant or Mixolydian b2 b6	b9,11,b13
Mixolydian b6	9,11,b13
Lydian dominant or Mixolydian #4	9,#11,13
Superlocrian	b9,#9,#11,b13
Half-whole diminished scale	b9,#9,#11,13
Whole-tone scale	9,#11,b13
Phrygian major 6th	b9,#9,11,13
Major pentatonic	9,13
Minor pentatonic	#9,11

Question: Is the following statement true?

$$X7(\#11) = X7(b5) \ ?$$

228

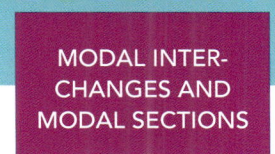

MODAL INTER-CHANGES AND MODAL SECTIONS

As you must know by now, a diminished 5th is enharmonically equal to an augmented 4th. For this reason, you may see the following notation:

$$X7(\flat5)$$

Now, although this chord does exist, it is NOT the same thing as an X7#11, which has a perfect 5th. So you CANNOT use one notation in place of the other.

So pay attention! Many people, even great musicians, make this mistake and confuse these two notations.

If you do encounter an X7b5, used in the proper way, and not just as a mistaken way of meaning X7#11, then you will have to exclude from your improvisation possibilities the modes that have a perfect 5th. This leaves you with the whole-tone scale and the Superlocrian.

MODAL INTERCHANGES AND MODAL SECTIONS

X7(b5)

Mixolydian	9,11,13
Phrygian dominant or Mixolydian b2 b6	b9,11,b13
Mixolydian b6	9,11,b13
Lydian dominant or Mixolydian #4	9,#11,13
Superlocrian	b9,#9,#11,b13
Half-whole diminished scale	b9,#9,#11,13
Whole-tone scale	9,#11,b13
Phrygian major 6th	b9,#9,11,13
Major pentatonic	9,13
Minor pentatonic	#9,11

X7(b9) This chord most often really implies Phrygian dominant.

Mixolydian	9,11,13
Phrygian dominant or Mixolydian b2 b6	b9,11,b13
Mixolydian b6	9,11,b13
Lydian dominant or Mixolydian #4	9,#11,13
Superlocrian	b9,#9,#11,b13
Half-whole diminished scale	b9,#9,#11,13
Whole-tone scale	9,#11,b13
Phrygian major 6th	b9,#9,11,13
Major pentatonic	9,13
Minor pentatonic	#9,11

MODAL INTER- CHANGES AND MODAL SECTIONS

X7(b9,b13)

This chord can strongly imply Phrygian dominant or Superlocrian.

Scale	Tensions
Mixolydian	9,11,13
Phrygian dominant or Mixolydian b2 b6	b9,11,b13
Mixolydian b6	9,11,b13
Lydian dominant or Mixolydian #4	9,#11,13
Superlocrian	b9,#9,#11,b13
Half-whole diminished scale	b9,#9,#11,13
Whole-tone scale	9,#11,b13
Phrygian major 6th	b9,#9,11,13
Major pentatonic	9,13
Minor pentatonic	#9,11

X7(b13)

This chord strongly implies Mixolydian b6 but can also be synonymous with Phrygian dominant.

Scale	Tensions
Mixolydian	9,11,13
Phrygian dominant or Mixolydian b2 b6	b9,11,b13
Mixolydian b6	9,11,b13
Lydian dominant or Mixolydian #4	9,#11,13
Superlocrian	b9,#9,#11,b13
Half-whole diminished scale	b9,#9,#11,13
Whole-tone scale	9,#11,b13
Phrygian major 6th	b9,#9,11,13
Major pentatonic	9,13
Minor pentatonic	#9,11

MODAL INTER-CHANGES AND MODAL SECTIONS

X7#5

This chord is very similar to the previous one, except it implies the absence of a perfect 5th in the chord. It usually indicates the whole-tone scale.

Scale	Tensions
Mixolydian	9,11,13
Phrygian dominant or Mixolydian b2 b6	b9,11,b13
Mixolydian b6	9,11,b13
Lydian dominant or Mixolydian #4	9,#11,13
Superlocrian	b9,#9,#11,b13
Half-whole diminished scale	b9,#9,#11,13
Whole-tone scale	9,#11,b13
Phrygian major 6th	b9,#9,11,13
Major pentatonic	9,13
Minor pentatonic	#9,11

X7(#9)

Scale	Tensions
Mixolydian	9,11,13
Phrygian dominant or Mixolydian b2 b6	b9,11,b13
Mixolydian b6	9,11,b13
Lydian dominant or Mixolydian #4	9,#11,13
Superlocrian	b9,#9,#11,b13
Half-whole diminished scale	b9,#9,#11,13
Whole-tone scale	9,#11,b13
Phrygian major 6th	b9,#9,11,13
Major pentatonic	9,13
Minor pentatonic	#9,11

MODAL INTER-CHANGES AND MODAL SECTIONS

X7(#9,#13)

Scale	Tensions
Mixolydian	9,11,13
Phrygian dominant or Mixolydian b2 b6	b9,11,b13
Mixolydian b6	9,11,b13
Lydian dominant or Mixolydian #4	9,#11,13
Superlocrian	b9,#9,#11,b13
Half-whole diminished Scale	b9,#9,#11,13
Whole-tone scale	9,#11,b13
Phrygian major 6th	b9,#9,11,13
Major pentatonic	9,13
Minor pentatonic	#9,11

X7(b9,#11)

X7ALT

Scale	Tensions
Mixolydian	9,11,13
Phrygian dominant or Mixolydian b2 b6	b9,11,b13
Mixolydian b6	9,11,b13
Lydian dominant or Mixolydian #4	9,#11,13
Superlocrian	b9,#9,#11,b13
Half-whole diminished scale	b9,#9,#11,13
Whole-tone scale	9,#11,b13
Phrygian major 6th	b9,#9,11,13
Major pentatonic	9,13
Minor pentatonic	#9,11

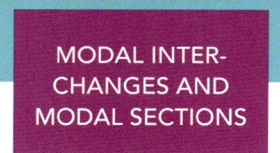

Connection between tritone subs and extended dom 7th

■ Tritone substitution and altered chords

In general, it is quite fascinating to notice that all the possible substitutions can be seen as ways to bring out different extensions, if you study the notes of the substitute chords, in relation to the root of the substituted chord.

Let's take the example of the following tritone substitution:

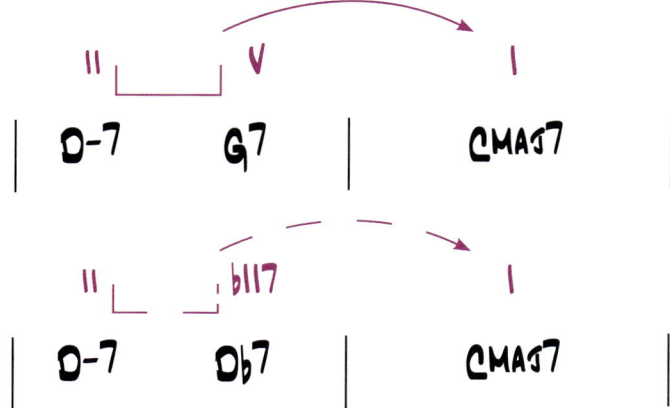

Now let's imagine that, underneath the substitute chord Db7, the bassist decided to stick to the original root (G). This is done quite often for it allows to add the tension brought by the substitution while preserving the V to I bass movement. What is the new created chord?.

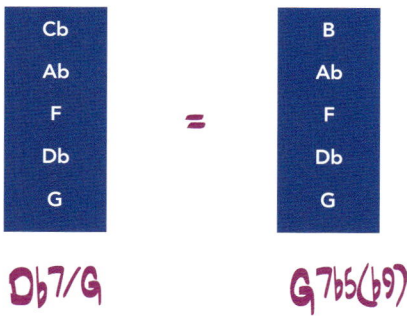

MODAL INTERCHANGES AND MODAL SECTIONS

Above, I explained that a tritone substitution was considered to be the first degree chord of the harmonization of the Lydian dominant mode. When harmonized fully, the Db7 chord becomes Db9(#11,b13). Let's go ahead and add those extensions and see what the chord becomes over a G on the bass:

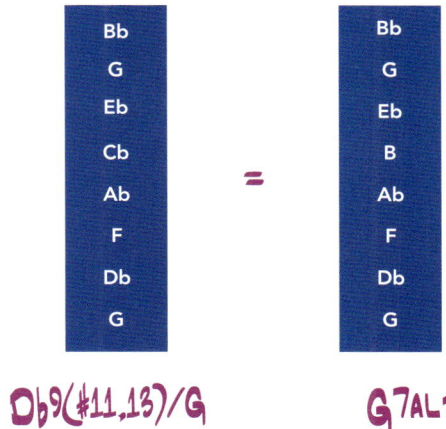

In other words, a tritone substitution, with all its extensions, is equivalent to playing the altered version of the original chord (the substituted chord), without its root. In terms of improvisation, what matters is the following equivalence:

Now remember, there is technically a difference between those two modes. But it's again a matter of mode thought, versus mode heard. In this case, on a V chord, it means that you can think Db Lydian dominant OR G Superlocrian. If the bass note is a Db, the mode heard will be Lydian dominant, and if the bass note is a G, the mode heard will be Superlocrian.

One last thing here…

Let's consider the Ab melodic minor scale and look at each of its modes.

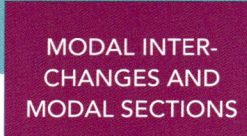

Degrees	1	b2	b3	b4	b5	b6	b7
Scale	Ab	Bb	Cb	Db	Eb	F	G
Mode	Melodic minor	Phrygian major 6th	Lydian #5	Lydian b7	Mixolydian b6	Locrian major 2	Superlocrian

Beautiful isn't it? Everything just makes perfect sense.

The mode that is borrowed from when using a tritone substitution of a dominant chord and the mode used when the dominant chord is extended in its most altered form, come from the harmonization of the same melodic minor scale: Ab melodic minor.

Tip: It can help to remember that within a given major or minor key, playing Superlocrian on the V7 degree dominant or Lydian dominant on the bII7, imply playing the bVI degree melodic minor scale.

If you prefer, you can also think that you should play the melodic minor scale that starts a minor second above the V note.

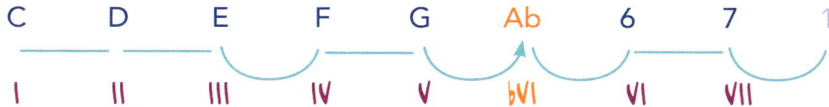

In general, any substitution, when studied over the original bass note (the bass note of the substituted chord) will bring out particular extensions. And this does not only apply to the substitutions of dominant chords.

For example, in a C major context, what are the extensions brought by substituting diatonically the Imaj7 with the III-7 chord?

MODAL INTERCHANGES AND MODAL SECTIONS

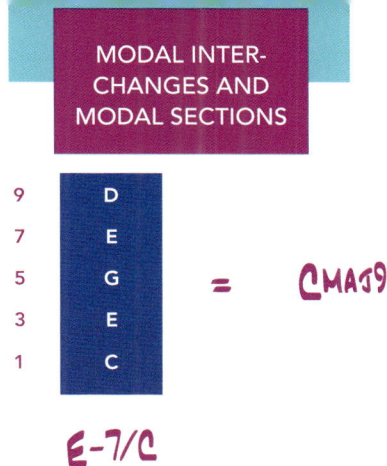

Voilà! This is extremely interesting, especially in an improvisational context, because it allows each musician to substitute chords as they wish, without compromising the global result. This will simply bring out different extensions. On the example above if I, as the pianist or guitarist, decided to use the substitution while the bassist stuck with the original bass, the result, for the listener, would have been a Cmaj9. If we consider the reverse situation where I stuck to a Cmaj7 and the bassist decided to play a E on the bass, the result would have been:

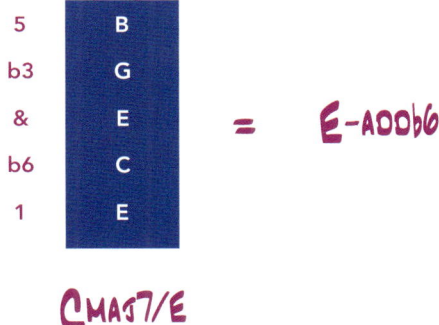

And that would sound perfectly fine. A little more tense, but hey, it's jazz baby! Now you still want to be in control of substitutions. Some could sound out of context or a little too much.

■ Diatonic substitutions and 9th chords

> In a major context, if you substitute the fifth degree dominant 7th chord with the seventh degree dominant (which is a half-diminished chord), it is equivalent to adding a major 9th to the original chord:

MODAL INTER-CHANGES AND MODAL SECTIONS

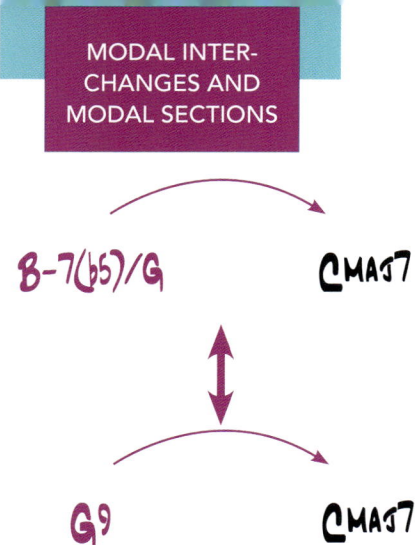

 In a minor context (or minor context with a minor borrowing), substituting the fifth degree dominant chord with the seventh degree dominant (fully-diminished chord) is equivalent to adding a minor 9th to the original chord:

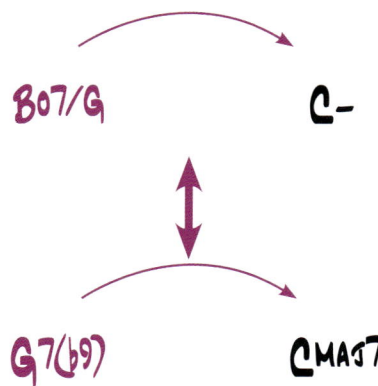

Well, that's about it for dominant chords… But there is still one thing we have to dive into. A style of music that is almost exclusively based on dominant 7th chord progressions and yet presents some very unique particularities. I'm of course talking about the style of BLUES. Oh, yeah!

THE BLUES

4

The Tonal Context

THE BLUES

THE BLUES

Introduction

When it comes to harmonic analysis, blues is something of its own. Again, you must remember that for the longest time, music was played without much theory to back it up. If you look at history in general and consider all the musicians that have existed and will exist, the vast majority of them did not know anything about theory. And any time we are tempted to get too pretentious about our understanding of music through theory, it just takes a good blues tune to bring us straight back to reality. It's said that Darwin, soon after he was supposedly done with his theory of evolution, happened to run into a platypus in Australia. This animal did not make much sense in the light of his new theory. This is why some creationists use this animal as an argument against evolution. Now this is hilarious isn't it? Well, it's exactly what happens when you put a blues chart in front of a classical musician or other firm believer of the Western vision of music theory. Blues is the platypus of music theory. And yet, it is one of the MOST POPULAR styles of music in the Western world, heard in every genre from pop to metal and jazz. But as we'll see, this style, harmonically, does not make any sense.

The reason for this is that Blues comes from what is unfortunately one of the darkest times of history: slavery. The word blues itself is said to come from the sadness and melancholy that black slaves or former slaves expressed through this music. Blues comes from the unfortunate cohabitation of African songs, chants and rhythms, with "white," Western music, instruments, and chord progressions. The fact that such a beautiful and now incredibly popular style of music, which constituted the bedrock of jazz, rock, R&B, hip hop, and many other genres, emerged as a side effect of human degradation is hard to make sense of, morally speaking. And to me it is just fair justice that this style, incredibly beautiful and efficient, still mocks the rules of Western harmony.

First of all, the blues scale, and I mean the actual blues scale and not just the "Westernized" blue scale (which we will talk about in a second) includes intervals that do not belong to our 12 note equal temperament system. Ouch. Well, we already know this is going to be a problem since, let's see, oh yes! Only EVERYTHING that we built so far was based on our 12 note system.

At this point, there are two options: we can build an entirely different theory from scratch that includes blues, or we can adapt our current theory to blues (which will imply approximations and simplifications) to make sense of it, and accept that sometimes, things just won't make sense. Well, it seems like the solution that was voted was the second one: we'll adapt our system to blues while acknowledging that it doesn't really make sense, and yet, sound freaking amazing!

THE BLUES

Secondly, African scales are based on **just intonation, which is a different tuning system** from the equal temperament system that western music is based on.

Remember (from the first volume) that the equal temperament system is based on the division of each octave in 12 equally-distanced half-steps. On the other hand, in just intonation, notes can be separated by less than a half-step.

■ Notion of cent

The cent is a unit of measurement used to describe intervals that cannot be defined with the equal temperament system. In other words, it is used to describe intervals which are smaller than a half-step or are not a multiple of a half-step.

The definition of a cent is very simple: each half-step in the equal temperament system is made of 100 cents.

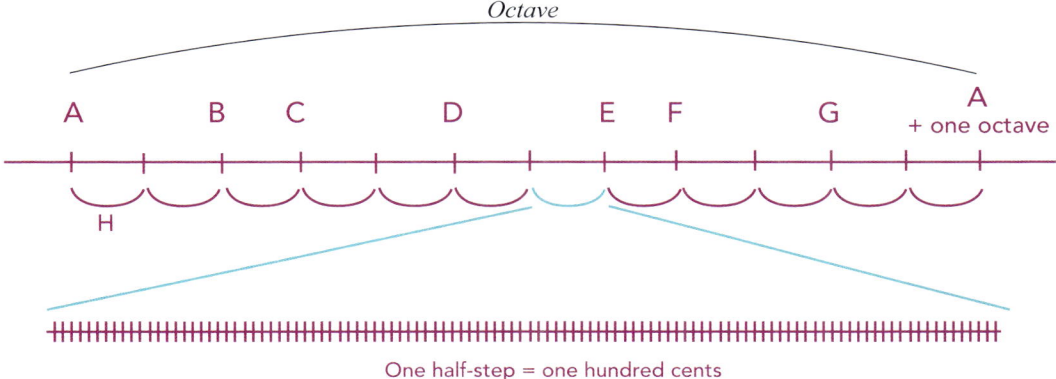

The cent allows much more precision when it comes to tuning and describing intervals.

■ The blues scale

In the previous book, we defined two different "blues scales": the major blues scale and the minor blues scale. As we will discover shortly, these scales are actually two variations of the actual blues scale.

THE BLUES

The full blues scale is a nine-note scale and corresponds to a major scale to which three notes, called blue or worried notes, are added. These notes do NOT belong to our 12-note system. And our fancy Western way of describing music, which uses intervals smaller than a half-step, is **microtonal music**. Again, this is a modern way to make sense of something that was obviously invented before the word microtonal even existed.

- The **blue 3rd is** most commonly found at 316 cents above the tonic, which is actually **somewhere between the b3 and the 3.** And when I say most commonly found there, it's because depending on the musician, the blue note can be played in different spots. That same blue note can be heard at 267 cents, which is between the 2 and the b3.

- The **blue 5th** is most commonly found at 583 cents, which corresponds to 2.9 full steps. This means this blue note is **slightly lower than the #4**.

- The **blue 7th** can be commonly found in two different spots: 969 cents, which is slightly lower than an actual b7, and 1018, which is slightly higher.

The main problem with the actual blue notes, as defined above, is twofold:

1. **The way modern music theory is built makes it difficult to properly define these notes and work with them from an analytical standpoint.**

2. **Many instruments, such as the piano, literally cannot reach or play the actual blue notes since they are tunned in half-steps. Only vocals or instruments which allow bending, such as guitar or saxophone, can reach the actual blue notes.**

This is why the blue notes are commonly approximated with the closest note belonging to the equal temperament system.

First blue note ⟶	#2	b3
Second blue note ⟶	#4	b5
Third blue note ⟶	b7	

This allows us to define an approximated version of the blues scale, adapted to the equal temperament system:

1 2 b3/#2 3 4 b5/#4 6 b7 7 1

THE BLUES

Scales used in place of the full blues scale

Because the actual blues scale is so different from what we are used to playing in the Western world of music, very few musicians actually use the proper "blues scale." Instead, most musicians use a combination of other more common scales and modes which include different combinations of the notes of the full blues scale.

The minor pentatonic scale and minor blues scale are obviously included in the full blues scale. If you sing or play an instrument which can bend, then you can obviously play an actual blue note instead of the approximated #4.

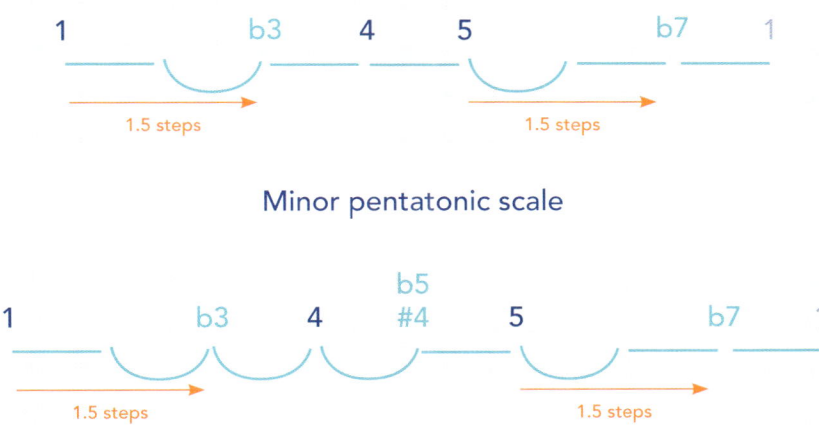

Minor pentatonic scale

Minor blues scale

■ The major pentatonic and major blues scale

The major pentatonic scale and major blues scale are also included in the full blues scale! The fact that both minor and major pentatonic scales can be used in a blues context is very unique to this genre. Just like for the minor blue scale, if your instrument allows it, feel free to play an actual blue note in place of the approximated #2 or b3.

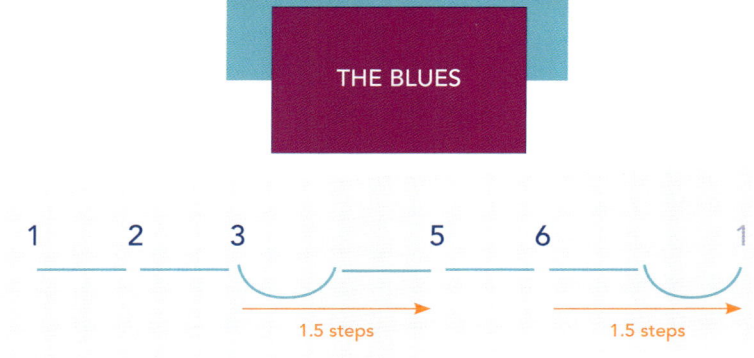

Major pentatonic scale

Major blues scale

Honestly, you can already get a lot done with the four scales above. Some blues musicians have built their entire career using only these scales. When it comes to blues, it's sometimes better to use a simple base tool to improvise and use your "ear" and "feeling" to add interesting notes around this basic minor pentatonic scale base.

Oh man… I said it. I said you should use "feeling." I feel a little ashamed of myself, being a big defender of theory. This explains why blues is SOO popular among guitar players more than any other instrument. Not only is it a style where you can get away with not knowing anything about theory, but you actually are ENCOURAGED to not overthink it. Just feel it, bro.

Now, while you CAN stop there to play blues, it doesn't mean you should. Indeed, all those ambiguous notes give us a perfect opportunity to use other modes and scales in a blues context.

■ The Mixolydian mode

The Mixolydian mode is also included in the blues scale and is very commonly used in a blues context.

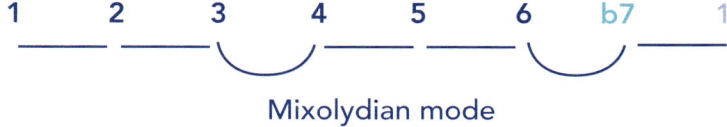

Mixolydian mode

THE BLUES

■ The Mixolydian bebop scale

Generally speaking, bebop scales are derived from regular modes with an added chromaticism, which allows them to add an extra tension note and mostly to have eight notes, which is handy when you want to play scales in sixteenth notes at 2000 bpm. It makes the scales more "symmetrical."

The Mixolydian bebop scale is simply a Mixolydian mode with an added major 7th, which brings out the ambiguity around the blue 7th and adds melodic tension to the scale by completing it with a leading tone.

This scale is used more often in jazz or jazz blues contexts (which we will study shortly). The name "bebop scale" actually comes from the subcategory of jazz referred to as bebop, which is a particularly fast and technical type of jazz.

Mixolydian Bebop Scale

■ The Dorian mode

The Dorian mode can be seen like a minor pentatonic with a added 2nd and major 6th (which both belong to the original blues scale). This mode can therefore be used in place of the blues scale and a base for your improvisation. Again however, you will want to add some blue notes here and there to sound bluesy.

Dorian Mode

■ The Dorian bebop scale

The Dorian bebop scale is simply a Dorian mode with an added major 3rd:

Dorian Bebop Mode

THE BLUES

■ The Lydian dominant mode

If you want to add some tension and spice to your blues, using the Lydian dominant is a very efficient way of doing so. This mode is also included in the full blues scale.

Lydian Dominant

■ The half-whole diminished scale

This scale is actually the closest one to the actual blues scale with the exception of its b2 interval, which does not belong to the blues scale. It is still used quite often to add a lot of tension to a blues. We will see that there is a specific place in a standard blues progression where it is particularly efficient.

The harmonic context of blues

Originally, African chants and melodies which inspired the blues scale and blues in general were mostly performed in a modal context. Again, this means a very simple harmonic context including only one chord or even sometimes one note p ayed in the background while melodies were created. The blues, however, comes from the intersection between Western tonal music and African modal music, which created very original and unique harmonic mechanisms.

This first question to be asked is, what chord or chords can be used to create a "blues modal context"? Again, this is a Western analysis of blues, since it is very unlikely that as it was being created, the blues musicians actually asked themselves these questions.

 The most common chord associated with a blues modal context is the dominant 7th chord.

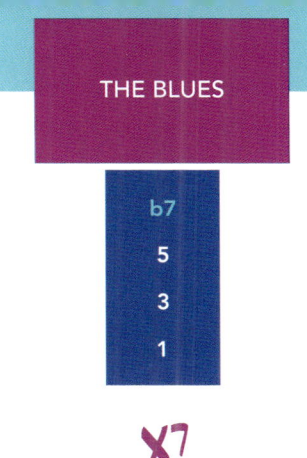

Technically, the b7 of this chord should be the "blue 7th," but it is often approximated with the minor 7th.

■ Extensions

The extensions allowed on these chords are based on the ones found in the blues scale.

Many blues tunes are based on a single dominant 7th chord. This makes sense since, once again, blues is at its origin a modal music. The interest is given to the melodist and/or the rhythms, not the harmonic progression.

 Repeating a chord over and over again for an undetermined amount of time is referred to as "vamping" on a chord.

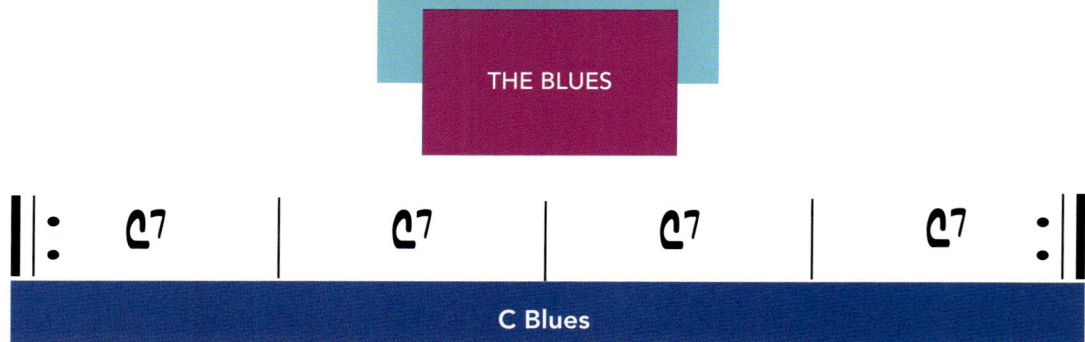

Notice that the improvisation guide only states "C blues." And indeed, if you are in a context where you are playing the blues, it wouldn't make any sense for me to give the exhaustive list of all the possible modes that can be played and mixed. As we saw, blues is a modal context of its own, so it makes much more sense to just indicate that you should play in a "blues" style.

This brings us to an important point: if you want to master the blues, you must first be comfortable playing over a single dominant 7th chord! So pick several dominant chords and start using the scales listed above. Remember that the only way you will sound "bluesy" is by having a clear idea of what blues sounds like, which means listening to a lot of blues! Theory can guide you to some extent, but I cannot teach you how to sound bluesy on paper!

Major and minor blues contexts

Although blues is most commonly played over dominant 7th chords, it can also be played over the minor version of the dominant chord, which is the minor 7th chord:

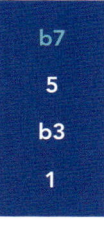

 A blues that is essentially based on dominant 7th chords is called a major blues, while a blues essentially based on minor 7th chords is called a minor blues.

THE BLUES

■ Extensions

The extensions of the minor 7th chord in a blues context are the following:

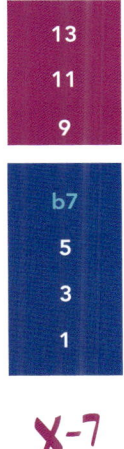

■ Scales and modes used

The most common scales used over a minor 7th chord in the context of a minor blues are not the same as in a major blues. In a minor context, we will exclude all the major modes (Mixolydian, Lydian dominant, major pentatonic, etc.) as they simply don't sound good in the minor context. Our list of options for improvising over a minor 7th chord in the context of blues is the following:

The minor pentatonic and minor blues scale

These two scales are the most efficient by far!

The Dorian mode

The Dorian mode is also very stable and efficient in this context.

The melodic minor scale

Remember that the melodic minor scale is simply a Dorian mode with a major 7th. It will work really well while adding a certain amount of tension and dissonance.

THE BLUES

Functional harmony and chord progressions in blues

Although the blues is technically mostly modal, it is not entirely devoid of tonality, since, if you remember, it was born from the fusion of African modal music and Western tonal music. Cultural interchanges always go both ways, and the white contribution to blues is definitely an aspect of tonality and a tonal center.

For this reason, a C blues commonly doesn't refer to a modal vamping in C, it also implies a series of chord progressions that emphasize the C blues scale as the center of gravity of the tune. And this is precisely what we call tonality. However, the chord qualities in blues do not depend on the harmonization of the blues scale like one could think. They are ALL dominant 7th in major or minor 7th in minor.

Degrees	1	4	5
Tetrads	I7	IV7	V7
Fuction	T	S.D	D

Major blues chord

Degrees	1	4	5
Tetrads	I-7	IV-7	V-7
Fuction	T	S.D	D

Minor blues chord

■ Common chord progressions in blues

While vamping on just one chord for the whole tune can be done, most blues includes the following mechanisms:

THE BLUES

- A modulation to the IV7 (in major) or IV-7 (in minor) chord. This modulation can be planned in advance (as in the 12-bar blues for example, which we will study soon) or cued which means that the musicians will agree, live, on where they decide to "go to the IV." If you are playing in a major blues jam and have been hanging out on the I7 for a while and someone shouts or raises four of his fingers, that means you are switching to the IV7. Then you will, unless otherwise indicated, keep vamping on the IV chord until the turnaround.

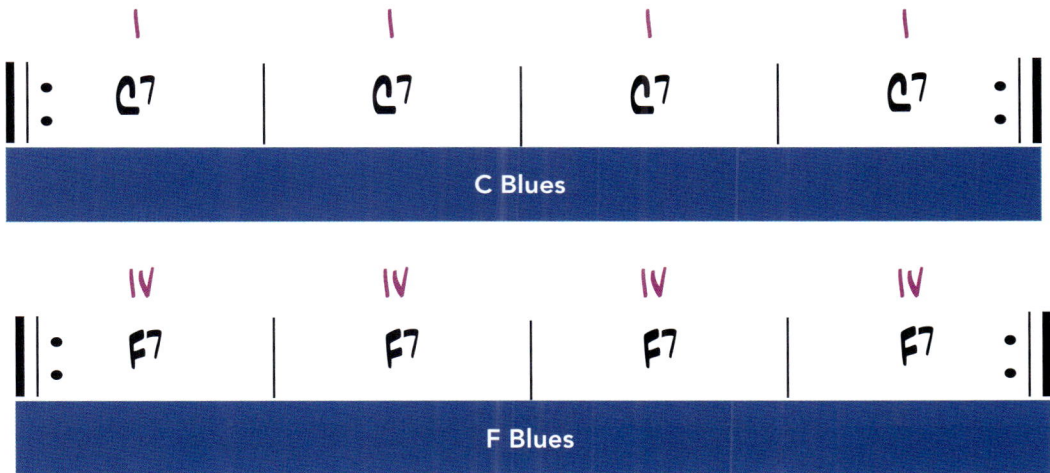

- The turnaround, as the name implies, indicates the end of the cycle and allows the musicians to all understand that they will be going back to the beginning of the form. A turnaround always at least includes a modulation to the V degree (V7 in major and V-7 in minor) for two bars, followed by the I chord for two bars. While the two previous parts can last an undetermined amount of time in some cases, the turnaround is almost ALWAYS the same length: 4 bars. It is also very common to replace the second bar of the V chord with a bar of the IV chord.

C major blues turnaround

THE BLUES

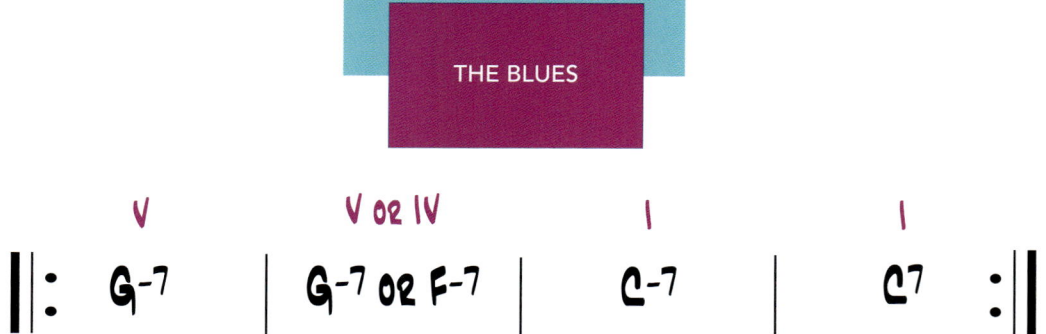

C minor blues turnaround

The 12-bar blues

You simply cannot avoid the 12-bar blues if you are looking for a valuable musical journey. It's definitely the most popular jamming progression. It's very simple: if you go to any jam session, in any genre, you will most likely play a 12-bar blues. This progression is simply a standardized version of the mechanisms we studied above. It starts with four bars of blues on the tonic chord (I), then to the (IV) and finishes with a turnaround. The advantage of this form is that you don't have to worry about cues because the number of bars played for each chord is predetermined. If you call a 12-bar blues, minor or major, in a particular key, everyone will know what you are talking about and you can just start playing!

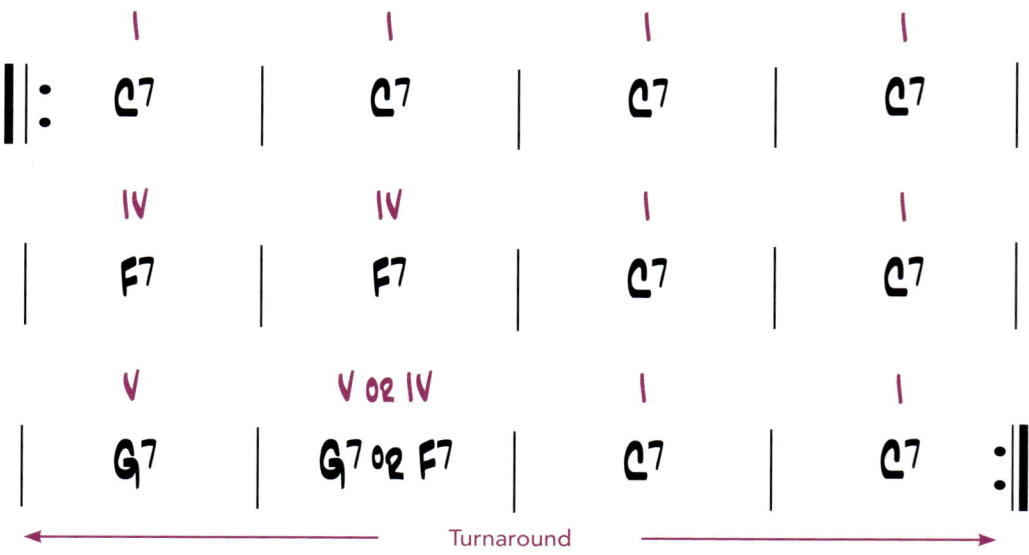

C major 12-bar blues

THE BLUES

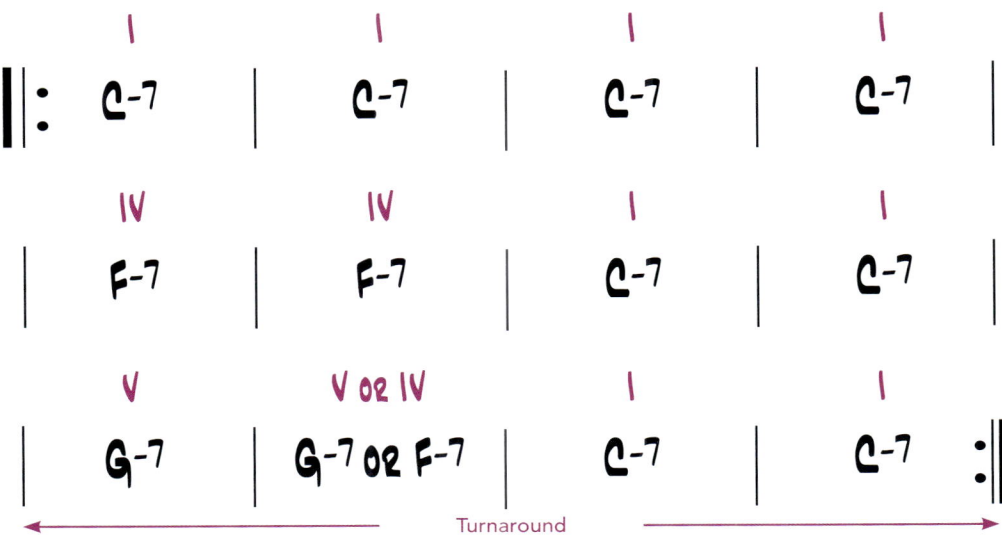

C minor 12-bar blues

■ Particularity of the minor blues

The main difference between the major and the minor blues is that the minor blues makes tonal sense. Indeed, if you look at a C minor blues for example, you notice that all the chords of the blues progression actually belong to the harmonization of the C natural minor scale.

This means that you can technically get away with playing the Aeolian mode or natural minor scale over the full minor blues progression. And it works really well! But again, you don't have to! For example, it's common to still hear a major 3rd as a passing note here and there, and very common to use the Dorian mode and blues scale on the I7 chord.

Degrees	1	2	b3	4	5	b6	b7
Tetrads	I-7	II-7(b5)	bIIIMAJ7	IV-7	V-7	bVIMAJ7	bVII7
Fuction	T	S.D	T	S.D	/	S.D	D

Improvisation guides

It's very challenging to give a guide on how to best improvise over the 12-bar blues. Considering that for each chord played you can technically play a combination of 10 different scales, things can get tricky. Moreover, as we previously discussed, blues can be appoached in many different ways depending on the type of blues and the player's personal preferences. There is a lot of feeling and playing by ear involed in blues.

Thankfully, you can always **default to the minor blues scale in any blues situation**. And you can always add notes to this scale to add more color if you are comfortable doing so. So the easiest improvisation guide in any blues, major or minor is the following:

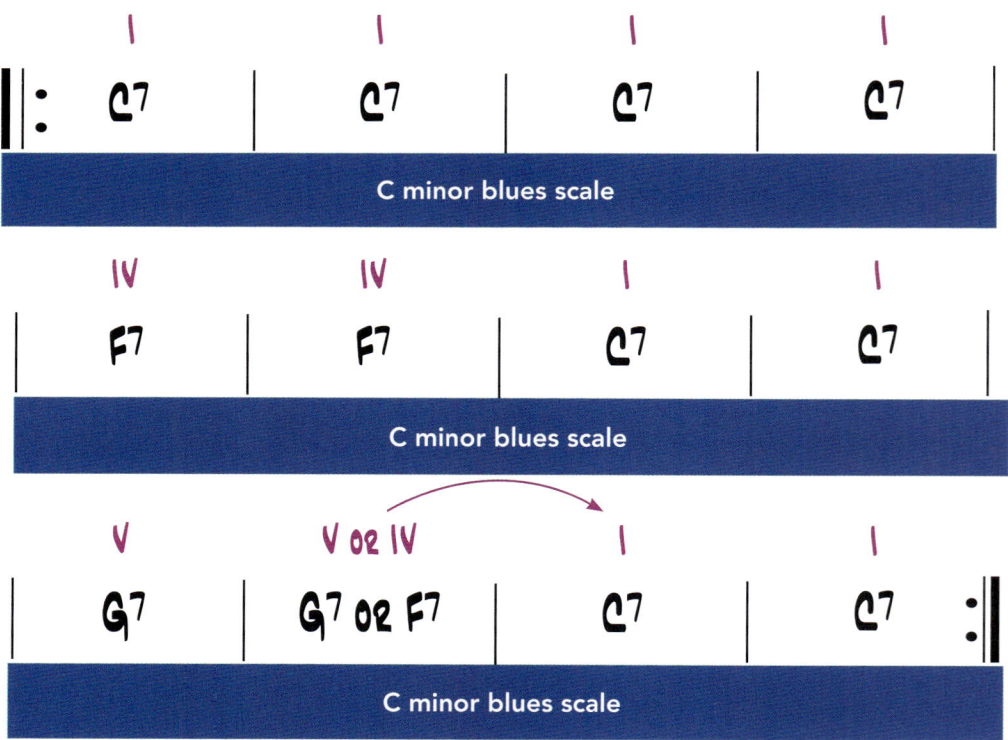

C major 12-bar blues

THE BLUES

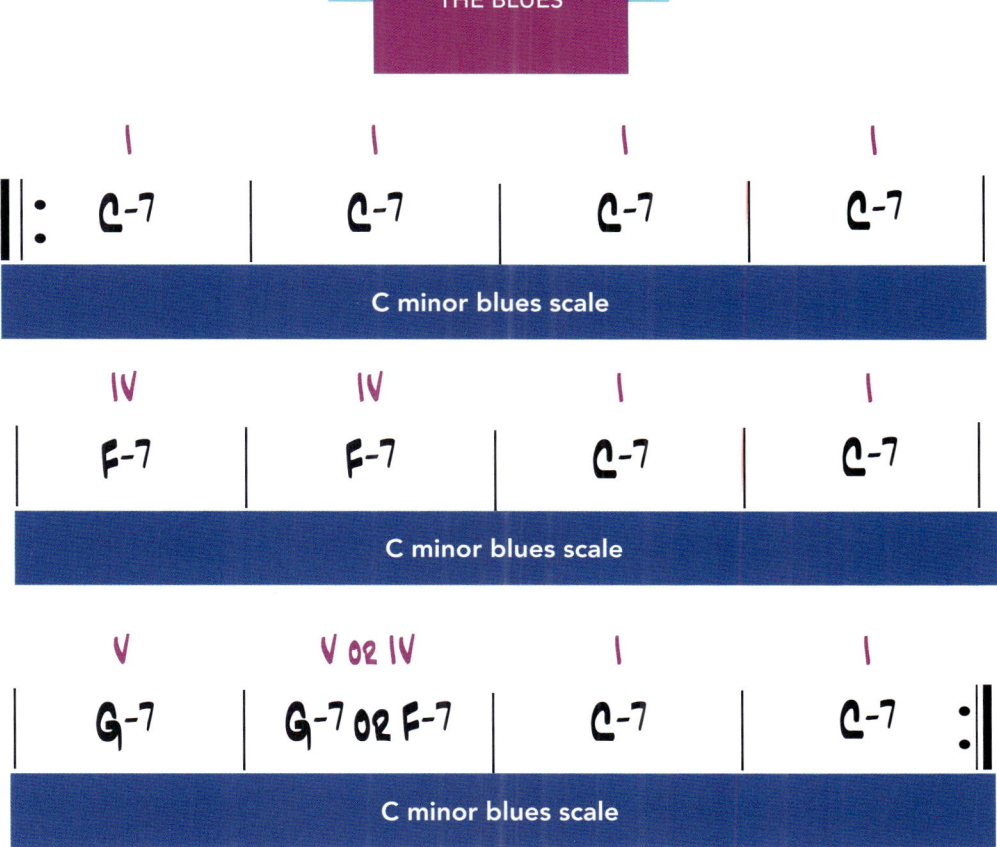

C minor 12-bar blues

Again, it's not surprising in a minor blues that the C minor blues scale can work over the whole progression, since a C minor 12-bar blues progression essentially puts you in a C minor key. But as to why this scale works over the three different dominant chords that make the major blues progression is a little bit mysterious, honestly. It can be very hard to make sense of blues the same way we have been analyzing tonal and even modal music before. So just take it as a given. Try it out! You will see that it works.

But even though the minor blues scale works the whole time, there are more pertinent and a little more advanced ways to improvice coherently over a major or minor 12-bar blues. Here are the guides that work the best in my opinion:

THE BLUES

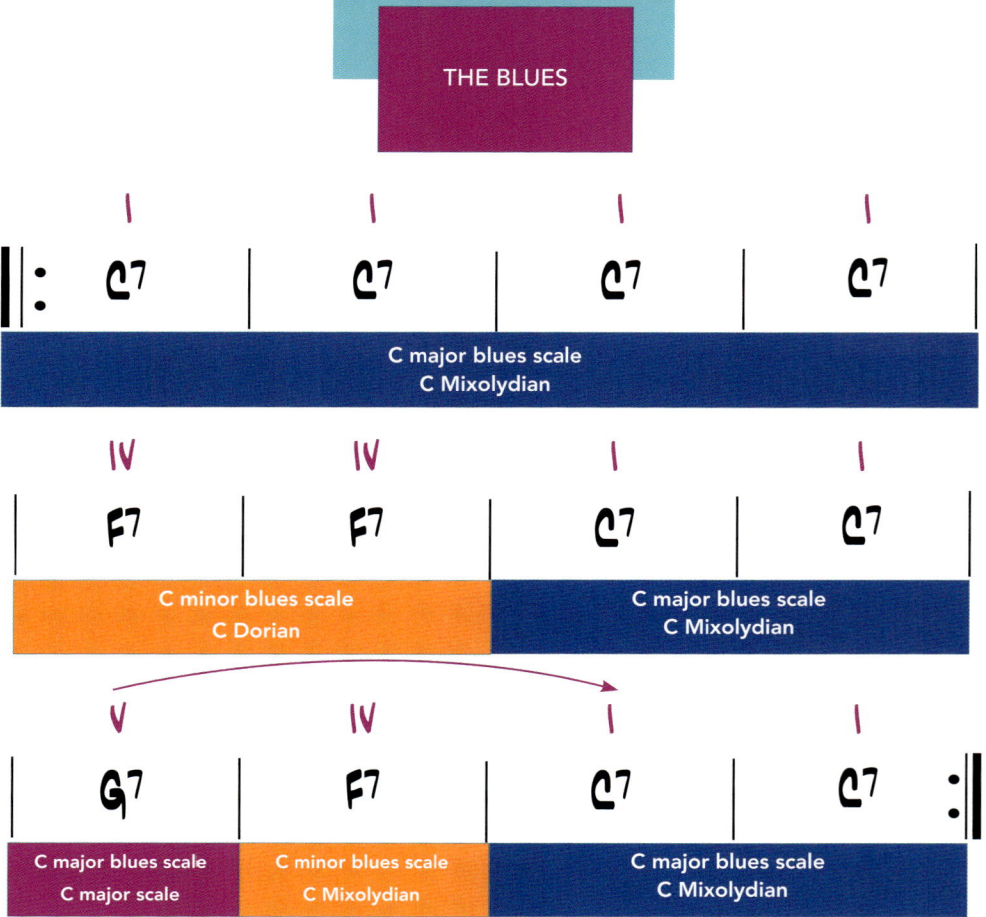

C major 12-bar blues

Notice that I think of C as the reference note over the whole progression to make things easier.

Using the major blues scale over the I7 chord is slightly more consonant than the minor blues scale since it includes the major 3rd of the chord. It therefore sounds a little more coherent.

On the IV chord, the C minor blues scale works very well, as well as the C Dorian mode, which has the same notes as the **F Mixolydian scale.** Technically, since the IV chord is an F7 chord, F Mixolydian will be the mode heard, but it doesn't mean you can't think of C Dorian instead to avoid switching reference notes.

The V chord is commonly seen as the dominant chord of C7, which temporarily puts us in the context of C major, which is equivalent to G Mixolydian. Therefore, the C major blues scale or pentatonic will work, as well as the C major scale or G Mixolydian.

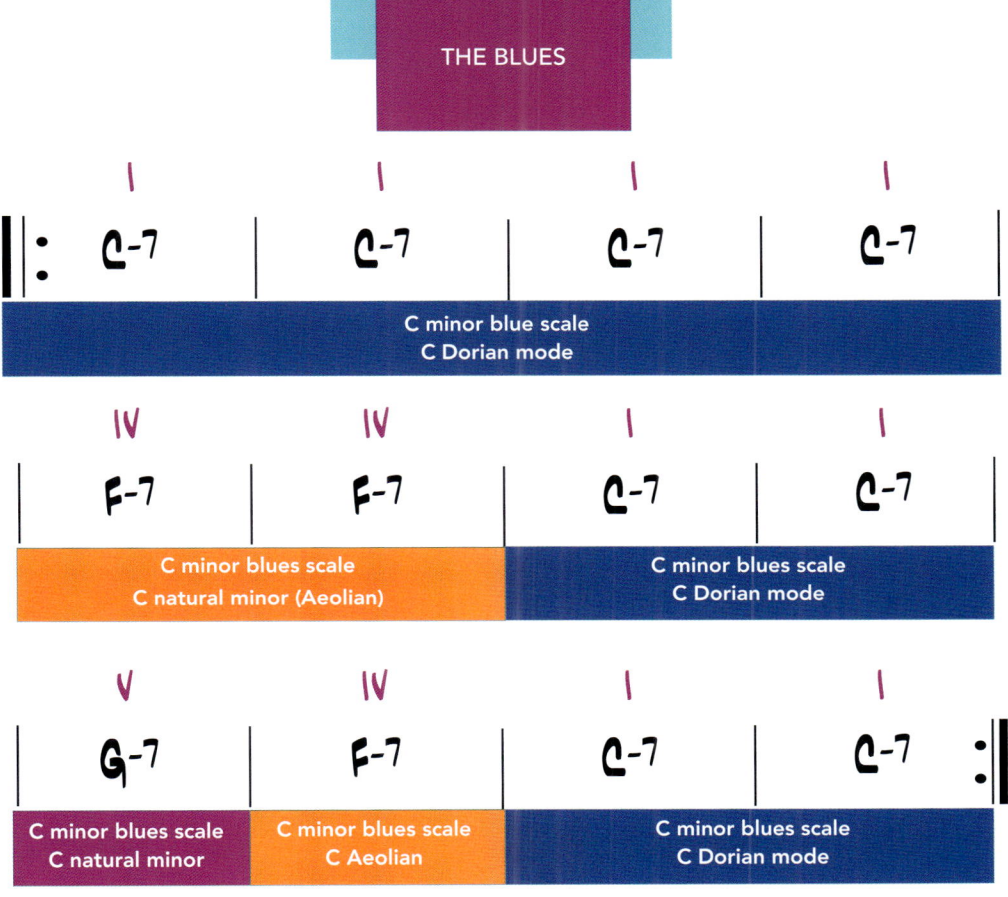

C minor 12-bar blues

Common variations of the standard 12-bar blues

There are countless variations of the standard 12-bar blues and most of these variations are simply the result of using the substitutions, secondary dominants, and progressions that are available in tonal harmony. This is now possible since we just added a tonal dimension and chord functions within the Blues. Obviously, each chord substitution or addition will also expand or change our melodic options, so pay close attention to the improvisation guide each time. Let's take a look at how we can enrich and modify our standard 12-bar blues!

THE BLUES

■ The "quick four"

The quick four is probably the most common variation of the standard 12-bar blues. A quick four refers to replacing the I chord in the second bar with the IV chord, thereby adding extra harmonic movement.

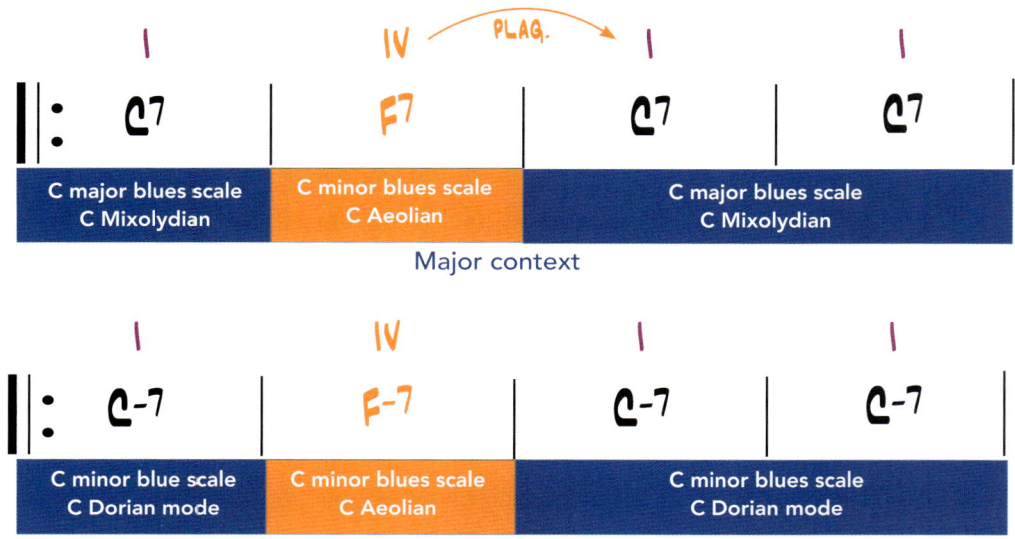

■ "Altered" dominant at the end of the turnaround

A very common addition to a standard turnaround is to play the V7 (whether in major or minor) in order to create a cadence resolving on the I chord (I7 or I-7) at the beginning of the tune. In this case, the goal of this secondary dominant is to add tension, so it will often be considered "altered." The only reason I put the word altered between quotes is because in this situation, it doesn't mean that ALL the extensions that make an altered chord must be present (#9, b9, #11, b13). It means that you CAN technically add any combination of extensions.

Just extend the chord as little or as much as you want, as long as you get the sound you want. The scale or mode you will play over this chord will depend on the extensions you choose, so make sure you study the previous chapter.

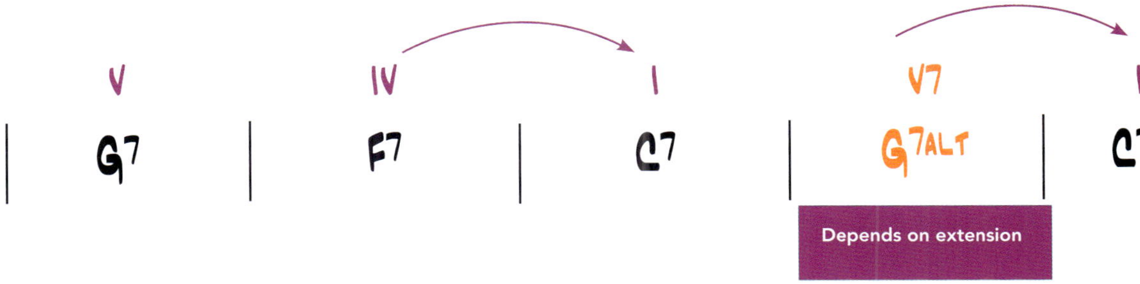

V
IV
I
V7
I
G7
F7
C7
G7ALT
C7
Depends on extension

Major context

V
IV
I
V7
I
G-7
F-7
C-7
G7ALT
C7
Depends on extension

Minor context

Altered dominant moving towards the IV

On the fourth bar, the I7 can be seen as a secondary dominant chord resolving on the IV7. In this case, it is common to make this chord "altered" to add more tensions. Just like above, this does not mean that the chord has to be fully altered per se; in this case it just means: create tension with the extensions you want.

I
I
I
V7/IV
C7
C7
C7
C7ALT
C major blues scale
C Mixolydian
Depends on extension
IV
IV
I
I
F7
F7
C7
C7
C minor blues scale
C Dorian
C major blues scale
C Mixolydian

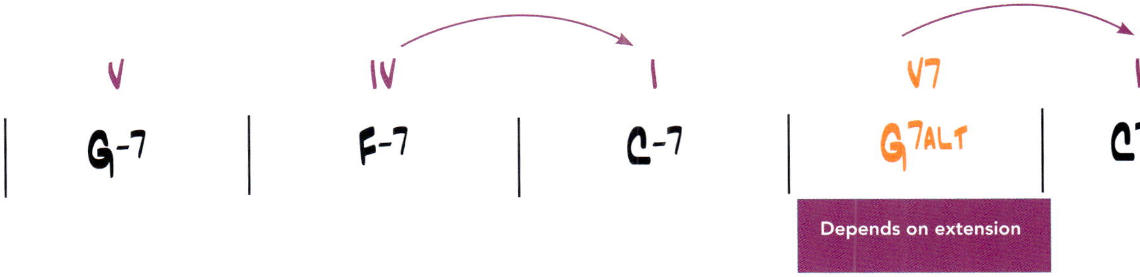

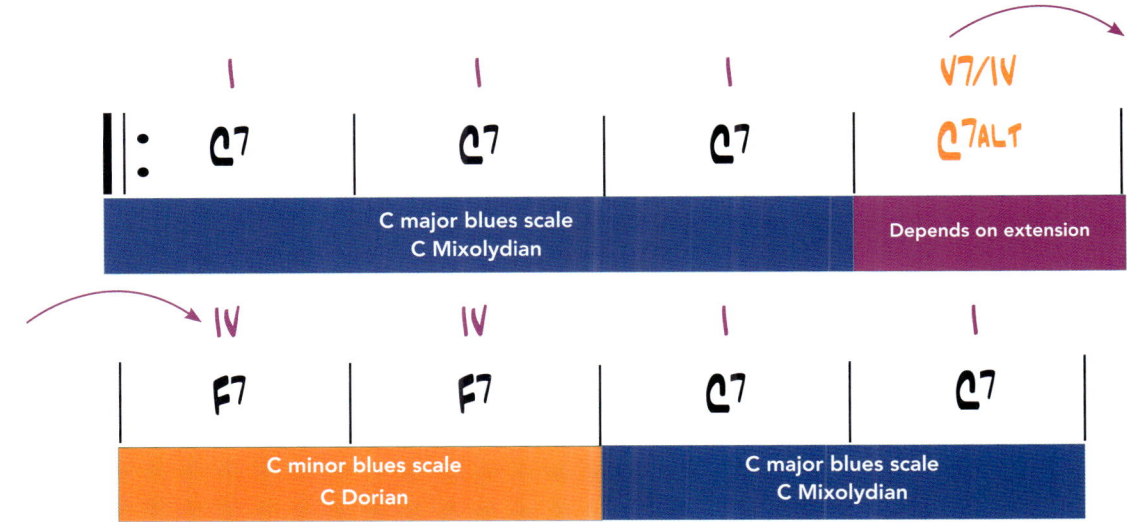

Major context

THE BLUES

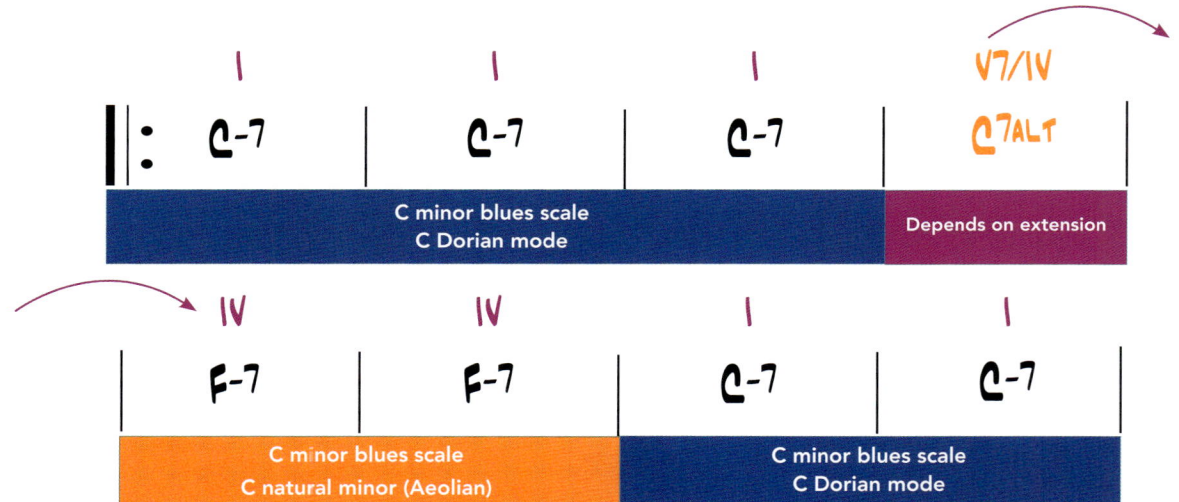

Minor context

■ Dominant moving back to I on bar 10

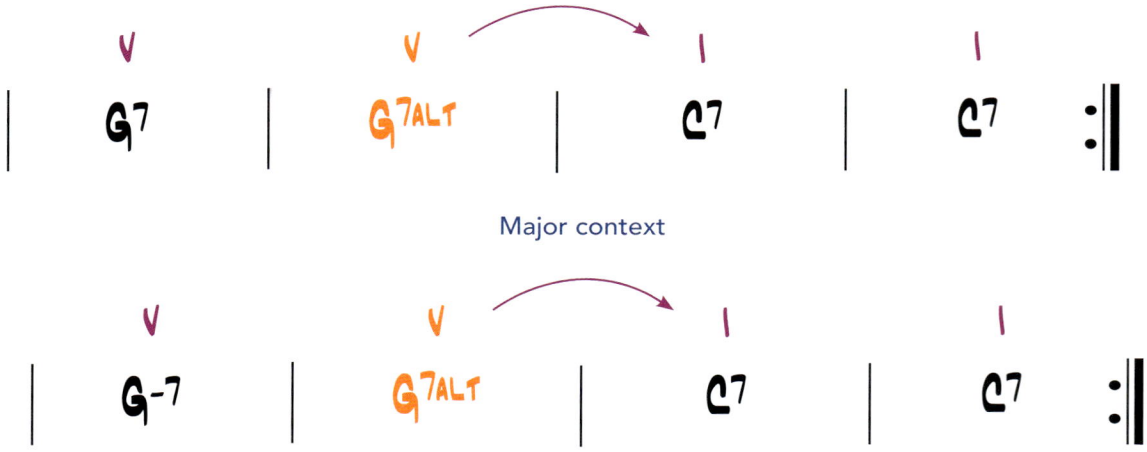

Major context

minor context

THE BLUES

■ Passing diminished chord on bar 6 in major 12-bar blues

This variation of the standard major 12-bar blues is definitely more used in jazz-influenced blues. This passing diminished chord is generated by moving the bass up from the 4 on bar 5 to the #4 (blue note) on bar 6. This adds extra harmonic movements and tension to a regular blues. Improvisation-wise, the C minor blues scale works very well, as well as a good old fashion F# arpeggio. Even though you should know by now that arpeggios always work when it comes to improvising, I find it useful to point it out here since it is particulary common and efficient.

Major context

■ Common secondary dominant chords and cadences

So what can you do when you add secondary dominant chords to a chord progression? That's right! You can add secondary subdominant chords to complete the cadences.

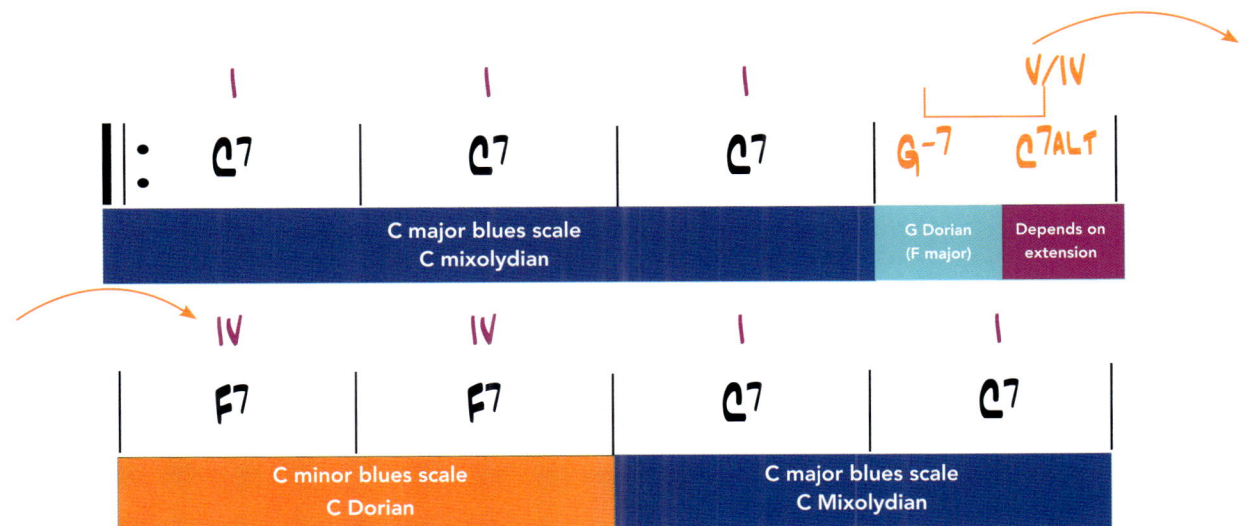

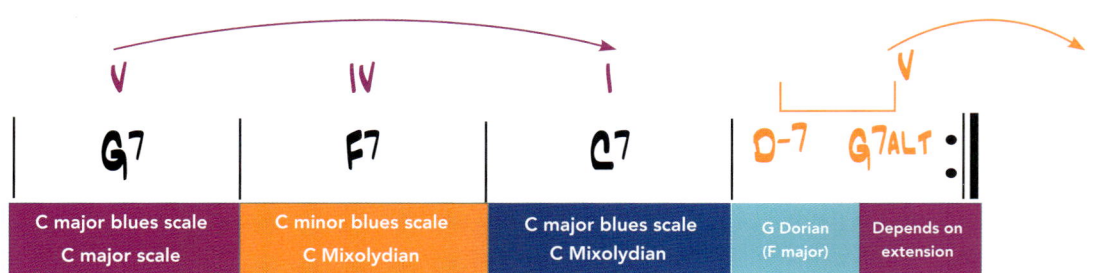

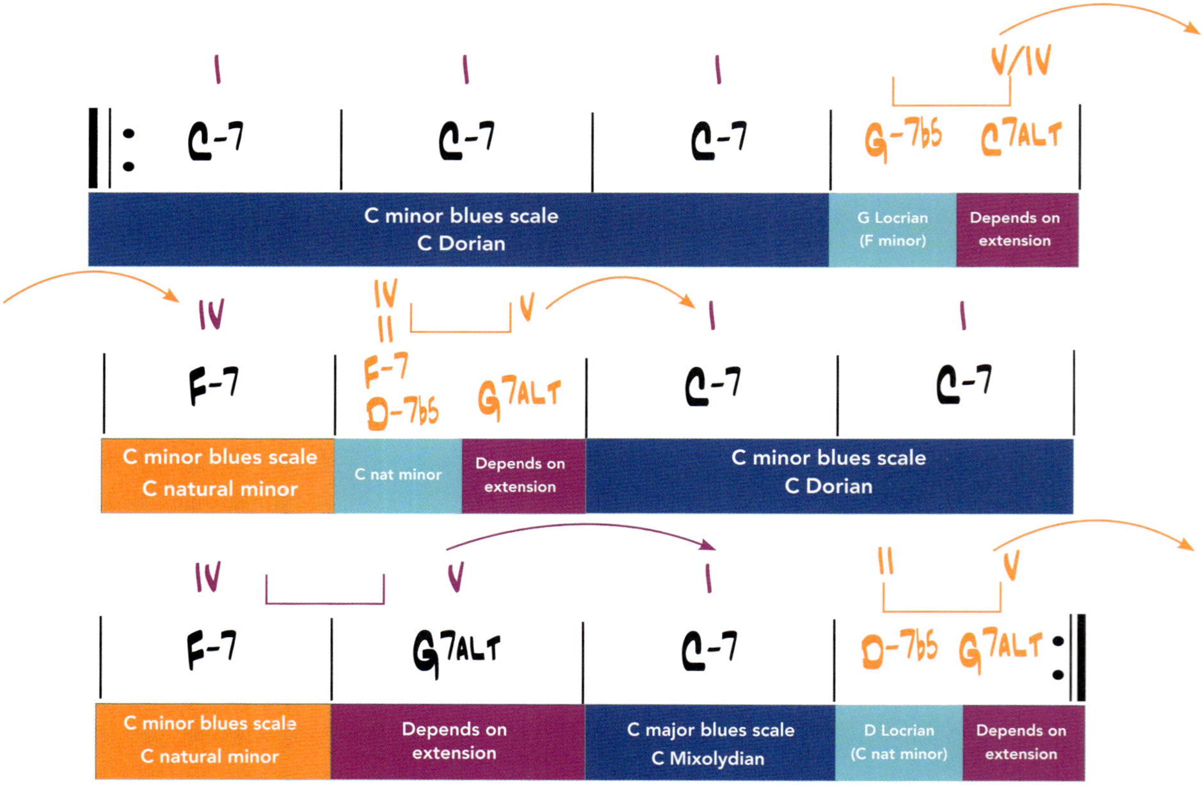

THE BLUES

■ Secondary cadences using tritone substitutions

Even though any the of the secondary cadences and dominant chords seen above can be replaced by a tritone substitution, the most common use of a tritone subsitution is found in the minor blues on bar 9.

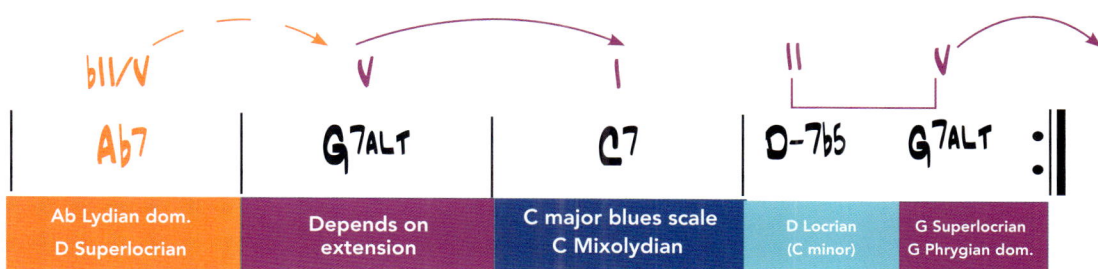

■ The most complex type of blues: the jazz blues

When there is an opportunity to make things complicated, you can always count on jazz musicians to take advantage of it and make things as complex as they can possibly be. The jazz version of the 12-bar blues is the result of what happens when you add as many secondary progressions as you can to a cute and simple three-chord blues.

Improvising over a jazz blues can be extreemly challenging. Considering all the options available over each dominant chord, it's very complicated to give a single improvisation guide. Fortunately, if you listen to enough jazz blues tunes and to how the masters of jazz navigate these chord progression, you can find some patterns of improvisation. I am going to give you what, according to me, seems to be the most standard way of improvising over a major and minor jazz blues. But feel free to explore more options!

Without further ado:

THE BLUES

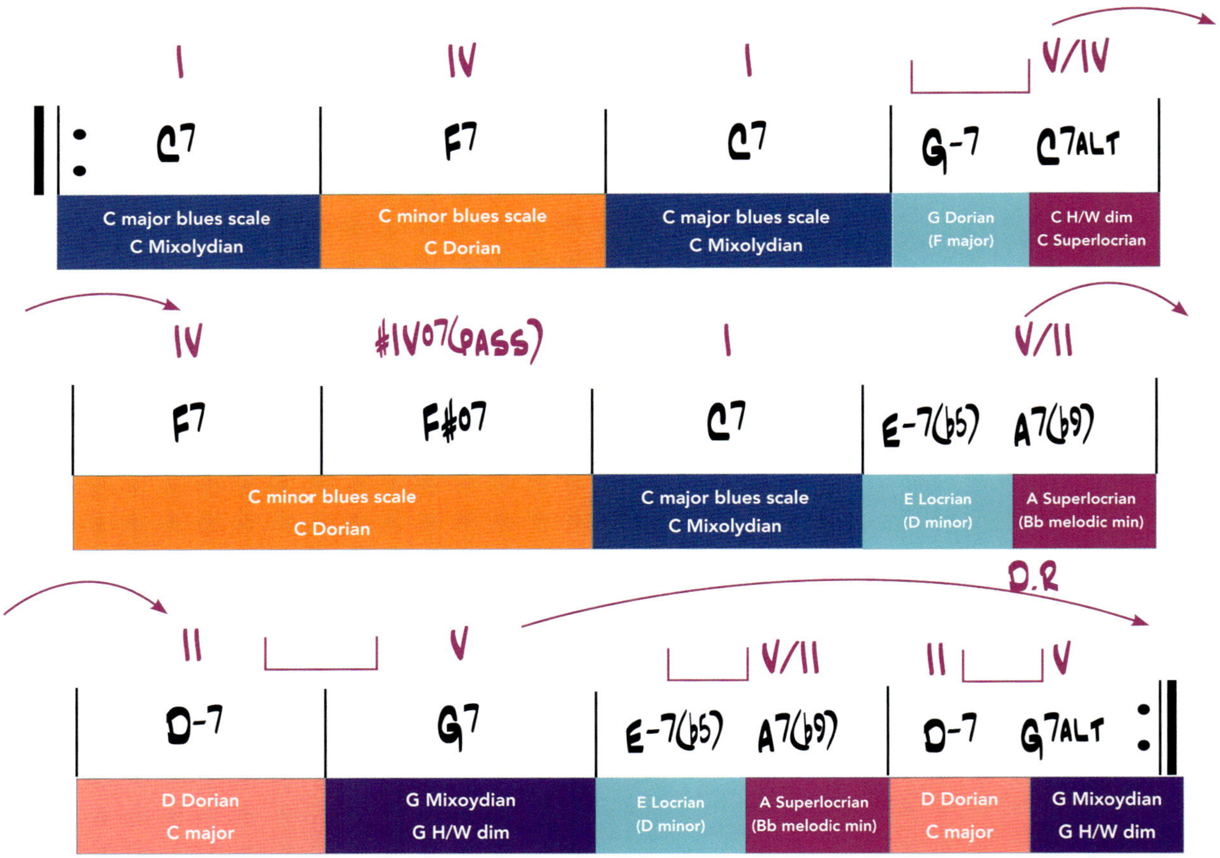

I	IV	I		V/IV
C7	F7	C7	G-7	C7ALT
C major blues scale / C Mixolydian	C minor blues scale / C Dorian	C major blues scale / C Mixolydian	G Dorian (F major)	C H/W dim / C Superlocrian

IV	#IVo7 (PASS)	I		V/II
F7	F#o7	C7	E-7(b5)	A7(b9)
C minor blues scale / C Dorian		C major blues scale / C Mixolydian	E Locrian (D minor)	A Superlocrian (Bb melodic min)

II	V		V/II	II	V
D-7	G7	E-7(b5)	A7(b9)	D-7	G7ALT
D Dorian / C major	G Mixoydian / G H/W dim	E Locrian (D minor)	A Superlocrian (Bb melodic min)	D Dorian / C major	G Mixoydian / G H/W dim

C major jazz blues

Well, great! Thanks, jazz… Look what you've done. It was so pure, so modal, so simple. Why did you have to add a bunch of chords and make me feel like I have no skills again? I want to make this clear: I love jazz. But sometimes I understand why it might annoy some musicians. Oh, and did I mention that unlike traditional blues, which tends to be pretty slow, jazz musicians tend to boost the tempo of blues to… say… 250 BPM?!! Just listen to "Billie's Bounce" for example. Anyways, this just takes a lot of practice and a lot of listening! It also takes a particular interest or even passion for jazz to find the patience to practice this.

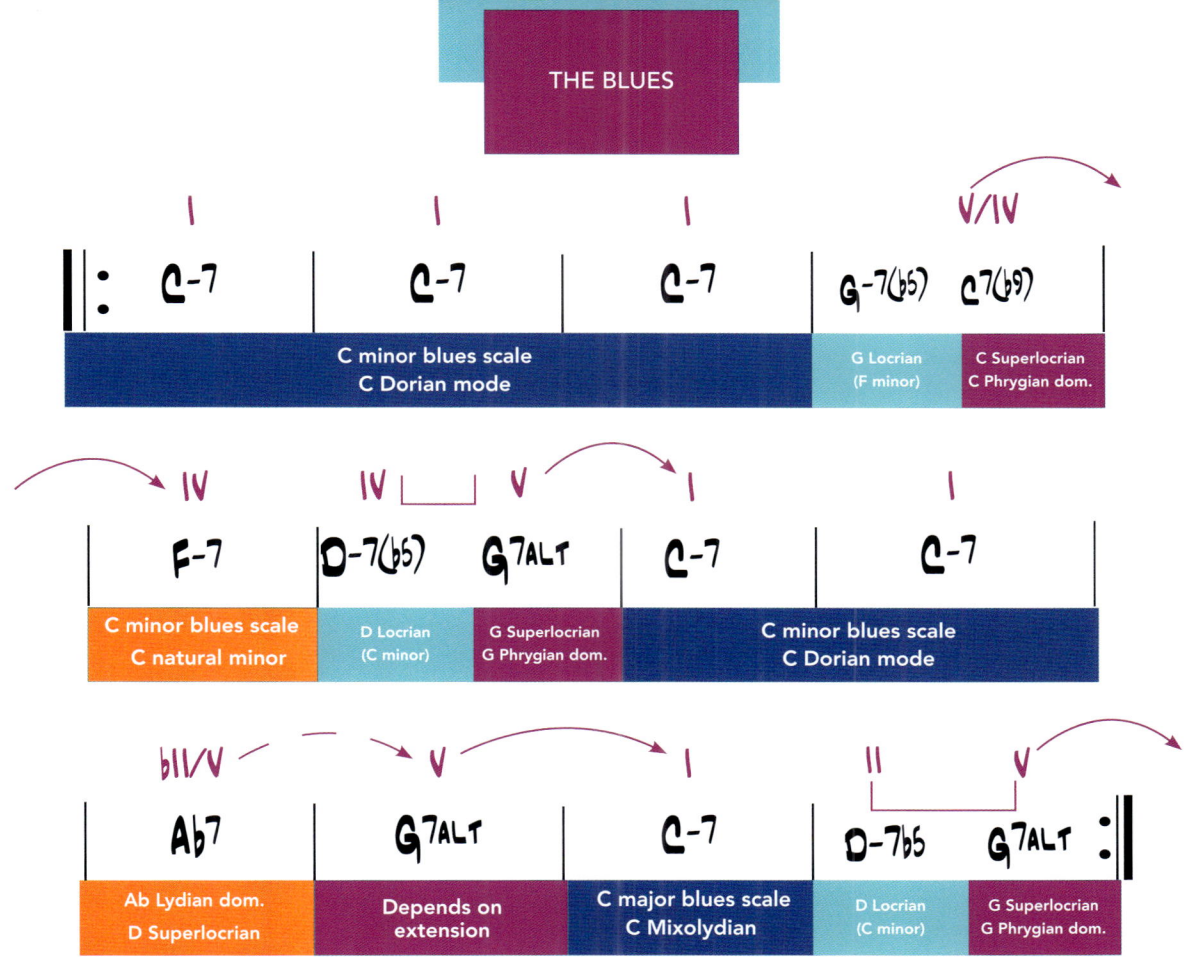

C minor jazz blues

Conclusion on blues

Blues is so different, fascinating, simple and yet potentially complex, and I could go on for many more pages about all the subtleties, variations, and different ways to approach it. However, I believe that if you understand what we've just studied, you will already have a very solid understanding of this unique style. At the very least, I hope you realize that it is NOT as simple as it seems. Sure, you can stick to the minor blues scale and the pentatonic scale and sound decent, but it goes way beyond that. First of all, if you want to sound good on a blues, you will have to work on your tone. The way you bend, trill, slide, and approach each note in general is VERY important when it comes to blues. Remember where this style comes from! There is passion and emotion in blues. Without these elements, you can play all the fanciest scales you want, it simply won't sound like blues. If you add all the harmonic possibilities and substitutions to the mix, you can create countless interpretations of the same basic blues. According to me, it takes a lifetime to truly explore and perfect the blues.

THE BLUES

Again, there is a perfect cooking metaphor for all of this: the omelette. What can possibly be simpler than an omelette, right? Eggs in a pan, that's it. And yet to this day, as the French chef Jacques Pépin said, "Anytime I want to assess the skills and experience of a chef, I ask him to make an omelette." Because simple as it may seem, making a REALLY GOOD omelette is actually very difficult. It's easy to make AN omelette, but making the perfect omelette takes a lot of experience and skills.

Well, there you go, blues is like the omelette of music: it's simple to play a blues, but to play a great blues, it takes a lot of skills in theory, feeling, touch, ear, and all the other musical skills you can think of. So if you want to judge a musician, don't ask him to make an omelette, but ask him to play a blues.

4

The Tonal Context

MODAL MIXTURE AND MODULATIONS

Minor borrowings and minor/major cadences

As we have seen before, dominant chords can resolve on minor or major chords equally well. This means that in a cadence, the tension chord (or suspension in the case of a plagal cadence) constitutes a perfect opportunity to trick and surprise the listener by resolving on a minor chord when you expect a major one and vice versa.

You can also use the extension on the dominant chord that should normally indicate a resolution on a minor chord for example, and resolve on a major chord instead. We have already seen this when using, for example, a seventh degree diminished chord (dominant) to resolve on the first degree major chord.

Let's see some other examples:

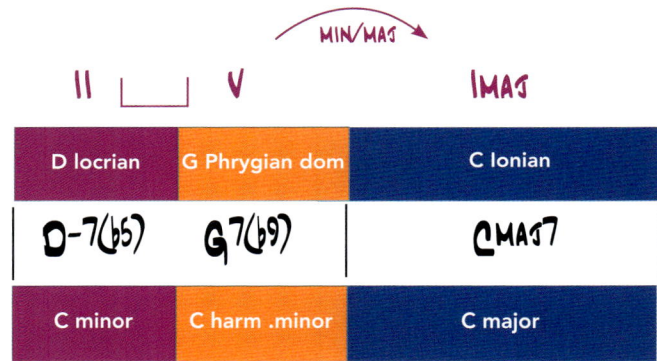

Here, the first bar should clearly indicate a minor cadence but resolves on a major chord instead.

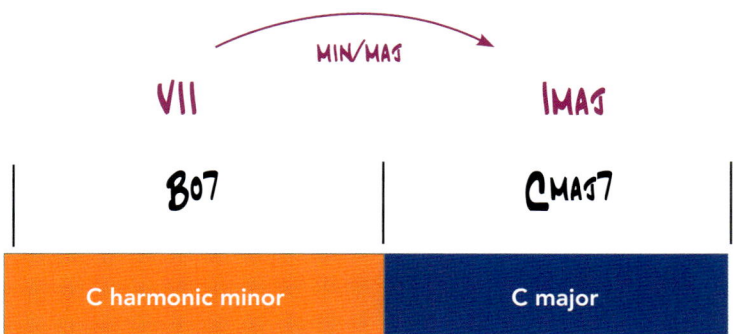

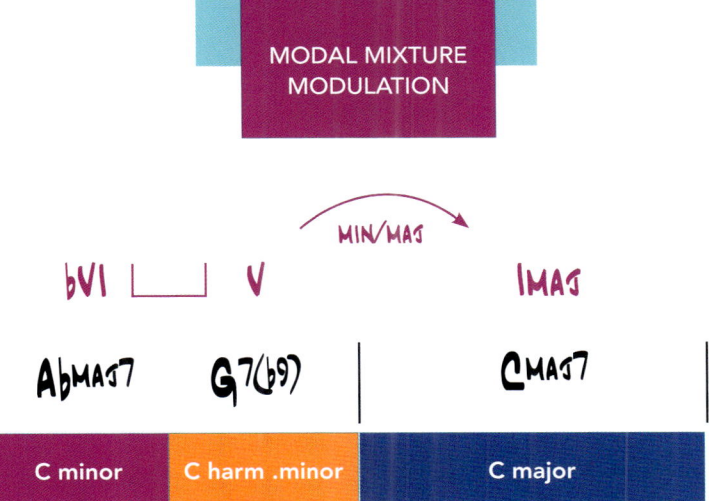

This is the case we've studied before where the diminished chord should resolve on a minor chord but resolves on a major chord instead.

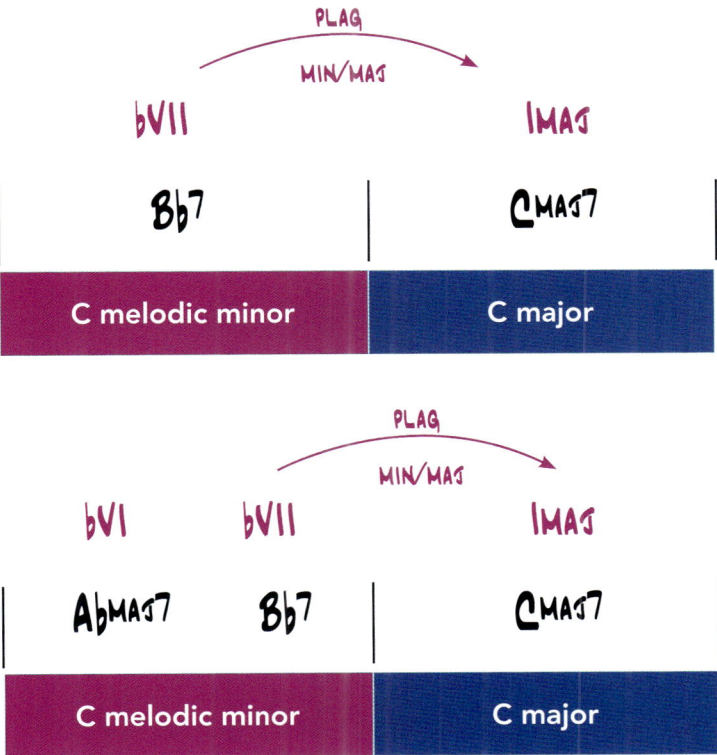

A bVII to I- progression is a common minor plagal progression which here, instead, resolves on the I major chord.

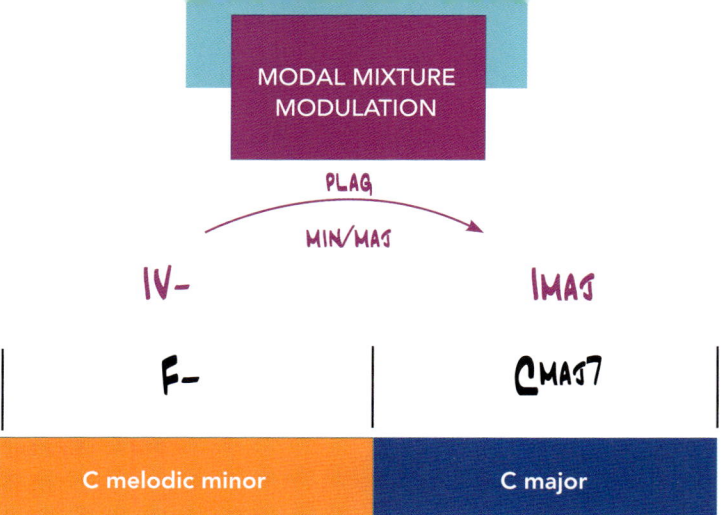

In the case of a minor/major plagal cadence, it is common to borrow from the first degree melodic minor scale, simply because it has more notes in common with the original major key.

Question: Can you also have major/minor cadence, which means that the borrowing goes the other way around? Namely, you are in a minor context and some cadences and chords are borrowed from the major key. Yes you can! But it isn't as common. For some reason, minor/major cadences have more impact.

Other common modal mixtures

Once again, a modal mixture or modal borrowing simply consists in temporarily seeing a chord in a tonal context, as a static modal context. The possibilities are therefore endless! But here are some common modal borrowings.

■ Dorian modal borrowing

In a minor context, it is very common to borrow the first degree tonic chord from the Dorian mode.

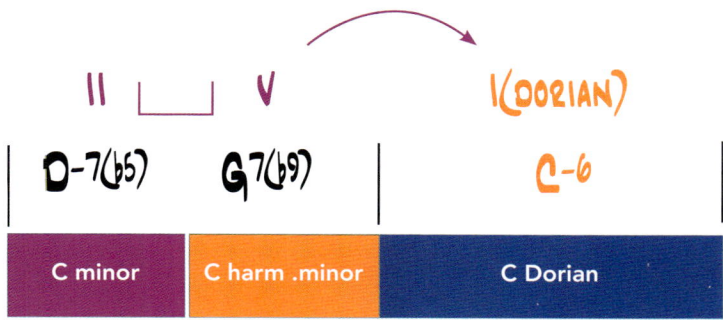

MODAL MIXTURE MODULATION

It turns out that the Dorian mode is a very stable minor mode, perhaps even more so than the natural minor scale. Its major 6th is rather soothing and more consonant than the minor 6th. The Dorian mode is strongly implied when a major 6th extension is added to the C- (C-6). Again, without any specifications, it's up to the improviser or composer to decide how to interpret the minor tonic chord.

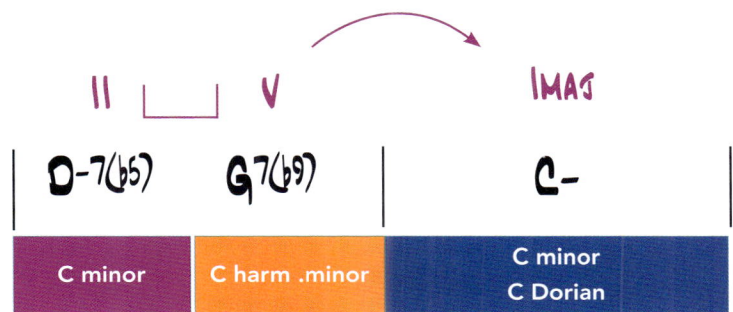

■ Melodic or harmonic minor modal borrowing

Another common modal borrowing is to use the melodic minor or harmonic minor scale in place of the natural minor or Dorian mode on the I chord of a minor key. This will add some tension and unique color notes, so make sure you know what you are doing before using this modal mixture. It won't work in every genre and context.

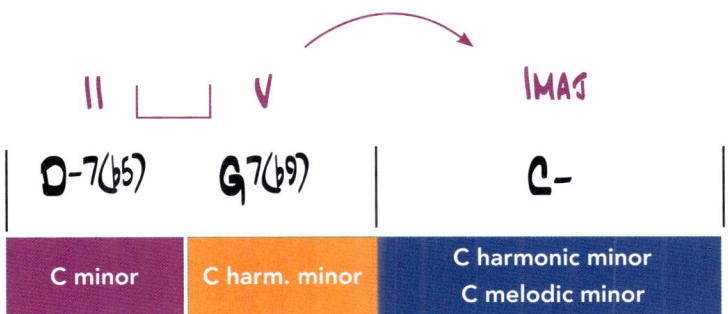

■ Lydian modal borrowing

In a major context, it is quite common to use the Lydian mode on the I chord. Indeed, the first degree chord of the harmonization of the Lydian mode is also a major 7th tetrad, which makes the major scale and the Ionian mode interchangeable. The only difference between these two scales is the nature of the 4th, which is perfect in the major scale and augmented in the Lydian mode.

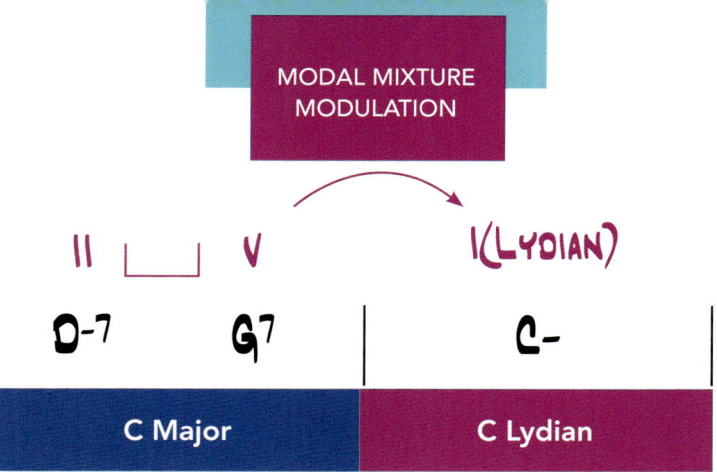

Back to square one…

Let's stop a second and reflect on all that we've seen. First, we started with modal contexts where the harmonic progressions were rather simple, but the melodic possibilities where more complex. Then, as the harmonic context got more complicated, the tonal interpretation of these chord progressions allowed us to, in a way, "unify" these chords within one single key. This allowed us to use a single scale to improvise over many different chords. And if things had stopped there, life would be pretty easy…

But now what do we have? Substitutions, borrowings, interchanges, tonal ambiguities between major and minor, and many other tricks that slowly but surely seem to bring us back to a point where each chord can be analyzed as, well… a context of its own! Did we really get back to the point where we were trying to avoid using the tonal context?

I mean, look at the chord progression above. Three chords and three different scales (one on each chord). What the heck?

Don't worry! Before you get discouraged, please keep the following things in mind:

1. **Just because all those tricks and mechanisms exist, it doesn't mean you should use them all the time! By understanding those mechanisms, you are broadening your spectrum of options! Again, this is a principle that always proves useful in music (and in life in general): just because you can, it doesn't mean you should.**

2. **The musical contexts and genres that allow you to use all the substitutions and borrowings and secondary progressions, etc., are rather limited! In jazz, you can for sure (and then again not excessively), in progressive rock and metal sometimes, but don't try to interpret a dominant chord as an opportunity to play Superlocrian if you are at a bluegrass jam or in a pop set.**

3. If you are in a tonal context, you ought to think "tonally" and please stick to the key scale as much as you need. And once you start understanding and hearing some particular modal colors or substitutions you could use, do it tastefully. There is a beauty in not taking every opportunity to complicate everything, technically OR harmonically.

And this last point is actually a perfect transition to what follows.

Improvisation in a tonal context with modal mixtures

When you are improvising in a tonal context that includes modulations, you should always keep in mind the bank of notes of the key of origin. And remember, the most consonant modulation, when you have several options, will always be the one that limits the number of notes that change.

 So when you encounter a modulation, the best thing to do is to focus on what note or notes change from the key of origin.

In a well-composed piece of music, most modulations will only change one or two notes.

Example:

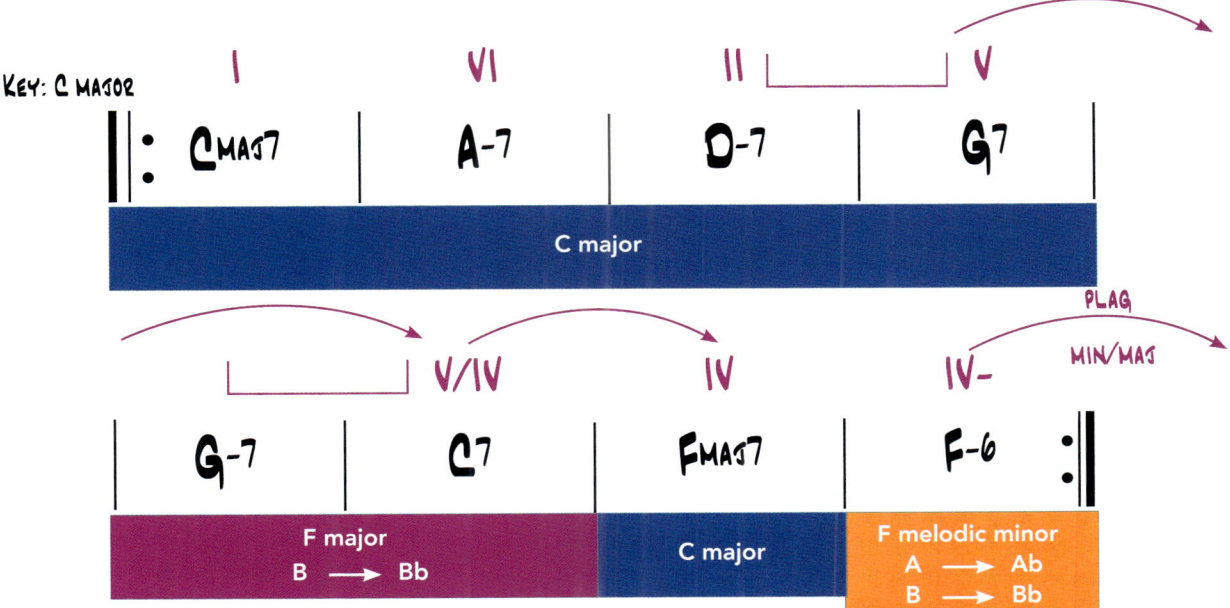

MODAL MIXTURE MODULATION

Notice that in the example above, the G-7 to C7 is a secondary cadence that resolves on the Fmaj7 (the IV chord in C major). This modulation is too short here to be considered an actual modulation per se, so it will simply be called a modal interchange (to the neighbor key of F major). Still, yet, when it comes to improvising, you are more than welcome to "think F major." Actual modulations are what we are just about to discuss.

Modulations

This is the LAST CASE that we really haven't studied, but knowing everything else, it will be very easy for you to understand. It's more a question of notations.

 **If you encounter a prolonged (usually four harmonic beats or more) of definitive change of key, you will actually reset the tonal center to the new key (this can be done by a change of tonic of major/minor quality, or a modulation to the relative minor key).**

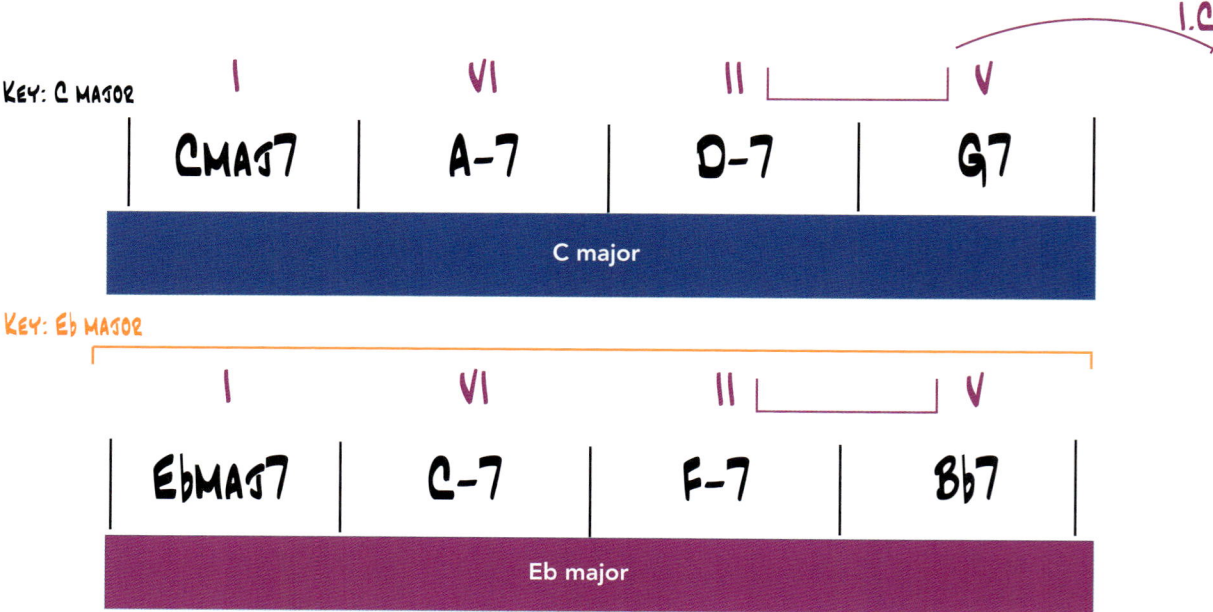

MODAL MIXTURE MODULATION

If you read sheet music, this is typically where you will see a change in key signature.

When it comes to improvisation, actual modulations and simple borrowings can be interpreted in the same way, except that in an actual modulation, you don't have to keep in mind the notes of the key of origin, you can really "reset" to the new key. But other than that, the differences are purely analytical. In both cases, you change the notes you play, basically.

Conclusion

Well, here we are… I think you are now ready! Everything we studied is much more than enough for you to analyze any music piece and thereby, create melodies in any harmonic context. Now obviously, there is much more to learn, potentially. But with this basis in harmonic analysis, you are ready to understand any new piece of information that could come your way. Also keep in mind the golden rule, which is that at the end of the day, what counts is the way it sounds to you and your listeners. My challenge was to educate you in understanding how harmony is to be analyzed for you to know all your options and choose the one that you deem most appropriate.

Now it's up to you to practice, listen, experiment, fail, and try again… Understanding everything we just covered is actually quite simple, but mastering it is the work of a lifetime. But by simply understanding, you will always be able to use your analyzing skills to dissect any complicated piece of music, practice it, experiment with your options, and find the one(s) you prefer.

This is a good guideline to remember:

1. **Analyze as many pieces of music you can, especially jazz tunes (because they are the most complex).**

2. Once you are done, and thereby know all your melodic options, try to improvise using all of these options just to try them all out.

3. Pick the ones you think sound the best and practice these more.

4. Try to improvise "by ear," and if you find something that sounds good, analyze what it is! You will most likely find out that you naturally use tools that are logical and will be part of the options that harmonic analysis suggests.

MODAL MIXTURE MODULATION

5. Always SING WHAT YOU PLAY.

So to finish this book, I will guide you through the analysis of four pieces of music that cover a lot of situations that you might encounter. This book will come with an exercise book full of analyzed tunes to allow you to practice more.

5

Harmonic Analysis & Case Studies

STANDARD MAJOR CHART

STANDARD MAJOR CHART

So you go to a jazz bar and someone gives you the following chart:

All Of Me
(Medium Swing) — Gerald Marks

A
| $\frac{4}{4}$ $C_{\Delta7}$ | ⁄. | E_7 | ⁄. |
| A_7 | ⁄. | D_{-7} | ⁄. ‖

B
| E_7 | ⁄. | A_{-7} | ⁄. |
| D_7 | ⁄. | D_{-7} | G_7 ‖

A
| $C_{\Delta7}$ | ⁄. | E_7 | ⁄. |
| A_7 | ⁄. | D_{-7} | ⁄. |

C
| $F_{\Delta7}$ | $F^\#_{o7}$ F_{-6} | $C_{\Delta7}/G$ E_{-7} | A_7 |
| D_{-7} | G_7 | C_6 $E^\flat_{o7}$ | D_{-7} G_7 ‖

Now they may also give you the chart as a lead sheet, with the melody underneath, but don't panic. Just ignore the staff and focus on the chords!!

278

STANDARD MAJOR CHART

So you go to a jazz bar and someone gives you the following chart:

Since you are not good at improvising yet, you fail quite miserably but then go home and decide: NEVER AGAIN! You decide to analyze this music.

1 - Harmonic rhythm

Some people overlook this step, but it is very important. You MUST start by looking at the harmonic rhythm. This means: How many chords are there per bar? Is the rhythm stable? Is it the same throughout the tune?

In this tune, you will notice that you have one chord per bar, except for the two last bars which don't really count as they constitute a turnaround (I will explain that later). We can therefore determine the weak and strong harmonic beats.

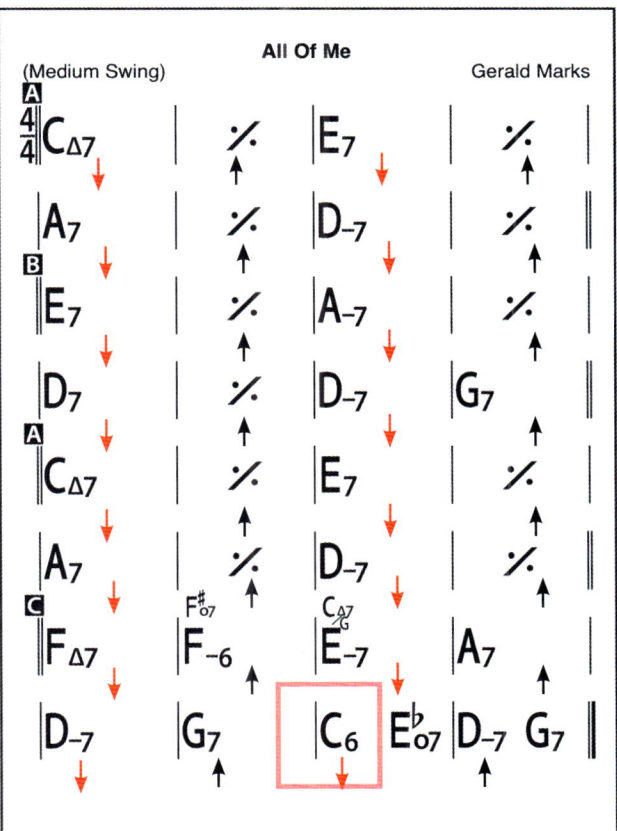

STANDARD MAJOR CHART

■ Changes in harmonic rhythm

There is, as we noticed, a punctual change in harmonic rhythm in the last two bars the this tune. It turns out that these two bars constitute a turnaround. Indeed, a chart like this one, unless otherwise indicated, is meant to be played in circles as many times as the musicians wish.

Most of the time, the first time through, the melody or head will be played, followed by many series of improvisations over the whole form. And just like in blues, it is customary to clearly indicate the end of the form or end of one circle by using a clear chord progression ending on a dominant chord on a weak beat which resolves on the I chord at the beginning of the form on a strong beat. Now, why four chords? Why this sudden acceleration in harmonic rhythm? It turns out this chord progression comes from harmonically enriching the following chord progression:

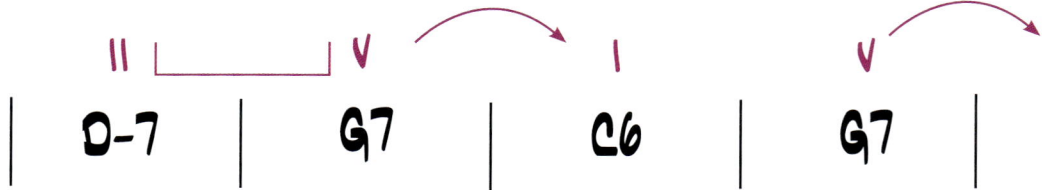

This would make a perfectly acceptable turnaround. But accelerating the harmonic rhythm by adding chords to the last two bars makes the turnaround even stronger!

Let's start by adding a sub-dominant chord on the last bar to complete the cadence. A complete cadence, again, is always stronger.

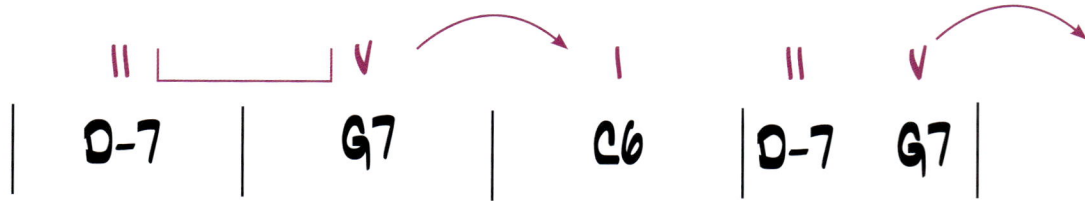

Now, where does that diminished chord come from? Well, there are two options, it can be a secondary dominant borrowed from a minor scale or, if not, a passing chromatic chord. In this case, by analyzing, you would notice that Ebo7 does not resolve on D-7. The VII diminished chord in D minor is C#dim7, and Ebdim7 does not correspond to any of its inversions.

STANDARD MAJOR CHART

So remember:

A jazz chart, unless there is a specific written ending, will not give you a clear indication on when and how to end it. Most of the time, the chart will include a turnaround in place of an ending. The way the tune ends will often be decided on the spot and will most likely be:

- A straight ending.
- An ending preceded by a tag.

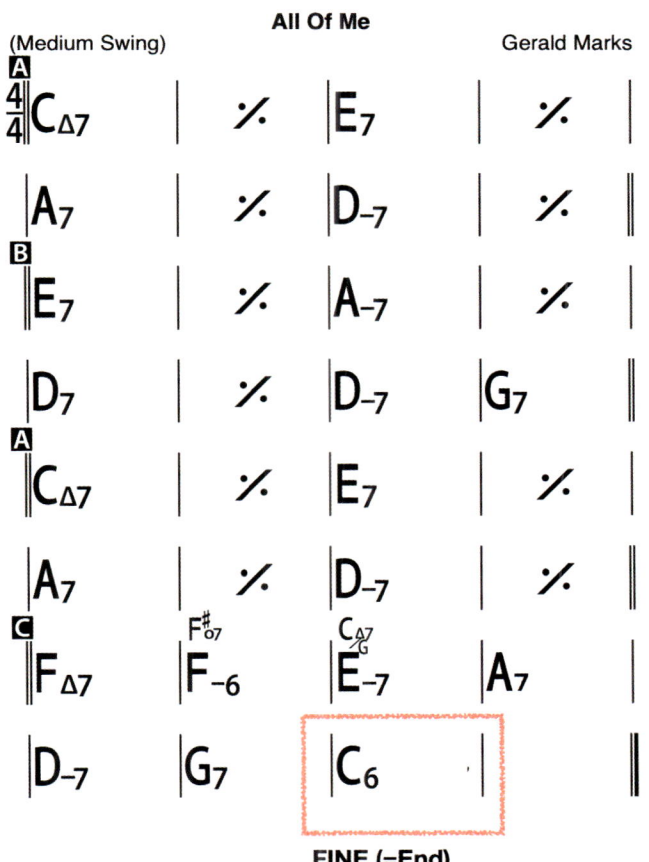

STANDARD MAJOR CHART

2 - The key

There are three indications that will allow you to determine the key of a tune. Usually, it takes at least two of the following points to figure out the key for sure.

1. **The key signature.**
2. **The first bar.**
3. **The last chord and the cadence that precedes it.**

Again, you should ALWAYS compare the results of these three clues to make a conclusion concerning the key.

■ 1. The key signature

The key signature is a clue, but is definitely not the most important one when it comes to determining the key. This is why in a chart that does not include the head, you won't even have a key signature. This is because the two other clues are more important and accurate.

Looking at the lead sheet, there are no flats or sharps in the key signature, which means we are either in C major or in A minor. Remember that these two keys have the same key signature. Now, there is a big difference between these two keys, and this is why the signature is too imprecise for us to make a well-informed decision.

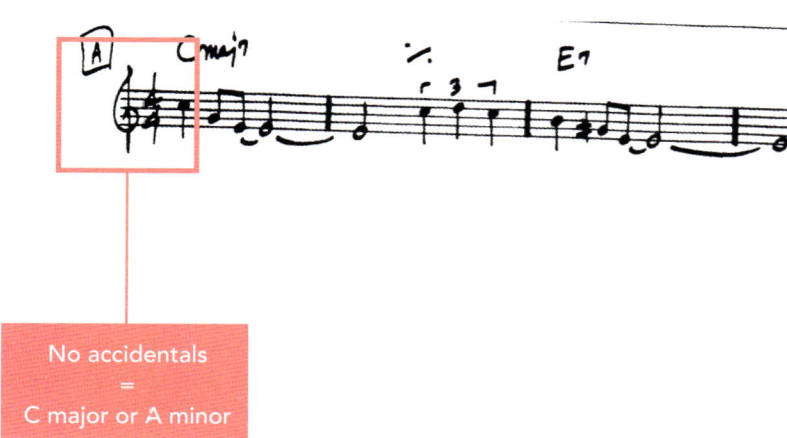

No accidentals
=
C major or A minor

STANDARD MAJOR CHART

■ 2. The most common chord on which authentic cadences resolve

The chord that seems to come back the most as a resolution chord for complete authentic cadences is clearly Cmaj7. This gives a strong indication on the key of the tune.

■ 3. The conclusive chord and conclusive cadence

Well, the last cadence is clearly a nice strong conclusive complete cadence resolving on a C6. Why not Cmaj7? Remember? The C6 is colorful but not as dissonant as a Cmaj7. Moreover, it is not rare to have the melody end on the root note (the C) which would be very dissonant with the B in the Cmaj7.

At this point there are no doubts, the key is **C major.**

If you are unsure, this last cadence will always be the strongest clue.

So you might think, why the heck would we even bother looking at the two first clues? Well, this is because some tunes can get quite tricky when you include potential modulations, interrupted conclusive cadences, and other trickeries.

Let's imagine that the tune modulated at some point to Ebmaj and stayed there for the rest of the time. Then our last conclusive cadence would indicate a key of Ebmaj… So what would be made of this? Well, not much.

Analyzing a piece of music is NOT a linear operation, it's a "layered process" that is best done in reverse, meaning that you start with the last cadence and work your way back to the first chord. Then you read the analysis forward to see if it is coherent. And as you are analyzing you may run into a chord that contradicts your analysis which makes you start again.

3 - Function of the main chords

Now we have an indication of the key of our tune. Since the name of this chapter is Major Chart, it's kind of a spoiler for you, and indeed it turns out this tuns is in C major the whole time. But remember, there could be modulations and modal sections. You don't know until you start analyzing. But having strong clues that point in the direction of C major, we will start analyzing the tune as if it were in C major. At this point, this could change, and when analyzing you must always be willing to change your mind. But this will give us something to start with.

STANDARD MAJOR CHART

Let's look at the harmonization of our C major scale.

Degrees	1	2	3	4	5	6	7
Tetrads	CMAJ7	D-7	E-7	FMAJ7	G7	A-7	B-7(b5)
Function	T	S-D	T	S-D	D	T	D

Now, reading backwards, start enciphering each chords in the following order:

- **Tonic chords**
- Dominant chords
- Sub-dominant chords

For now, simply ignore all the chords that don't belong to the harmonization of the scale.

STANDARD MAJOR CHART

```
       I
||: CMAJ7    |    %    |    E7     |    %     |
                                  II
 |   A7      |    %    |   D-7     |    %     |
                                  VI
 |   E7      |    %    |   A-7     |    %     |
                                  II          V
 |   D7      |    %    |   D-7     |   G7     |
       I
 |  CMAJ7    |    %    |    E7     |    %     |
                                  II
 |   A7      |    %    |   D-7     |    %     |
    IV                      III
 |  FMAJ7    |   F-6   |   E-7     |   A7     |
    II          V           I           II   V
 |   D-7     |   G7    | CMAJ7  Eb°7 | D-7  G7 :||
```

STANDARD MAJOR CHART

```
         I
||: CMAJ7    |  %  |  E7        |  %  |
                       II
 |  A7       |  %  |  D-7       |  %  |
                       VI
 |  E7       |  %  |  A-7       |  %  |
                       II      V
 |  D7       |  %  |  D-7       |  G7  |
         I
 |  CMAJ7    |  %  |  E7        |  %  |
                       II
 |  A7       |  %  |  D-7       |  %  |
    IV              III
 |  FMAJ7    | F-6 |  E-7       |  A7  |
    II          V       I         II  V
 |  D-7      |  G7 | CMAJ7 Ebo7 | D-7 G7 :||
```

STANDARD MAJOR CHART

5 - Secondary dominant chords and cadences

Now we need to make sense of all the chords that do not directly belong to the harmonization of the scale. The best thing to do is to start with secondary dominant chords, keeping in mind that each of these chords have many possible substitutions!

Again, since cadences resolve going forward, it is best to analyze going backward (start from the end).

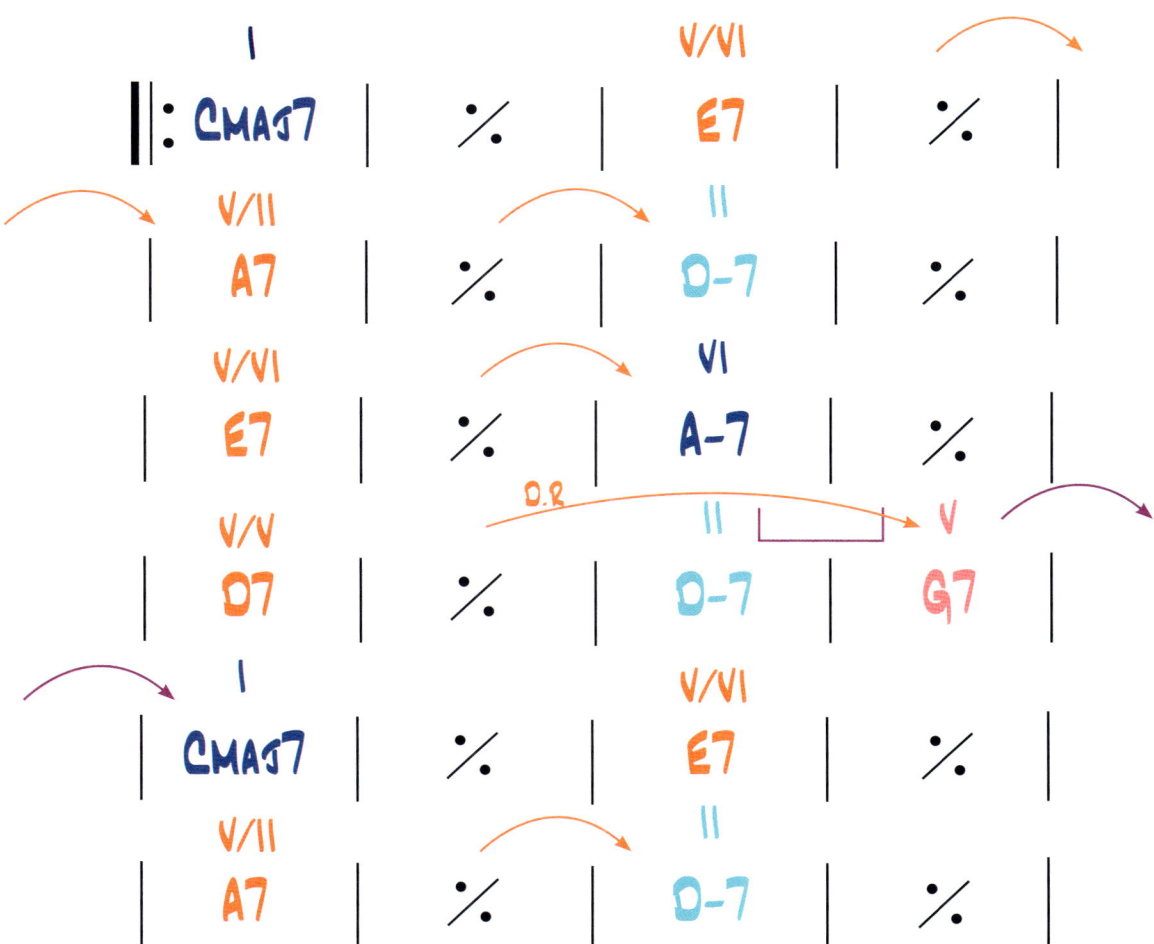

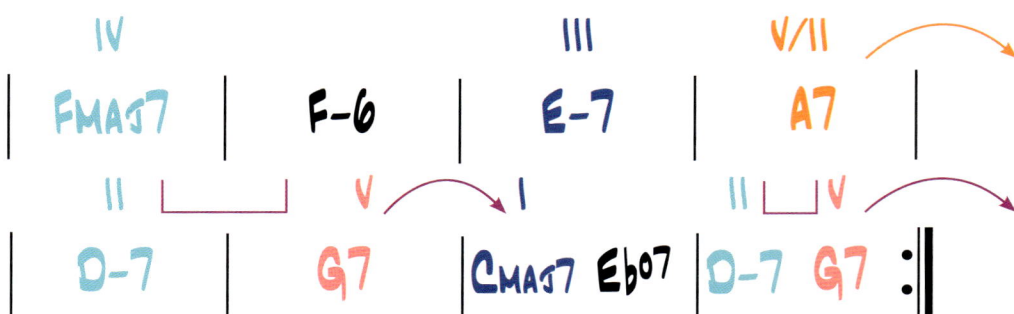

6 - Remaining progression

For the other chords, you don't really have a choice, you need to think about all the possible harmonic mechanisms you know and figure it out.

Let's start with the F-6 chord. When in doubt, you can simply encipher it very literally by just replacing the root of the chord by the appropriate roman numeral and see if you recognize a progression that makes sense:

| IV | IV- | III | V/II |
| FMAJ7 | F-6 | E-7 | A7 |

Now is this a progression that we know?

| IV- | III |
| F-6 | E-7 |

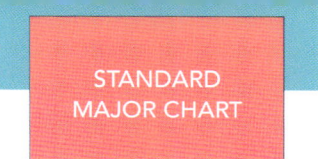

No? How about now?

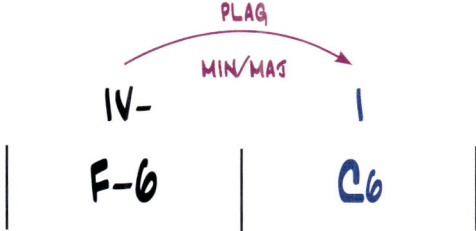

Oh yes!! We know that. And we also know that E-7 is a diatonic substitution of Cmaj7 (they are both tonic chords in C major). Well, that was easy. Now we are left with the following chord progression:

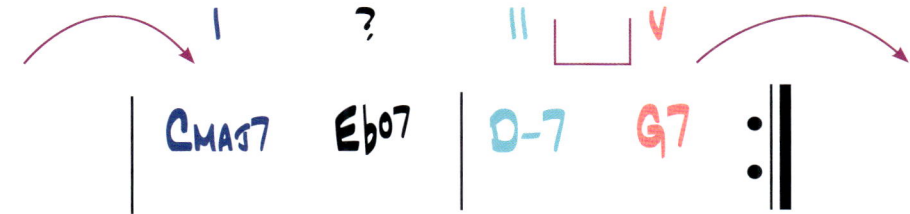

We already figured this out before and saw it was a diminished passing chord.

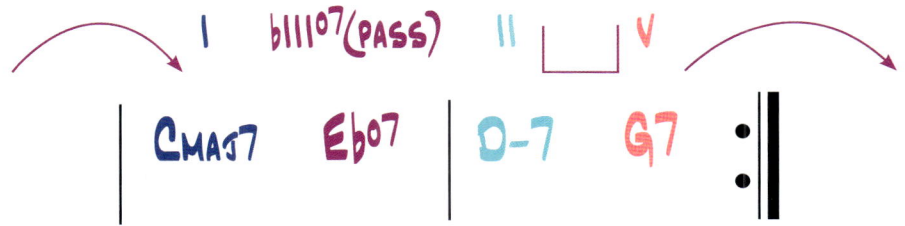

We're done. Crushed it. Goodbye.

7 - Interpretation and improvisation

So how do we improvise over this tune? Well, remember, the center of gravity of the tune is C major, so you should always have the C major scale as a reference in mind while you improvise. But this tune does modulate, however, mostly because of all the secondary dominants. Now again, there are many ways of improvising somewhere in the following spectrum:

Weak playing	Playing too much
In this case you mainly use the key scale (C major here) and only change the smallest amount of notes when there is a modulation. Your goal is to stay as close to the tonal as possible.	Here, you take every opportunity to see each chord as a modal context and go further away from the key of origin. You will use many altered scales on dominant chords and will even sometimes use modal interchanges on the tonic chords.

You can even move around this spectrum throughout the improvisation.

So what I'm going to do is analyze the tune on each extreme of this spectrum. Again, I will indicate on the bottom the thought mode, and the heard mode on the top.

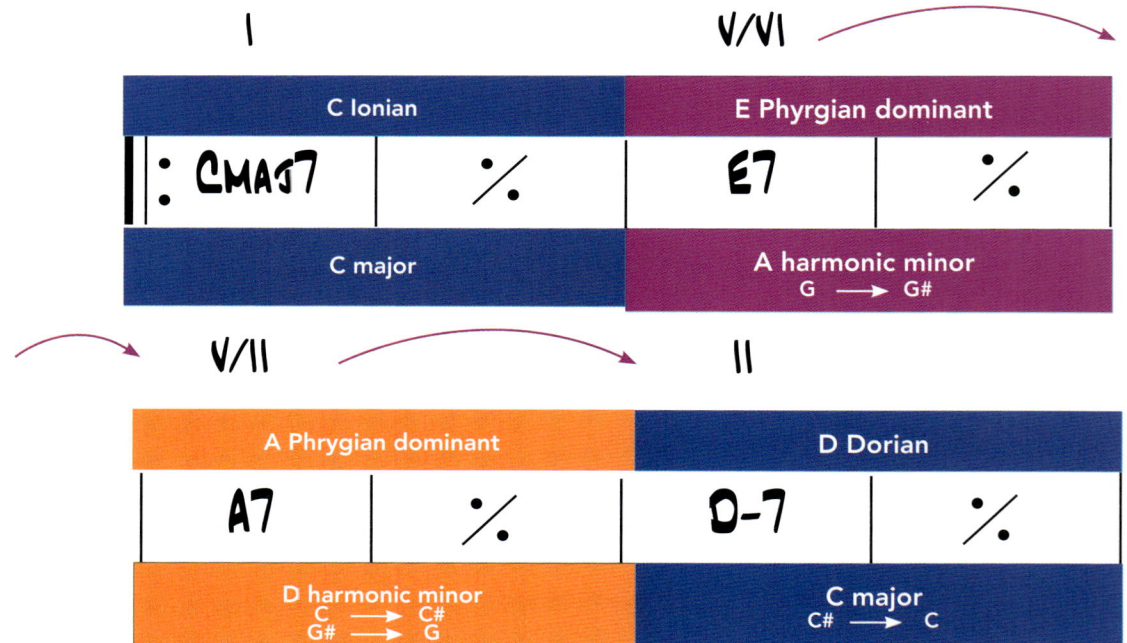

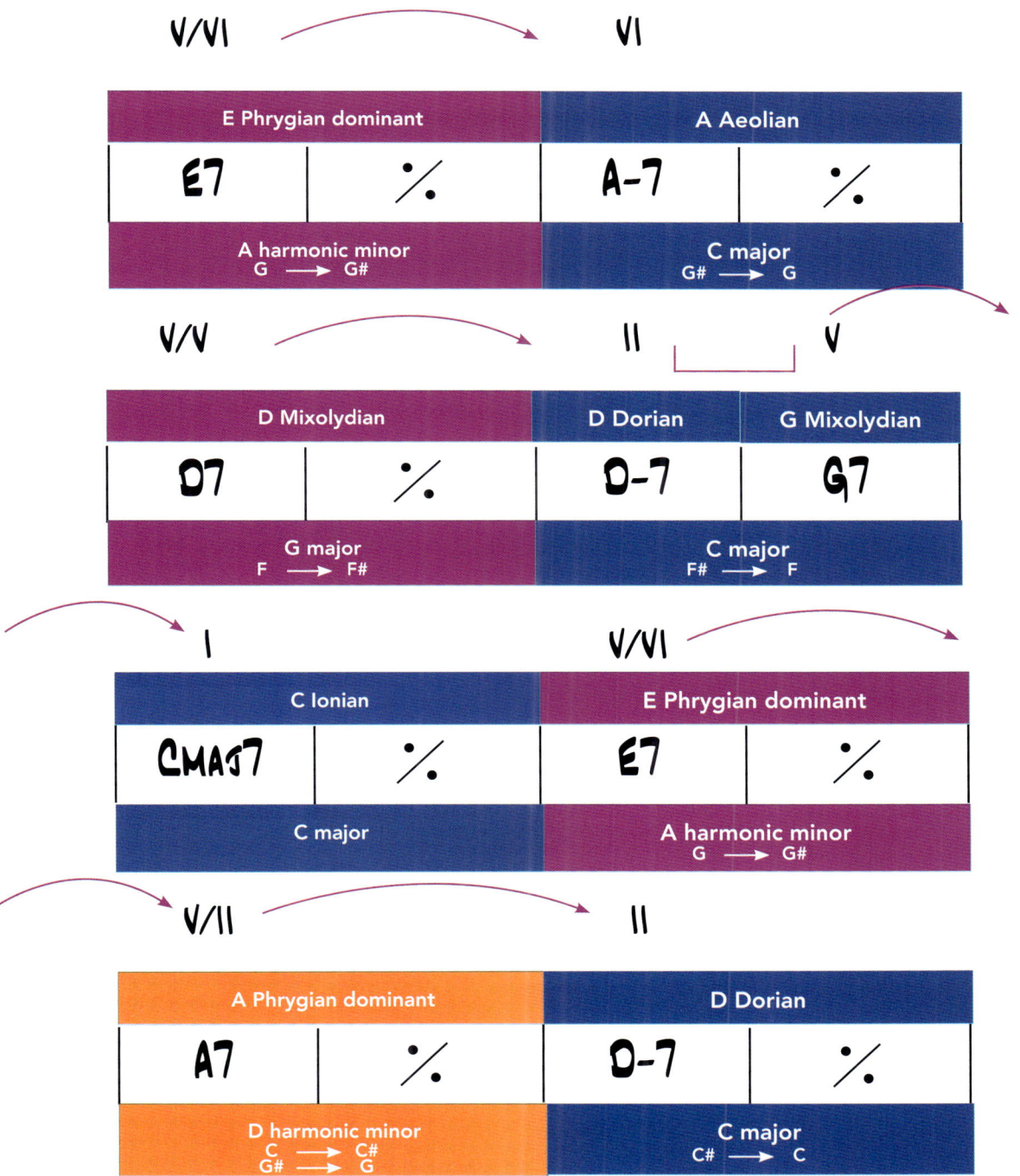

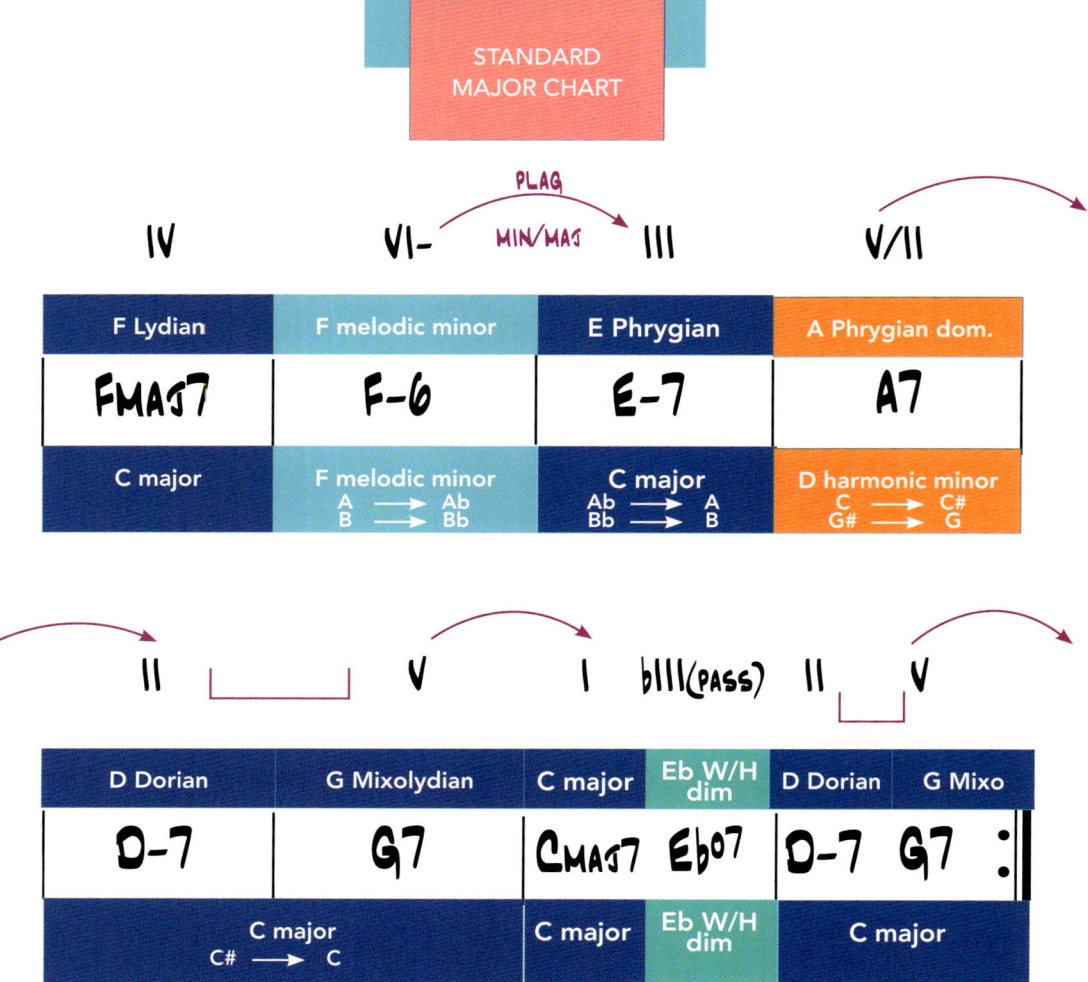

"So you mean, this was the simplest option to improvise???"

Well, yes… You can simplify by using arpeggios or pentatonic scales, but if you want to use regular heptatonic scales, this is your simplest option. It's a jazz tune, so it's normal that you will have to use modulations and borrowings. Rare are the jazz tunes that don't use at least ONE modulation at some point. The good news is that jazz is probably the most complicated genre to analyze. So when you encounter a rock tune or pop tune, it will seem almost too easy.

Example: "No Women No Cry," by Bob Marley:

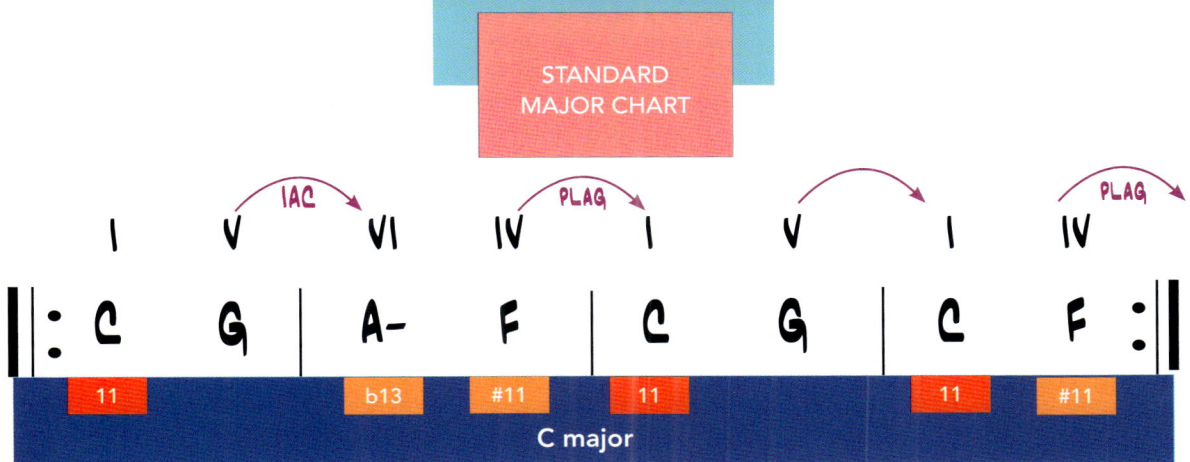

Now, isn't that much easier? Other than a few tension notes which you might want to avoid, you can use the C major scale over the entire progression.

Oh and just for fun... want to try a little reharmonization?

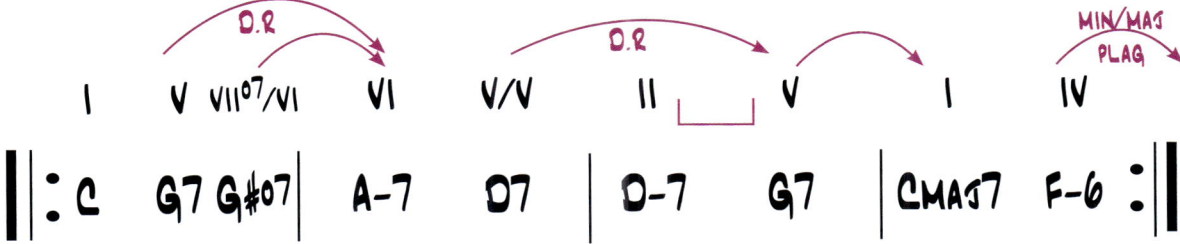

Modal analysis

Okay, now it's time to look into a more "sophisticated" analysis. Unlike the tonal analysis where there is only one possible result most of the time, the modal context is more open to interpretation.

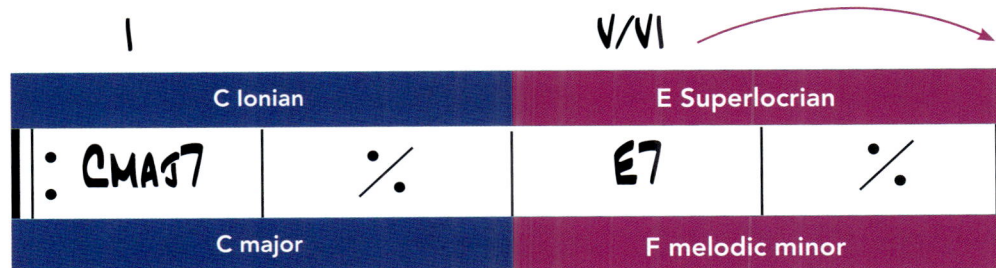

Here you can technically use any mode compatible with a dominant chord (as seen earlier). Just remember that some modes naturally sound better when the progression resolves on a minor chord. The Superlocrian works great here.

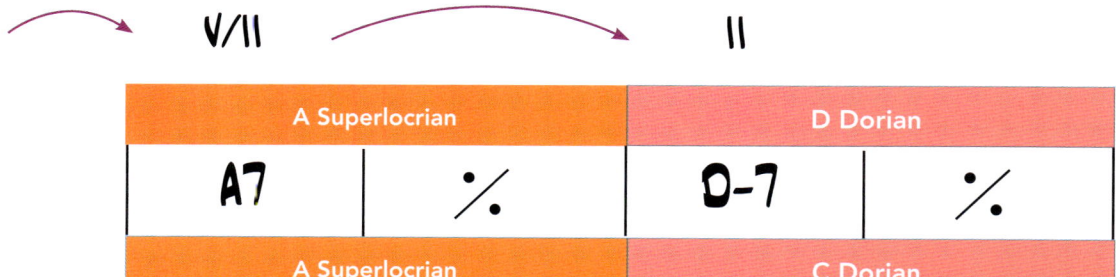

Technically, as seen earlier, you should avoid the 6th on the second degree in a tonal context. But this chord is not part of a cadence and is played long enough that you could actually THINK in terms of D Dorian and bring out the major 6th (B).

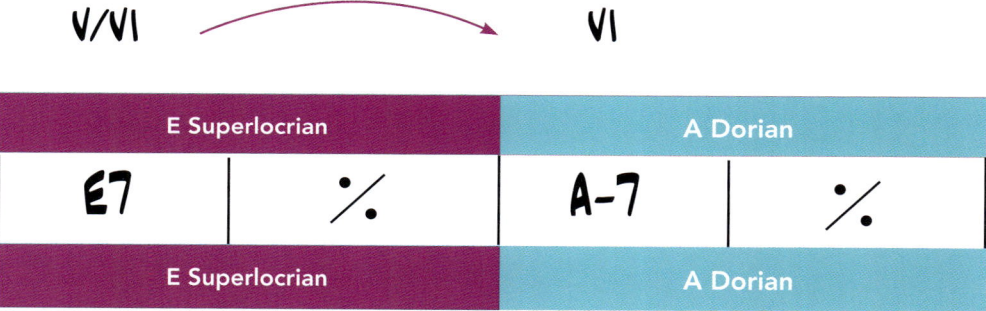

For the same reasons, you can use the A Dorian mode (which comes from the G major scale) on the VI chord instead of the C major scale. This will surprise the listener and bring out some interesting colors.

STANDARD MAJOR CHART

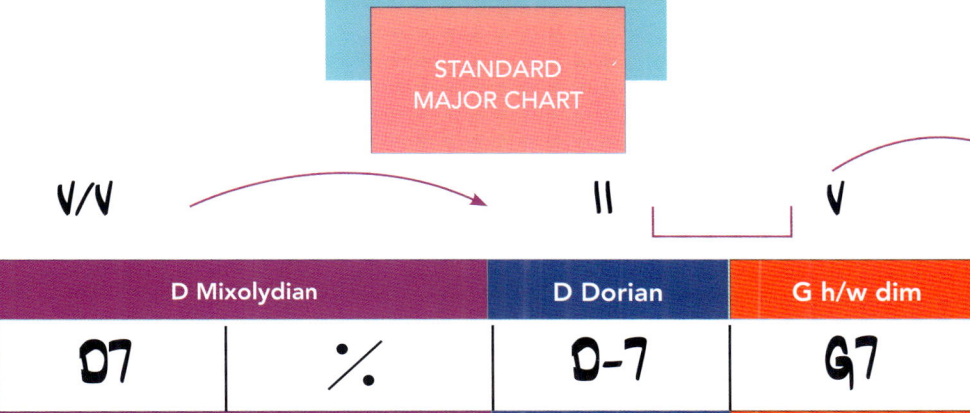

This scale works great on the dominant chord of major cadences.

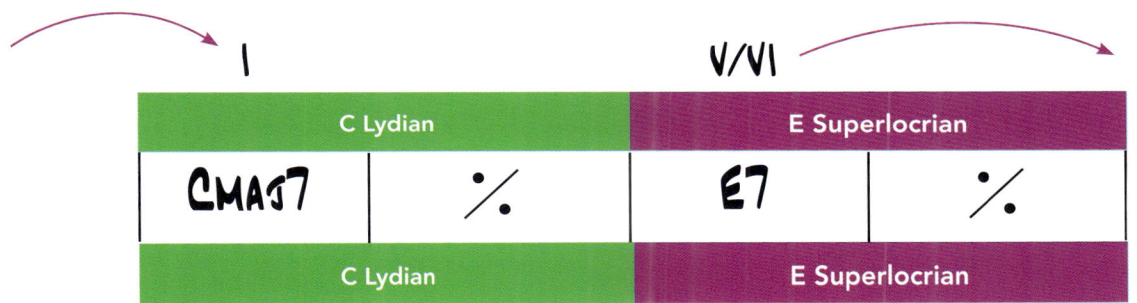

The Cmaj7 created an opportunity for a modal interchange between the Ionian (major) mode and the Lydian mode, also based on a Cmaj7 tetrad.

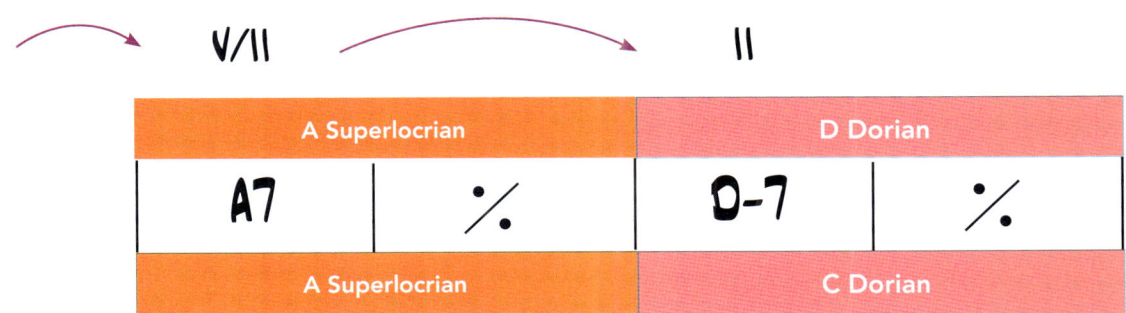

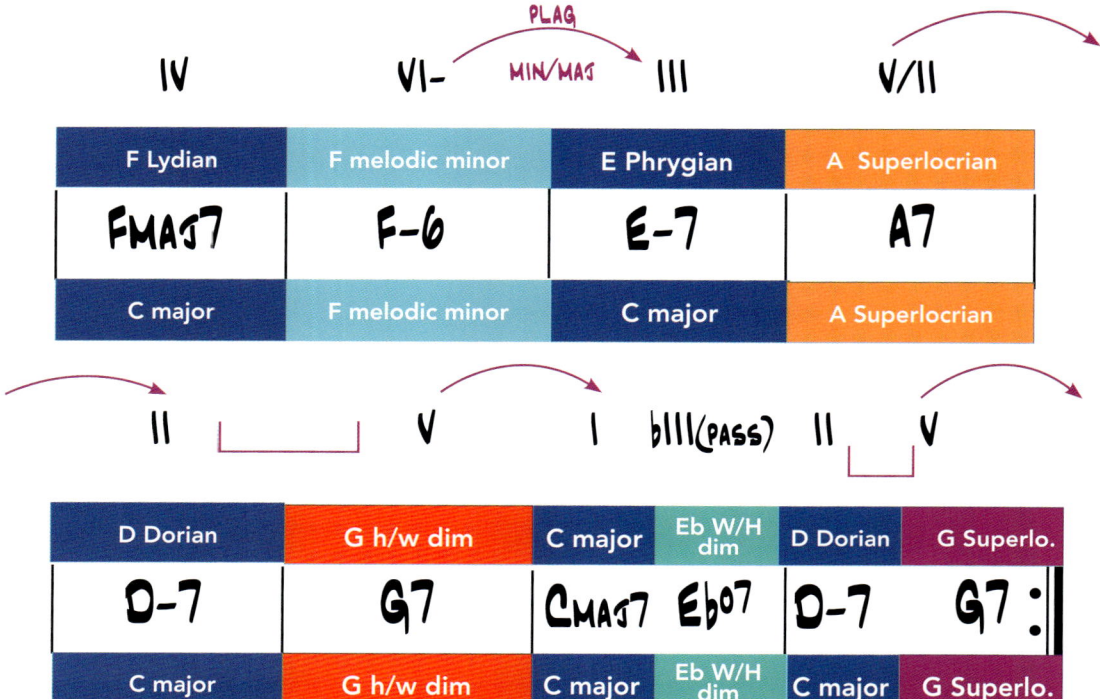

    Well, that's a lot of work… But again don't panic. Start with a simple tonal playing and add new colors or modes or intervals little by little. You need to hear what you play and most importantly LIKE what you play. If Superlocrian doesn't sound that good to you in a context (or any context), it doesn't matter how cool the name of that mode is, you won't make it sound good! It will be coming from the wrong place. The improvisation guide I wrote above can sound good if played by someone who really masters all those modes, but it could also sound very boring and dissonant and inappropriate if not done naturally. So again, start simple, add complexity, take your time and LISTEN. The best thing to do here probably is to pick up some cool solos from good jazz musicians and analyze them. What are they playing? Why does it sound good? How can I incorporate it into my solos?

    Now I'm going to be very honest with you. I'm not sure I would be able to play according to the interpretation above… Why? Because it would be forcing myself! Most of the time when I improvise, my brain is not so active. I play what I hear. And sometimes what I hear will bring out Superlocrian, sometimes another mode. I don't know. And I don't care anymore. But this became possible BECAUSE I did the work of trying out all those modes. I strongly recommend getting software such as iReal Pro to practice all those jazz standards, slow down the tempo and try out all those options.

5

Harmonic Analysis & Case studies

MINOR CHART WITH MODULATION

MINOR CHART WITH MODULATION

```
4/4 ||: A-        | B-7(b5)  E7(b9) |  A-      | B-7(b5)  E7(b9) |
    |  A-        | D-7      G7     |  CMAJ7   | A7(b9)          |
    |  D-7       | G7              |  CMAJ7   | FMAJ7           |
    |  B-7(b5)   | E7(b9)          |  A-      | B-7(b5)  E7(b9) ||
    |  A-        | B-7(b5)  E7(b9) |  A-      | %               |
    |  E-7(b5)   | A7(b9)          |  D-      | %               |
    |  D-7       | B-7(b5)  E7(b9) |  A-      | FMAJ7           |
    |  B-7(b5)   | E7(b9)          |  A-      | B-7(b5)  E7(b9) :||
```

All right, now since it is our second analysis, I'll try to go just a little bit faster. The principle that we will use is the same as for the major chart.

1 - Harmonic rhythm

The harmonic rhythm is mostly of one chord per bar for the whole tune with some little punctual irregularities that don't really change the harmonic rhythm in general.

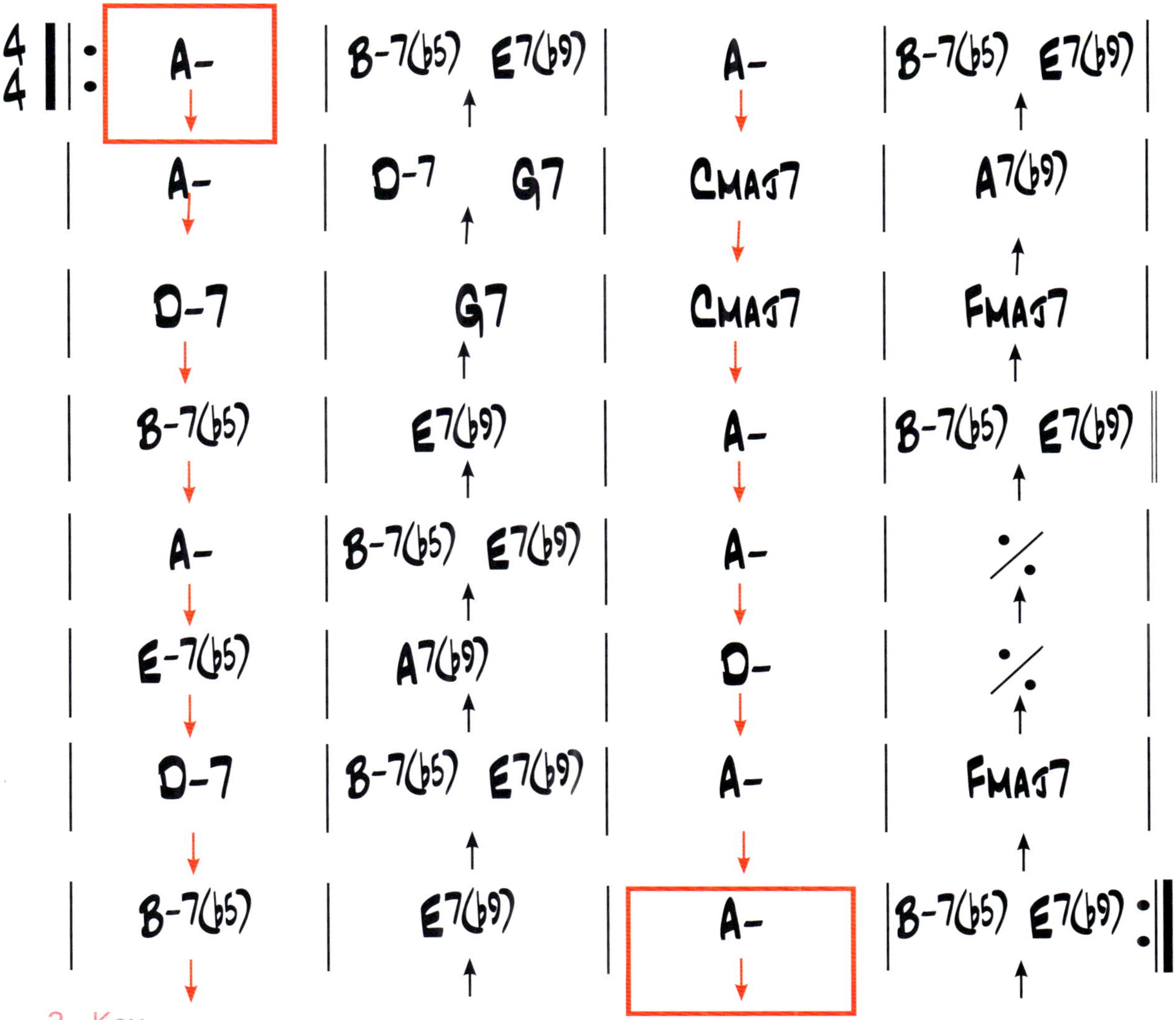

MINOR CHART WITH MODULATION

```
4/4 ||: | A-       | B-7(b5)  E7(b9) | A-     | B-7(b5)  E7(b9) |
       | A-       | D-7      G7     | CMAJ7  | A7(b9)          |
       | D-7      | G7              | CMAJ7  | FMAJ7           |
       | B-7(b5)  | E7(b9)          | A-     | B-7(b5)  E7(b9) ||
       | A-       | B-7(b5)  E7(b9) | A-     | %               |
       | E-7(b5)  | A7(b9)          | D-     | %               |
       | D-7      | B-7(b5)  E7(b9) | A-     | FMAJ7           |
       | B-7(b5)  | E7(b9)          | A-     | B-7(b5)  E7(b9) :||
```

2 - Key

■ 1. The key signature

If you had the lead sheet, you would see this:

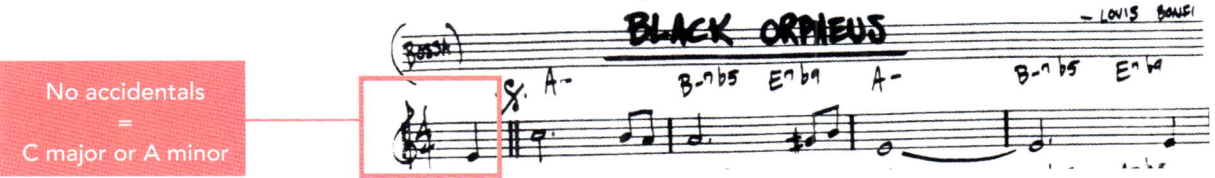

No accidentals = C major or A minor

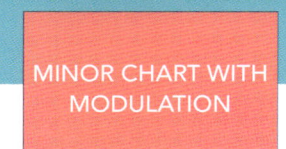

2. The most common chord on which authentic cadences resolve

A quick glance at the chart shows that most authentic cadences seem to resolve on an A- chord.

3. The conclusive chord and conclusive cadence

The last cadence is a complete authentic conclusive cadence that ends on an A-.

Conclusion? The key of this tune is clearly A minor.

3 - Function of the main chords

Let's harmonize the A minor scale and A harmonic minor scale and look at the function of each chord degree. In a minor context, you should always harmonize the natural minor and the harmonic minor scale (sometimes the melodic minor scale), since the cadences require borrowing from these scales.

Degrees	1	2	b3	4	5	b6	b7
Tetrads	A-7	B-7(b5)	CMAJ7	D-7	E-7	FMAJ7	G7
Function	T	S-D	T	S-D	/	S-D	S-D

Natural minor scale

Degrees	1	2	b3	4	5	b6	7
Tetrads	AMIN(MAJ7)	B-7(b5)	CMAJ7(#5)	D-7	E7	FMAJ7	G#DIM7
Function	T	S-D	T	S-D	D	S-D	D

Harmonic minor scale

Let's see what we can find in the chart:

MINOR CHART WITH MODULATION

```
         I              II        V             I              II        V
4 ||:   A-       | B-7(b5)  E7(b9) |    A-       | B-7(b5)  E7(b9) |
4
```

1
```
         I              IV       bVII          bIII                     
|       A-       | D-7      G7    |   Cmaj7    |    A7(b9)       |
         IV             bVII           bIII           bVI
|       D-7      |        G7     |   Cmaj7    |    Fmaj7        |
```
```
         II             V              I             II        V
|     B-7(b5)    |    E7(b9)     |    A-       | B-7(b5)  E7(b9) ||
```

```
         I              II        V             I
|       A-       | B-7(b5)  E7(b9) |    A-       |      %          |
```

2
```
|     E-7(b5)    |    A7(b9)     |    D-       |      %          |
         IV             II        V             I                      bVI
|       D-7      | B-7(b5)  E7(b9) |    A-       |    Fmaj7        |
         II              V             I             II        V
|     B-7(b5)    |    E7(b9)     |    A-       | B-7(b5)  E7(b9) :||
```

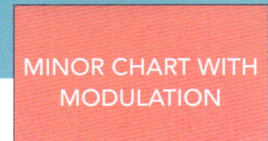

We can see that we are almost done!

But even though this way of enciphering is completely correct, there is something to pay attention to in the zones 1 and 2 highlighted above. How? Well, there are clues that after a while should become obvious to you, but the best clue is actually to LISTEN to the tune.

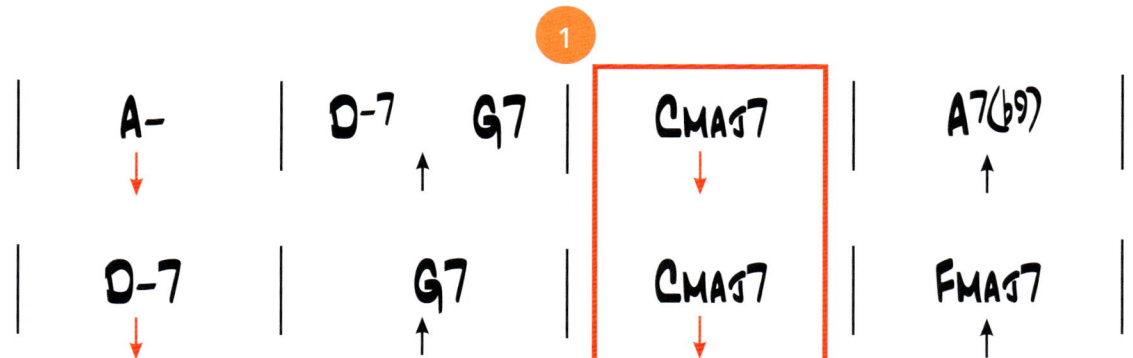

In zone 1, the center of gravity seems to switch to C major. Notice that C△ is used to resolve two strong perfect complete cadences. Had this been the case just for one or two bars, no big deal, but here, you MUST interpret the section as a modulation to C major.

This beautiful minor perfect cadence is to a D-. Notice that the minor 7th is also absent in this chord, and this is another indication that we are modulating to D minor.

The next bar starts with a D minor as well, but with a minor seventh, which is an indication that we are back in A minor. A D-7 is seen as a sub-dominant chord.

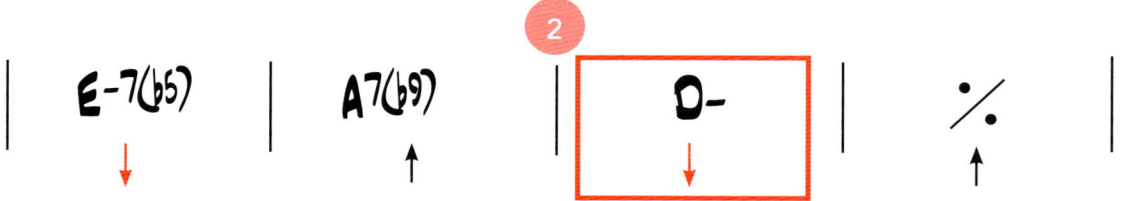

MINOR CHART WITH MODULATION

4 - Main cadences

Pay attention to how the modulations are indicated and to how they change the analysis.

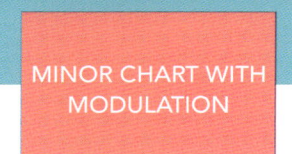

MINOR CHART WITH MODULATION

5 - Secondary dominant chords and cadences

There is just one secondary dominant chord on bar 8 (see above).

6 - Remaining progression

We've already analyzed all the chords at this point, so we are done! Nothing to add in this section.

7 - Interpretation and improvisation

Again, you can interpret this tune in different ways and use different improvisation options. I will simply give you one of the possibilities. Feel free to explore different alternatives by using the rules explored before.

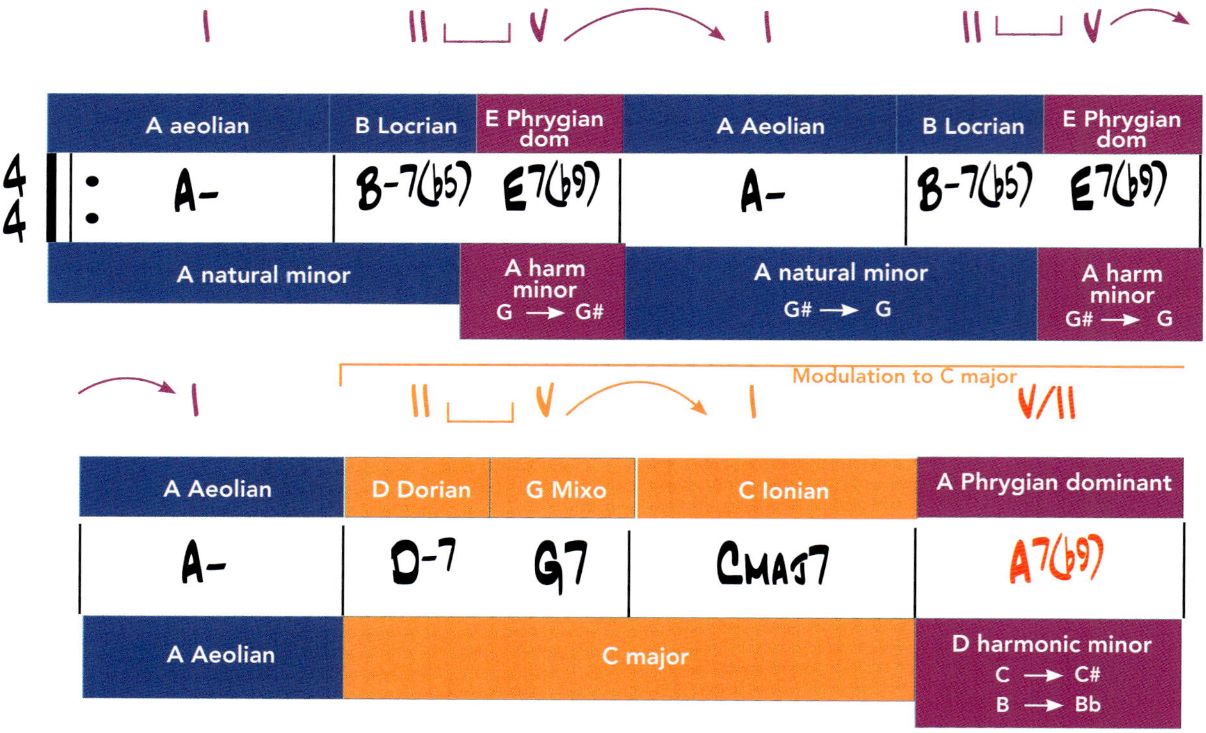

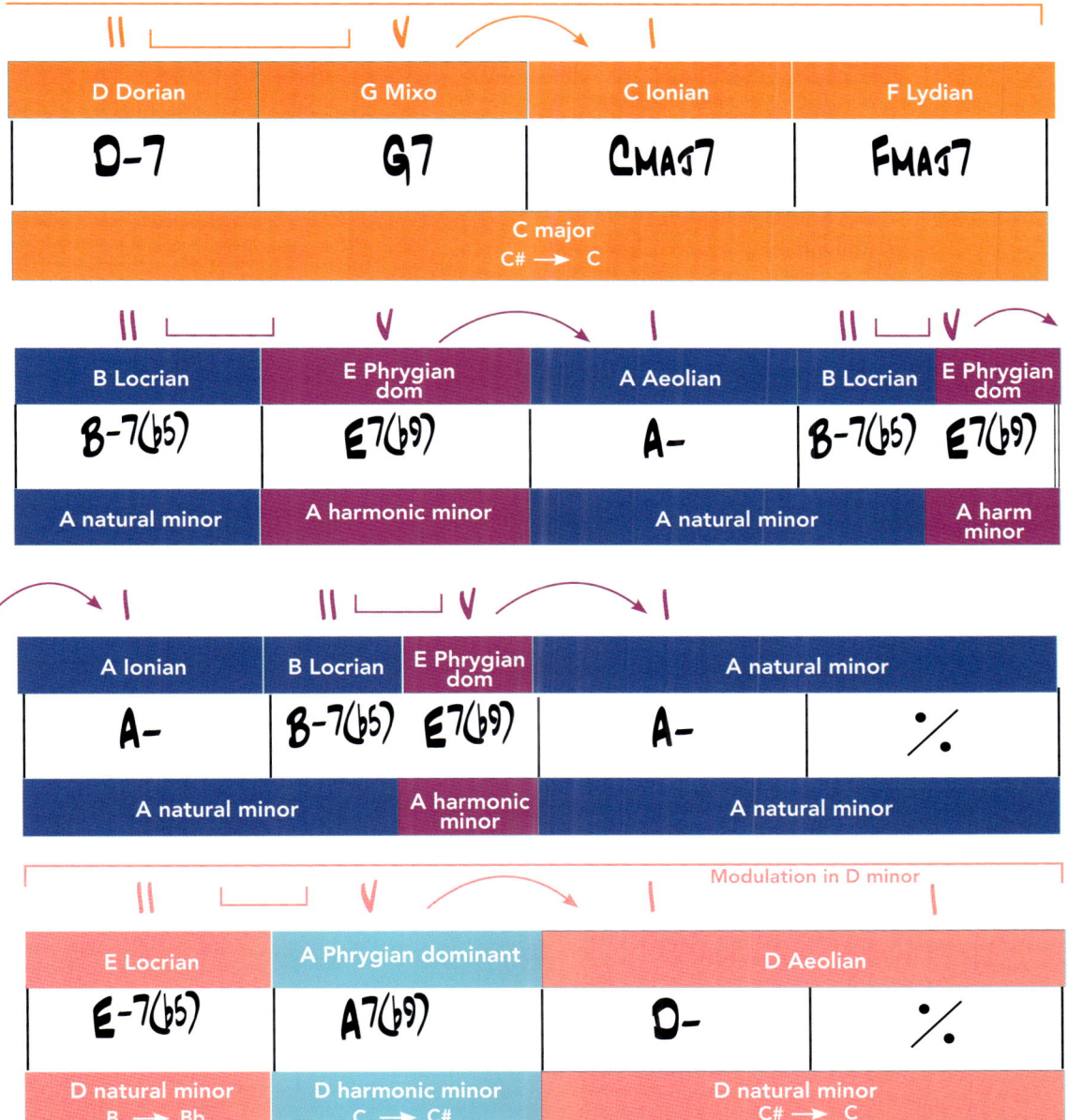

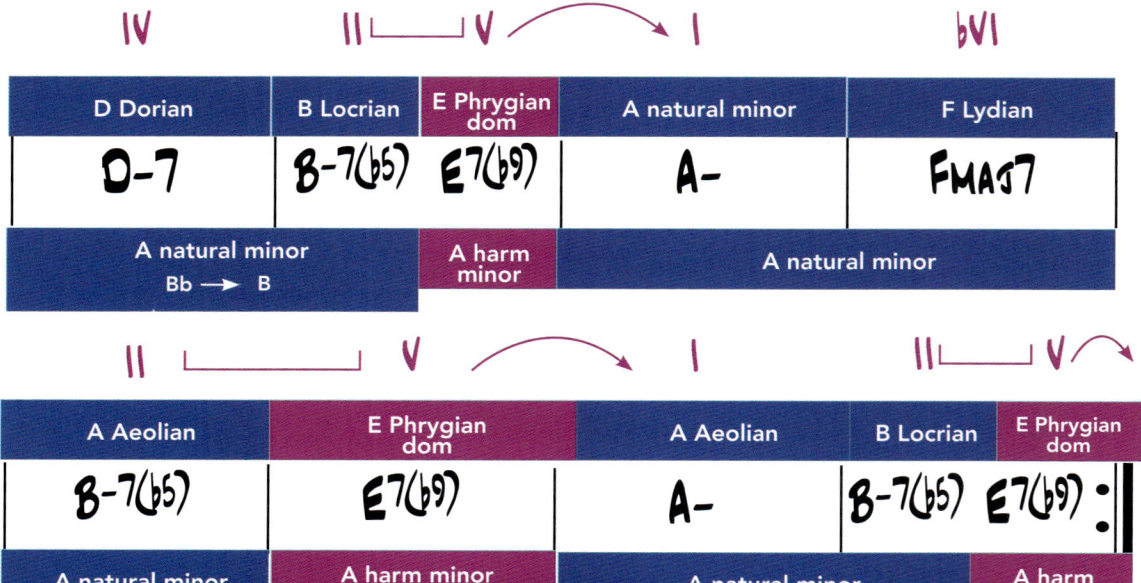

CHART WITH
MODAL SECTION

5

Harmonic Analysis & Case Studies

MODAL CHART

CHART WITH MODAL SECTION

For this last example, I decided to analyze a more "modal" tune. This simply means that the tune includes one or several modal sections that are not the result of a modal interpretation, but are actually brought out by the harmonic progression. You will find some of the modal cadences that we discovered at the beginning of the book.

$\frac{3}{4}$ ‖: F-7 | G-7 | AbMAJ7 G-7 | F-7 |
| F-7 | G-7 | AbMAJ7 G-7 | F-7 |
| Eb | Eb | Db Eb | F-7 |
| Eb | Eb | Db Eb | F-7 :‖

There are some clues that you can look for to determine rather easily that a tune is modal.

- A big clue is the fact of not having a key signature and yet having a chord progression that does not indicate the keys of C major or A minor. Again, normally, no sharps or flats implies C major or A minor. But in some modal tunes, composers simply don't put a key signature because there is NO tonal center.

- However, in most cases, especially if the main mode implied in the tune includes many sharps or flats, it will be easier to add a key signature, not to indicate a key, BUT to avoid repeating the accidentals throughout the tune. In this case, the key signature used will be that of the major or minor scale that is closest (in terms of notes) to the actual mode. (And this will be the case in the tune we are about to analyze.)

My tip? I always assume that by default, a tune is tonal. If during the analysis, I encounter clues that show the tune must me modal, I will simply change my interpretation on the fly.

CHART WITH MODAL SECTION

1 - Harmonic rhythm

The tune is in 3/4, but in this case it doesn't matter, the harmonic rhythm is of one chord per bar.

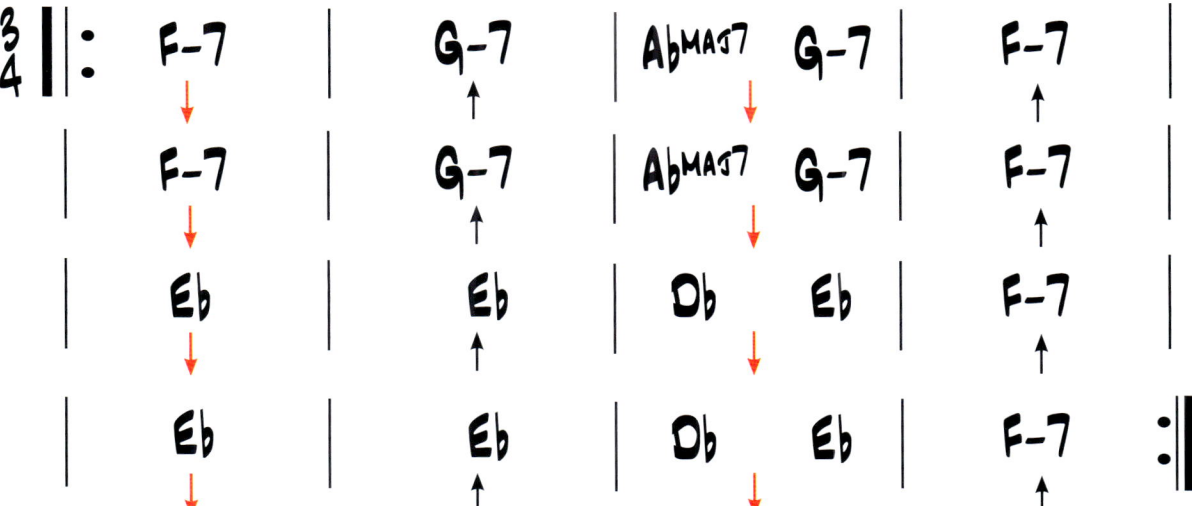

2 - Key

1. The key signature

If you had the lead sheet, you would see this:

4 flats = Ab major or F minor

CHART WITH MODAL SECTION

■ 2. The most common chord

The most common chord in this tune is obviously F-7. So up to this point, it seems like we might be in F minor.

■ 3. The last bar or cadence

The last cadence is a weak cadence (ends on a weak harmonic beat) AND does not end with an authentic cadence. That's unusual for a tonal tune… very unusual. At this point, you should be suspicious. But still, **it seems like we should be in F minor.**

3 - Function of the main chords

Okay, let's harmonize F minor.

Degrees	1	2	b3	4	5	b6	b7
Tetrads	F-7	G-7(b5)	AbMAJ7	Bb-7	C-7	DbMAJ7	Eb7
Function	T	S-D	T	S-D	/	S-D	S-D

Natural minor scale

Degrees	1	2	b3	4	5	b6	7
Tetrads	FMIN(MAJ7)	G-7(b5)	AbMAJ7(#5)	Bb-7	C7	DbMAJ7	EDIM7
Function	T	S-D	T	S-D	D	S-D	D

Harmonic minor scale

Let's look for those chords in the chart.

CHART WITH MODAL SECTION

```
     I              I           bIII           I
3/4 ‖: F-7    |    G-7    |  AbMAJ7  G-7  |   F-7    |
     I              I           bIII           I
    | F-7    |    G-7    |  AbMAJ7  G-7  |   F-7    |
    bVII           bVII         bVI   bVII       I
    | Eb     |    Eb     |   Db     Eb   |   F-7    |
    bVII           bVII         bVI   bVII       I
    | Eb     |    Eb     |   Db     Eb   |   F-7   :‖
```

Ok… well again this looks a little odd. No V chords? Something is different but let's keep going.

4 - Main cadences

```
     I              I           bIII           I
3/4 ‖: F-7    |    G-7    |  AbMAJ7  G-7  |   F-7    |
```

There are two identical lines each time, so I'm not going to repeat them. Let's save the trees.

```
    bVII           bVII         bVI   bVII  PLAG   I
    | Eb     |    Eb     |   Db     Eb   |   F-7    |
```

So, just ONE cadence, and a plagal one, which concludes on a weak beat. Something here is not normal. A tonal tune that only includes ONE cadence towards the tonic, it's simply impossible.

5' - Modal analysis

$$\frac{3}{4} \|: \overset{I}{F{-}7} \ | \ \overset{?}{G{-}7} \ | \ \overset{bIII}{A\flat MAJ7} \ G{-}7 \ | \ \overset{I}{F{-}7} \ |$$

Let's look at this line. What is this G-7 doing here? Does it belong to the harmonization of F minor? Nope. Is it a secondary dominant or sub-dominant, or a substitution chord? Nope.

Remember, when you are analyzing music, you should always be willing to change your mind. Here, we must change our mind.

There HAS to be something modal going on here. At least, let's give it a try.

Let's look at some common minor modes, starting with the Dorian mode:

Degrees	1	2	b3	4	5	6	b7
Tetrads	F-7	G-7	AbMAJ7	Bb7	C-7	D-7(b5)	EbMAJ7

Miracle!! This works!

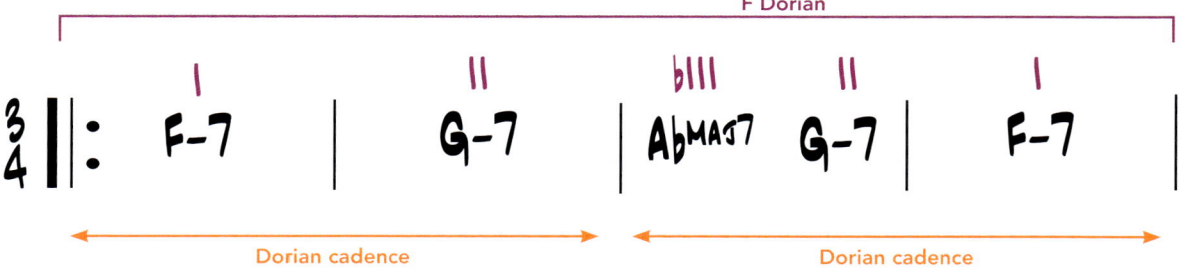

However, there is another problem if we consider this tune as Dorian:

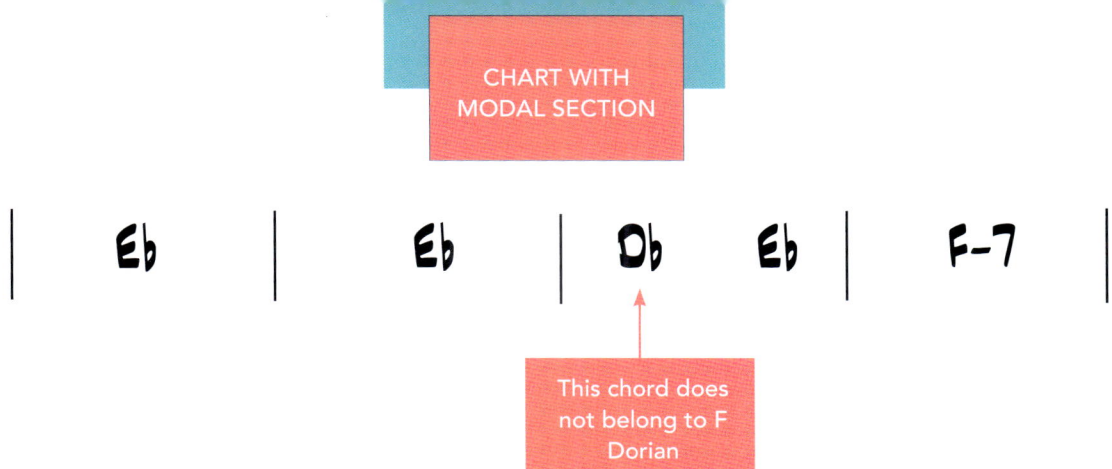

However, this chord made sense in the key of F minor. Yes, but we just said this tune was most obviously not tonal. This is confusing.

Here, my friends, we have just noticed the subtle (actually not so subtle) difference between the minor key and the aeolian mode. These two concepts are similar in a lot of ways. The minor key and Aeolian mode are based on the same scale and have the same harmonization. BUT, the Aeolian mode, unlike the minor key, is not based on the same mechanism. Its goal is not to emphasize a key, but the colors of the Aeolian mode.

This means you don't even have to indicate the plagal cadence here. It is not the point! If we wanted to emphasize the key using this cadence, we would at least make it land on a strong beat. This is obviously not what's going on here. This progression is an Aeolian modal progression.

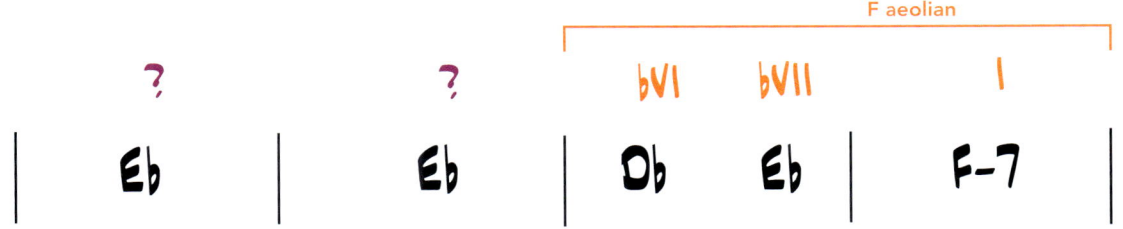

We are almost done, but not quite yet. The Eb triad belongs to the F Dorian mode AND the F Aeolian mode. Without any indications about the 7th, however, we cannot tell for sure if this chord is to be interpreted in one context or the other.

Answer: It's really up to you. This is another example of an opportunity for modal interchanges. Both will sound good for different reasons.

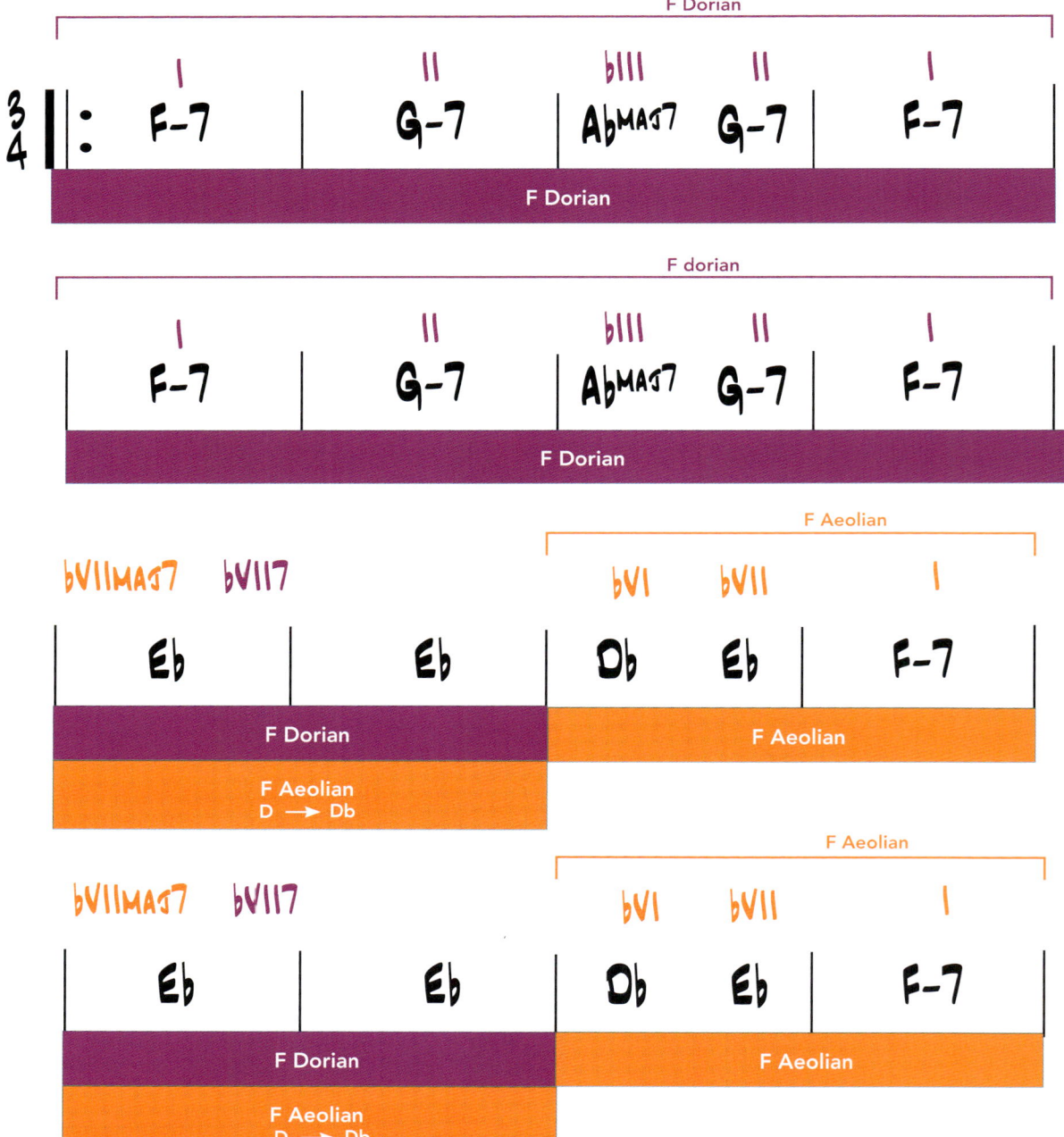

CONCLUSION

Well... What an adventure this has been, hasn't it? If this is your first time reading this book and you have actually managed to read it through, from start to finish, then please take a second to congratulate yourself. Hopefully, you can also reflect on all the knowledge you have acquired. And if you feel like many notions are still unclear, it's completely normal. At the end of the day, you cannot truly master improvisation and composition on paper only. After your first read, all I expect from you is to at least feel relieved by realizing that improvisation and composition are not divine gifts that some people have and others simply don't. There are guides and rules on how to navigate these two fields, which are undoubtedly the most fulfilling and inspiring aspects of one's musical journey. There is no better feeling than that of creating your own material, be it on the spot with improvisation, or through the process of composition.

I also hope that even if you don't understand or remember everything (and you most likely won't unless you have an IQ of 400), you will at least realize that it is not rocket science. Grasping each concept only requires a bit of common sense, but there are so many of them that you will most likely get overloaded at some point. It's okay...

Because between the understanding and the mastery of the mechanisms of harmony is a gap that can only be crossed through practice, curiosity, perseverance, and passion. It takes passion to muster the energy and patience required to truly master all the notions in this book. Therefore, you will most certainly have to come back to each notion in this book, understand it, practice it, and implement it for a while, and then move on to the next one. I know this virtue seems to be vanishing these days, but the key word here is patience! Don't try to rush things. Because most of the notions in this book are not ones that you can just practice for a bit and then be done with. I still work on my two-five-ones every day, for example, and I probably will keep working on them for the rest of my life. But at least the theory behind them has no secret for me anymore, and I know what to practice. This, if anything, is really what I wish you could get out of this book: a clear vision of what to work on to get to where you want to be as a creator of music.

Moreover, don't feel like you necessarily have to master everything in this book to become a good composer or improviser. Depending on your goals and the genres of music that you wish to focus on, you might not need to know how to navigate all of the musical contexts I introduced and analyzed. But if you want to go all the way or explore the more harmonically advanced genres such as jazz, then you have the tools to do so.

This book is truly everything I know about music theory. I wrote it to help you, my friend, and all the musicians who, like me, were confused about the rules of musical creation. And while there are still some areas of theory that I have not explored, this book should give you all tools to venture into some even more advanced and nerdy concepts if you wish to do so.

I truly wish you the best of luck in your musical adventure and hope from the bottom of my heart that this book will have given you massive amounts of value. Just remember: you too can create, and I know you have a musical voice that deserves to be expressed and heard. And nothing would make me happier than knowing that my humble work could have helped this voice reach its full potential.

EXERCISES

Let me remind you that the following exercises are more than practice exercises. Their goal is to show you how to build the knowledge yourself by using the definitions I gave you. You should:

1. Be able to remember the results of these exercises.
2. Understand how I made these exercises so that you can make your own!

EXERCISES

Exercise 1: Harmonizing scales in different intervals

Using the step-by-step process for harmonizing a scale, complete the harmonization of the following scales:

Diatonic harmonization of Ab major in 4ths

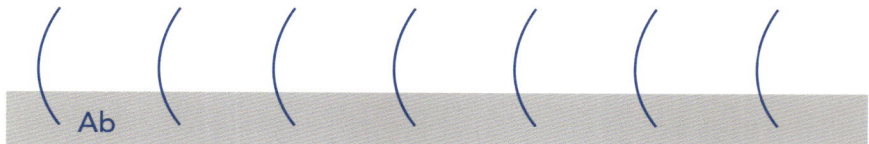

Diatonic harmonization of E harmonic minor in 6ths

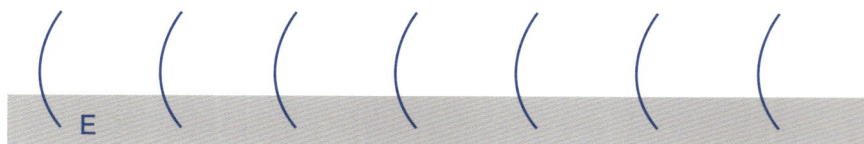

Diatonic harmonization of C half-whole diminished scale in 3rds

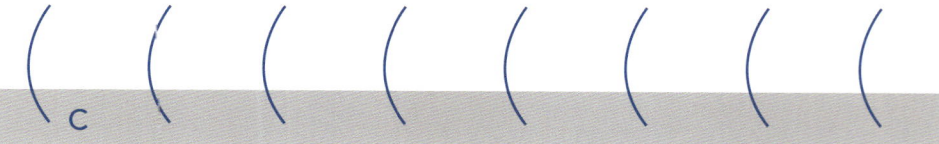

Here you should notice something interesting! If you harmonized the scale correctly, you should find out that harmonizing the diminished scale in 3rds only generates minor 3rds! This makes sense since, if you remember from the previous book, the diminished scale is symmetrical in minor 3rds.

Diatonic harmonization of A major in 7ths

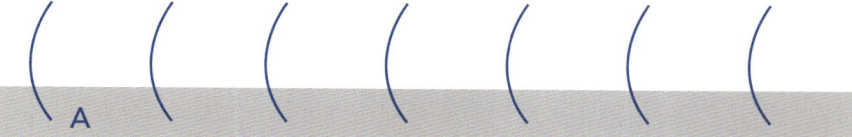

EXERCISES

Exercise 2: Diatonic harmonization of the major scale in sus2 and sus4 triads

Again, you can harmonize a scale using any polyphonic tool you want. In this exercise, you will have to harmonize the major scale in sus2 and sus4 triads. Since the results of this exercise are relatively important, I will guide you through it and give you the result. Try not to cheat!

Step 1: Definition of a sus2 and sus4 triad.

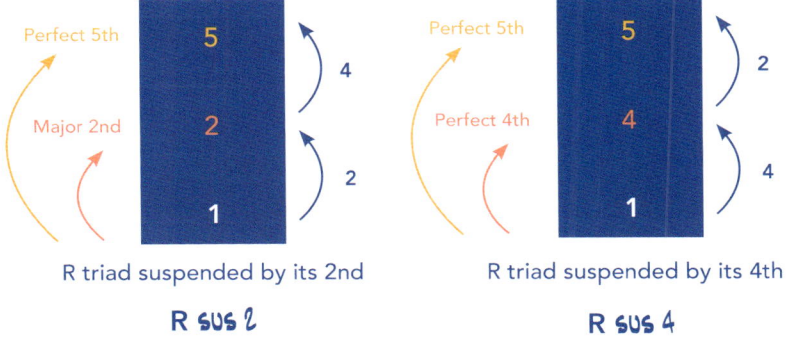

Step 2: Harmonize the C major scale in sus2 triads and sus4 triads. Remember that the harmonization is diatonic.

Diatonic harmonization of C major scale in sus2 triads

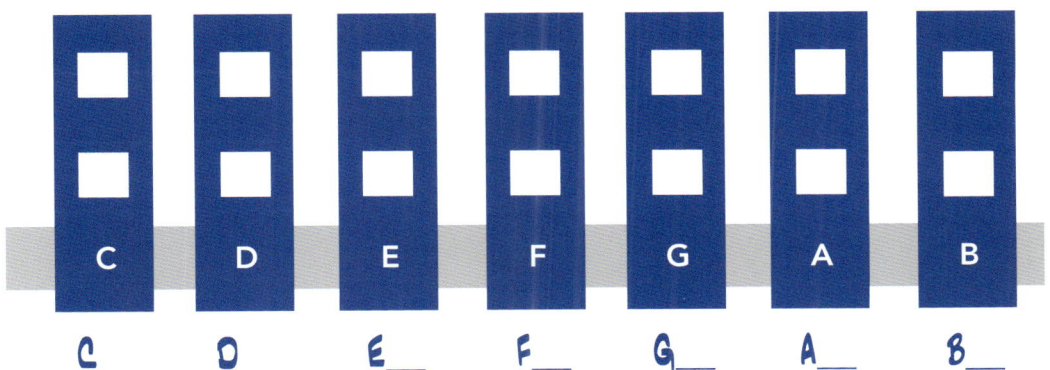

EXERCISES

Diatonic harmonization of C major scale in sus4 triads

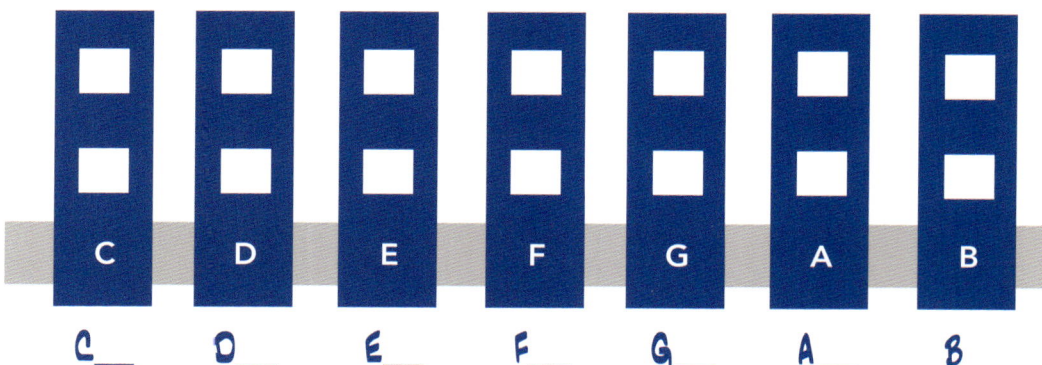

At this point you might have encountered a little problem...

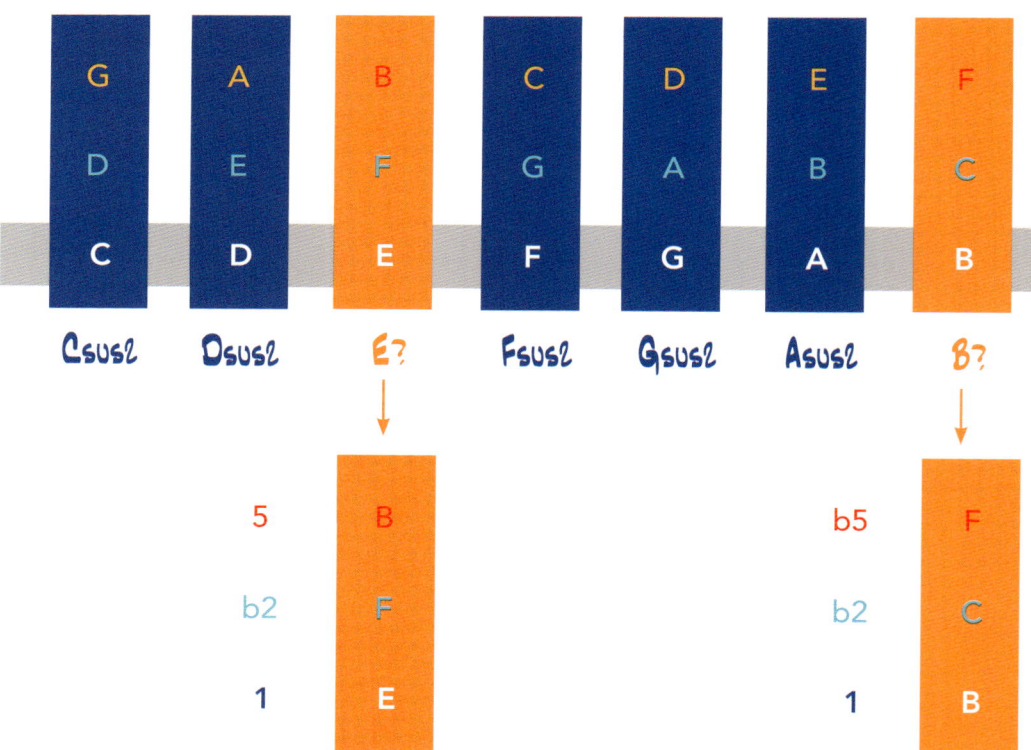

EXERCISES

These two triads are not really sus2 triads... If we made them sus2 triads, we would have to use notes which do not belong to the C major scale, which would make the harmonization non-diatonic. These two triads are actually named after the mode they originate from. We've seen them in the first book, but I won't blame you if you don't remember.

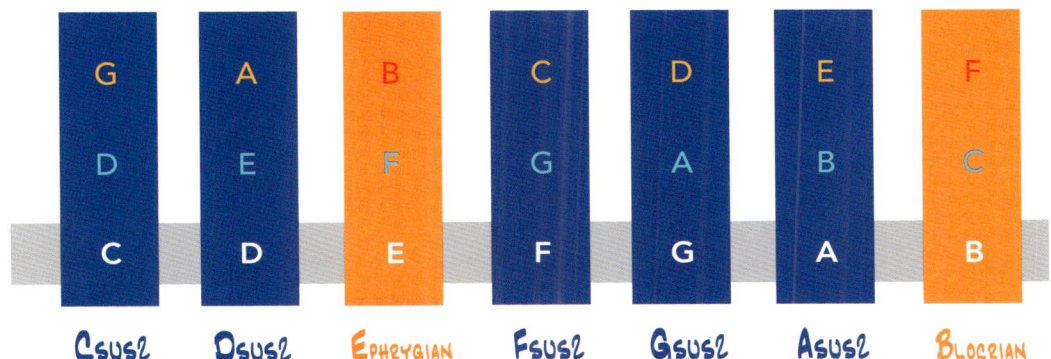

Same principle for the sus4 triads:

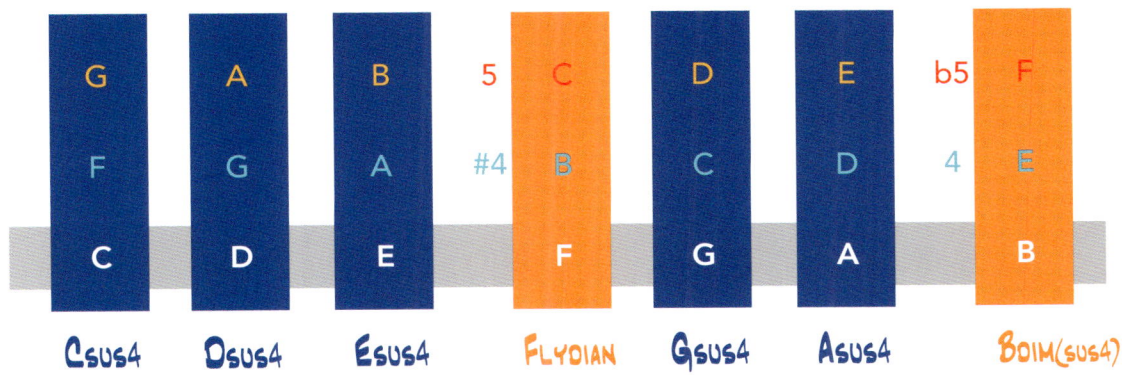

Step 3: Generalize the results to a generic major scale. At this point I'm sure you can do this on your own.

Harmonization of the major scale in sus2 triads

EXERCISES

Harmonization of the major scale in sus4 triads

1	2	3	4	5	6	7

Exercise 3: Harmonizing all the modes of the major scale

Complete the following tables:

Complete diatonic harmonization of the Dorian mode

Degrees	1	2	b3	4	5	6	7
Tetrads							
Extensions							

Complete diatonic harmonization of the Phrygian mode

Degrees	1	b2	b3	4	5	b6	b7
Tetrads							
Extensions							

EXERCISES

Complete diatonic harmonization of the Mixolydian mode

Degrees	1	2	3	4	5	6	b7
Tetrads							
Extensions	— — —	— — —	— — —	— — —	— — —	— — —	— — —

Complete diatonic harmonization of the Aeolian mode

Degrees	1	2	b3	4	5	b6	b7
Tetrads							
Extensions	— — —	— — —	— — —	— — —	— — —	— — —	— — —

Complete diatonic harmonization of the Locrian mode

Degrees	1	b2	b3	4	b5	b6	b7
Tetrads							
Extensions	— — —	— — —	— — —	— — —	— — —	— — —	— — —

EXERCISES

Exercise 4: Determining the different melodic possibilities over different intervals

Simply highlight or circle the different melodic possibilities that could be played over the following intervals.

G3

Major scale modes	Harmonic minor scale modes	Melodic minor scale modes	Pentatonic scales	Blues scales	Whole-tone	Diminished
Ionian	Harmonic minor	Melodic minor	Major	Major	Whole-tone	Half-whole
Dorian	Locrian maj 6	Phrygian maj 6	Minor	Minor		Whole-half
Phrygian	Ionian #5	Lydian #5				
Lydian	Dorian #4	Lydian b7				
Mixolydian	Phrygian dom.	Mixolydian b6				
Aeolian	Lydian #2	Locrian maj 2nd				
Locrian	Superlocrian bb7	Superlocrian				

Bb6

EXERCISES

Major scale modes	Harmonic minor scale modes	Melodic Minor scale modes	Pentatonic Scales	Blues Scales	Whole-tone	Diminished
Ionian	Harmonic minor	Melodic minor	Major	Major	Whole-tone	Half-whole
Dorian	Locrian maj 6	Phrygian maj 6	Minor	Minor		Whole-half
Phrygian	Ionian #5	Lydian #5				
Lydian	Dorian #4	Lydian b7				
Mixolydian	Phrygian dom.	Mixolydian b6				
Aeolian	Lydian #2	Locrian maj 2nd				
Locrian	Superlocrian bb7	Superlocrian				

Exercise 5: Determining the different melodic possibilities over different chords

Simply highlight or circle the different melodic possibilities that could be played over the following chords.

D-9

Major scale modes	Harmonic minor scale modes	Melodic minor scale modes	Pentatonic scales	Blues scales	Whole-tone	Diminished
Ionian	Harmonic minor	Melodic minor	Major	Major	Whole-tone	Half-whole
Dorian	Locrian maj 6	Phrygian maj 6	Minor	Minor		Whole-half
Phrygian	Ionian #5	Lydian #5				
Lydian	Dorian #4	Lydian b7				
Mixolydian	Phrygian dom.	Mixolydian b6				
Aeolian	Lydian #2	Locrian maj 2nd				
Locrian	Superlocrian bb7	Superlocrian				

EXERCISES

B7(♭9)

Major scale modes	Harmonic minor scale modes	Melodic minor scale modes	Pentatonic scales	Blues scales	Whole-tone	Diminished
Ionian	Harmonic minor	Melodic minor	Major	Major	Whole-tone	Half-whole
Dorian	Locrian maj 6	Phrygian maj 6	Minor	Minor		Whole-half
Phrygian	Ionian #5	Lydian #5				
Lydian	Dorian #4	Lydian ♭7				
Mixolydian	Phrygian dom.	Mixolydian ♭6				
Aeolian	Lydian #2	Locrian maj 2nd				
Locrian	Superlocrian ♭♭7	Superlocrian				

E♭-11

Major scale modes	Harmonic minor scale modes	Melodic minor scale modes	Pentatonic scales	Blues scales	Whole-tone	Diminished
Ionian	Harmonic minor	Melodic minor	Major	Major	Whole-tone	Half-whole
Dorian	Locrian maj 6	Phrygian maj 6	Minor	Minor		Whole-half
Phrygian	Ionian #5	Lydian #5				
Lydian	Dorian #4	Lydian ♭7				
Mixolydian	Phrygian Dom.	Mixolydian ♭6				
Aeolian	Lydian #2	Locrian maj 2				
Locrian	Superlocrian ♭♭7	Superlocrian				

EXERCISES

Exercise 6: Identifying modal contexts based on chord progressions

Determine the modal context for each of the following chord progressions. You have two main methods to do so:

Use one of the common modal progressions given to you in the chapter.

Try to reconstitute the "big 7-note chord" from the chords of the progression. If you don't know where the first degree chord is, rely on the harmonic rhythm! It will most definitely be on a strong bar.

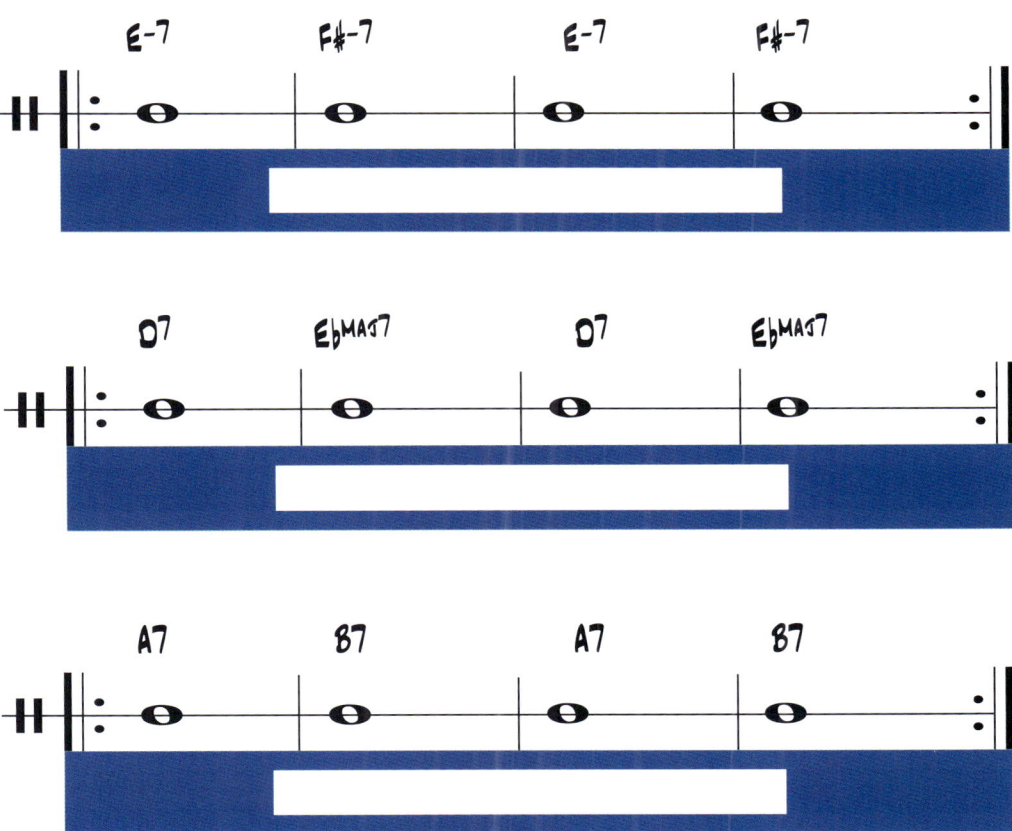

EXERCISES

Exercise 7: Find the major and relative minor key associated to key signatures

For each of the following key signatures, determine the major and relative minor key as well as which notes carry the accidentals.

Remember the process! All you have to do is count the number of sharps or flats and use the circle of 5ths to determine the key. You don't need to know how to read. For example:

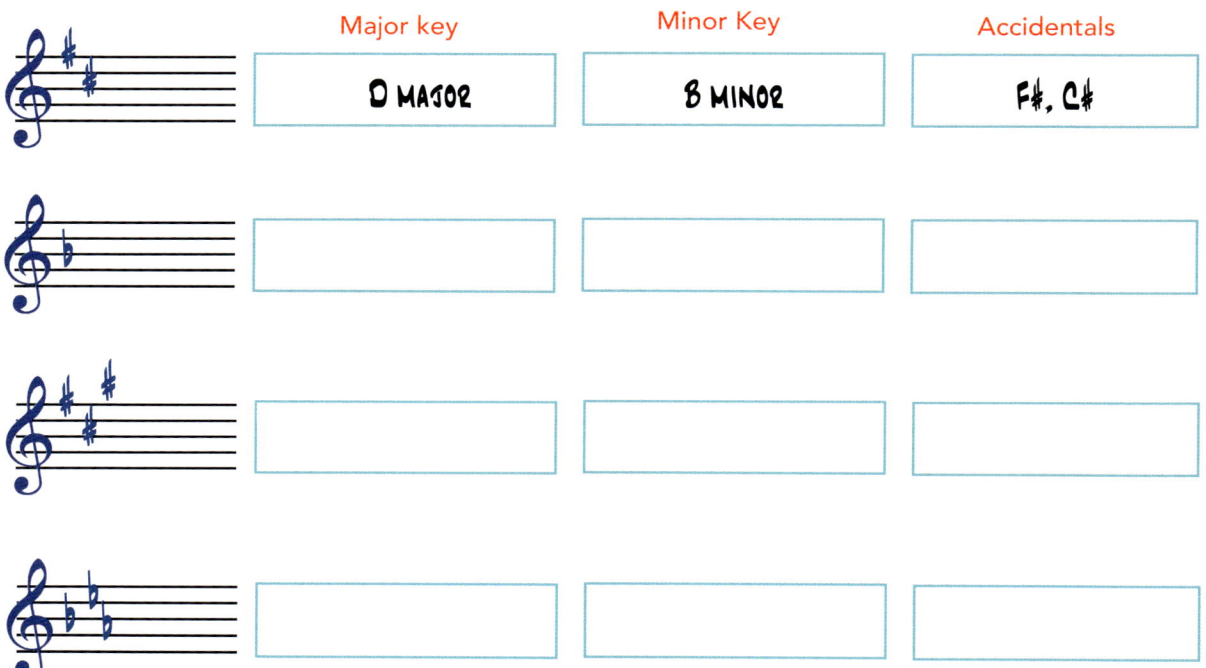

Exercise 8: Recognizing perfect authentic cadences

In the following chord progressions, find the perfect authentic cadences and use the proper notation to indicate their presence. Simply look for dominant 7th chords and see if it resolves on a major chord. Make sure that the root of the dominant chord is a 5th above that of the major chord.

EXERCISES

Key: F Major

| F6 D-7 | G-7 C7 | FMAJ7 | G-7 C7 |

Key: Modal

| BMAJ7 D7 | GMAJ7 Bb7 | EbMAJ7 | A-7 D7 |

Key: Eb Major

| F7 | F-7 Bb7 | EbMAJ7 | C7 |

Exercise 9: Recognizing complete cadences

Same as the previous exercise, but you need to recognize complete cadences in the following chord progressions.

Key: F Major

| F6 D-7 | G-7 C7 | FMAJ7 | G-7 C7 |

Key: Eb Major

| F7 | F-7 Bb7 | EbMAJ7 | C7 |

Key: Ab Major

| Bb-7 Eb7 | AbMAJ7 F-7 | Bb-7 Eb7 | AbMAJ7 |

EXERCISES

Exercise 10: Finding and analyzing secondary dominant chords

Using the correct notation, indicate the presence of secondary dominant chords in the following chord progressions.

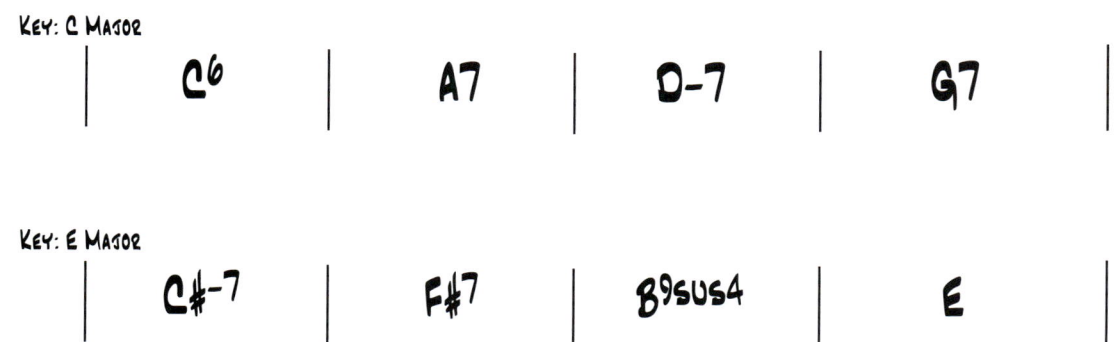

Exercise 11: Determine the improvisation guide of progressions including secondary dominants.

Write the improvisation options underneath the given chord progressions.

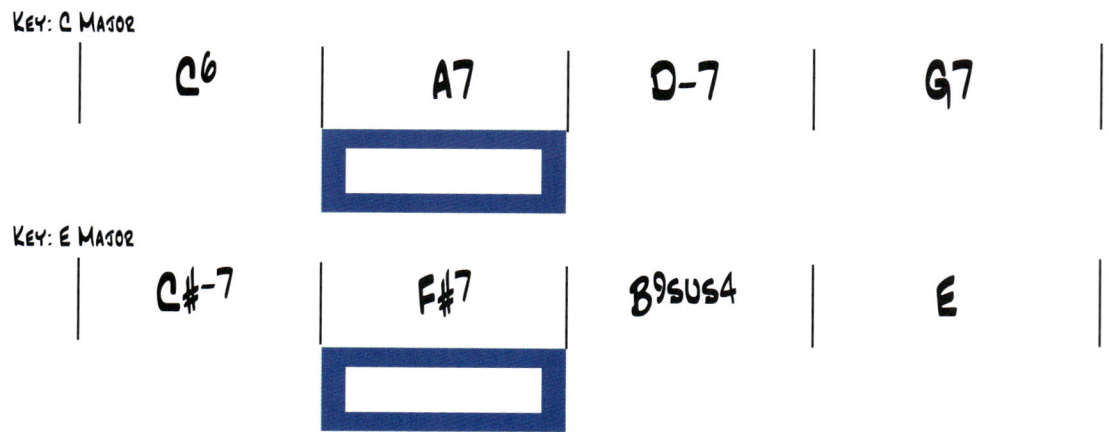

EXERCISES

Exercise 12: Finding the tritone substitution of secondary dominant chords

Write the tritone substitution underneath the following secondary dominant chords.

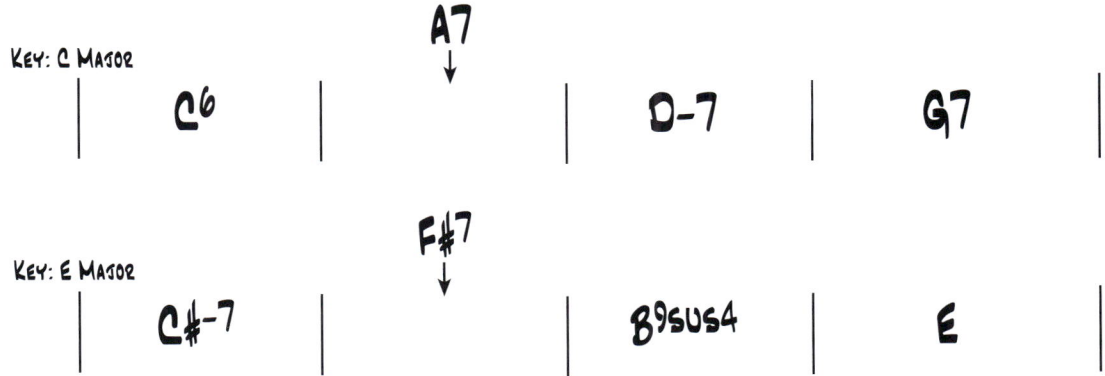

APPENDIX

Appendix A: More about tonality

During the editing process, I was advised to clarify some points of potential confusion with regards to my use of the word "tonality", and how I contrast with with the notion of modal music. Many people would argue that "tonality" is also present in modal music and that the true opposite of tonal music would be **atonal music**. A good example of this type of music would be Arnold Schoenberg's Sechs Kleine Klavierstücke.

However, the problem with atonal music is that it stands, by definition, outside of the realm of what can be rationally analyzed for the purpose of composition and improvisation. In other words, the only "rule" per se, in atonal music, is to create the impression that there is no tonal center at all, no "home", no one chord, note, scale or key around which the music gravitates.

I know people love debates when it comes to niche subjects such as music theory, and most of the time, these debates are useful and constructive. But sometimes, they are just a matter of semantics and are simply due to people not agreeing on the definitions they are using upon entering the debate . My goal in this book is more practical than philosophical. It is to guide you with composition and improvisation in the contexts you will bee most likely to encounter. The number of times you will be asked to create melodies in a purely atonal context will most likely be close to none which is why I did not even evoke it.

So in order to prepare you for potential debates around this subject, allow me to clarify one more time: for lack of a better term, I define tonal music as music which is built mostly upon harmonic complexity, and harmonic mechanisms of tension and release such as cadences. I contrast this with modal music defined as music based mostly on simple harmonic contexts which leave room to bring out the colors of one or several modes. Admittedly, both of these systems present a sense of "centeer" or "home", but the means by which it is brought out as well as the effect on the listener are very different.

I hope this clarification serves its purpose and doesn't turn out to be more counterproductive than not, thereby leaving you more confused than before. To sum it up simply, there are several potential definitions of "tonality". Some are based exclusively on the sense of feeling like there is a "center" around which the music is articulated. In this case, the opposite of tonal music would be atonal music. My definition is based on HOW the center is emphasized and on the harmonic mechanisms which allow this emphasis. In this case, tonal music contrasts with modal music.